Pro JavaScript with MooTools

Learning Advanced JavaScript Programming

Mark Joseph Obcena

Apress®

Pro JavaScript with MooTools: Learning Advanced JavaScript Programming

ISBN-13 (pbk): 978-1-4302-3054-0

ISBN-13 (electronic): 978-1-4302-3055-7

Printed and bound in the United States of America (POD)

President and Publisher: Paul Manning
Lead Editors: Frank Pohlmann and Ben Renow-Clarke
Technical Reviewer: Simo Kinnunen
Editorial Board: Steve Anglin, Mark Beckner, Ewan Buckingham, Gary Cornell, Jonathan Gennick, Jonathan Hassell, Michelle Lowman, Matthew Moodie, Duncan Parkes, Jeffrey Pepper, Frank Pohlmann, Douglas Pundick, Ben Renow-Clarke, Dominic Shakeshaft, Matt Wade, Tom Welsh
Coordinating Editor: Mary Tobin
Copy Editor: Sharon Terdeman
Compositor: MacPS, LLC
Indexer: Julie Grady
Artist: April Milne
Cover Designer: Anna Ishchenko

Distributed to the book trade worldwide by Springer Science+Business Media, LLC., 233 Spring Street, 6th Floor, New York, NY 10013. Phone 1-800-SPRINGER, fax (201) 348-4505, e-mail orders-ny@springer-sbm.com, or visit www.springeronline.com.

For information on translations, please e-mail rights@apress.com, or visit www.apress.com.

Apress and friends of ED books may be purchased in bulk for academic, corporate, or promotional use. eBook versions and licenses are also available for most titles. For more information, reference our Special Bulk Sales–eBook Licensing web page at www.apress.com/info/bulksales.

The source code for this book is available to readers at www.apress.com.

To the one who owns my heart.

Contents at a Glance

Contents

Foreword

I began working on MooTools in 2005, and, after a year of development, I released the very first version to the public. MooTools slowly gained popularity, ascending to its current position as one of the top JavaScript frameworks.

MooTools, however, has a rather steep learning curve and a very big codebase. It was never written with absolute beginners in mind, so users are often intimidated about trying to learn it. This is unfortunate; they're missing out on the great power and customizability MooTools offers, simply because it looks scary.

It is not all MooTools' fault, of course. There's a distinct lack of useful information available on the subject, though I must admit that MooTools itself hasn't done enough to correct the situation. People who want to learn the framework are left to their own devices—and that can get really at times.

Fortunately, that's where this book comes in. *Pro JavaScript with MooTools* will take you on a journey from the building blocks of JavaScript, through the prototypal concepts, to the very inner workings of MooTools. By the time you're finished reading it, MooTools will hold no more secrets from you.

When I think about the best MooTools articles I have ever read on the Web, Mark's blog, *Keetology*, comes immediately to mind. Mark has been writing awesome JavaScript and MooTools material for years, in articles (like his "Up the Moo herd" series) and in actual code (Raccoon!). His blog is a must-read for anyone wanting to learn or expand his knowledge of MooTools, or JavaScript in general.

Pro JavaScript with MooTools isn't simply a well-written technical book. This book thoroughly explains how object-oriented programming works in JavaScript, and then gradually takes advantage of your newly acquired knowledge to explain how MooTools operates, and how you can build awesome stuff with it.

And awesome stuff is what we want you to build! MooTools is no longer an obscure framework that sprang from a simple effects library. It's now a full-fledged development tool with a great set of core developers, an active and growing community, and a huge roll of user-developed applications and extensions.

But development doesn't end with the recent successes. While this book is about MooTools 1.3, the most recent release, it is also a preparation of sorts for version 2.0. MooTools 1.3 reflects the direction we're heading in the future—toward a better, faster, and more powerful MooTools. We're working to make the strong parts of the framework even stronger, and we're going to improve the parts that need improvement.

However, we want you to share in these exciting developments, and the first step toward that is learning more about MooTools. You don't need to be an expert to learn MooTools, as this book will show you. All you need is a little patience, creativity—and a whole lot of milk.

Back in 2005, MooTools was just a small framework I created for fun and experimentation. It never occurred to me that it would eventually become the subject of a book, a book whose range, I must say, is as impressive as its depth. It makes me proud of what MooTools has achieved.

Things are just gonna get more awesome from here…

Valerio Proietti
MooTools Founder and Lead-Developer

About the Author

 **Mark Joseph Obcena** is a freelance software developer, graphic designer, and writer from Manila, Philippines. Popularly known as keeto online, Mark is a big fan of open source development and regularly contributes to several open source projects, including MooTools where he's a member of the official Community Team. He's currently experimenting with new programming languages while working on several CommonJS projects, which are available from his Github page, and he sometimes gets bullied by the MooTools community into writing a post for his web site, *Keetology* (http://keetology.com).

Mark also owns a cat named Shröddy, who may or may not exist.

About the Technical Reviewer

Simo Kinnunen, originally from Helsinki, lives in Tokyo, where he combines the study of the Japanese language with being a web expert and JavaScript hacker. He is also a Zend engineer, and he spent quite a large part of this spare time building a rather complicated web text replacement hack called cufón.

Acknowledgments

I've often thought of myself as a one-man show: Mark, the Developer for Every Occasion™. This book, however, is not mine alone. A lot of people have contributed in one way or another to make this book possible, and I'd like to take a piece of it to thank them.

First, I want to give a big thank-you to Valerio Proietti, MooTools Founder and Lead Developer, who has not only given his time to read early drafts of the work, but has also graced this book with a foreword. You, sir, are truly awesome.

I'd also like to thank the MooTools team—the builders, the contributors, and the creators—who have tirelessly given their love to the framework. This book would literally not have been possible if not for the great work that you've put into MooTools. Special thanks to Christoph, Djamil, William, David, and Thomas, who have given their input, pings, and thumbs-up for the book.

A thank-you also goes out to the members of the MooTools community, especially the regulars of the #mootools IRC channel. Your constant need for updates about the book and unending encouragement drove me to make this work worthy of the highlights. Thanks and [ ]/ are also due to the regulars of the "other" mootools IRC channel: Jabis, Michael, Graham, and Rud. You guys are all awesome.

Of course, I won't forget to thank Simo, my dear technical reviewer, who has given his time and effort in reviewing the drafts of this work. Thank you for putting up with my dangling semicolons. Chocolates and thank-yous are sent to Tokyo for you.

Another round of cheers and claps are also given to the people at Apress who believed enough in this work to put their time into it. To Frank, thank you for giving me the chance to broadcast my ideas to the world, and thank you for believing that I could pull off this work. To Mary and Ben, thank you for putting up with my haphazard writing styles and weird submission schedule. And to Sharon, thank you for adding more awesome to my writing.

Of course, I'd also like to give thanks and hugs to my family. To my mom and dad who have always believed in me in their own quirky way, to my siblings Christine and Jan Raleigh who are now learning the value of being connected, and to my aunt and uncle who have stood by me like a second set of parents, thank you.

Finally, I'd like to give the biggest thanks to three people by dedicating parts of the book to them.

Part I is dedicated to my friend Garrick Cheung. Without you, this book would have never been started. Thank you for the input, the critiques and the ideas. You are a great man, an awesome person, and a very good friend. *To Happiness.*

Part II is dedicated to my very good friend Tim Wienk. Without you, this book would never have been completed. Thank you for listening to my rants, thank you for keeping me company, thank you for keeping me sane, and thank you for being a good friend. *To Friendship.*

And Part III is dedicated to P.E.M. Without you, I would have never gotten the courage to find happiness. Thank you for showing me what's wrong, what's changing, and what's possible. I'll always be your Marquito. *To Love.*

Preface

The universe, perhaps, is just a crazy runtime environment with sparse documentation and seemingly random side effects, and life is nothing more than a program written in a language called "Universcript." I conclude that this might be the case because, when I decided to invoke my audition method in the fall of 2008 to try out for the role of Moritz Stiefel in a local production of *Spring Awakening*, I never expected that it would return a Book object.

Fortunately, not all things are that quirky. The universe might think that it's a great idea to take my botched audition and turn it into a writing opportunity—an API decision I *fully* approve, by the way—but most programming languages behave more predictably. Some languages behave predictably well, some languages behave predictably well with some exceptions, and some languages behave predictably weird.

The fascinating thing, though, is that a language's predictability often has less to do with the language itself and more to do with its users. The more we learn about a programming language, the more predictable it becomes. The key, then, isn't coding blindly and whining (quite loudly for some) about a language's apparent shortcomings, but learning, experimenting, and applying. The quirks will stay quirky, but at least now we can appreciate their quirkiness.

This book is about JavaScript as it relates to the MooTools framework. Like any other language, JavaScript's predictability has a lot to do with the people who code with it. While it is pretty predictable, JavaScript does have some quirks and unique features that might not be apparent at base level. Unfortunately, a lot of us who proudly proclaim to be JavaScript developers don't take time to learn the language enough to appreciate these quirks and features.

A big part of this problem, surprisingly, comes from the popularity of frameworks. JavaScript's almost prodigal-son-like comeback into the limelight of web development has brought forth a slew of libraries and frameworks that promise an easier experience when working with the language. While most of them do deliver on the promise, it comes with the cost of dependency: developers get so comfortable with a framework that they forget there's a powerful language underneath the abstraction.

This book tries to address this particular issue for the MooTools framework. MooTools is in the unique position of being one of the more popular frameworks that extend and improve JavaScript rather than bury it in the guise of an API. MooTools works with native JavaScript, uses native JavaScript, and feels like native JavaScript. MooTools users, therefore, are exposed to the power of JavaScript at every level—all they have to do is look at it.

If you're looking for a recipe book, a how-to book, or a book of source code that you can copy and paste into your next application, I'm afraid this is not that book. This book is all about exploring JavaScript and looking at how JavaScript is used for the internals of the MooTools framework. This book will show you how the features of JavaScript are used inside the framework, and how they come together to create the very powerful set of APIs we know as MooTools.

In essence, this book is an extension and expansion of the *Up the MooTools Herd* series I previously wrote for my blog. As with that series, this book is not aimed at beginners, but at intermediate and advanced users. So, if you're new to MooTools or JavaScript, I suggest you put this book on your to-read list and grab a beginner's book first.

This book is divided into three parts. The first part is all about JavaScript as ECMAScript, and focuses on the native features of the language—functions, objects, and types—and the subsystems inside MooTools that work with these parts. The second part of the book focuses on JavaScript in the browser and explores subjects such as elements, events, and animation. Finally, the last part of this book is a short exploration of JavaScript outside the browser and gives an introduction to CommonJS and MooTools using Deck.

As you'll learn in the next chapter, MooTools is divided into two main projects: MooTools Core and MooTools More. In writing this book, I've decided to focus solely on MooTools Core, so there's no mention of any of the features or extensions found in MooTools More. Also, I've limited myself to MooTools version 1.3 for this book, so any features from or incompatibilities with previous versions are not mentioned.

And with those words out of the way, it's time for us to start our exploration. It's best that we begin with the opening credits and get to know our dramatis personae. So if you're ready, let's meet the cast: JavaScript and MooTools.

PART I

Exploring JavaScript and MooTools

CHAPTER 1

■■■

JavaScript and MooTools

Before we begin our exploration of how to get the most out of JavaScript using the powerful MooTools framework, let's focus a little on JavaScript and MooTools individually. We'll also talk about the JavaScript developer's toolkit, and what you need to develop applications in JavaScript.

JavaScript

JavaScript started out as a small language called *Mocha,* which was created by Brendan Eich back in May of 1995. Mocha was designed for scripting web pages, and the plan was to bundle it with Netscape's Navigator browser. Before the browser's release, though, Netscape acquired a trademark license from Sun Microsystems to use the name "Java" and the language was renamed to **JavaScript**. This move was somewhat political on Netscape's part: the release of JavaScript coincided with the new Navigator support for Java, a popular programming language, and the name *JavaScript* was chosen to market the language as a new and powerful programming language.

This marketing ploy, although somewhat disingenuous since JavaScript and Java bear no relation except for a very superficial similarity in naming conventions and some syntax, was quite successful and JavaScript started gaining traction among web developers. This led Microsoft to create a similar implementation for its Internet Explorer browser, which was released in August of 1996. Microsoft named its language *JScript* in order to bypass having to license the name Java from Sun Microsystems.

Netscape sought standardization for the language and submitted it to Ecma International for work on the specification, and in June 1997, the first version of *ECMAScript* was adopted by the Ecma General Assembly. The name ECMAScript was a compromise: None of the parties involved in the standardization wanted to donate their trademark, so Ecma decided to invent a new name for the language.

■ **Note** ECMAScript is the real name of the language as it's described by the Ecma standards and specification; JavaScript and JScript are dialects that have extra features that may not be compatible with the standard. The JavaScript language and its development are now handled by Mozilla, and JScript continues to be developed by Microsoft. For the most part, this book is about ECMAScript, but we'll use the name JavaScript throughout since it's the more popular name.

While JavaScript became popular among web developers, the rest of the programming world dismissed the language as nothing more than a curiosity. This was probably due to the fact that web design was still in its infancy, and most of the developers who used JavaScript were considered amateurs in comparison to other programmers who were developing systems in other languages. JavaScript, being quite new and intended for scripting web pages, was seen as a "toy language" compared with the established languages of the time.

That didn't stunt JavaScript's growth, though, and by 1999 a new specification of ECMAScript was approved and browsers started implementing ECMAScript 3. By 2003, more complex JavaScript-powered web applications started appearing. The huge leap from simple dynamic web pages to powerful web applications was staggering, and JavaScript was once again in the spotlight as the main technology that powered these applications. The revolution finally got its name in 2005 when Jessie James Garrett published his article "Ajax: A New Approach to Web Applications." Ajax, which stands for "Asynchronous JavaScript and XML", became the banner name for several technologies used to create rich and complex web applications—at the top of which was JavaScript. We'll learn more about Ajax in Chapter 11.

JavaScript rose from being a dismissed language to the star of the web. However, as applications became increasingly complex, the need for much more powerful JavaScript implementations became more apparent and browser makers started developing more robust versions of their JavaScript engines. JavaScript development took off from that point, and browser adoption of new features of the most current version of the language (ECMAScript 5, which was approved in December 2009) is growing—and there are a host of other new features still being standardized.

Another milestone was reached in January of 2009 when the *CommonJS* project was founded with the aim of moving JavaScript outside the web browser. Several CommonJS implementations began to emerge, and it's now possible to create JavaScript applications that run outside the browser and on the server, making JavaScript truly an all-around programming language.

MooTools

During the height of the Ajax period, JavaScript developers realized that some of the programming tasks they were doing were repetitive and could be simplified, so developers started releasing frameworks and libraries that included utility functions for common tasks as well as other helper methods and objects that simplified JavaScript programming. Throughout the years, though, most of these early frameworks and libraries became extinct, but a few of them survived and gained quite a following.

One of those frameworks is **MooTools**, which had its humble beginnings in a small animation library called *Moo.Fx*. Back in 2005, the dominant JavaScript framework was *Prototype* and its effects library called *Script.aculo.us*. Dissatisfied with Scriptaculous, Valerio Proietti created a new lightweight effects library for Prototype that emphasized code quality and size, and Moo.Fx ended up being only 3KB—uncompressed.

Moo.Fx became the seed that sprouted the MooTools library. While Moo.Fx solved the immediate effects problem with Prototype, the library itself was still a source of dissatisfaction for Valerio and he sought to create a new framework that focused not only on quality and size, but on code modularity as well. Eventually, Moo.Fx became the core of the MooTools effects module, and additional utility functions and modules were added to create a standalone framework. With the release of MooTools 0.87, the framework was born.

The framework gathered a steady community and established a capable team of core developers, and the code underwent several revisions: 1.0 became a milestone release with several new features, and the 1.11 release is still usable today; the 1.2 release marked another milestone, with more modular code and revisions to the base native augmentation code. During preparation of the release that followed 1.2.1, the framework was split into two codebases: *MooTools Core*, which represented the "core" modules of the framework, and *MooTools More*, which included the plug-ins and extensions to the core. The launch of the official MooTools Forge in December of 2009 also heralded another milestone for the framework: A web application dedicated to bringing together community-submitted plug-ins, the MooTools Forge opened an official avenue where the MooTools community could share their code.

And with the release of version 1.3, MooTools has once again reinvented itself with a simpler Type system, an improved Class implementation and a fast new selector engine. From its 3 KB beginnings as an effects library, MooTools has grown into one of the best and most powerful JavaScript frameworks around.

The Language Extension

MooTools complements JavaScript in a way that no other library could. When people refer to MooTools, they call it a JavaScript library or a JavaScript framework. Though these descriptions aren't necessarily wrong, they don't encapsulate the main idea behind MooTools—which is to leverage and improve the JavaScript language itself. Therefore, I prefer to call MooTools something else: *a language extension*.

Developers using MooTools are expected to be JavaScript programmers first, MooTools users second. In the MooTools community, a lot of emphasis is given to learning how to properly write JavaScript, and everyone is expected to know at least the basics of programming. This is because MooTools itself is so intertwined with JavaScript that learning the framework without having a basic grasp of the language would be impossible.

What's often surprising for new users is just how much MooTools feels like native JavaScript. Often, people in the official MooTools IRC channel are asked whether a specific feature is from MooTools or from native JavaScript, and for the most part it's hard to differentiate unless you look at the documentation. Unlike other JavaScript frameworks that impose new rules and syntax on the language, MooTools does not aim to transform JavaScript into another language. It adheres to JavaScript conventions, the syntax and the defined rules, and improves the language by adding new features that leverage and improve the existing ones.

This love for the language itself is apparent in some of the main features of MooTools: the Type system (called Natives in pre-1.3 versions) was created to provide an easier way to augment natives; the Class system was included to simplify object-oriented programming; and the DOM modules were crafted to provide a simpler alternative to its native counterpart for working with web documents. MooTools makes the process of working with JavaScript easier on so many levels and it inspires developers to add more features to the language.

In the chapters that follow you'll see just how much MooTools complements the language. While this is primarily a JavaScript book, MooTools is used as an exemplar of what's possible with the language, and how you—using only the tools available in the language itself—can create complex and powerful new features that add value to JavaScript.

Your Toolkit

Before we venture further, you'll need to get your toolkit together in order to run the example code snippets in this book, as well as to build the arsenal you'll need to develop your own JavaScript applications.

Thankfully, working with JavaScript doesn't require a lot of tools or any complicated software. In fact, much of what you'll need probably came preinstalled on your computer, and some you can easily download for free. So without further ado, here are the components of a JavaScript developer's toolkit.

JavaScript Interpreter

A **JavaScript interpreter** (or **engine**) is a program that parses and executes JavaScript programs. You'll need an interpreter that implements at least JavaScript version 1.5, which is equivalent to ECMAScript 3. An ECMAScript 5 conforming interpreter is nice to have, though not necessary.

You don't have to look far to get yourself a usable interpreter: all major graphical web browsers have JavaScript interpreters built in and, due to the recent popularity of the language, turned on by default. At the time of writing, there are five web browsers that have enough marketshare to be classified as "major":

- **Firefox** (www.mozilla.com/firefox/)

- **Google Chrome** (www.google.com/chrome/)

- **Internet Explorer** (www.microsoft.com/windows/internet-explorer/)

- **Opera** (www.opera.com/)

- **Safari** (www.apple.com/safari/)

Of course, not all browsers are created equal. For working with JavaScript, I recommend Firefox, Chrome, or Safari. These three are the popular choices for JavaScript development because of their support for standards, language implementation completeness, and availability of proper development tools. In fact, an impromptu survey I conducted revealed that these three browsers are the browsers of choice for most developers in the MooTools IRC channel.

Aside from a web browser, you can also obtain a JavaScript interpreter by downloading a **CommonJS implementation**. These standalone JavaScript interpreters are used for out-of-the-browser JavaScript applications. However, CommonJS implementations lack the necessary environment to run browser-based JavaScript programs, which will be discussed more in Part Two of this book. We'll talk more about these CommonJS implementations and how to get them in Chapter 13.

JavaScript Console

Some of the programs we'll be working with in the first part of this book aren't graphical; they are very basic programs that produce text-based output. In the old days, you might display such text output using the native alert function. However, this could be very obtrusive, and having multiple alert calls in one page could lead to a lot of unnecessary clicking.

Instead, the snippets in this book will use the console object and its log method to display code output. The console object is a special browser object that's exposed by the **JavaScript console**, which is part of the development tools that come with most browsers these days. The JavaScript console is used to display errors, warnings, and other information about running scripts, and user-generated output can be displayed using a special call to console.log.

Safari and Chrome have a built-in JavaScript Console that can be accessed through the Webkit *Web Inspector* (called *Developer Tools* in Chrome). For Safari, you can activate the Web Inspector by going to **Preferences ➤ Advanced** and checking the **Show Develop menu in menu bar** option. You can then use this menu to access the Web Inspector by selecting the **Show Web Inspector** menu item. Chrome, on the other hand, has its Developer Tools enabled by default and you can access it by clicking the "wrench menu," then selecting **Tools ➤ JavaScript Console** (Figure 1–1).

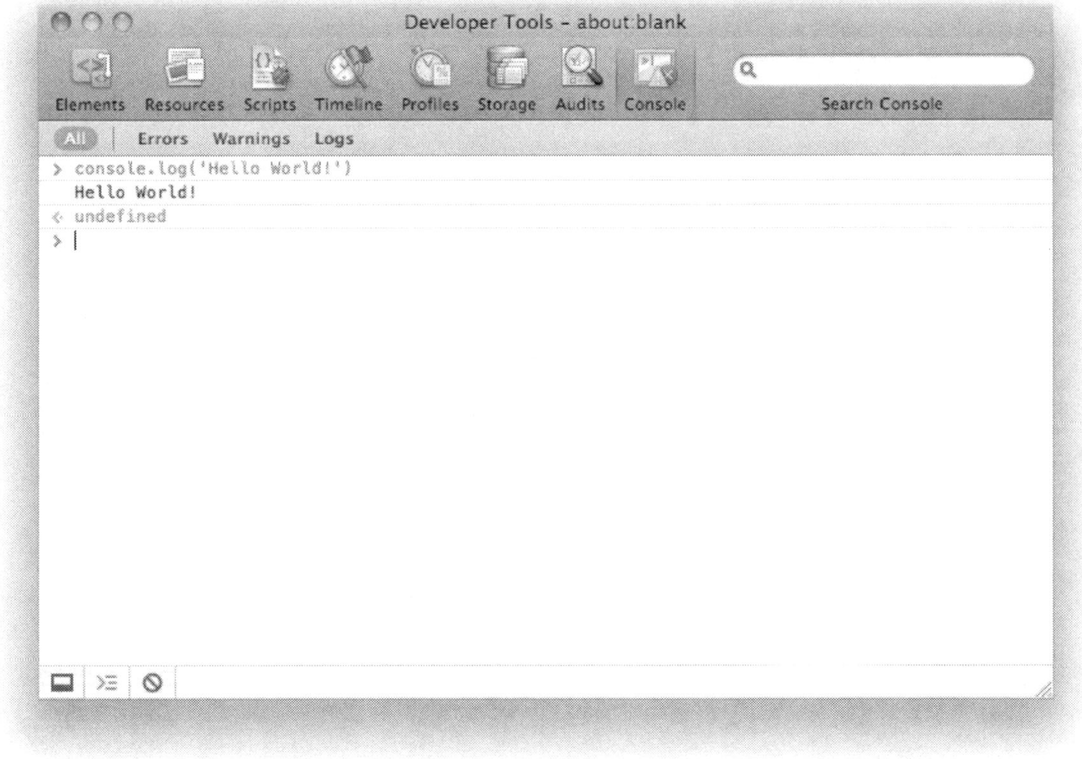

Figure 1–1. Webkit Web Inspector (Developer Tools) in Chrome

Firefox doesn't have a JavaScript console or developer tools built in, but it does have a fantastic developer extension called *Firebug* (http://getfirebug.com/). Like Webkit's Web Inspector, Firebug is a set of web development tools and includes its own JavaScript console, which can be accessed by clicking the Firebug icon at the status bar or by pressing the F12 key (Figure 1–2).

When running the snippets from this book in your browser, make sure you open up your browser's JavaScript console so you can see the output of the code. Also, take note that the JavaScript console allows you to evaluate code directly by entering it into the input that's provided and hitting the Return or Enter key, giving you a chance to dynamically perform experiments during runtime.

In this book, we'll limit ourselves to using the console.log method for result output. The console object, though, as well as the developer tools themselves, has a rich set of features that are essential to JavaScript development. As these are a bit beyond the scope of this book, I advise you to refer to the browsers' respective documentation for more information.

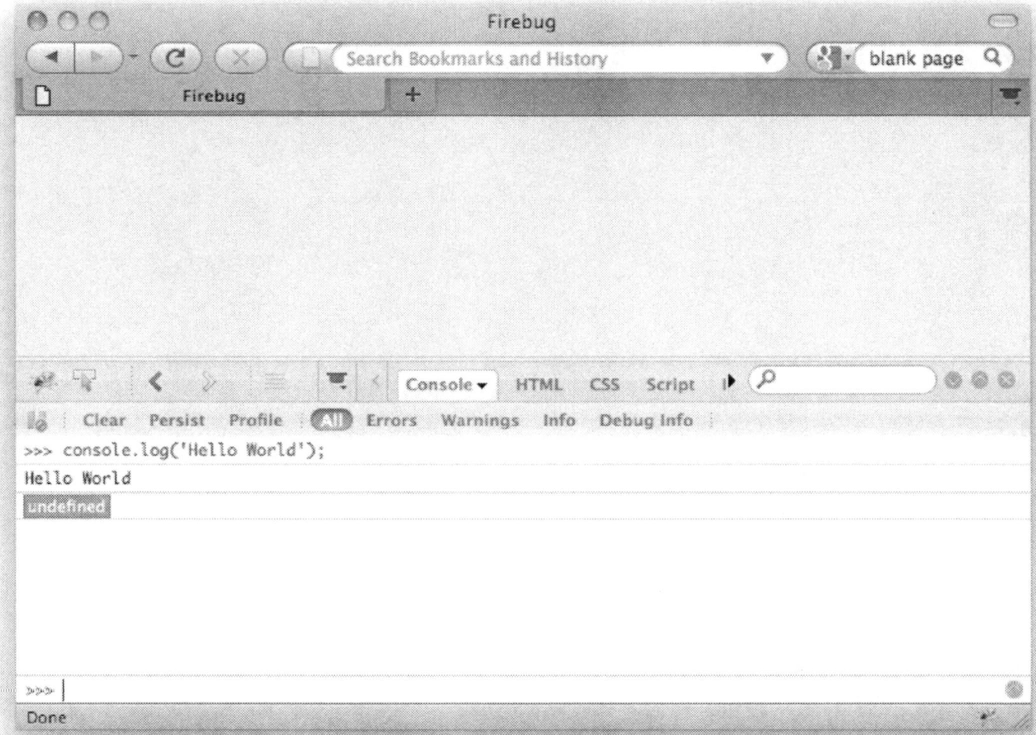

Figure 1–2. Firebug's JavaScript Console on Firefox

MooTools Core and the Snippet Runner

Since this is a book about MooTools as much as it is a book on JavaScript, you'll need to get yourself a copy of the MooTools framework. The easiest way to do that is to head over to http://mootools.net/download/ and download the prepackaged release.

   This book focuses on MooTools Core 1.3, so you'll need to download that version from the site. Older versions of MooTools have incompatibilities with the 1.3 release, so make sure you have the latest version or the snippets and examples in this book might not work. I also recommend you use the uncompressed version of MooTools Core when working with this book so that you'll be able to look at the original source code and so it'll be easier to debug errors that might be thrown from the framework itself.

   You'll also need to prepare a "snippet runner," which is a basic HTML page where you can type in the snippet you want to run. It doesn't need to be fancy, and I used this very simple template to execute the code while I was writing this book:

```
<!doctype html>
<html>
<head>
    <title>Snippet Runner</title>
    <script type="text/javascript" src="path-to-your-mootools-src.js"></script>
    <script type="text/javascript">
        // insert snippet to run here
    </script>
</head>
<body>
</body>
</html>
```

As you can see, my snippet runner is just a plain HTML page that has two `<script>` tags: one to link the MooTools source file and the other to contain the snippet I'd like to run. Because most of our output will be displayed in the JavaScript console, no special structures are needed in the script runner.

Code Editor and JSLint

To complete your toolkit, you'll need a proper programmer's editor for writing your code. Because the subject of text editors often brings heated debate, I won't go into a detailed discussion about the pros and cons of each available editor. However, there are certain things an editor needs to be considered usable for our purpose: syntax highlighting, line-number display, and support for JavaScript and HTML.

■ **Note** In case you're wondering, I use Vim (`www.vim.org`) as my editor for JavaScript development—and for writing this book. (To be exact, I use MacVim: `http://code.google.com/p/macvim/`.)

Most programmers' editors these days support extensions or plug-ins and, if yours does, make sure you find a way to integrate **JSLint** into your editor. JSLint is a static code analysis tool that checks your JavaScript code and warns you of any errors you might have failed to notice. Because JSLint can analyze your code without having to execute it, you'll be able to correct errors before you even open your JavaScript interpreter.

JSLint was originally created by Douglas Crockford, and you can find an online version of the tool at `www.jslint.com/`. You can also download an offline version of JSLint that uses the Java-based *Rhino* JavaScript interpreter, which you can run on your own computer. However, I recommend you use an alternative implementation called **JavaScript Lint** or **JSL** (`www.javascriptlint.com/`), created by Matthias Miller, that's more flexible than Crockford's original version and uses the C-based *Spidermonkey* JavaScript interpreter from Mozilla. JSL also has better support for editor integration, and you can find instructions for integrating it into the more popular editors at its site.

JSL uses a config file to tell it which particular rules to check against. Because some of the rules conflict with the standard MooTools style, you'll have to setup your JSL config file to limit warnings regarding MooTools code.

The Wrap Up

Now that we have all of the preliminaries out of the way, it's time to get started on our journey. It's quite a ride we have in front of us, but I'm positive we'll be able to pass through all our pitstops with ease.

Our first destination will take us to functions, one of the best features of the JavaScript language. So if you have your seatbelt buckled, let's start our exploration.

CHAPTER 2

■ ■ ■

Functions

One of JavaScript's best features is the language's implementation of functions. Whereas other languages present different function types for different purposes, JavaScript only has one function type that covers all use cases—from subroutines to lambdas to object methods.

A JavaScript function may look simple on the outside but don't be fooled—the architecture that hides underneath a basic function declaration is quite complex. And while topics like function forms, scope, context, and function execution may seem too complicated for practical consideration, learning about these details that usually go unnoticed improves your knowledge of the language and provides you with an arsenal to solve even the most complex of problems.

There won't be much mention of MooTools in this chapter or the one that follows, so don't be surprised! Instead, we'll be turning our focus on the two essential features of the JavaScript language—functions and objects—and what we learn in these chapters will not only help us understand the MooTools framework but will also assist us further on in developing complex applications.

The Function

Let's start by agreeing on some terms. From here on, we'll define a **function** as a *separate block of code that performs a certain action and returns a value*. It can receive **arguments**, which are values passed to the function, it can be used to compute the resulting **return value**, and it can be executed multiple times by **invoking** it.

```
// a basic function with two arguments:
function add(one, two){
    return one + two;
};

// invoking the function and passing arguments:
var result = add(1, 42);
console.log(result); // 43

// invoking the function again, but with different arguments:
result = add(5, 20);
console.log(result); // 25
```

JavaScript is a language with **first-class functions**. A first-class function is a function that can be stored in variables, passed as arguments to other functions, and even be used as return values for other functions. This is possible because functions, like almost everything else in JavaScript, are objects. The language also lets you create new functions and transform defined functions at runtime, which, as we'll see later on, enables MooTools to add improvements to native JavaScript.

One Function, Multiple Forms

While there is only one function type in JavaScript, there are multiple function forms, which are the different ways to create a function. The base syntax for most of these forms is called a **function literal** and it looks like this:

```
function Identifier(FormalParameters, ...){
    FunctionBody
}
```

First is the `function` keyword followed by a space and an optional **identifier** that references your function; next comes an optional comma-separated list of **formal parameters** wrapped in a pair of parentheses, which are turned into local variables that will be available from inside of your function; and finally, you have the optional **function body** where you'll write statements and expressions. Take note that those are not typos: a function has a lot of optional parts. We won't elaborate on why these parts are optional right now, but we'll learn more about them throughout the chapter.

▓ **Note** You'll see the term *literal* in several parts of this book. In JavaScript, literals are values defined directly from your code. `"mark"`, `1`, and `true` are examples of string, number, and Boolean literals, while `function(){}` and `[1, 2]` are function and array literals respectively.

A function is called using the **invocation operator** `()` appended to the identifier (or, as we'll see later, to the object itself). The invocation operator can also be used to pass in actual arguments or values for the function's use.

▓ **Note** The formal parameters of a function refer to the named variables you declare inside the parenthesis when you create your function, while the actual arguments refer to the values you pass when you invoke a function.

Because functions are objects, they also have methods and properties. We'll talk more about methods and properties of objects in Chapter 3, but for now, let's remember that a function has two basic properties:

- `name` – contains the string value of the function's identifier;
- `length` – is an integer corresponding to the number of formal parameters defined for the function (or 0 if there are no formal parameters).

Function Declaration

From the base syntax, we can create the first function form, called a **function declaration**. A function declaration is the simplest of all function forms, and most developers use this form for their code. The following code defines a new function called add:

```
// a function named `add`
function add(a, b){
    return a + b;
};

console.log(typeof add);     // 'function'
console.log(add.name);       // 'add'
console.log(add.length);     // 2

console.log(add(20, 5));     // 25
```

The identifier in a function declaration is required, and it will be used to create a variable in the current scope whose value is the function. In our example, an add variable is created in the global scope with the name property of add, equivalent to the function identifier, and the length property is 2 because we have two formal parameters.

Because JavaScript is *lexically scoped*, identifiers are scoped based on where they are defined rather than on their syntax or where they are executed. This is important to remember because JavaScript allows us to define functions inside other functions and scoping rules might get confusing:

```
// outer function, global scope
function outer(){

    // inner function, local scope
    function inner(){
        // ...
    };

};

// check the outer function
console.log(typeof outer);  // 'function'

// run outer to create the new functions
outer();

// check the inner function
console.log(typeof inner);  // 'undefined'
```

In this example, an outer variable is created in the global scope and given the value of our outer function. When it is invoked, the outer function creates a local variable called inner that is given the value of our inner function. When we check the values using the typeof operator, the outer function appears available in the global scope but the inner function is available only from inside the outer function—because the inner function is stored in a local variable.

Because a function declaration also creates a variable with the same name as its identifier, you have to make sure that there are no variables with the same name as the identifier in your current scope. Otherwise, it'll override the value of that variable with the function:

```
// a variable in the current scope
var items = 1;

// a function declaration with the
// same name; overrides value
function items(){
    // ...
};
```

13

```
console.log(typeof items); // 'function', not 'number'
```

We'll learn more about the details of JavaScript's scoping in a while, so let's first take a look at other function forms.

Function Expression

The next form takes advantage of the fact that functions can be stored in variables. This form is called a **function expression** because rather than explicitly defining a function, you "express" a function as a value of a variable.

Here's the same add function we declared above, but using a function expression.

```
var add = function(a, b){
    return a + b;
};

console.log(typeof add);    // 'function'
console.log(add.name);      // '' or 'anonymous'
console.log(add.length);    // 2

console.log(add(20, 5));    // 25
```

In this example, we create a function literal that becomes the value of our variable add. We can then use this variable to invoke our function, as illustrated on the last line where we use the function to add two numbers.

You'll notice that the length property of the function is the same as its function declaration counterpart, but the name property is different. In some JavaScript interpreters, its value will be a blank string (''), while in others it'll be 'anonymous'. This happens because we didn't specify an identifier for the function literal. In JavaScript, a function without an explicit identifier is called an **anonymous function**.

The scoping rules for function expressions are a bit different from function declarations because they depend on variable scoping. Remember that in JavaScript, the var keyword defines a variable to be scoped locally, and omitting the keyword creates a global variable instead:

```
// outer function, global scope
var outer = function(){

    // inner function, local scope
    var localInner = function(){
        // ...
    };

    // inner function, global scope
    globalInner = function(){
        // ...
    };

};

// check the outer function
console.log(typeof outer);          // 'function'
```

```
// run outer to create the new functions
outer();

// check the new functions
console.log(typeof localInner);     // 'undefined'
console.log(typeof globalInner);    // 'function'
```

The function outer is defined to be of global scope, because while we use the var keyword, it's on the top level of the application. Inside the function are two other functions, localInner and globalInner. The localInner function is stored in a variable that's local to the inside of the outer function and can't be accessed in the global scope. However, globalInner is stored in a variable that's defined without the var keyword, making both the variable and the function it contains global.

Named Function Expression

Although function expressions are usually written using anonymous functions, you can also specify an explicit identifier for your function. This is a variation of the function expression called a **named function expression**.

```
var add = function add(a, b){
    return a + b;
};

console.log(typeof add);     // 'function'
console.log(add.name);       // 'add'
console.log(add.length);     // 2

console.log(add(20, 5));     // 25
```

This example is the same as a function expression that uses an anonymous function, but we specify an identifier for the function literal. Unlike in the previous example, the name property of this function is 'add', which is consistent with the identifier we specified, rather than 'anonymous' or an empty string.

JavaScript allows an explicit identifier for function expressions so that a function can reference itself from the inside. You might be asking why you'd need this feature, so let's look at two different examples.

```
var myFn = function(){
    // reference the function
    console.log(typeof myFn);
};

myFn(); // 'function'
```

In the example above, the function myFn could easily reference itself via the variable holding it because the variable that contains the function is available inside the function scope. However, consider the next example:

```
// global scope
var createFn = function(){

    // result function
    return function(){
        console.log(typeof myFn);
    };

};
```

```
// different scope
(function(){

    // put the result function of `createFn`
    // into a local variable
    var myFn = createFn();

    // check if reference is available
    myFn(); // 'undefined'

})();
```

This example might be a little too complex, but we'll tackle the details later. Right now, just focus on the functions. In our global scope, we create a new function called createFn, which returns a new logging function like our previous example. Next, we create a new localized scope and define a variable myFn and assign the return value of createFn.

The code is similar to the earlier example, but here we use the function value that's returned from another function instead of directly assigning the function literal to the variable. Also, the variable myFn is on a different localized scope, which is not accessible to our resulting function value. Thus, it'll log 'undefined' rather than 'function' in this case, because the scoping doesn't allow the function to reference itself via the variable holding it.

By adding an explicit identifier to our result function, we'll be able to reference the function itself even if we don't have access to the variable holding it:

```
// global scope
var createFn = function(){

    // result function, with identifier
    return function myFn(){
        console.log(typeof myFn);
    };

};

// a different scope
(function(){

    // put the result function of `createFn`
    // into a local variable
    var myFn = createFn();

    // check if reference is available
    myFn(); // 'function'

})();
```

Adding an explicit identifier is like creating a new variable that's available from inside the function that can be used to reference the function itself, making it possible for the function to call itself from the inside (for recursive operations) or perform actions on itself.

A named function declaration has the same scoping rules as a function declaration with an anonymous function: the scope of the variable determines whether the function will be local or global. However, the additional identifier has a different scoping rule: *it's only available from inside the function.*

```
// a function with different identifiers
var myFn = function fnID(){
    console.log(typeof fnID);
};

// the variable
console.log(typeof myFn);    // 'function'

// the identifier
console.log(typeof fnID);    // 'undefined'

myFn(); // 'function'
```

This example shows that while the variable `myFn` could be used to reference the function, the identifier `fnID` isn't accessible from the outside. However, accessing this identifier variable from the inside of the function itself works.

Single-Execution Function

We touched on the subject of anonymous functions in passing when creating function expressions, but they have much broader use than that. One of the most important is a technique that uses an anonymous function to create a function that's executed immediately, without storing references to it. This form is called a **single-execution function**.

```
// create a function and invoke it immediately
(function(){

    var msg = 'Hello World';
    console.log(msg); // 'Hello World'

})();
```

Here we create a function literal and wrap it inside a pair of parentheses. We then use the function invocation operator ( ) to execute the function immediately. The function isn't stored in a variable, nor is any reference to it created. It's a "run-once" function: create it, do whatever it does, and then move on.

To understand how a single-execution function works, you need to remember that functions are objects and objects are values. Because JavaScript values can be used immediately without having to store them in variables, you can create anonymous functions that you immediately execute just by appending a function invocation operator.

However, notice that we wrap our function inside a pair of parentheses in the previous example, instead of doing it like this:

```
// this is considered a syntax error
function(){

    var msg = 'Hello World';
    console.log('msg'); // 'Hello World'

}();
```

A JavaScript interpreter will throw a syntax error when it encounters these lines because it interprets the code as a function declaration. It sees a function literal but no identifier, and it throws an error because a function declaration requires an identifier to follow the function keyword.

We need to wrap the function in parentheses in order to tell the JavaScript interpreter that it is not a function declaration but, rather, that we are creating a function and we use its value immediately. Because we have no identifier we can use to reference the function, we need to wrap it in parentheses in order to create a direct reference to the function and be able to directly call it. This wrapping in parentheses is needed only when we have no direct reference to the function, like with single-execution functions.

■ **Note** The invocation operator can be included within the parentheses or outside it, like so: `(function(){...` `}())`. Putting the operator outside is more common, though, and it's considered as the proper MooTools style.

A single-execution function is useful in a lot of cases and the most important of these is to keep variables and identifiers inside a localized, protected scope. Consider the following example:

```
// top level scope
var a = 1;

// localize scope with a single
// execution function
(function(){

    // local scope
    var a = 2;

})();

console.log(a); // 1
```

Here, our first variable a is declared in the top scope, making it available globally. We then create a single execution function and redeclare a inside, changing its value to 2. But because this is a localized variable, the original top-level a variable does not change.

This technique is popular, especially with library developers, because localizing variables into a separate scope avoids identifier clashing. If you include two scripts that define the same identifier within your application, the chance of one of them overwriting the value of the other is high—unless one of them localizes their scope via a single-execution function.

Another way of using a single-execution function is when you want to perform a task with a function and use its return value in a throwaway function:

```
// Store a single-execution function's
// return value to a variable
var name = (function(name){

    return ['Hello', name].join(' ');

})('Mark');

console.log(name); // 'Hello Mark'
```

Don't get confused by this code: this is not a function expression. What's happening is that we create a single-execution function that's immediately invoked and returns the value we want to store in our variable.

Another feature of single-execution functions is their ability to have an identifier, just like with a function declaration:

```
(function myFn(){

    console.log(typeof myFn); // 'function'

})();

console.log(typeof myFn); // 'undefined'
```

While it may seem like this is a function declaration, it's actually a single-execution function. Even though we specify an identifier for the function, it does not create a variable in the current scope as a function declaration does. This lets you reference the function from inside itself without creating a new variable inside the current scope. This is especially useful to prevent overwriting the original values of variables that already exist in the current scope.

Like any other function, single-execution functions can receive arguments passed via the invocation operator. Combine this with an identifier available from inside the function and the ability to store the return value of a single-execution function and you can create quick recursive functions for your code:

```
var number = 12;

var numberFactorial = (function factorial(number){
    return (number == 0) ? 1 : number * factorial(number - 1);
})(number);

console.log(numberFactorial); // 479001600
```

Function Object

The last function form, the **function object**, is different from all the rest because it does not use a function literal. The basic syntax of this form is as follows:

```
// a function object
new Function('FormalArgument1', 'FormalArgument2', ..., 'FunctionBody');
```

Here, we use the Function constructor to create a new function by passing strings as arguments. The first arguments define the named arguments for the function, and the last argument defines the function body.

■ **Note** While we call this form a function object, remember that all functions are objects. We simply use this term to differentiate between a function created via a literal and one created via an object constructor, which will be discussed in the next chapter.

Here's our add function using this form:

```
var add = new Function('a', 'b', 'return a + b;');

console.log(typeof add);    // 'function'
```

```
console.log(add.name);      // '' or 'anonymous'
console.log(add.length);    // 2

console.log(add(20, 5));    // 25
```

You'll notice that the code is similar to using an anonymous function literal. Like an anonymous function, a function object has either a blank string or 'anonymous' for its name property value. In the first line, we create a new function using the Function constructor, passing in the arguments 'a', 'b', and 'return a + b;'. The first two strings will become the named arguments of the function, and the final string will become the function body. Using this form is like using eval: the last string argument is turned into executable JavaScript code and used as the body of the function.

■ **Note** You don't need to pass the named arguments as separate strings. The Function constructor also allows for a single string containing comma-separated name values, like so: new Function('a, b', 'return a + b;');

While this form has its uses, as we'll see in later in this book where it'll be used as a templating engine, a Function object has a disadvantage over a function literal because the function's scope is limited to the global scope:

```
// global variable
var x = 1;

// localized scope
(function(){

    // local x variable
    var x = 5;

    // a function object
    var myFn = new Function('console.log(x);');
    myFn(); // 1, not 5.

})();
```

Even though we have a local variable x in our separate scope, the function object will not be able to reference this because it's evaluated in the global scope.

Arguments

All functions have access to their formal arguments from the inside. These formal arguments are turned into local variables within the function and their values correspond to the values passed when the function was invoked. The mapping of arguments is based on the order they were passed: the first value corresponds to the first named argument and so on.

When the number of actual arguments passed is greater than the number of formal arguments, the additional actual arguments are not stored in any formal argument variable. On the other hand, if the number of actual arguments passed is less than the defined formal arguments, the remaining formal arguments will have the value of undefined.

```
var myFn = function(first, second){
    console.log('first: ' + first);
    console.log('second: ' + second);
};

myFn(1, 2);
// first: 1
// second: 2

myFn('a', 'b', 'c');
// first: a
// second: b

myFn('test');
// first: test
// second: undefined
```

Because JavaScript allows a function to receive a mutable number of arguments, it also provides a way to access the arguments passed to the function even if there are no corresponding formal arguments defined. This is done via the arguments object, which is an array-like object that contains the values of all actual arguments passed to a function:

```
var myFn = function(){
    console.log('length: ' + arguments.length);
    console.log('first: ' + arguments[0]);
};

myFn(1, 2);
// length: 2
// first: 1

myFn('a', 'b', 'c');
// length: 3
// first: a

myFn('test');
// length: 1
// first: test
```

The arguments object has a length property that can be used to find out the number of arguments passed to a function. The values of the arguments can be accessed by providing a zero-based index to the arguments object: arguments[0] is the first value passed, arguments[1] is the second value passed, and so on.

By using the arguments object instead of named arguments, you can create functions that take a different number of arguments for processing. For example, we can modify our add function to accept multiple arguments and add them:

```
var add = function(){
    var result = 0,
        len = arguments.length;
    while (len--) result += arguments[len];
    console.log(result);
};
```

```
add(15); // 15
add(31, 12, 92); // 135
add(19, 53, 27, 41, 101); // 241
```

There is one big problem with the `arguments` object that you need to remember: it is a mutable object. You can replace the values inside arguments or even change it entirely to another object:

```
var rewriteArgs = function(){
    arguments[0] = 'no';
    console.log(arguments[0]);
};

rewriteArgs('yes'); // 'no'

var replaceArgs = function(){
    arguments = null;
    console.log(arguments == null);
};

replaceArgs(); // true
```

The first function shows that we can overwrite the values of the `arguments` object, and the second function changes the value of the object to `null`. The only constant item would be the `length` property of the object: as long as you don't overwrite the `arguments` object or change its value entirely, the `length` would still reflect the number of arguments passed even if you append new objects to it:

```
var appendArg = function(){
    arguments[2] = 'three';
    console.log(arguments.length);
};

appendArg('one', 'two'); // 2
```

When writing code, take care to ensure you don't overwrite the `arguments` object or change its values so you don't end up with weird side effects.

There's another property of the `arguments` object, `callee`, and it's a reference to the function itself. In the previous section we used the function identifiers to refer to the function, and that's similar to how `arguments.callee` works:

```
var number = 12;

var numberFactorial = (function(number){
    return (number == 0) ? 1 : number * arguments.callee(number - 1);
})(number);

console.log(numberFactorial); // 479001600
```

Notice that the function here is an anonymous one: we have no identifier yet we're able to call it recursively via the `arguments.callee` property. This is the exact purpose of this property: to enable a function to call itself without using its identifier (if it even has one).

But while it's a useful property, `arguments.callee` has been deprecated in ECMAScript 5 and using it in ES5 Strict Mode will throw an error. So, if possible, don't use this property; instead use the identifier techniques discussed earlier.

While JavaScript allows for a variable number of arguments to be passed to a function, it does not enable default values. However, you can mimic default argument values by checking the passed values and setting them if they're undefined:

```
var greet = function(name, greeting){

    // check if arguments are defined;
    // if not, use a default value..
    name = name || 'Mark';
    greeting = greeting || 'Hello';

    console.log([greeting, name].join(' '));
};

greet('Tim', 'Hi'); // 'Hi Tim'
greet('Tim');        // 'Hello Tim'
greet();             // 'Hello Mark'
```

Because named arguments that don't have corresponding passed values are given the value of `undefined` (and thus have a "falsy value" or a value that evaluates to the Boolean *false*), we can use the logical OR operator (||) to reassign a default value to the variable.

It's also important to remember that native type arguments (such as strings or integers) are passed to a function by value, which means that changes to these values aren't reflected in the outside scope. However, when used as arguments to functions, objects are passed by reference, reflecting any changes inside the function scope:

```
var obj = {name: 'Mark'};

var changeNative = function(name){
    name = 'Joseph';
    console.log(name);
};

changeNative(obj.name); // 'Joseph'

console.log(obj.name);  // 'Mark'

var changeObj = function(obj){
    obj.name = 'Joseph';
    console.log(obj.name);
};

changeNative(changeObj);    // 'Joseph'

console.log(obj.name);  // 'Joseph'
```

In the first function, we pass the `obj.name` as an argument and because it's a native string type, changing it from within the function does not affect the original value. But in our second function, we pass the object itself and the function receives a direct reference to the object, enabling us to change the property, which is reflected outside the function.

Finally, you'll recall that I mentioned that the arguments object is array-like. This means that while the arguments object seems to be like an array (in the sense that its values can be accessed via numeric indices), it's not actually an array and it doesn't have array methods. You can, however, turn the arguments object into a real array using the `Array.prototype.slice` function:

```
var argsToArray = function(){
    console.log(typeof arguments.callee); // 'function'
    var args = Array.prototype.slice.call(arguments);
    console.log(typeof args.callee); // 'undefined'
```

```
        console.log(typeof args.splice); // 'function'
};

argsToArray();
```

You'll see how this is useful in later sections when we deal with more advanced techniques. For now, just keep in mind that you can turn your arguments object into an array if you need to.

Return Values

The return keyword is used inside a function body to explicitly return a value. JavaScript allows multiple return statements from within the code, and the function exits as soon as one is executed:

```
var isOne = function(number){
    if (number == 1) return true;

    console.log('Not one..');
    return false;
};

var one = isOne(1);
console.log(one);
// true

var two = isOne(2);
// 'Not one..'
console.log(two);
// false
```

The first time we call this function, we pass it the argument 1. This argument meets the condition of our if statement within the function body, so the return statement is executed and the function halts. However, in the second call, the value 2 does not meet the condition so the function continues until the next return statement.

Multiple return statements are useful for limiting the execution of a function, and it's common practice to halt the function at the beginning using variable checks in order to save processing time and prevent errors, as the following snippet of code for getting a data property from a DOM element illustrates:

```
var getData = function(id){
    if (!id) return null;
    var element = $(id);
    if (!element) return null;
    return element.get('data-name');
};

console.log(getData());                   // null
console.log(getData('non existent id'));  // null
console.log(getData('main'));             // 'Tim'
```

Because retrieving an element from the DOM and getting its property are expensive tasks, we place checks within the code to immediately halt further execution in order to save processing power. The second check also functions as a guard to prevent the code from throwing an error when calling the get method of the object if its value is null.

As a final note on return values, remember that all JavaScript functions return values—whether or not you explicitly return one. If you don't specify a return value via an explicit statement or if your return statements are never executed, the return value of the function will be undefined.

Function Internals

While function forms, arguments, and return values are part of the core function topics, there are a lot of things underneath the visible source code that require our attention. In the next sections, we'll take a behind-the-scenes look at the internals of functions as well as a peek at what happens when JavaScript interpreters encounter a function. We won't go into deep technical details, but we'll focus on the most important parts we need to know in order to understand functions.

Some people find parts of JavaScript arbitrary and the rules of the language seem hard to grasp at first. Learning the internals helps a lot in understanding these seemingly random rules, and as we'll see throughout the next sections, knowing the inner workings of JavaScript actually contributes to making your code much more reliable and powerful.

▓ **Note** The actual implementation of JavaScript interpreters is mostly creator-dependent, and therefore some details we'll discuss in the next sections may not be true for all JavaScript interpreters. However, the ECMAScript specification does describe general rules on how interpreters should implement functions, so we do have an official guide to function internals.

Executable Code and Execution Contexts

JavaScript differentiates between three kinds of executable code:

- **Global code** is the code that's found on the top level of the application source.

- **Function code** is the code that's inside functions or what we called before the bodies of functions.

- **Eval code** is the code that's passed and executed by the JavaScript function eval().

The following example shows these different kinds of executable code:

```
// this is global code
var name = 'John';
var age = 20;

function add(a, b){
    // this is function code
    var result = a + b;
    return result;
};

(function(){
    // this is function code
    var day = 'Tuesday';
```

```
    var time = function(){
        // this is also function code,
        // but it is separate from the code
        // above
        return day;
    };
})();
```

```
// this is eval code
eval('alert("yay!");');
```

The variables name, age, and most of the functions we created all reside in the top level, which mean they're global code. However, the code inside functions is function code, and it's seen as separate from the global code. In cases where there are functions inside other functions, the content of the inner functions is also treated as separate function code—which is why the code inside the time function is separate.

So why do we have different types of code in JavaScript? In order to keep track of exactly where it is when interpreting code, the JavaScript interpreter uses an internal mechanism called an **execution context**. During the course of running a script, JavaScript will create and enter several execution contexts, not only to keep track of its location within the program but also to store data that's used for proper execution of the program.

A JavaScript program will have at least one execution context, normally called the **global execution context**. When a JavaScript interpreter starts executing your program, it "enters" the global execution context and begins interpreting the code using this execution context. When it encounters a function, the interpreter creates a new execution context and then enters this new context and executes the function code using this context. When the function has finished executing or when it has returned a value, the interpreter exits the execution context and returns to the previous one.

This might get confusing, so let's clear it up a bit with a little example.

```
var a = 1;

var add = function(a, b){
    return a + b;
};

var callAdd = function(a, b){
    return add(a, b);
};

add(a, 2);

callAdd(1, 2);
```

This code is simple enough to understand, and it's a good example of how JavaScript creates, enters, and leaves execution contexts. Let's go through it step by step:

1. When the program starts, the JavaScript interpreter enters the global execution context and starts evaluating the code. It creates the variables a, add, and callAdd, and defines their values to be the number 1, a function, and another function, respectively.

2. The interpreter encounters a function invocation for the add function. It creates a new execution context, enters it, and evaluates the expression a + b, then returns the value of this expression. After it returns the value, it leaves the new execution context it created, discards it, and goes back to the global execution context.

3. The interpreter then encounters another function invocation, this time for callAdd. Like in step 2, it creates a new execution context and enters it before interpreting the callAdd function body. As it evaluates the contents of the function, though, it encounters another function invocation—to the add function—and as for every other function invocation, the interpreter creates a new context and enters it. At this point, we have three execution contexts: the global execution context, one for callAdd, and another for add, the last one being the active execution context. When the add function is finished, its execution context is discarded and the interpreter enters the execution context of callAdd, which also returns a value, thereby signaling the interpreter to exit and discard this execution context and reenter the global one.

Execution contexts may be a bit confusing but since you'll never actually deal with them directly with your code, it's acceptable if you don't understand them fully at first. Still, a question comes to mind: if we're not gonna deal directly with execution contexts, why do we need to discuss them?

The answer lies in the other uses for execution contexts. I already mentioned that JavaScript interpreters use execution contexts to keep track of their position in the code, but aside from this important use, several internal objects are also associated with execution contexts that directly affect your JavaScript program.

Variables and Variable Instantiation

The first of these internal objects is the **variable object**. Each execution context has its own variable object that's used to keep track of all the variables that are defined within that context.

The process of creating variables in JavaScript is called **variable instantiation**. Because JavaScript is a lexically-scoped language, the scope of a variable depends on where it is instantiated in your code. The only exceptions to this rule are global variables created by omitting the var keyword:

```
var fruit = 'banana';

var add = function(a, b){
    var localResult = a + b;
    globalResult = localResult;
    return localResult;
};

add(1, 2);
```

In this snippet, the variable fruit and the function add are globally scoped and can be used throughout the whole script. On the other hand, the variables localResult, a, and b are locally scoped and are available only inside the add function. The variable globalResult, however, is globally scoped because the var keyword is omitted.

Variable instantiation is the first thing that happens when a JavaScript interpreter enters an execution context. The interpreter creates a variable object for the execution context and then checks for var declarations in the current context. These variables are then created and added in the variable object and given the value undefined. When we consider this with our example code, we can say that the variables fruit and add are instantiated using the variable object of the global execution context, while the variables localResult, a, and b are instantiated using the variable object of the local execution context of the add function. The variable globalResult, however, is a tricky one, and we'll discuss its implications later.

An important point to remember about variable instantiation is that it's connected with execution contexts in a deeper way. If you recall, we have three types of executable code in JavaScript: global code, function code, and eval code. In turn, we can say we also have three types of execution contexts: the *global execution context, function execution contexts*, and *eval execution contexts*. And since variable instantiation uses the variable object of an execution context, it follows that we can have only three main types of variables in JavaScript: *global variables, variables that are local to a function*, and *variables from evaluated code*.

This leads us to one of the things that confuse a lot of people about the language: *JavaScript has no block scope*. In other C-like languages, code inside a pair of curly braces form what is called a **block**, which has its own separate scope. However, because variable instantiation happens at the level of the execution context, a variable that's instantiated anywhere in a current execution context will be available throughout that context, not just in the current block.

```
var x = 1;

if (false) {
    var y = 2;
}

console.log(x); // 1
console.log(y); // undefined
```

In a language that has block scope, the line `console.log(y)` should produce an error since you're trying to access a variable that's not been instantiated (because the line `var y = 2;` will never be evaluated). However, JavaScript doesn't throw an error with this code, but instead tells us that the value of y is undefined, which is the value of a variable that's been instantiated but not given a value. Seems like curious behavior, doesn't it?

However, if we remember that variable instantiation happens at the level of the execution context, we'll know that this behavior is expected. When JavaScript interprets the snippet above, it starts by entering the global execution context and then does variable instantiation by looking for all variable declarations throughout the whole context and adds these variables to the variable object. So our code is really interpreted like this:

```
var x;
var y;

x = 1;

if (false) {
    y = 2;
}

console.log(x); // 1
console.log(y); // undefined
```

The same context-level instantiation also applies to functions:

```
function test(){
    console.log(value); // undefined
    var value = 1;
    console.log(value); // 1
};

test();
```

Even though our variable is defined after the first call to `console.log`, we still get a log of undefined rather than an error because variable instantiation happens before any other code inside the function is run. Our variable is already instantiated and given the value of undefined before the first line of the function body is executed, but it is only given a value of 1 on the second line. This is why it's always good to put all your variable declarations at the start of your code or at the beginning of a function. By declaring all variables at the beginning, you make it clear that the variable will be available across the whole of the current scope.

As you can see, the process of creating the variable (*instantiation*) and the process of assigning a value to a variable (*declaration*) are done separately by the JavaScript interpreter. This leads us back to a previous example:

```
var add = function(a, b){
    var localResult = a + b;
    globalResult = localResult;
    return localResult;
};

add(1, 2);
```

In this snippet, the variable `localResult` is local to the function, but the variable `globalResult` becomes global. The most common explanation for this is that when you omit the `var` keyword, the variable will be global, but that's a very naive explanation. Since we know that the processes of variable instantiation and declaration are separate, we can rewrite the function to look like how the interpreter might see it:

```
var add = function(a, b){
    var localResult;
    localResult = a + b;
    globalResult = localResult;
    return localResult;
};

add(1, 2);
```

The variable `localResult` will be instantiated and a reference to it will be stored in the variable object of the execution context. When the interpreter sees the line `localResult = a + b;`, it checks the variable object of the current execution context to see if there's a variable with the same name stored, and because there is such a variable in our example, the value is assigned to that variable. However, when it executes `globalResult = localResult`, it does not find any references so it proceeds to check whether the variable is present in the variable object of the previous context (in this case, the global execution context). But because it still does not find a reference to this variable, the interpreter assumes that it's new and creates a new variable in the last execution context it checked—which is always the global execution context. Therefore, the variable becomes a variable of the global execution context.

Scoping and the Scope Chain

That process of looking up variables in an execution context's scope is called **identifier resolution** and it's powered by another internal object associated with execution contexts, the **scope chain**. As its name implies, the scope chain is an ordered list containing objects that the JavaScript interpreter uses to figure out which variable a particular identifier is referring to.

Each execution context has its own scope chain that's created before the interpreter enters the execution context. A scope chain can contain several objects, one of which would be the variable object of the current execution context. Let's consider this simple code:

```
var fruit = 'banana';
var animal = 'cat';

console.log(fruit); // 'banana'
console.log(animal); // 'cat'
```

The code runs within the global execution context, so the variables `fruit` and `animal` are stored in the variable object of the global execution context. When the interpreter encounters the line `console.log(fruit)`, it sees the identifier `fruit` and looks for the value of this identifier by searching through the current scope chain—which contains a single object, the variable object of the global execution context. The interpreter then figures out that the variable has the value of `'banana'`. The same thing happens to the line after that.

Coincidentally, the variable object of the global execution context is used for another purpose, as the **global object**. This global object has its own internal representation inside the interpreter, but it's also available through JavaScript itself via the `window` object in the browser or the `global` object in certain JavaScript interpreters. All global variables are actually members of the global object: in the example above, you can reference the variables `fruit` and `animal` via `window.fruit` or `global.fruit` and `window.animal` or `global.animal`, depending on where you're running the script. The global object is present in all scope chains for all execution contexts, and in the case of global code, the global object is the only object inside the scope chain.

It gets more complicated with functions, though. Aside from the global object, the scope chain of a function also contains the variable object of its own execution context.

```
var fruit = 'banana';
var animal = 'cat';

function sayFruit(){
    var fruit = 'apple';

    console.log(fruit); // 'apple'
    console.log(animal); // 'cat'
};

console.log(fruit); // 'banana'
console.log(animal); // 'cat'

sayFruit();
```

For code within the global execution context, the identifiers `fruit` and `animal` refer to the variables with the values `'banana'` and `'cat'` respectively, because those are the references stored in the variable object (i.e., the global object) of the execution context. However, inside the `sayFruit` function the identifier `fruit` has a different value because another variable `fruit` was also declared inside that function. Since the variable object of the current execution context is in the front of the chain before the global object, the interpreter knows that we are referring to a local variable rather than the global one and correctly resolves the identifier.

Since JavaScript is a lexically-scoped language, identifier resolution also respects the position of functions in the code. A function inside another function can see the variables from the outer function, as in this example:

```
var fruit = 'banana';

function outer(){
    var fruit = 'orange';

    function inner(){
        console.log(fruit); // 'orange'
    };

    inner();
};

outer();
```

The variable `fruit` inside the inner function has the value `'orange'` because the scope chain of the function not only contains its own variable object but also the variable object of the function where it was declared in the code (in this case, the outer function). When the interpreter encounters the identifier `fruit` inside the `inner` function, it first looks at its own variable object. Since there's no such identifier there, it goes to the next object, which is the variable object of the outer function. The interpreter then finds the identifier it needs, so it stops there and concludes that the value of fruit is `'orange'`.

That, however, only applies to functions created using function literals. Function objects created using `new Function()` that are inside other functions behave differently as they won't be able to access the variables from their external function:

```
var fruit = 'banana';

function outer(){
    var fruit = 'orange';

    var inner = new Function('console.log(fruit);');

    inner(); // 'banana'

};

outer();
```

In this example, our `inner` function wasn't able to access the local variable `fruit` inside the `outer` function, so the output of `console.log(fruit)` inside the `inner` function is `'banana'` rather than `'orange'`. This happens because functions created using the `new Function()` form have scope chains that contain only their own variable objects and the global object. The variable objects of any surrounding functions aren't added to the scope chain of these functions, and this limits scope resolution to only local and global variables.

The creation of the scope chain happens right after the interpreter creates the execution context and before variable instantiation. In the case of global code, the interpreter first creates the global execution context, then the scope chain. It then proceeds to create the variable object of the global execution context (which also becomes the global object), then it does variable instantiation before adding the variable object to the scope chain. In the case of function code, the same thing happens but the global object is added to the function's scope chain first, then the variable objects of surrounding functions (if any), with the function's own scope chain being added last. Since the scope chain is technically a logical stack, the order of lookup during identifier resolution depends on which object was added first, so the most local of variable objects is added last to ensure that the local variable objects would be searched first during identifier resolution.

Closures

The presence of first-class functions in JavaScript and the ability of these functions to reference variables from surrounding functions give the language the base for another powerful function feature: **closures**. This language feature makes JavaScript functions extra useful, though it's also one of the more difficult to understand parts of the language. But because we already discussed how JavaScript functions work internally in the previous sections, we should be able to figure out how exactly closures work and how we can use them in our code.

Normally, the lifetime of a JavaScript variable is limited by where it was declared. A global variable will persist until the program is finished while a variable local to a function will only be available until the function is done. When the function exits, the local variables are destroyed by the interpreter via garbage collection and are no longer available. However, when an inner function inside another function retains a reference to a variable from the outer function and this inner function is then kept in reference even after the execution of the outer function, the variable persists even though the outer function has finished. When this happens, we get a closure.

Confusing? Let's check some examples:

```
var fruit = 'banana';

(function(){
    var fruit = 'apple';
    console.log(fruit); // 'apple'
})();

console.log(fruit); // 'banana'
```

Here, we have a single execution function that creates a variable fruit. Within that function, the value of the variable fruit is 'apple'. When the function is done, the variable fruit with the value of 'apple' is destroyed. We're left with the global variable fruit that has the value 'banana'. No closure was created. Let's take a look at another one.

```
var fruit = 'banana';

(function(){
    var fruit = 'apple';

    function inner(){
        console.log(fruit); // 'apple'
    };

    inner();
})();

console.log(fruit); // 'banana'
```

This example is similar to one we saw in another section. The single execution function creates a variable fruit and a function called inner. When the inner function gets called, it references the variable fruit from the outer function and we get the value 'apple' rather than 'banana'. Unfortunately, the inner function is local to the single execution function, which means it also gets destroyed after the function is done. Still no closure, so let's look at one more.

```
var fruit = 'banana';
var inner;

(function(){
    var fruit = 'apple';

    inner = function(){
        console.log(fruit);
    };

})();

console.log(fruit); // 'banana'
inner(); // 'apple'
```

And now it gets interesting. In this code we declared a variable called inner in the global scope and, within our single execution function, we gave this global variable the value of a function that logs the value of the fruit variable. Normally, the variable fruit inside the single execution function should be destroyed after the function is done, like in our previous examples, but because we referenced this variable inside our inner function, it is retained, which is why we get the value 'apple' when we call the function. And this is a closure.

A closure is created when a function inside another function gets stored outside the outer function's scope while retaining references to a variable from the outer function. Even though the function no longer operates inside its surrounding function, references to the variables from the surrounding function are still retained because the internal scope chain of the function still contains the variable object of the surrounding function, even though the surrounding function may no longer exist.

Remember that a function's scope chain is tied to its execution context, and like every other object associated with an execution context, it is created right after the creation of the execution context and destroyed together with the execution context when the function exits. Also, the interpreter only creates a function's execution context (and therefore its scope chain) when the function is invoked. In the case of our example above, the inner function is invoked during the last line of our code and, by that time, the execution context (along with its scope chain and variable object) of the original anonymous function has already been destroyed. So how can the inner function reference the local variable fruit inside the anonymous function when the original variable object containing it is already long gone by then?

The answer lies in a function's internal property called the **scope property**. All JavaScript functions have their own internal scope property that contains references to the objects that will be used to build the scope chain. When the interpreter creates the scope chain for a function, it looks at the function's scope property to see which items to add to the scope chain. Since this scope property is associated with the function itself rather than the execution context, it persists until the function is finally destroyed— making it usable no matter how many times the function is invoked.

A function created in the global context has a scope property that contains the global object, so its scope chain consists only of the global object and its own variable object. A function created inside another function has a scope object that contains all the objects inside the encapsulating function's scope property and the encapsulating function's variable object.

```
function A(){
    function B(){
        function C(){
        };
    };
};
```

In this snippet, the A function's scope property contains only the global object. The B function's scope property will inherit the contents of the A function's scope property (in this case, only the global object) plus the variable object of the A function because it's nested inside. Finally, the C function will have a scope property that inherits all of the objects from the B function's scope property—the global object and the variable object of A—plus the preceding function's variable object.

Function objects created with the new Function() form, on the other hand, only have one item in their scope property (which is the global object). This means that they can't access the local variables from surrounding functions, and therefore can't be used to create closures.

The "this" Keyword

We'll wrap up these sections on function internals in a bit, but we have one final item to discuss: the this keyword. If you have experience in other object-oriented programming languages, you might have come across a similar keyword, usually called this or self, that's used to refer to the current instance (more on this in Chapter 3). However, JavaScript's this keyword is a little trickier, since its value is dependent upon the execution context and the caller of the function. It's also mutable, which means its value can be changed during runtime.

The value of this will always be an object, and there are several rules that dictate which object will become the this in a particular piece of code. The simplest rule is that in the global context, this refers to the global object:

```
var fruit = 'banana';

console.log(fruit); // 'banana'
console.log(this.fruit); // 'banana'
```

If you recall, all variables that are declared in the global context are actually properties of the global object. Here we see that this.fruit correctly resolves to the fruit variable, showing us that the this keyword in the snippet is in fact the global object. Functions declared in the global context will also have the this keyword pointing to the global object inside their function bodies:

```
var fruit = 'banana';

function sayFruit(){
    console.log(this.fruit);
};

sayFruit(); // 'banana'

(function(){
    console.log(this.fruit); // 'banana'
})();

var tellFruit = new Function('console.log(this.fruit);');

tellFruit(); // 'banana'
```

For functions that are created as properties of objects (often termed methods), the this keyword will refer to the object itself rather than the global object:

```
var fruit = {

    name: 'banana',

    say: function(){
        console.log(this.name);
    }

};

fruit.say(); // 'banana'
```

We'll get further into the topic of objects in the next chapter, but for now, notice how the line this.name resolves properly to the name property of the fruit object. In essence, it's the same for previous examples: since the functions in the previous examples were properties of the global object, the this keyword inside the function body referred to the global object. So it follows that functions that are properties of any object will have the object itself as the this value in their body.

Nested functions, on the other hand, follow one simple rule: they always have the global object as their default this value, no matter where they appear:

```
var fruit = 'banana';

(function(){
```

```
    (function(){
        console.log(this.fruit); // 'banana'
    })();
})();

var object = {

    fruit: 'orange',

    say: function(){
        (function(){
            console.log(this.fruit); // 'banana'
        })();
    }

};

object.say();
```

Here, we see that the identifier this.fruit inside our two nested single execution functions resolved to the global fruit variable. In the case of the single execution function inside the say function, the value of this.fruit was still 'banana' even though the say function itself has its this keyword pointing to the object object. This means that the outer function doesn't affect the this value of the inner nested function.

Earlier I said that the this value is mutable and this ability to change the value of the keyword has several uses in JavaScript. Functions have two methods that can be used to change the this value: apply and call. These methods are actually used to invoke the function without the invocation operator (i.e., without the use of ( ) after the function identifier), but you can also provide arguments to these methods to change the behavior of the function.

The apply method takes two arguments: thisValue, which is used as the value of this inside the function, and params, which is an array of arguments to pass to the function. When the apply method is called on a function without any arguments or when the first argument passed is null, the this value of the function becomes the global object and no arguments are passed:

```
var fruit = 'banana';

var object = {

    fruit: 'orange',

    say: function(){
        console.log(this.fruit);
    }

};

object.say(); // 'orange'
object.say.apply(); // 'banana'
```

Reusing a snippet from the last example, we see that when we used apply without arguments to the object.say function, the this value of the function becomes the global object rather than the object itself—thereby resolving this.fruit to be 'banana' rather than 'orange'.

To set the this value of a function to another object, you simply have to pass a reference to the object using the apply function:

```
function add(){
    console.log(this.a + this.b);
};

var a = 12;
var b = 13;

add(); // 25

var values = {a: 50, b: 23};

add.apply(values); // 73
```

The `apply` method's second argument can be used to pass arguments to the function being called. This argument should be in the form of an array containing values that correspond to the function's formal parameters:

```
function add(a, b){
    console.log(a); // 20
    console.log(b); // 50
    console.log(a + b); // 70
};

add.apply(null, [20, 50]);
```

The other function method, `call`, works the same way as `apply` and thus follows the same rules indicated above. The only difference is that `call` can take multiple arguments after the `thisValue` argument, and these arguments will correspond to the formal parameters of the function in the order they were declared:

```
function add(a, b){
    console.log(a); // 20
    console.log(b); // 50
    console.log(a + b); // 70
};

add.call(null, 20, 50);
```

Advanced Function Techniques

The previous sections are meant as a base from which to start our explorations of functions. However, in order to fully utilize the power of JavaScript functions, we must be able to apply the various bits and pieces we've learned from those sections.

In the next sections, we'll discuss some of the advanced function techniques we can use in our code and we'll explore various uses for the things we've learned so far. Like everything else in this book, the information here is not meant to be exhaustive, but rather a starting point for further experimentation.

Limiting Scope

Let's say we have a program that needs to keep track of the user's name and age. We have a variable, user, which is an object where we keep the necessary data and two sets of functions, setName and getName, setAge and getAge, that we'll use to set and get the data:

```
// the `user` object where we keep the data
var user = {name: 'Mark', age: 23};

function setName(name){
    // make sure the name is a string
    if (typeof name == 'string') user.name = name;
};

function getName(){
    return user.name;
};

function setAge(age){
    // make sure the age is a number
    if (typeof age == 'number') user.age = age;
};

function getAge(){
    return user.age;
};
// set a new name
setName('Joseph');
console.log(getName()); // 'Joseph'

// set a new age
setAge(22);
console.log(getAge()); // 22
```

So far, so good. Our setName and setAge functions have checks to ensure that our values are of the correct type before setting them. However, we notice that the user variable is in the global scope and it's accessible everywhere. This presents a problem since you could just set the names without using the functions we've declared:

```
user.name = 22;
user.age = 'Joseph';

console.log(getName()); // 22
console.log(getAge()); // 'Joseph'
```

This isn't good, since we want the values to be correctly typed.

So what can we do? If you recall, variables declared inside a function are local to the function itself and are not accessible outside, and closures provide a way for a function to retain references to the local variables of its surrounding function. We can combine both of these points to limit our user variable to a local scope and then use closures for our setter and getter functions:

```
// create a single execution function
// to encapsulate the code and localize the user variable
(function(){

    // our variable is now local
    var user = {name: 'Mark', age: 23};

    // make our functions global
    setName = function(name){
```

```
        if (typeof name == 'string') user.name = name;
    };

    getName = function(){
        return user.name;
    };

    setAge = function(age){
        if (typeof age == 'number') user.age = age;
    };

    getAge = function(){
        return user.age;
    };

})();

// set a new name
setName('Joseph');
console.log(getName()); // 'Joseph'

// set a new age
setAge(22);
console.log(getAge()); // 22
```

Now, if someone tries to set the values of user.name or user.age without going through the functions, it will result in a runtime error since the user object is no longer available to any other code except our getter and setter functions.

Currying

One of the best things about having first-class functions is the ability to create these functions during runtime and store them in variables. Say we have the following snippet:

```
function add(a, b){
    return a + b;
};

add(5, 2);
add(5, 5);
add(5, 200);
```

Our last three lines call the function add to add 5 and another number. We're adding the same base number (5) to different numbers multiple times and it seems better if we could just set the function to add 5 instead of having to type it every time. We could modify our add function to use 5 + b instead, but other parts of our program might already use the add function, so this won't do. Wouldn't it be nice if we could dynamically modify our add function without changing it entirely?

It turns out we can. This technique is called **partial application** or **currying**, and it involves creating a function that "applies" some of the arguments ahead of time:

```
function add(a, b){
    return a + b;
};
```

```
function add5(b){
    return add(5, b);
};

add5(2);
add5(5);
add5(200);
```

Here, we create an add5 function that calls our add function with a preset value (in this case, 5). The add5 function is essentially our add function but with an argument already applied (hence, partial application). However, the snippet above doesn't show the dynamic part. What if we have other parts in our code where we can use this? If we were to do as we did above, we'd have to create a new function for each of the partially applied functions we want.

This is where first-class functions come in handy. Instead of explicitly declaring our new add5 function, we can have another function that takes a function as its argument and then returns a modified copy of that function. In our case, we can create a function that modifies our add function dynamically to create a new partially applied function:

```
function add(a, b){
    return a + b;
};

function curryAdd(a){
    return function(b){
        return add(a, b);
    };
};

var add5 = curryAdd(5);

add5(2);
add5(5);
add5(200);
```

In this snippet we introduce a new function called curryAdd. It takes a single argument, a, which will be the value passed as the a argument to the original add function. It then returns a new function that has one formal parameter, b, which will be used as the b argument to add. When we call this new function via curryAdd(5), it returns a new partially applied function that we store in a variable. Because we have a closure, the partially applied function retains a reference to the a variable from our curryAdd function, making it usable for the next invocations.

This, of course, is a very trivial application of curried functions, but it suffices to show how the technique works. You'll find uses for currying in many parts of your code and it's a technique that comes in handy during day-to-day development.

Decoration

Another technique that uses dynamic modification of functions and closures is **decoration**. The operative word is "decorate," and function decoration involves taking a function and adding new "features" to it dynamically.

Say we have a function that takes a single object as its argument and stores the key-value pairs in another object:

```
(function(){

    var storage = {};

    store = function(obj){
        for (var i in obj) storage[i] = obj[i];
    };

    retrieve = function(key){
        return storage[key];
    };

})();

console.log(retrieve('name')); // undefined

store({name: 'Mark', age: 23});
console.log(retrieve('name')); // 'Mark'
```

What if we want our store function to take in a pair of arguments instead of just a single object? So instead of doing store({name: 'Mark'}), we also want to be able to do store('name', 'Mark'). We could modify our store function to do this, but we've also used a similar style in other parts of our code, so it's better if we can do this dynamically.

What we can do is to create a decorator function that will wrap our store function:

```
var decoratePair = function(fn){
    return function(key, value){
        if (typeof key == 'string'){
            var _temp = {};
            _temp[key] = value;
            key = _temp;
        }
        return fn(key);
    };
};

(function(){

    var storage = {};

    store = decoratePair(function(obj){
        for (var i in obj) storage[i] = obj[i];
    });

    retrieve = function(key){
        return storage[key];
    };

})();

console.log(retrieve('name')); // undefined

store('name', 'Mark');
console.log(retrieve('name')); // 'Mark'
```

This is one of the more complex examples we've seen so far, so let's take it step by step. First, we declared a new function called decoratePair that takes a single argument, fn, which is the function we're decorating. decoratePair then returns a new decorated function that takes two arguments, key and value. Since our original store function takes only a single object as its argument, the decorated function checks whether the first argument is an object or a string. If it's not a string, the wrapped function will immediately be called. However, if it's a string, the function turns it into an object before it calls the wrapped function. When we define the store function, we pass the original function to decoratePair as a literal.

Our decorator above ensures that we have proper arguments for the wrapped function before calling it, but decorators can also add features after the function is called. Here we have a simple decorator that takes the arguments from our add function and multiplies them by the second argument:

```
var add = function(a, b){
    return a + b;
};

var decorateMultiply = function(fn){
    return function(a, b){
        var result = fn(a, b);
        return result * b;
    };
};

var addThenMultiply = decorateMultiply(add);

console.log(add(2, 3)); // 5
console.log(addThenMultiply(2, 3)); // 15
```

Here we created the function addThenMultiply dynamically by passing the original add function to decorateMultiply. The result is a function that saves the results of the add function and modifies it before returning the value.

Function decoration is useful for a lot of tasks and it enables you to extend functions without having to modify them directly. This is especially handy for built-in functions that you can't modify directly, as well as third-party code you can't control.

Combination

A similar technique to decoration is **combination**, which involves putting together two functions to create a new function. Unlike decoration, combination involves directly passing the results of one function to another.

Here's a simple example of how it works:

```
var add = function(a, b){
    return a + b;
};

var square = function(a){
    return a * a;
};

var result = square(add(3, 5));
console.log(result); // 64
```

The square(add(3, 5)) code shows how combination works, but it's not exactly a combined function. Here, the value returned from add(3, 5), which is 8, is passed to the square function, which in turn returns 64. To make this a combined function, we have to automate the process so that we don't have to type square(add(a, b)) all the time.

While we could simply create a function that has the square(add(a, b)) code inside it, the better way is to write a **combinator** function that takes two functions and combines them:

```
var add = function(a, b){
    return a + b;
};

var square = function(a){
    return a * a;
};

var combine = function(fnA, fnB){
    return function(){
        var args = Array.prototype.slice.call(arguments);
        var result = fnA.apply(null, args);
        return fnB.call(null, results);
    };
};

var addThenSquare = combine(add, square);

var result = addThenSquare(3, 5);
console.log(result); // 64
```

Our new combinator in this snippet, called combine, is a function that takes two arguments, fnA and fnB, which correspond to the two functions to be combined. It then returns a new combined function. The innards of the combined function are more complex than what we've seen in past examples, but it essentially takes the arguments passed to the function, turns them into an array, uses the apply method of functions to invoke the first function, fnA, and then stores the result in a variable. The result is then passed to the second function, fnB, before it's returned. We then create a new function, addThenSquare, by passing the references to our add and square functions to our combinator. The result is a function that combines our two small functions together.

Note that the order is important when combining functions, as well the number of arguments. In our example, we can't have a squareThenAdd function, since square takes only one argument and returns one value while add needs two arguments. And since JavaScript only allows for one return value, combined functions are usually limited to functions that take a single argument.

MooTools and Functions

You'll notice that, so far, much of our discussion has centered on functions in the context of JavaScript, and MooTools is strangely out of the picture. This is not so unusual if you remember that MooTools doesn't try to turn JavaScript into something else but rather uses the available features of the language to make it more powerful. The information we've learned so far is core to how MooTools implements new features, and a cursory glance at the MooTools source code will show its extensive use of features like single execution functions for limiting scope, closures, currying, and decoration and other techniques.

In the next sections, we'll take a look at some of the features that MooTools adds to functions, and see how they can be used for our own applications.

Function Binding

If you recall from a previous section, we learned that a function's this value is mutable and that we can change it using the apply and call methods. However, there are cases when it's time-consuming if we have to use apply and call each time:

```
function setName(name){
    this.name = name;
};

var object = {name: 'Mark'};

setName.call(object, 'Joseph');
setName.call(object, 'Olie');
setName.call(object, 'Patrick');
```

A better solution would be to create a new version of the setName function that would be automatically bound to the object:

```
function setName(name){
    this.name = name;
};

var object = {name: 'Mark'};

function setObjectName(name){
    setName.call(object, name);
};

setObjectName('Joseph');
setObjectName('Olie');
setObjectName('Patrick');
```

This technique is called **binding**, and it's much better than the earlier example since it eliminates the need to use call all the time. But it's a bit time-consuming to declare new functions for all functions you want to rebind. Fortunately, MooTools gives us an easier way to do this using the bind method of functions. Our code above can be simplified using this method:

```
function setName(name){
    this.name = name;
};

var object = {name: 'Mark'};

var setObjectName = setName.bind(object);

setObjectName('Joseph');
setObjectName('Olie');
setObjectName('Patrick');
```

The first argument to the bind method is an object that will be the this value of the new function. The method then returns a new function similar to the example we had in the previous snippet.

All arguments passed to bind after the first argument are passed as arguments to the function being bound. If we have several calls to setName.call(object, 'Mark') in our code, we could simply create a new function using var setObjectToMark = setName.bind(object, ['Mark']), and replace our previous calls with setObjectToMark(). Note, however, that bind does not do partial application: if we leave out any arguments to the function, they will be set to undefined.

Extending Functions with Methods

While MooTools already includes several useful function methods, it also allows developers to add new function methods easily. We'll discuss much of how this native extension mechanism works in Chapter 6, but right now we'll focus on how we can use this MooTools feature to add new methods.

The MooTools way to add new function methods is via Function.implement. Here's an example:

```
// create a new function method `thenAdd`
Function.implement('thenAdd', function(num){
    var self = this;
    return function(){
        var args = Array.prototype.slice.call(arguments);
        var result = self.apply(null, args);
        return result + num;
    };
});

var add = function(a, b){
    return a + b;
};

// modify the add function to add 5 to the result
var addThenAdd5 = add.thenAdd(5);

console.log(addThenAdd5(2, 3)); // 10

var square = function(a){
    return a * a;
};

// modify the square function to add 2 to the result
var squareThenAdd2 = square.thenAdd(2);

console.log(squareThenAdd2(5)); // 27
```

To create the new method, we called Function.implement with two arguments: a string with the value 'thenAdd', which will be the name of the method, and a function, which will be the actual method. Our actual thenAdd method is a function that takes one argument, num, which is the number to add to the result of the function we're modifying. It then returns a new function that wraps the original function.

You'll notice that we didn't have to specify the function itself that we were modifying in our thenAdd method. Since it's a function method, the this keyword inside our method body already points to the function, so when we called add.thenAdd(5), this referred to the add function, and the same thing happens for the square.thenAdd(2) call. One other thing we did was to save the reference to the function to a local variable via the line var self = this; so that we can reference the function inside the new function we're creating. If we didn't do this, we'd lose reference to the function since the value of this inside the new function would be the global object instead of the function we're modifying.

As in previous examples, you'll see that a closure is created, enabling us to reference both the original function via self and the number argument to the thenAdd method. We also used the Array.prototype.slice.call(arguments) technique to turn our arguments object into an array so that we can use it with the apply method, and this also gives our new function flexibility to handle a variable number of arguments. The result is a new function method that adds a number to the result of the original function.

In the previous section on combination, we used a combinator function to join two functions. We could rewrite our old combinator function into a new function method to make it easier to reuse the function:

```
Function.implement('combine', function(fn){
    var self = this;
    return function(){
        var args = Array.prototype.slice.call(arguments);
        var result = self.apply(null, args);
        return fn(result);
    };
});

var add = function(a, b){
    return a + b;
};

var square = function(a){
    return a * a;
};

var addThenSquare = add.combine(square);

var result = addThenSquare(3, 5);
console.log(result); // 64
```

If you're creating more than one method, you can pass Function.implement a single object argument instead of a string and a function. If we were to add our two methods above in one go, we could do this by passing an object instead:

```
Function.implement({

    addThen: function(num){
        var self = this;
        return function(){
            var args = Array.prototype.slice.call(arguments);
            var result = self.apply(null, args);
            return result + num;
        };
    },

    combine: function(fn){
        var self = this;
        return function(){
            var args = Array.prototype.slice.call(arguments);
            var result = self.apply(null, args);
            return fn(result);
        };
    }

});
```

The Wrap Up

As we've seen in this chapter, JavaScript's implementation of functions is truly amazing. JavaScript functions are powerful and complex—both from the developer's and the interpreter's points of view. We saw the different forms of functions available to us and discussed seemingly simple elements such as arguments and return values. We also dived deep into the internals of functions and learned about execution contexts, variable instantiation, and scoping. Finally, we discussed the various advanced techniques and features of JavaScript functions like closures, currying, decoration, and dynamic modification, and we toured the additional features that MooTools provides.

I hope you've learned a lot about how powerful and complex JavaScript functions are and that you picked up a few nifty techniques to use in your own programs. However, we're just getting started in our exploration and this chapter is meant to be the starting point for more complex JavaScript topics.

In the next chapter, we'll learn about objects and dive headfirst into JavaScript's own flavor of object-oriented programming. So if you're ready, turn to the next chapter and let's get started.

CHAPTER 3

■■■

Objects

The specification document for ECMAScript defines the language as "an object-oriented programming language for performing computations and manipulating computational objects within a host environment." To put it simply, JavaScript is an object-oriented (OO) language.

The object-oriented approach focuses on objects, their composition, and how they interact with each other. While the whole area that is object-oriented programming is beyond the scope of this book, we'll discuss JavaScript's own flavor of object-oriented programming in this chapter.

Like the previous chapter on functions, there won't be much talk about MooTools here. The MooTools framework is an object-oriented framework at its core and we need to get a solid grasp of JavaScript's native object implementation to truly appreciate it. Don't worry, though, this is the last chapter where everything's vanilla JavaScript. We'll spend the rest of the book talking more about MooTools.

JavaScript is Prototypal(-ish)

While all OO languages deal with objects at their core, the process by which objects are created and composed divides most OO languages into two camps:

- *Classical (or class-based) object-oriented languages* use classes to create objects. A class is a special data type that serves as a blueprint for creating objects. In a classical OO language, you define the structure of an object by creating a class for it and then create the object itself by creating an instance of the class, in a process called instantiation.

- *Prototypal (or prototype-based) object-oriented languages*, on the other hand, do not have classes but rely on other objects as blueprints. In a prototypal language, you create an actual object called the prototype that reflects the structure you want and this object is then used as a blueprint for your other objects. You create new instances by copying the prototype itself in a process called cloning. In pure prototypal languages, all objects can be used as prototypes.

JavaScript, at its core, is a prototypal language: there are no classes in JavaScript and objects are created from other objects. However, JavaScript is not a purely prototypal language. In fact, it has traces of classical features that we'll see later on in this chapter. If you're already familiar with other object-oriented languages, you'll probably find JavaScript to be weird, since the language has a unique—and somewhat quirky—object implementation.

However, don't be turned off too quickly: JavaScript—as an object-oriented language—is quite flexible and its fusion of classical and prototypal features give it a highly powerful base for complex and rich applications.

A Language of Objects

A JavaScript **object** is essentially an aggregate of **key-value pairs**. It's a complex data type, in contrast to "simple" data types like strings and numbers. Each key-value pair in an object is called a **property**, the key being the **property name** and the value being the **property value**.

The property name is always a string, but the property value can be any data type: primitives like strings, numbers, or Booleans, or complex data types like arrays, functions, and other objects. Although JavaScript makes no distinction about what data type a property contains, properties with functions as their values are often called **methods** to distinguish them from other properties. To avoid confusion, we'll adopt this practice in our discussion: properties with values other than functions will be called "properties" and properties with functions as their values will be called "methods". When we need to refer to both the properties and methods of an object, we'll use another term from object-oriented programming: **members**.

▪ **Note** The lack of distinction between properties and methods in JavaScript arises from the fact that the language has first-class functions. From the perspective of the interpreter, any member of an object—regardless of value—is a property, since functions themselves can be used as values.

There are no limits to the number of properties an object can have, and an object can also have zero properties (making it an *empty object*). Depending on its use, an object can sometimes be called a *hash* or a *dictionary* or a *table*, reflecting its structure as a set of key-value pairs. However, we'll stick to object in our discussion.

The easiest way to create a new object in JavaScript is using the **object literal**:

```
// an object literal
var person = {
    name: 'Mark',
    age: 23
};
```

Here, we create a new object with two properties, one with the key name and the other with the key age, and store it in our person variable—giving us a person object with two members. Notice that we didn't wrap the keys in quotes even though keys have to be strings. This is allowed in JavaScript as long as the keys are valid identifiers and not reserved words. Otherwise, we have to wrap our keys in quotes:

```
// object literal with different keys
var person = {
    'name of the person': 'Mark',
    'age of the person': 23
};
```

To access a member of an object, we can use **dot notation**, which involves appending a period to the object's identifier and then the name of the key we want to access, or **bracket notation**, which involves appending a pair of square brackets, [ ], to the end of the identifier containing a string value corresponding to the key:

```
var person = {
    name: 'Mark',
    age: 23
```

```
};

// dot notation
console.log(person.name); // 'Mark'

// bracket notation
console.log(person['age']); // 23
```

The dot notation is actually just a shortcut—or *syntactic sugar*—for the bracket notation, although it's common practice to use dot notation most of the time. Of course, dot notation is limited to keys that are proper identifiers; for everything else, you'll have to use bracket notation.

```
var person = {
    'name of the person': 'Mark',
    'age of the person': 23
};

console.log(person['name of the person']); // 'Mark'
```

You'll also use bracket notation when you're not using a string literal for the key, but a variable that holds a string literal:

```
var person = {
    name: 'Mark',
    age: 23
};

// variable to hold the key
var key = 'name';

console.log(person[key]); // 'Mark'

Accessing an object's member that's not set will return the value undefined:

var person = {};

console.log(person.name); // undefined
```

You can set the value of an object's member by explicitly defining it during the creation of the object like we did in the previous examples, but you can also set or modify a member's value by simply assigning a new value:

```
var person = {name: 'Mark'};

person.name = 'Joseph';
console.log(person.name); // 'Joseph'

console.log(person.age); // undefined
person.age = 23;
console.log(person.age); // 23
```

You can create methods by simply assigning a function value to an object's member:

```
var person = {
    name: 'Mark',
    age: 23,
```

```
    sayName: function(){
        console.log(this.name); // 'Mark'
    }
};

console.log(typeof person.sayName); // 'function'
person.sayName();

person.sayAge = function(){
    console.log(this.age); // 23
};

console.log(typeof person.sayAge); // 'function'
person.sayAge();
```

You'll notice that we referred to the name and age members of our person object using this.name and this.age in our methods. If you recall our discussion in the previous chapter, you know that the this keyword for functions that are properties of objects refers to the object itself. In our case, the sayName and sayAge functions are methods of the person object, and therefore the value of the this keyword in their function bodies points to the person object.

The Building Blocks of Objects

While object literals are an easy way to create new objects, they don't showcase JavaScript's full object-oriented capabilities. For one, limiting yourself to object literals would be time-consuming: if you need 30 objects to represent people with the properties name and age and logName and logAge methods, it would be impractical to create literals for each of these objects. In order to be efficient, we need a way to define the structure of our objects and use this definition to create new instances of the objects.

In a classical object-oriented language, we can create a new Person class to define the structure of our objects. In a prototypal object-oriented language, we can simply create a base Person object for the structure, then clone this object to create new instances. JavaScript—while nominally a prototypal language—takes an approach that fuses both the classical and prototypal way.

Constructor Functions

The first half of JavaScript's approach involves **constructor functions** (or simply, **constructors**). Object literals are actually syntactic sugar for creating objects without having to use a constructor. The following objects are equivalent:

```
// using an object literal..
var personA = {
    name: 'Mark',
    age: 23
};

// using a constructor..
var personB = new Object();
personB.name = 'Mark';
personB.age = 23;
```

The function `Object` is our constructor function, and using `var personB = new Object()` is the same as using `var personB = {}`. By using `new Object()`, we create a new blank object and this new object is said to be an instance of `Object`.

The `Object` constructor is special because it represents the "base" object in JavaScript: all objects in JavaScript, regardless of which constructor was used to create them, are instances of `Object`. You can check whether an object is an instance of a constructor using the `instanceof` operator:

```
// object literal
var personA = {};

// constructor
var personB = new Object();

// check whether objects are instances of Object
console.log(personA instanceof Object); // true
console.log(personB instanceof Object); // true
```

All objects also have a special property called `constructor`, which is a reference to the constructor function that was used to create it. In the case of our simple objects above, the value of this property will be the `Object` constructor:

```
// object literal
var personA = {};

// constructor
var personB = new Object();

// check whether objects used Object constructor
console.log(personA.constructor == Object); // true
console.log(personB.constructor == Object); // true
```

As the name implies, constructor functions are, obviously, functions. In fact, any JavaScript function (with the exception of *host* or interpreter-implemented functions) can be used as a constructor. This is one of the unique aspects of the language's object implementation: instead of creating a new construct for instantiating objects, JavaScript just relies on the readily available function construct.

Of course, you won't be using every function you create as a constructor. In almost all cases, you'll create your own functions that serve the sole purpose of being constructors for your classes. A constructor function is just like any other function—with slight changes in its internals—and it's common practice to define functions with their names capitalized to denote their nature as constructors:

```
// our Person constructor
var Person = function(){};

// using the Person function as a regular function
var result = Person();
console.log(result); // undefined

// using the Person function as a constructor
var person = new Person();

console.log(typeof person); // 'object'
console.log(person instanceof Person); // true
console.log(person.constructor == Person); // true
```

We created a new constructor called Person by simply defining a blank function. When the Person function is called like a normal function, it returns undefined. However, when we use the new keyword in conjunction with the Person() invocation, something different happens: it returns a new object. It is this combination of the new keyword and a call to a constructor function that makes object instantiation happen.

In our example, new Person() returns a blank object, just like the object returned by new Object(). The only difference in this case is that the object returned is no longer just an instance of Object, it's also be an instance of Person, and the constructor property of the object now points to our new Person constructor rather than Object. But the object returned is still a blank object.

If you recall from the last chapter, the this keyword inside functions refers to an object. In the case of our Person function, it should refer to the global object when the function is used as a regular function (because it was declared in the global scope). However, something changes when the Person function is used as a constructor: this no longer points to the global object, but instead points to the new object created:

```
// a global object
var fruit = 'banana';

// our constructor
var Person = function(){
    console.log(this.fruit);
};

// Person as a regular function
Person(); // logs 'banana'

// Person as a constructor
new Person(); // logs undefined
```

We get undefined for the last line because this.fruit no longer points to any identifier available. It's the job of the new keyword to create a new object and change the this value of the constructor function to point to the new object.

At the start of this section, we ran into a problem with using simple object literals for object creation. We needed a way to create several copies of the person object without having to type each one of them via literals. Now that we know that constructor functions can be used to create objects and that the this keyword refers to the new object, we can use this to solve our problem:

```
var Person = function(name, age){
    this.name = name;
    this.age = age;
};

var mark = new Person('Mark', 23);
var joseph = new Person('Joseph', 22);
var andrew = new Person('Andrew', 21);

console.log(mark.name); // 'Mark'
console.log(joseph.age); // 22
console.log(andrew.name + ', ' + andrew.age); // 'Andrew, 21'
```

The first thing you'll notice is that we changed our constructor a bit to accept arguments. This is allowed because constructors are just like regular functions, with the exception of having their this keyword pointing to the newly created instance. When the call to new Person is interpreted, a new object is created and the Person function is invoked. Inside the constructor function, the arguments to name and age are set as the values of the object properties of the same name. The object is then returned.

Using constructors makes instantiating new objects of the same structure easier. Instead of explicitly defining the structure of each object via literals, you can simply create a constructor function that defines the structure ahead of time. This comes in handy when you need to add more members to your objects, especially when it comes to methods:

```
var Person = function(name, age){
    this.name = name;
    this.age = age;
    this.log = function(){
        console.log(this.name + ', ' + this.age);
    };
};

var mark = new Person('Mark', 23);
var joseph = new Person('Joseph', 22);
var andrew = new Person('Andrew', 21);

mark.log(); // 'Mark, 23'
joseph.log(); // 'Joseph, 22'
andrew.log(); // 'Andrew, 21'
```

Here we added a new method called log to our objects by simply declaring the value of this.log as a logging function inside our constructor. If we were still using object literals, we would have to define the log function for each of our objects—and that would take too long. But by using a constructor function, we can define the function once for all our objects.

Prototypes

While constructor functions might seem like the end point for JavaScript's object implementation, they're only half of the picture. And if we limit ourselves to using constructor functions, we'll run into several problems.

One such problem is code organization. At the start of the last section, we wanted an easier way to create person objects with the properties name and age, and the methods setName, getName, setAge, and getAge. If we modify the Person constructor from the previous section according to our specification, we end up with something like this:

```
var Person = function(name, age){

    // properties
    this.name = name;
    this.age = age;

    // methods
    this.setName = function(name){
        this.name = name;
    };

    this.getName = function(){
        return this.name;
    };

    this.setAge = function(age){
        this.age = age;
    };
```

```
        this.getAge = function(){
            return this.age;
        };

};
```

Our `Person` constructor has suddenly ballooned—and we only have two properties and four methods! Imagine if you start creating complex objects with lots of members and complex methods. Your code would soon get hard to manage if you put everything inside your constructor.

Another issue that arises is extensibility. Suppose we have the following code:

```
// constructor.js
var Person = function(name, age){
    this.name = name;
    this.age = age;
    this.log = function(){
        console.log(this.name + ', ' + this.age);
    };
};
```

```
// program.js
var mark = new Person('Mark', 23);
mark.log(); // 'Mark, 23'
```

In this example, the `Person` constructor comes from another file we load from an external source into our program and we don't have access to change the code. But for our program, we need to add the new methods getName and getAge to our `Person` instances. Since we can't modify the constructor itself, we can't add these new methods inside the constructor.

Then we get a brilliant idea: let's add the methods to the instances! Since new members can easily be added to methods by assignment, this would be easy to do. However, we quickly run into some problems:

```
// program.js
var mark = new Person('Mark', 23);
mark.log(); // 'Mark, 23'

mark.getName = function(){ return this.name; };
mark.getAge = function(){ return this.age; };

mark.getName(); // returns 'Mark'
mark.getAge(); // returns 23

var joseph = new Person('Joseph', 22);
joseph.log(); // 'Joseph, 22'

// the following lines will produce an error:
joseph.getName();
joseph.getAge();
```

Even though we successfully managed to add new methods to our mark instance, our joseph instance didn't get the same methods. We end up with the same problem we had with object literals: we have to define the same set of members for each of our objects. This isn't very practical, even if we build a helper function to do it.

At the beginning of this chapter, we learned that JavaScript is a prototypal language and that the main feature of a prototypal language is its reliance on creating copies of an original object—the prototype—to define new objects instead of using classes. But looking back, we haven't seen any copying involved, nor did we see any original objects that serve as prototypes. All we saw were functions used as constructors and that new keyword.

And that's our clue: the new keyword. Remember that when we use new Object(), the new keyword creates a new object and uses that object as the this value of our constructor function. Actually, the new keyword isn't creating a new object: it's copying an object. And the object it's copying is none other than the **prototype**.

All functions that can be used as constructors have a special property called the prototype, which is an object that defines the structure of your instances. When you use new Object(), a new copy of Object.prototype is made and this becomes your new object instance. This is another unique trait of JavaScript: unlike other prototypal languages where any object can be a prototype, JavaScript defines special prototype objects for the sole purpose of prototyping.

■ **Note** There is a way to mimic the prototypal style of other languages in JavaScript, though, wherein you directly clone any object to create a new object, instead of relying on prototypes. We'll learn how to do this in the last section of this chapter.

The prototype object, like any other object, can have an unlimited number of members, and adding new members to it is simply a matter of assigning new values. We could rewrite our original Person code in this way:

```
var Person = function(name, age){
    this.name = name;
    this.age = age;
};

Person.prototype.log = function(){
    console.log(this.name + ', ' + this.age);
};

var mark = new Person('Mark', 23);
mark.log(); // 'Mark, 23'
```

Here, we moved the declaration of our log method outside of the constructor. By assigning Person.prototype.log, we tell the interpreter that all objects created from the Person constructor should have a log method, and this is reflected in our last line where we call mark.log(). The rest of the constructor stays the same: we didn't move our this.name and this.age properties to the prototype because we want to be able to set them when we invoke our constructor.

With prototypes in mind, we could also rewrite the code we had at the start of this section into something more manageable:

```
var Person = function(name, age){
    this.name = name;
    this.age = age;
};

Person.prototype.setName = function(name){
```

```
        this.name = name;
};

Person.prototype.getName = function(){
    return this.name;
};

Person.prototype.setAge = function(age){
    this.age = age;
};

Person.prototype.getAge = function(){
    return this.age;
};
```

This new code is much cleaner because we're not cramming everything inside our constructor and we can easily add more methods in the future without having to rearrange the constructor.

Another problem we had was how to add new methods when we can't change the constructor function. But since we already have access to the constructor function (and therefore its prototype), we can easily add new members without any access to the constructor itself:

```
// person.js
var Person = function(name, age){
    this.name = name;
    this.age = age;
};

// program.js
Person.prototype.log = function(){
    console.log(this.name + ', ' + this.age);
};

var mark = new Person('Mark', 23);
mark.log(); // 'Mark, 23'

var joseph = new Person('Joseph', 22);
joseph.log(); // 'Joseph, 22'
```

We actually already saw a sample of dynamic prototype augmentation in the previous chapter on functions. One function form, the function object, used the Function constructor and we were able to add new function methods through the MooTools function called Function.implement. All JavaScript functions are actually instances of Function, and Function.implement actually modifies Function.prototype. Even though we didn't have access to the Function constructor itself—which is a built-in constructor that's provided by the interpreter—we're still able to add new function methods by augmenting Function.prototype. The augmentation of native types will be discussed later on in the chapter on Types and Natives.

Inheritance

To understand prototypal programming in JavaScript, we need to be able to distinguish between prototypes and instances. As we learned earlier, a *prototype* is an object we use like a blueprint to define the structure of objects we want. When we copy the prototype, we create an *instance* of the prototype:

```javascript
// Animal constructor
var Animal = function(name){
    this.name = name;
};

// Animal prototype
Animal.prototype.walk = function(){
    console.log(this.name + ' is walking.');
};

// Animal instance
var cat = new Animal('Cat');
cat.walk(); // 'Cat is walking.'
```

In this example, Animal and its prototype define the structure of our Animal objects, and our object cat is an instance of Animal. When we execute new Animal(), a copy of Animal.prototype is created and we call this copy as an **instance**. Animal.prototype is an object with a single member, walk, which is a method and therefore all instances of Animal also have the same walk method.

But what happens if we change Animal.prototype after we created an instance?

```javascript
// Animal constructor
var Animal = function(name){
    this.name = name;
};

// Animal prototype
Animal.prototype.walk = function(){
    console.log(this.name + ' is walking.');
};

// Animal instance
var cat = new Animal('Cat');
cat.walk(); // 'Cat is walking.'

// Does an Animal have an eat method?
console.log(typeof cat.eat); // undefined, so no.

// Add an eat method to Animal
Animal.prototype.eat = function(){
    console.log(this.name + ' is eating.');
};

console.log(typeof cat.eat); // 'function'
cat.eat(); // 'Cat is eating'
```

Something interesting happened here. When we first checked the value of cat.eat after we created the cat object, we found that cat.eat was undefined. We then added a new method to Animal.prototype called eat and checked again: cat.eat is no longer undefined but is now a function. In fact, it's the same function we defined for Animal.prototype.

It seems that defining new properties for a prototype updates all instances of the prototype, regardless of when they were created. Remember that when we create a new object, the new operator creates a new copy of the prototype and when we created cat, the prototype only had one method. If it's a real copy, it shouldn't have the eat method after we defined it in the prototype. After all, if you take a document and copy it on a photocopy machine and then write something on the original using a pen, you wouldn't expect that new change to automatically appear in the photocopied version, right?

Perhaps the interpreter knows when new properties are added to the prototype and automatically adds them to the instances? Maybe after we add the new eat method to Animal.prototype, it searches for all instances of Animal and then adds this new method to them? We can easily check if this is the case by doing a simple experiment. After creating a cat instance, we'll give it its own eat method, and then we'll update the prototype. If the interpreter indeed copies methods from the prototype, the eat method of our cat instance should be overwritten:

```
// Animal constructor
var Animal = function(name){
    this.name = name;
};

// Animal prototype
Animal.prototype.walk = function(){
    console.log(this.name + ' is walking.');
};

// Animal instance
var cat = new Animal('Cat');
cat.walk(); // 'Cat is walking.'

// Add a new eat method to cat
cat.eat = function(){
    console.log('Meow. Cat is eating!');
};

// Add an eat method to Animal
Animal.prototype.eat = function(){
    console.log(this.name + 'is eating.');
};

cat.eat(); // 'Meow. Cat is eating!'
```

Clearly, that's not the case. The JavaScript interpreter does not update the instances, because our cat.eat method points to the one we defined for the cat object rather than the one from Animal.prototype. So what's really happening?

All objects have an internal property called proto that points to the object's prototype. This property is used by the interpreter to "link" the object to its prototype. While it's true that the new keyword creates a copy of the prototype, it actually just creates a "superficial" copy, in the sense that the object it creates looks like the prototype. But the truth is that the object created by new is nothing more than a blank object that has its internal proto property set to the prototype of the constructor.

You're probably asking, "Wait, if it's a blank object, why does it have methods and properties like the prototype? Where do those come from?" This is where the proto property comes in. Objects are linked to their prototype so that the methods and the properties of the prototype can be accessed from the object. In our example, our cat object didn't really have its own walk method—it was actually the walk method of Animal.prototype. When the interpreter comes across the identifier cat.walk(), it checks whether the cat object has its own walk method. Since we didn't explicitly define a walk method for our cat object, it checks the proto property of the object to find its prototype, then checks the prototype to see if it has a walk method. And seeing that there is indeed such a method in the prototype, the interpreter uses this method for the instance.

This also explains the eat method of our other example: because we explicitly defined an eat method for our cat object, the eat method of our Animal.prototype wasn't called. An object overrides the members of the prototype if it has a member of the same key, and the members of an object's prototype are available only when they aren't overridden by the object's own members.

An object's member that's from the prototype (as opposed to a member that was explicitly defined for it) is said to be *inherited,* and the process of obtaining members from an object's prototype is called **inheritance**. You can check if an object has its own member using the hasOwnProperty method that's available to all objects:

```
var Animal = function(){};
Animal.prototype.walk = function(){};

var dog = new Animal();

var cat = new Animal();
cat.walk = function(){};

console.log(cat.hasOwnProperty('walk')); // true
console.log(dog.hasOwnProperty('walk')); // false
```

Here we explicitly defined a walk method for our cat object, but we didn't do the same for our dog object. When we call cat.hasOwnProperty('walk'), it returns true because cat now has its own walk member. In contrast, dog.hasOwnProperty('walk') returns false because there's no explicitly defined walk member for dog. Interestingly, if we do cat.hasOwnProperty('hasOwnProperty'), it'll return false, because the hasOwnProperty method itself is inherited from Object.

One thing to consider is the value of this: inside a constructor, the value of this always points to the instance and never to the prototype. Functions defined from the prototype have another rule: if they are called directly from the prototype, the this value will point to the prototype object, but when they are called from an object inheriting from the prototype, this will point to the instance rather than the prototype:

```
var Animal = function(name){
    this.name = name;
};

Animal.prototype.name = 'Animal';

Animal.prototype.getName = function(){
    return this.name;
};

// Call `getName` directly from the prototype
Animal.prototype.getName(); // returns 'Animal'

var cat = new Animal('Cat');
cat.getName(); // returns 'Cat'
```

Here we changed our code a bit so that the Animal.prototype object will have its own name property. When we called the function directly, this.name points to the value of the name property of Animal.prototype. However, when we called cat.getName(), this.name points to the value of cat.name (which we set in our constructor).

The prototype and its instances are separate objects, and the link between them goes only one way: changes to the prototype are reflected to all its instances but changes to the instances affect only the instances. However, weird behavior occurs when complex types come into play wherein changes to one instance affect all other instances.

Remember that in JavaScript we have both primitives and complex types. Primitives such as strings, numbers, and Booleans are always used by value: a copy is made when they are passed to functions or assigned to variables. However, complex types like arrays, functions, and objects are always used by reference, which means that they aren't copied but rather a "pointer" to the original complex type is created:

```
// Create an object
var object = {name: 'Mark'};

// "Copy" the object into another variable
var copy = object;

console.log(object.name); // 'Mark'
console.log(copy.name); // 'Mark'

// Change the value of our copy
copy.name = 'Joseph';

console.log(copy.name); // 'Joseph'
console.log(object.name); // 'Joseph'
```

When we did var copy = object, no new object was created. Rather, our variable copy was assigned a reference to the same original object that was the value of object. Therefore, both copy and object now reference the same object. A change made to copy was therefore reflected to object because they're really pointing to the same object.

Objects can have members that are complex types, such as an object with a property that's another object. Prototypes, being objects themselves, can also have complex types as properties. The problem arises when you define a property in a prototype that points to a complex object, because this property will then be inherited by all instances and they will all therefore point to a single object:

```
var Animal = function(){};

Animal.prototype.data = {name: 'animal', type: 'unknown'};

Animal.prototype.setData = function(name, type){
    this.data.name = name;
    this.data.type = type;
};

Animal.prototype.getData = function(){
    console.log(this.data.name + ': ' + this.data.type);
};

var cat = new Animal();
cat.setData('Cat', 'Mammal');
cat.getData(); // 'Cat: Mammal'

var shark = new Animal();
shark.setData('Shark', 'Fish');
shark.getData(); // 'Shark: Fish'

cat.getData(); // 'Shark: Fish'
```

Both the cat and shark objects don't have their own data property, so they inherit the object from Animal.prototype. Because of this inheritance, cat.data and shark.data both point to the same object that was defined from Animal.prototype. Any change in one instance therefore gets reflected in other instances and gives us unwanted behavior.

The easiest way to solve this would be to remove the data property from `Animal.prototype` and give our instances their own data property. This could easily be done inside the constructor:

```
var Animal = function(){
    this.data = {name: 'animal', type: 'unknown'};
};

Animal.prototype.setData = function(name, type){
    this.data.name = name;
    this.data.type = type;
};

Animal.prototype.getData = function(){
    console.log(this.data.name + ': ' + this.data.type);
};

var cat = new Animal();
cat.setData('Cat', 'Mammal');
cat.getData(); // 'Cat: Mammal'

var shark = new Animal();
shark.setData('Shark', 'Fish');
shark.getData(); // 'Shark: Fish'

cat.getData(); // 'Cat: Mammal'
```

Because the this keyword inside our constructor points to the instance itself, setting `this.data` inside it would give the instance its own data property and won't affect our prototype. The end result is that all our instances now have their own data properties, and changing these properties will no longer affect other instances.

The Prototype Chain

The `Object` constructor and its corresponding prototype is the base object in JavaScript. All objects, regardless of how they are constructed, inherit from Object. In the case of the following code, this is simple enough to understand:

```
var object = new Object();

console.log(object instanceof Object); // true
```

Because we constructed object using the `Object` constructor, we can say that the internal proto property of object points to `Object.prototype`. However, consider the following code:

```
var Animal = function(){};

var cat = new Animal();

console.log(cat instanceof Animal); // true
console.log(cat instanceof Object); // true
console.log(typeof cat.hasOwnProperty); // 'function'
```

We know for a fact that cat is indeed an instance of Animal, since it was created using new Animal(). We also know that all objects have a method called hasOwnProperty, which they inherit from Object. But how can our cat object inherit from `Object` when its internal `proto` property points to Animal? And how can cat be an instance of both `Animal` and `Object` at the same time when we didn't even use the `Object` constructor?

The answer lies within the prototypes. By default, a constructor's `prototype` is a basic object that has no methods or properties of its own. Sound familiar? Yes, it's like an object that's created using `new Object()`! We could have written our code in the following form:

```
var Animal = function(){};

Animal.prototype = new Object();

var cat = new Animal();

console.log(cat instanceof Animal); // true
console.log(cat instanceof Object); // true
console.log(typeof cat.hasOwnProperty); // 'function'
```

And now it's clearer that `Animal.prototype` inherits from `Object`. Aside from inheriting from its own prototype, an instance also inherits from the prototype of the prototype of the prototype.

Sound confusing? Let's examine this in our code above. Our cat object is created using `new Animal`, so it inherits properties and methods from `Animal.prototype`. The value of `Animal.prototype` is an object created using `new Object()`, so it inherits the properties and methods from `Object.prototype`. In turn, these properties and methods that our `Animal.prototype` inherits from `Object.prototype` are also passed to any instances of Animal. And, therefore, we can say that our cat object *indirectly inherits* from `Object.prototype`.

The internal `proto` property of our cat object points to `Animal.prototype`, and, in turn, the internal `proto` property of our `Animal.prototype` points to `Object.prototype`. This continuous linking between the prototypes is called the **prototype chain,** and we can say that the cat object's prototype chain extends from the cat object itself to `Object.prototype`.

■ **Note** `Object.prototype` is always the end of the prototype chain, and this prototype's `proto` property does not point to any other object—otherwise there would be no end to the prototype chain and it would be impossible to traverse it. `Object.prototype` itself is not created using any constructors, but rather set by the interpreter internally, thus making it the only object that is not an instance of `Object`.

The process of looking up properties and methods of an object through the prototype chain is called **traversal**. When the interpreter encounters `cat.hasOwnProperty`, it first looks at the object itself to see if there's a member called hasOwnProperty in the object. When it doesn't find one, it looks at the next object in the prototype chain, which is `Animal.prototype`. As there's still no such member in this object, it moves on to the next object in the prototype chain, and so on. If it finds the member we're looking for in one of the objects in the chain, it stops the traversal and uses this member. If it reaches the end of the chain (which is `Object.prototype`) and still does not find what it's looking for, it returns the value undefined for the member. In our example, the traversal ends at `Object.prototype`, where the hasOwnProperty method comes from.

An object is always an instance of at least one constructor: for objects created using literals and objects created using `new Object()`, they're instances of `Object`. For objects created using a different constructor, they will be an instance of both the constructor used to create them as well as an instance of all the constructors used to create the prototypes in their prototype chain.

Deliberate Chains

The prototype chain becomes useful once we start creating more complex objects. Say we want to have an Animal object: all animals have a name, and all animals should be able to eat to survive. Therefore, we could write the following code:

```
var Animal = function(name){
    this.name = name;
};

Animal.prototype.eat = function(){
    console.log('The ' + this.name + ' is eating.');
};

var cat = new Animal('cat');
cat.eat(); // 'The cat is eating.'

var bird = new Animal('bird');
bird.eat(); // 'The bird is eating.'
```

So far so good. But now we want our animals to make noises, so we need to add methods. Moreover, these animals make different sounds: a cat meows and a bird tweets, so a cat needs a meow method and a bird needs a tweet method. Of course, we can simply create these methods on the animals themselves, but it would be impractical since we plan on creating many cat and bird objects. We could also simply add both these methods to Animal.prototype, but that would be wasteful since birds never meow and cats never tweet.

What if we simply create separate constructors for both objects? We can create Cat and Bird constructors and modify their prototypes to fit the particular animal. But both these animals eat—do we really need to define an eat method for each of the animals? That would mean quite a number of repeated declarations should we decide to add more types of animals.

With our knowledge of the prototype chain, we realize that there's a better solution. We can code our program so that we have separate Cat and Bird objects with proper methods and still inherit the methods that both animal share from our original Animal prototype:

```
var Animal = function(name){
    this.name = name;
};

Animal.prototype.eat = function(){
    console.log('The ' + this.name + ' is eating.');
};

var Cat = function(){};

Cat.prototype = new Animal('cat');

Cat.prototype.meow = function(){
    console.log('Meow!');
};

var Bird = function(){};

Bird.prototype = new Animal('bird');
```

```
Bird.prototype.tweet = function(){
    console.log('Tweet!');
};

var cat = new Cat();
cat.eat(); // 'The cat is eating.'
cat.meow(); // 'Meow!'

var bird = new Bird();
bird.eat(); // 'The bird is eating.'
bird.tweet(); // 'Tweet!'
```

We left our original Animal constructor and prototype as they were and created two new constructors, Cat and Bird. We used empty functions for our new constructors since we didn't have anything to set inside them, but we could have as easily added some other statements inside them if needed. The default prototypes for Cat and Bird were replaced with instances of Animal, so our Cat and Bird objects will also inherit from Animal.prototype. Finally, we added proper methods to the prototypes—meow for Cat and tweet for Bird. When we finally instantiated our objects, the results were two objects that inherit from both their immediate prototypes and from Animal.prototype.

In classical programming languages, the process of creating a specialized version of a class by creating a new class and inheriting directly from the original class is called *subclassing*. JavaScript, being a prototypal language, does not have classes and, in essence, the only thing we are doing is creating a *deliberate prototype chain*. We say "deliberate" because we explicitly set which objects will be included in the prototype chain of our instances.

There is no limit to the size of your prototype chain, and you can extend your chain to allow for more specialization:

```
var Animal = function(name){
    this.name = name;
};

Animal.prototype.eat = function(){
    console.log('The ' + this.name + 'is eating.');
};

var Cat = function(){};

Cat.prototype = new Animal('cat');

Cat.prototype.meow = function(){
    console.log('Meow!');
};

var Persian = function(){
    this.name = 'persian cat';
};

Persian.prototype = new Cat();

Persian.prototype.meow = function(){
    console.log('Meow...');
};

Persian.prototype.setColor = function(color){
```

```
    this.color = color;
};

Persian.prototype.getColor = function(){
    return this.color;
};

var king = new Persian();
king.setColor('black');
king.getColor(); // 'black'
king.eat(); // 'The persian cat is eating.'
king.meow(); // 'Meow...'

console.log(king instanceof Animal); // true
console.log(king instanceof Cat); // true
console.log(king instanceof Persian); // true
```

Here we created a new specialized version of Cat called Persian. You'll notice that we created a Persian.prototype.meow method, which overwrites (during traversal) the original Cat.prototype.meow method for instances of Persian. If you check, you'll see that the king object is an instance of Animal, Cat, and Persian, which means our prototype chain was correctly set.

The real power of prototype chains (deliberate or not) is when we see it in conjunction with inheritance and prototype chain traversal. Because all of the prototypes are linked, a change at one point in the chain will be reflected in the items below that point. If we add a new method or property to Animal.prototype, for instance, all prototypes that inherit from Animal will also receive those new members. This gives us a way to extend several objects easily and quickly.

As your programs grow in complexity, deliberate chains help keep your code organized. Instead of jamming all your code into one prototype, you can create multiple prototypes that have deliberate chains to reduce the amount of code you're working with and keep your program manageable.

Simplified Prototypal Programming

You should realize by now that JavaScript's object-oriented flavor is in a class of its own. JavaScript's status as a prototypal language is largely nominal: constructor functions and the new keyword are elements you'd expect to find in classical languages, and JavaScript's use of inheritance from prototypes—while clearly a prototypal characteristic—relies on specialized prototype objects, making them similar to classes. The design of the language's object implementation was in part affected by language politics: JavaScript was created during a time when classical languages were the standard, and it was decided to give the language some features that would be familiar to classical programmers.

However, JavaScript is a flexible language. While we may not be able to change the core implementation of objects, we can leverage what's already available to give the language a more pure prototypal feel (and as we'll see in the next chapter, even a more classical feel).

In this "simplified" prototypal model, we'll forgo the complexities of JavaScript prototyping and focus on objects themselves. Instead of creating a constructor and setting prototypes, we'll use real objects as the prototypes and create new objects by "cloning" these prototypes. To get a better idea of what we're going to do, let's first use an example from another prototypal programming language called *Io*:

```
Animal := Object clone
Animal name := "animal"

Cat := Animal clone
Cat name := "cat"

myCat := Cat clone
```

Since this isn't a book about Io, we'll stick to the basics. Like JavaScript, the base object of Io is called Object. However, Io's Object isn't a constructor (i.e., not a function), but rather a real object. At the start of our code, we created a new object, Animal, by cloning the original Object object. Object clone in Io means "access the clone method of Object and execute it," since Io uses spaces instead of periods or brackets to access properties. Next we set the name property of Animal to the proper string and then created a new object called Cat by cloning the Animal object and also set a name property for it. Finally, we created our myCat object by cloning our final Cat object.

We can do something similar in JavaScript:

```
var Animal = function(){};
Animal.prototype = new Object();
Animal.prototype.name = 'animal';

var Cat = function(){};
Cat.prototype = new Animal();
Cat.prototype.name = 'cat';

var myCat = new Cat();
```

Similar, but not exactly the same. In our Io example, the final myCat object inherits directly from Cat, Animal, and Object, which are all actual objects and not constructors. In our JavaScript example, our final myCat object inherits from Cat, Animal, and Object via their prototype properties, and Cat, Animal, and Object are functions rather than objects. In other words, Io does not have constructors and it clones directly from objects, while JavaScript has constructor functions and clones prototypes rather than real objects.

We could have the same feature in JavaScript if we could control the internal proto property of objects. For instance, if we have an Animal object and a Cat object, we could change the proto property of the Cat object so that it links directly to the Animal object (as opposed to linking to a prototype) so that Cat would inherit directly from it.

While the proto property itself is internal and can't be changed, several JavaScript engines have introduced a special object property called __proto__ that's accessible from the JavaScript API. The __proto__ property of an object can be used to change an object's internal proto property, making it possible to directly inherit from another object:

```
var Animal = {
    name: 'animal',
    eat: function(){
        console.log('The ' + this.name + ' is eating.');
    }
};

var Cat = {name: 'cat'};
Cat.__proto__ = Animal;

var myCat = {};
myCat.__proto__ = Cat;

myCat.eat(); // 'The cat is eating.'
```

There are no constructors in this example: Animal and Cat are real objects created using literals. By setting Cat.__proto__ = Animal, we told the interpreter that the internal proto property of Cat should be the Animal object. In the end, myCat inherits from both Cat and Animal and its prototype chain does not have any objects that are prototype. This is a simplified prototypal model that doesn't involve any constructors or prototype but instead relies on setting the prototype chain to use real objects.

You can take a similar approach via Object.create, a new function introduced in ECMAScript 5. It takes a single argument, an object, and creates a new blank object with the internal proto property set to the object passed to it:

```
var Animal = {
    name: 'animal',
    eat: function(){
        console.log('The ' + this.name + ' is eating.');
    }
};

var Cat = Object.create(Animal);
Cat.name = 'cat';

var myCat = Object.create(Cat);
myCat.eat(); // 'The cat is eating.'
```

Notice that Object.create is similar to the clone method from Io, and internally, they actually do the same thing. When we did var Cat = Object.create(Animal), the interpreter created a new object and set its internal proto property to point to the Animal object. We can reproduce the original Io example using Object.create and the results will be strikingly similar:

```
var Animal = Object.create({});
Animal.name = 'animal';

var Cat = Object.create(Animal);
Cat.name = 'cat';

myCat = Object.create(Cat);
```

Unfortunately, while both these approaches are nice, they're not available everywhere. The __proto__ property is not a part of the ECMAScript specification, so not all JavaScript engines support it. Object.create, while included in the specs, is from ECMAScript 5—which is less than a year old at the time of writing and isn't implemented in all engines yet. If you need multiple engine support for your programs (especially if it's a web application), keep in mind that these approaches won't work on all platforms.

There is, however, a way to implement Object.create on older engines. Remember that JavaScript objects are used by reference. If you store an object in a variable x and then do y = x, both x and y will now point to the same object. Also, the prototype property of a function is an object and the default object can be overridden by simply assigning a new object to it:

```
var Animal = {
    name: 'animal',
    eat: function(){
        console.log('The ' + this.name + ' is eating.');
    }
};

var AnimalProto = function(){};
AnimalProto.prototype = Animal;

var cat = new AnimalProto();
```

```
console.log(typeof cat.purr); // 'undefined'

Animal.purr = function(){};

console.log(typeof cat.purr); // 'function'
```

This should be familiar by now. We created an `Animal` object with two members, a `name` property and an eat method. We then created an "intermediate" constructor called `AnimalProto` and set its prototype property to the `Animal` object. Because of references, `AnimalProto.prototype` and `Animal` both point to the same object, and thus, when we created our `cat` instance, it was actually inheriting directly from the `Animal` object—just like an object produced by `Object.create`.

With this in mind, we can mimic `Object.create` for JavaScript engines that don't support it:

```
if (!Object.create) Object.create = function(proto){
    var Intermediate = function(){};
    Intermediate.prototype = proto;
    return new Intermediate();
};

var Animal = {
    name: 'animal',
    eat: function(){
        console.log('The ' + this.name + ' is eating.');
    }
};

var cat = Object.create(Animal);

console.log(typeof cat.purr); // 'undefined'

Animal.purr = function(){};

console.log(typeof cat.purr); // 'function'
```

To start, we used `if (!Object.create) ...` in the first line to check whether `Object.create` already exists so that we won't overwrite it. Our `Object.create` function is simple enough: it creates a new constructor called `Intermediate` and sets this constructor's `prototype` to the `proto` object passed. It then returns an instance of this intermediate constructor. Because it uses the features already available in older implementations, our `Object.create` function is compatible with almost every modern engine.

The Wrap Up

In this chapter we learned all about JavaScript's object implementation and how it differs from other languages. While at its core a prototypal language, JavaScript has features that put it in a different category as a blend of both classical and prototypal languages. We saw how we can create objects using simple literals and constructors with prototypes. We examined inheritance and how JavaScript traverses the prototype chain, and we implemented a simple prototypal model that hides the complexity of prototypes.

Because JavaScript is an object-oriented language at its core, the concepts we've learned here will help us in developing complex programs in JavaScript. And while the mechanics of object-oriented programming are beyond the scope of this book, I hope I've given you enough information to help you explore the topic further.

Now that we've learned how objects work with native JavaScript, we're left to ask a new question: "But what about MooTools?" This is a very interesting question because we didn't see much of MooTools in this chapter. Thankfully, we're just getting started and we still have room to learn one unique way MooTools handles objects. I call it unique because MooTools doesn't just use the concepts presented here to create simple features—it uses them to do something far more dramatic. And that's the subject of our next chapter.

So if you have your cup of tea or coffee ready, I suggest you sit back and relax as we explore MooTools in depth.

CHAPTER 4

■■■

Classes

In the previous chapter, we learned about JavaScript's object implementation and discovered how ideas from both prototypal and classical languages were incorporated into the language. This merging of approaches is somewhat unique to the language and sometimes makes it harder for new developers to learn how object-oriented programming in JavaScript works.

MooTools, with its focus on modularity and simplicity, provides an elegant alternative to the native implementation. To put it succinctly, MooTools turns JavaScript into a classical language. In this chapter, we'll learn how this class system works, and we'll examine some of the techniques used by MooTools to add a major language feature to JavaScript.

From Prototypes to Classes

Suppose we need to create several JavaScript objects to represent people. These objects need to have two properties, name and age, and a method called log to print out the values of these properties. Recalling what we learned from the last chapter, we come up with this snippet:

```
var Person = function(name, age){
    this.name = name;
    this.age = age;
};

// Properties
Person.prototype.name = '';
Person.prototype.age = 0;

// Methods
Person.prototype.log = function(){
    console.log(this.name + ', ' + this.age);
};

// Creating a new Person instance
var mark = new Person("Mark", 23);
mark.log(); // 'Mark, 23'
```

First, we created a Person constructor by assigning a function to our variable. We then defined the name, age, and log members by augmenting our constructor's prototype object. Finally, we created a new instance object using new Person(). We know that the new keyword creates a new object that inherits from Person.prototype, and we stored our newly created object in our mark variable.

So the whole process—without thinking too much of the details—can be summed up in three steps: create a constructor function, modify its prototype property, and instantiate it using new. Of course, this is from a JavaScript perspective—in true prototypal languages (like our Io example in the last chapter), the process is much simpler: create an object, and clone it to create a new object.

Unlike their prototypal counterparts, though, classical programming languages don't use objects to define other objects but instead rely on a special construct called a **class** to define objects. A class—much like a prototype—defines the structure of an object by specifying its properties and methods. For example, here's an implementation of a Person class in a classical language called *ooc*:

```
Person: class {

    // Properties
    name := ""
    age  := 0


    // Methods
    init: func (name: String, age: Int) {
        this name = name
        this age = age
    }

    log: func {
        printf("%s, %d", this name, this age)
    }

}

// Creating a new Person instance
mark := Person new("Mark", 23)
mark log() // "Mark, 23"
```

First, we created a new class called Person and then we defined several members: the properties name and age, which are a string and an integer respectively, and two methods, init and log. We then created a new object instance of Person called mark and called its log() to print out the name and age of our instance. You'll notice that we didn't have a constructor function, although we did have an init method that looks similar to our original constructor. We'll learn more about this difference later. The important thing to note right now is that both our JavaScript and ooc examples are doing the same task of defining objects to represent people, even though they're using different constructs to do it.

While they are both defining the structure of objects, classes and prototypes are different within the languages themselves. In a true prototypal language (which JavaScript is not), prototypes are always objects and any object can be a prototype. In contrast, classes can be objects or primitive types, depending on the language implementation. Classical languages also use special syntax to define classes, as in our ooc example, while prototype languages define prototypes like regular objects. This special syntax for classes makes the structure of instances immutable in most cases: you won't be able to add new members to objects without defining them first through the class—something you can freely do in prototypal language. For instance, you won't be able to do mark occupation := 'JavaScript Developer' in our ooc example above because the property occupation wasn't defined in our class.

But the biggest difference is in terms of inheritance and types. Objects in classical languages inherit from classes and, because the word class implies a group of things, these objects are seen not only as instances of those classes but also *members* of that group defined by class. In the case of our ooc example, the object mark not only inherits from the Person class but it's also a member of a group that is composed of all Person objects. We commonly refer to this grouping as a **type**. It's the job of a class not only to define the structure of objects but also define the type of those objects.

However, we can't have the same grouping in true prototypal languages. Since objects are cloned and inherit directly from other objects, there's no separate construct that defines the type of the objects.

For example, we have a Person object and we clone it to create a mark object. We can say that the mark object inherits from Person and that it's a copy of the Person object. But this doesn't mean that the mark object is of the type Person because Person itself is just an object and it doesn't define a grouping.

So where does JavaScript stand in this? Interestingly, it's somewhere in the middle. JavaScript is technically a prototypal language but it also contains classical influences. For one, a JavaScript object doesn't inherit from just any plain object but from the special prototype object defined as a property of the constructor. In essence, JavaScript prototypes are similar to classes because they're special language constructs. The existence of these special language constructs—prototypes and constructor functions— means we could have "types" in JavaScript because they create groupings for our objects. But because the prototype is still an object, JavaScript still implements prototypal rather than classical inheritance.

The MooTools Class System

Take a look at the previous JavaScript and ooc examples. Clearly, the class declaration in ooc is cleaner than the declarations in JavaScript. In our ooc example, all the properties and methods of our object were declared inside the class {...} declaration and you could easily see what members our instances would have. Our JavaScript example, on the other hand, is more verbose and repetitive: there's no visual grouping for our constructor and prototype members and we had to write Person.prototype several times.

This becomes even more apparent as you start writing large JavaScript applications where you need to declare many different kinds of objects. I don't know about you, but typing stuff over and over again seems counterproductive and tedious to me.

Developers were quick to see this problem and they developed many techniques to simplify object-oriented programming in JavaScript. The best solution, of course, was to implement a class system in JavaScript. There are many class systems available from different frameworks, each with its own feature set, but arguably the best among all of them is the MooTools class system.

That's quite a big assertion on my part, so let me give you a few reasons:

- The syntax of MooTools classes is similar to what's found in actual classical languages.

- The MooTools class system is built on the native JavaScript object implementation—all the magic is already in the language itself.

- The class system abstracts and extends the native object implementation, adding useful features that simplify object-oriented programming.

- Inheritance is handled by the class itself—including direct inheritance and "multiple inheritance" using "mixins" (more on these later and in the next chapter).

- The system itself is extensible, which means you can add new features easily.

We'll discuss these points more thoroughly throughout this chapter, but here's the most important thing to consider: MooTools doesn't give you a half-baked class system that's nothing more than syntax changes. Instead, the MooTools class system is a complete implementation of class-based programming for JavaScript.

The first point is actually easy to prove. To give you a taste, here's how we implement the previous examples using a MooTools class:

```
var Person = new Class({

    // Properties
    name: '',
```

```
    age: 0,

    // Methods
    initialize: function(name, age){
        this.name = name;
        this.age = age;
    },

    log: function(){
        console.log(this.name + ', ' + this.age);
    }

});

// Creating a new Person instance
var mark = new Person('Mark', 23);
mark.log(); // 'Mark, 23'
```

Pretty, isn't it? In fact, it looks strikingly similar to our ooc example. But even with the syntax change, using the class is no different from how we'd use a constructor: we still used the new keyword, we still passed arguments to our constructor function, and we still got a new object that inherits from Person.

In MooTools, we create a class using the Class constructor. This constructor takes a single object argument called params, the key-value pairs that will become the members of the class. The object passed to the class constructor is your blueprint, and it defines how you want your instances to look. It then returns a constructor function. Let's take a look at another class:

```
var Animal = new Class({

    name: 'Animal',

    eat: function(){
        console.log(this.name + ' is eating.');
    },

    walk: function(){
        console.log(this.name + ' is walking.');
    }

});

var myAnimal = new Animal();
myAnimal.eat(); // 'Animal is eating.'
myAnimal.walk(); // 'Animal is walking.'

console.log(myAnimal instanceof Animal); // true
```

Here we create a new class called Animal by passing an object to the Class constructor. Our object literal has three members: a property called name and two methods, eat and walk. The Class constructor returns a new constructor function and then we create an instance of the class called myAnimal using new Animal(). Because we declared the eat and walk methods for our class using the object literal, we are able to call these methods on our myAnimal object. Finally, we use the instanceof operator to verify that our new myAnimal object is indeed an instance of Animal.

I mentioned that the MooTools class system is built upon the native object implementation, and we saw that the Class constructor takes an object that describes the members of the class we're creating and then returns a constructor. If we connect these two pieces of information, we get the gist of how the Class constructor works: it creates a new constructor function, goes through the keys we specified in the object argument, appends these keys to the new constructor's prototype property, and returns the constructor.

It might sound too simple, but that's exactly how the core of the MooTools class system works. A MooTools class is nothing more than a simple abstraction of the constructor-prototype pair with additional extensions to make working with them simpler. This means that everything we learned in the previous chapter about objects and prototypes still applies to classes.

Of course there are major differences, particularly in how we'll look at things from now on. Because MooTools abstracts the native prototypal implementation, there's almost no need for us to work directly with prototypes—and in most cases, you won't even notice you're working with prototypes.

Another thing we have to change is how we talk about object-oriented programming itself. Since we'll be dealing with classes rather than prototypes, we'll be using classical terms from here on. It's a weird shift to talk about JavaScript in a classical manner, but because MooTools provides a complete system for classical programming, we'll need to use proper terms when working with the class system.

Constructors and Initializers

In the MooTools class system, there's no distinction between the constructor and the prototype because we have only one blueprint object: the class. Before, we had to create a constructor function and then augment its prototype property to add new methods. But since we're only going to deal with classes from now on, we'll only have to worry about the class itself and the members we'll be defining in our class.

One shift we'll have to make when switching from the prototypal model to the classical one is to forget about the actual constructor function. In the prototypal model, we used the constructor function to prepare the object. In the case of our Person constructor, we set the name property of the instance to the value of the argument passed. When it comes to more complex programs, constructor functions tend to be more complex than this, performing lots of operations that set up the new instance.

But we didn't declare a constructor function in our implementation of the Person class using the MooTools class system. Instead, the stuff we usually place inside the constructor's body was placed in a special method called initialize in our class declaration. This method is called the **initializer** and it effectively replaces the constructor function from the prototypal model.

In essence, both the constructor and the initializer are used for the same thing: to set up the new instance. The main difference is that the constructor in the prototypal model is technically separate from its prototype and is not inherited by its instances, while an initializer is an actual method that's inherited by objects:

```
var Person = new Class({

    // Properties
    name: '',
    age: 0,

    // Methods
    initialize: function(name, age){
        this.name = name;
        this.age = age;
    },

    log: function(){
        console.log(this.name + ', ' + this.age);
    }
```

```
});

var mark = new Person('Mark', 23);
console.log(typeof mark.initialize); // 'function'

console.log(typeof Person); // 'function'
console.log(typeof Person.prototype.initialize); // 'function'
```

However, having an `initialize` method doesn't mean we don't have an actual constructor. In our Person class example, `Person` is our constructor and `Person.prototype.initialize` is the initializer. Since the MooTools class system still uses the native prototype-based object implementation, we still need constructor functions to augment their prototype properties and to create new objects using the new keyword.

One misconception is that the `initialize` function we declare in our class will become the constructor function for the class, but this isn't the case. All classes actually use a common constructor function. We say "common constructor" not because all classes use the exact same function, but because all of them have a constructor that looks like this:

```
// the common constructor function
function(){
    reset(this);
    if (newClass.$prototyping) return this;
    this.$caller = null;
    var value = (this.initialize) ? this.initialize.apply(this, arguments) : this;
    this.$caller = this.caller = null;
    return value;
}
```

Most of the stuff inside this common constructor might look like gibberish right now, but for the moment let's focus on the line that starts with `var value`. This is the most important line in the common constructor and it invokes the instance's `initialize` method, passing any arguments given to the common constructor. Also, note that the return value of the `initialize` method is stored in the variable value and returned at the end of our common constructor.

Applying this to our previous example, the call to new `Person('Mark', 23)` first invoked the Person function (which is the common constructor) and then the instance's `initialize` method was called, passing the argument `'Mark'` to it. These invocations are transparent: when looking at it from the outside, it seems that the initialize method was invoked directly.

The separation of the constructor function and the initialize method might seem redundant—after all, we could just remove the common constructor and use the `initialize` function as the constructor itself. This distinction, however, is important because of the difference between instantiation and initialization.

Instantiation is the process of creating a new object, while **initialization** is the process of setting up the object. With our original prototypal model, both the instantiation and initialization phases happen: first instantiation via the new keyword and then initialization by calling the constructor.

But there are times when we want to create an object without initializing it. It's probably hard to think of why we'd want to do this, but we'll see how it's useful later on. What we do need to realize right now is that with our original prototypal model, we can't separate instantiation and initialization, because the constructor always gets called after creating a new object. Having a separate method for initialization solves this problem because we can now bypass the initialization phase if necessary.

The common constructor also enforces some workarounds for the language, like removing object references and adding private methods. Since we already have a function automating these tasks for us, we can focus our attention on the class itself rather than having to write these workaround codes every time.

Rethinking Members

In the prototypal model, we had to worry about the separation of the constructor and the prototype. While the constructor is still invoked to process the instance, it's not part of the instance itself—which can lead to some confusion later on. In contrast, the MooTools class system eliminates this distinction by making the constructor "irrelevant" and instead turning to the `initialize` method. With a class, the only things you have to worry about are the actual members of your object.

The MooTools class system still uses the native prototypal implementation, and members are still added to the `prototype` of the constructor of the class. Because properties and methods still behave the same way, we can easily apply what we already learned about them from the last chapter.

The process of adding members to the prototype of the class isn't straightforward, though. It may seem that the `Class` constructor simply takes the members of the object argument passed and adds them directly to the `prototype`, but there's a more complex process happening underneath.

Before we go any further, let's revisit a problem we encountered in the last chapter. Suppose we have the following class:

```
// person.js
var Person = new Class({

    name: '',
    age: 0,

    initialize: function(name, age){
        this.name = name;
        this.age = age;
    },

    log: function(){
        console.log(this.name + ', ' + this.age);
    }

});
```

This class is found in a file called `person.js`, which is an external file that's not accessible to us. Now we want to add new methods to this class: `getName`, `setName`, `getAge`, and `setAge`. We don't have access to the class declaration itself, so we can't edit it directly. What we did in the last chapter was to augment `Person.prototype` to add the new members. Since classes use the native prototypal implementation, we could use the same technique to augment our `Person` class.

That also works with classes, but it's not considered proper MooTools style. Classes abstract prototypes, so there's no need to directly augment the `prototype` object. The proper way is to use a class method known as `implement` to add these new members:

```
// program.js
Person.implement({

    getName: function(){
        return this.name;
    },

    setName: function(name){
        this.name = name;
    },

    getAge: function(){
```

```
        return this.age;
    },

    setAge: function(age){
        this.age = age;
    }
```
});

We call the `implement` method of our `Person` class and then pass it an object literal containing the methods we want to add to our class. The result is that all instances of `Person` will now have those methods, just like the result we'd get if we augmented the `prototype` object directly.

All classes have the `implement` method: it's a part of the simplified abstraction of the MooTools class system. I said that it's not proper MooTools style to directly augment the prototype of a class, but that's an understatement. What I should have said was this: *always use the implement method*. Unless you know what you're doing and unless you have a real need to do so, *never directly augment the prototype of a class*.

Some might think that this is too strict a rule. If MooTools classes just abstract the native prototypal implementation, augmenting class prototypes should work. This isn't the case, though: part of the abstraction provided by classes is ensuring proper object behavior. The `implement` method doesn't just add members to the prototype directly, but instead processes the members first to make sure that everything will work as expected.

You might have noticed that the `implement` syntax is similar to the `Class` constructor's syntax, with both requiring an object literal describing the properties and methods to be added to the `prototype` of the class. That's because the `Class` constructor itself uses `implement` to add the members. All class members go through the `implement` method—even the ones passed through the `Class` constructor.

The `implement` method looks through each of the items from the object argument and checks whether it should process that particular item before it adds it to the `prototype`. The processing depends on the type of the item: properties undergo different processing from methods, and there is special processing done to items with particular keys. Since we're talking about members now, we won't go into detail about those keys here; instead we'll focus on how `implement` processes methods and properties.

Rethinking Methods

In the prototypal model, adding methods is done simply by adding a property to the `prototype` with a function value:

```
var myFn = function(){
    console.log('Hello');
};

var Person = function(){};
Person.prototype.log = myFn;

var mark = new Person();

console.log(typeof mark.log); // 'function'
console.log(mark.log == myFn); // true

mark.log(); // 'Hello'
```

Here, we assign the function that's stored in the `myFn` variable to `Person.prototype.log`. Because functions are referenced, both `myFn` and `Person.prototype.log` now point to a single function, which we confirm by comparing `myFn` and `mark.log`. No surprises here. However, the behavior is different with classes:

```
var myFn = function(){
    console.log('Hello');
};

var Person = new Class({
    log: myFn
});

var mark = new Person();

console.log(typeof mark.log); // 'function'
console.log(mark.log == myFn); // false

mark.log(); // 'Hello'
```

We know that the `log` method is our original `myFn` function, because `mark.log()` outputs as expected. But when we compare `mark.log` and `myFn`, we're told that they're not the same function. This means that `myFn` and `Person.prototype.log` point to different functions. But how come `mark.log()` still works as if both functions are the same?

This is one of the changes brought about by the `implement` method. We learned about function decoration in Chapter 2; well, the `implement` method decorates all methods in a class. All class methods you pass to `implement` are changed to the following decorated function:

```
function(){
    if (method.$protected && this.$caller == null) throw new Error('The method "' + key + '"
cannot be called.');
    var caller = this.caller, current = this.$caller;
    this.caller = current; this.$caller = wrapper;
    var result = method.apply(this, arguments);
    this.$caller = current; this.caller = caller;
    return result;
}
```

Don't get scared yet—right now you can ignore most of the lines in this extremely confusing function. The most important line here is the one that starts with `var result`. The identifier `method` in this function points to the actual method you passed in your declaration. In the case of our previous example, `method` points to the same function as `myFn`. Because it's simply a decorator, calling this function also invokes the original function. The results of your original function are then stored in a variable and returned. The whole process is transparent, and you won't notice what's happening when you're working with classes.

This decorated function also stores the original method in a special property called `$origin`. We can compare the methods as follows:

```
var myFn = function(){
    console.log('Hello');
};

var Person = new Class({
    log: myFn
});

var mark = new Person();
```

```
console.log(typeof mark.log); // 'function'
console.log(mark.log == myFn); // false

console.log(mark.log.$origin == myFn); // true

mark.log(); // 'Hello'
```

Arguably, this function seems like the most complex of all functions in MooTools, and it does take a while to understand it. This complex decoration might be overwhelming right now, but we'll learn how it works throughout this chapter and the next. While understanding how this function works internally isn't essential to working with classes, it'll help you see how MooTools implements classical features like calling overridden methods and hiding private methods.

Rethinking Properties

If you look back at all the prototype-based examples we've seen so far, you'll notice that we never declared properties for most of them. Instead of augmenting them to the prototype itself, we created the properties inside the constructor. We did this so we wouldn't encounter this particular behavior:

```
var data = {name: '', age: 0};

var Person = function(name, age){
    this.data.name = name;
    this.data.age = age;
};

Person.prototype.data = data;

Person.prototype.log = function(){
    console.log(this.data.name + ', ' + this.data.age);
};

var mark = new Person('Mark', 23);
mark.log(); // 'Mark, 23'

data.name = 'Joseph';
data.age = 22;

mark.log(); // 'Joseph, 22'

console.log(data == Person.prototype.data); // true
```

We discussed why this problem occurs in the last chapter, but the basic explanation is that both data and Person.prototype.data point to the same object, so any changes to one are reflected in the other.

However, this approach isn't recommended when using classes. In fact, it's advised to declare all properties for classes when possible. But unlike our previous example, the problem doesn't come up when using classes, and changing the value of the data object doesn't affect the data property of our mark object:

```
var data = {name: '', age: 0};

var Person = new Class({
```

```
    data: data,

    initialize: function(name, age){
        this.data.name = name;
        this.data.age = age;
    },

    log: function(){
        console.log(this.data.name + ', ' + this.data.age);
    }
});

var mark = new Person('Mark', 23);
mark.log(); // 'Mark, 23'

data.name = 'Joseph';
data.age = 22;

mark.log(); // 'Mark, 23'

console.log(data == Person.prototype.data); // false
```

This is another effect of using the `implement` method. Properties declared for a class undergo a process called **dereferencing**, which removes any reference from the object. This is done by creating a copy of an object that's exactly like the original. For instance, both the `data` and `Person.prototype.data` objects above might look like the same object, but the latter is really just a copy. Instead of augmenting it directly into the prototype, a copy of `data` was created and assigned to `Person.prototype.data`. Any references to `data` were removed, and changes to this object no longer affect the copy.

The dereferencing done by `implement` is recursive: if an object contains another object, the inner object is also dereferenced. In an array of objects, for example, not only is a copy of an array created, but each object inside the array is also copied. However, dereferencing is limited to only some kinds of objects: arrays, objects created using literals or `new Object()`, and objects created using user-defined constructors. Objects like functions, dates, and DOM objects aren't dereferenced since they're host objects, and primitives like strings and numbers don't need to be dereferenced because they're not reference types. For example, the date object won't be dereferenced in the following:

```
var date = new Date();

var Item = new Class({
    date: date
});

var obj = new Item();

console.log(obj.date == date); // true
```

Dereferencing, however, doesn't just happen on the class level: instances are also dereferenced. To understand why, we need to take a look at a variation of the original problem:

```
var Person = function(name, age){
    this.data.name = name;
    this.data.age = age;
};
```

```
Person.prototype.data = {name: '', age: 0};

Person.prototype.log = function(){
    console.log(this.data.name + ', ' + this.data.age);
};

var mark = new Person('Mark', 23);
mark.log(); // 'Mark, 23'

var joseph = new Person('Joseph', 22);
joseph.log(); // 'Joseph, 22'

mark.log(); // 'Joseph, 22'

console.log(mark.data == joseph.data); // true
```

This is an even bigger problem: because both mark and joseph inherit from Person.prototype, their data properties both point to the same object. Therefore, any changes made to one instance also affect all other instances. This is what we'd expect from objects, and if you recall our discussion in the previous chapter, we solved this by moving the data declaration into the constructor to give each instance its own separate data property.

The MooTools class system, on the other hand, solves this automatically for us:

```
var Person = new Class({

    data: {name: '', age: 0},

    initialize: function(name, age){
        this.data.name = name;
        this.data.age = age;
    },

    log: function(){
        console.log(this.data.name + ', ' + this.data.age);
    }

});

var mark = new Person('Mark', 23);
mark.log(); // 'Mark, 23'

var joseph = new Person('Joseph', 22);
joseph.log(); // 'Joseph, 22'

mark.log(); // 'Mark, 23'

console.log(mark.data == joseph.data); // false
```

The dereferencing here is no longer done by implement, but by the common constructor. If you look back at the code for the common constructor in the section on Constructors and Initializers, you'll see that the first line is a function call: reset(this). The this keyword in that code points to the newly created instance of the class, and the reset function is the private dereferencing function for class instances.

When we called new Person(), a new instance is created and then the Person constructor is called. The first thing the constructor does is to call reset to dereference the instance. This instance, of course, already inherits from Person.prototype, so the properties declared in our prototype are copied and reassigned in the object to give each instance its own copy. This automated process ensures that all our instances have their own copies of the objects declared in the prototype.

Inheritance

Because classes are just abstractions of the native prototypal implementation, instances still inherit from the prototype of their constructors, and the prototype chain is still traversed to look for members. Setting up the prototype chain, though, is different with classes.

In the last chapter, we were able to make objects that inherit from multiple prototypes by creating deliberate chains:

```
var Animal = function(name){
    this.name = name;
};

Animal.prototype.eat = function(){
    console.log('The ' + this.name + ' is eating.');
};

var Cat = function(){};

Cat.prototype = new Animal('cat');

Cat.prototype.meow = function(){
    console.log('Meow!');
};

var cat = new Cat();
cat.eat(); // 'The cat is eating.'
cat.meow(); // 'Meow!'
```

Here we created a Cat constructor and then set its prototype to be an instance of Animal. Because of how the prototype chain works, all instances of Cat not only inherit from Cat.prototype but also from Animal.prototype. To set the deliberate chain, we had to assign an actual object as the prototype of the new constructor. This is the essence of prototypal inheritance: objects inherit from other objects.

Classical inheritance has a different view: objects—and classes themselves—inherit from classes. If we were to write the example above in a classical language, we would have to declare that the Cat class inherits from the Animal class. This inheritance is direct: the Cat class won't be inheriting from an instance of the Animal class, like in our JavaScript example, but from the Animal class itself. In classical terms, we then say that the Cat class is a **subclass** of the Animal class, and the Animal class is the **superclass** of the Cat class.

The MooTools class system provides classical inheritance with a simple interface. When we implement the example above using classes, we get the following:

```
var Animal = new Class({

    name: '',

    initialize: function(name){
        this.name = name;
```

```
    },

    eat: function(){
        console.log('The ' + this.name + ' is eating.');
    }

});

var Cat = new Class({

    Extends: Animal,

    initialize: function(){
        this.name = 'cat';
    },

    meow: function(){
        console.log('Meow!');
    }

});

var cat = new Cat();
cat.eat(); // 'The cat is eating.'
cat.meow(); // 'Meow!'
```

As you've probably guessed, the important line in this snippet is Extends: Animal. Extends is one of the special keywords processed by the implement method, and it's actually connected to a function that we'll talk about more in the next chapter. The important point to know right now is that this line declares that our Cat class is a subclass of Animal, and sets the prototype chain of the Cat class to inherit from Animal.

▓ **Note** Extends, like other special keywords, is case-sensitive. Always remember to capitalize the first letter.

Unlike our prototypal example, we passed Animal in our declaration instead of new Animal(). Extends allows us to declare inheritance using classes themselves instead of instances of those classes. Aside from being easier to write, this has the added benefit of being easier to read: a quick glance at our Cat class informs us that it's a subclass of Animal because we can easily see the Extends declaration.

The Extends inheritance mechanism is another MooTools abstraction. Since we're still using prototypes beneath the class system, JavaScript expects our prototype chain to be declared using the prototypal model. Extends does this automatically for us: when the implement method sees the Extends keyword, it creates a new instance of the class we declared and uses this new instance to set up the prototype chain.

In our example above, implement goes through each of the items in our object literal to build the Cat class. When it encounters Extends: Animal, it creates a new instance of the class by instantiating new Animal(). It then sets the prototype of the common constructor to the new Animal instance and adds the other members of the class to the prototype. Finally, the Class constructor returns the common constructor and it becomes the final Cat class.

In our section on the common constructor, we found out that the class system distinguishes between instantiation and initialization. I also said that there are times we would want to create instances without initializing them. Extends is one of those times: the instance of the superclass created via Extends isn't initialized:

```
var Superclass = new Class({

    initialize: function(name){
        console.log('Initializing Superclass.');
    }

});

var Subclass = new Class({

    Extends: Superclass,

    initialize: function(){
        console.log('Initializing Subclass.');
    }

});

var obj = new Subclass(); // 'Initializing Subclass.'
```

In this code, we get only the 'Initializing Subclass' log in our console. When Subclass was created, an instance of Superclass was created to become the value of Subclass.prototype. But this instance of Superclass wasn't initialized, which we confirm because there's no log in the console.

This behavior happens because of how initializers work. It's the job of the initializer to prepare an instance and to set it up in a way that's unique to the instance. Often, this is done using special arguments that are passed when creating an instance. Take a look at the following snippet:

```
var Postable = function(element){
    this.element = element;
    this.element.method = 'POST';
};
```

When we create instances of Postable, we are expected to pass an element argument to the constructor. The instance is then initialized by setting the value of its element member to the element argument we passed, then a new property called method is added to the member. A problem occurs, though, when we try to create a subclass:

```
var Postable = function(element){
    this.element = element;
    this.element.method = 'POST';
};

var SubPostable = function(){};

SubPostable.prototype = new Postable(); // this will throw an error
```

To make SubPostable a subclass of Postable, we had to declare SubPostable.prototype to be a new instance of Postable. But since Postable had a combined constructor and initializer, we get an error when we create the instance without passing an element argument.

Of course, we can simply pass an argument when we create the new instance, but what argument should we pass? Remember that during the process of subclassing, we don't yet know which arguments are going to be passed—those items will be available when we instantiate the class. We could pass a dummy object, but doing so just to bypass an error isn't good programming.

On the other hand, we'll never run into such a problem with the MooTools class system because constructors and initializers are separate. Even though the class system creates an instance of Postable and sets it as the prototype of Subpostable, the initialized method of the Postable instance never gets called:

```
var Postable = new Class({

    element: null,

    initialize: function(element){
        this.element = element;
        this.element.method = 'POST';
    }

});

var SubPostable = new Class({

    Extends: Postable

});
```

To fully understand why MooTools does this, we need to think back to the prototype chain. We create deliberate chains in order to create extensions and variations of our original prototypes. An Animal prototype, for instance, should contain members that are shared by all animals, such name, eat(), and sleep(). It could then be specialized to make Cat, Bird, or Dog prototypes, each with its own set of methods that are unique to cats, birds, or dogs. These specializations could be further divided into specific types of cats, birds, or dogs. The important thing to consider is that we're doing this in order to inherit members from all these classes without having to rewrite members again: an instance of Magpie, for example, might inherit properties and methods from Magpie.prototype, Bird.prototype and Animal.prototype.

JavaScript's object implementation requires us to declare a prototype as an instance of another prototype in order to create a deliberate chain. Unfortunately, the use of constructor functions as initializers in the prototypal model works against us, since the processes of instantiation and initialization are merged into one function. If the only reason we set the prototype to an instance of another prototype is to inherit members, we shouldn't need to initialize the instance into a usable state, because we're not going to use it except for traversal.

This concern is handled properly by the MooTools class system: because we only need to instantiate the superclass in order to access its properties and methods for our subclass, the superclass is instantiated without being initialized. When we need to finally initialize our object, we can do so in the subclass itself without having to worry about how the superclass handles initialization.

Overridden Methods

The prototype chain is invisible: there's no direct way to check whether a prototype inherits from another object. MooTools classes, on the other hand, have visible links to their superclass, which is called parent:

```
var Animal = new Class({

    name: '',
```

86

```
        initialize: function(name){
            this.name = name;
        }

});

var Cat = new Class({

    Extends: Animal,

    initialize: function(){
        this.name = 'cat';
    }

});
```

```
console.log(typeof Animal.parent); // 'undefined'
console.log(typeof Cat.parent); // 'function'
console.log(Cat.parent == Animal); // true
```

The parent property of a class is a reference to its superclass. In our example, Animal.parent is undefined, since it doesn't have a superclass, but Cat.parent correctly points to Animal, since Cat is a subclass of Animal. While the parent property of classes doesn't have much use in development, there's another parent that is important. Before we talk about it, though, let's tackle a problem that arises with inheritance: how to access overridden methods.

When we look back at how the prototype chain is traversed, we remember that each object in the chain is checked for the property being accessed. If a property isn't found in the first item in the chain, the next item is checked—and so on until we find the property.

```
var Animal = function(){};

Animal.prototype.log = function(){
    console.log('This is an Animal.');
};

Animal.prototype.eat = function(){
    console.log('The animal is eating.');
};

var Cat = function(){};

Cat.prototype = new Animal();

Cat.prototype.eat = function(){
    console.log('The cat is eating.');
};

var tibbs = new Cat();
tibbs.log(); // 'This is an Animal.'
tibbs.eat(); // 'The cat is eating.'
```

In this example, tibbs.log() refers to Animal.prototype.log. Because we didn't declare Cat.prototype.log, the original log method from our Animal.prototype is the one inherited by our Cat instances. However, we specified our own Cat.prototype.eat method, and because of the way the prototype chain is traversed, our Cat instances inherit this method instead of Animal.prototype.eat. We therefore say that Cat.prototype.eat overrides Animal.prototype.eat.

Overridden methods are very straightforward as long as you're not doing anything fancy. However, one problem that often comes up is how to access the overridden methods of a superclass. Because you won't be able to access the scope chain directly, you'll have to call the overridden method from the superclass directly via its prototype:

```
var Animal = function(){};

Animal.prototype.log = function(){
    console.log('This is an Animal.');
};

Animal.prototype.eat = function(){
    console.log('The animal is eating.');
};

var Cat = function(){};

Cat.prototype = new Animal();

Cat.prototype.eat = function(){
    Animal.prototype.eat.apply(this);
    console.log('The cat is eating.');
};

var tibbs = new Cat();
tibbs.log(); // 'This is an Animal.'
tibbs.eat();
// 'The animal is eating.'
// 'The cat is eating.'
```

Here, we called the overridden eat method of Animal.prototype by directly invoking it using Animal.prototype.eat.apply(this). We need to use apply or call when accessing the overridden method because we want the function to be bound to the current instance.

MooTools classes use a more elegant approach. All subclasses are given a new method called parent, which can be used to call the overridden method:

```
var Animal = new Class({

    log: function(){
        console.log('This is an Animal.');
    },

    eat: function(){
        console.log('The animal is eating.');
    }

});

var Cat = new Class({

    Extends: Animal,

    eat: function(){
```

```
        this.parent();
        console.log('The cat is eating.');
    }

});

var tibbs = new Cat();
tibbs.log(); // 'This is an Animal.'
tibbs.eat();
// 'The animal is eating.'
// 'The cat is eating.'
```

If you look at our eat method in the Cat class, we called the parent method to call the overridden eat method of the Animal superclass. Like our original prototypal example, the call to this.parent() inside the eat method calls Animal.prototype.eat. Unlike our prototypal example, though, we no longer need to use apply or call, since the parent method already does this for us.

The parent method becomes really handy when used in conjunction with overridden methods that do lots of processing, like initializers:

```
var Animal = new Class({

    name: '',

    initialize: function(name){
        this.name = name;
    },

    getName: function(){
        return this.name;
    }

});

var Cat = new Class({

    Extends: Animal,

    initialize: function(name){
        this.parent(name);
        this.name += ', the Cat.';
    }

});

var tibbs = new Cat('Tobias');
console.log(tibbs.getName()); // 'Tobias, the Cat.'
```

In this example, we first call the initialize method of the Animal class using this.parent, passing the necessary argument, before doing our own processing, which involves adding the string ', the Cat.' to the name property. In essence, the parent method not only makes it possible to call the overridden method, but also provides a way to "extend" it with our own property.

The parent method is available only to subclasses that inherit through the Extends property. If we tried to call this.parent() inside the Animal class, for instance, we'd get an error about not having a parent method.

Inside this.parent()

The parent method itself is an interesting function, and it's one of the most ingenious parts of the MooTools codebase. If you look at the source, you'll see that the parent method looks like this:

```
function(){
    if (!this.$caller) throw new Error('The method "parent" cannot be called.');
    var name = this.$caller.$name, parent = this.$caller.$owner.parent;
    var previous = (parent) ? parent.prototype[name] : null;
    if (!previous) throw new Error('The method "' + name + '" has no parent.');
    return previous.apply(this, arguments);
}
```

There's only one parent method in a subclass, but it changes depending on where it was called. We don't really need to learn how it works, but it's an interesting topic that will help us understand exactly how MooTools solves the problem of overridden methods. But before we can fully understand how the parent method works, we have to retrace a few steps.

Remember that before adding methods to the prototype, implement decorates the functions using the wrapper function we saw earlier. The wrapper function has several special properties, the most important ones being $owner and $name:

```
var Animal = new Class({

    name: '',

    initialize: function(name){
        this.name = name;
    },

    getName: function(){
        return this.name;
    }

});
```

```
console.log(Animal.prototype.getName.$owner == Animal); // true
console.log(Animal.prototype.getName.$name); // 'getName'
```

The $owner property points to the class itself, while $name is the name of the method you declared. In our example, Animal.prototype.getName.$owner points to the Animal class, while Animal.prototype.getName.$name has the value 'getName'. Take note that the $name property isn't taken from the identifier of the function itself, but from the key we used when we declared the method.

The main purpose of the wrapper function is to keep track of which method is currently called. When we call a method from an instance, the wrapped method sets the internal $caller property of the instance to itself. The $caller property is used to determine which current function is running. When we call tibbs.getName() for example, the $caller property will be set to the getName method.

Now when we call this.parent() inside a method, the function checks the $caller property to determine which of the methods invoked it. If there's no $caller property, it will throw an error, preventing parent from being called from outside a method. If there's a $caller, though, the parent method will store its $name property to determine the name of the method and then access the superclass using $owner.parent. The method then checks whether there's an overridden method from the superclass and invokes it, returning the arguments.

Let's trace how it all works with this example:

```
var Animal = new Class({

    name: '',

    initialize: function(name){
        this.name = name;
    },

    getName: function(){
        return this.name;
    }

});

var Cat = new Class({

    Extends: Animal,

    initialize: function(name){
        this.parent(name);
        this.name += ', the Cat.';
    }

});

var tibbs = new Cat('Tobias');
console.log(tibbs.getName()); // 'Tobias, the Cat.'
```

First, we call new `Cat()`, thereby calling the initialize method. The `$caller` property is then set to initialize, with `$caller.$owner` pointing to the `Cat` class and `$caller.$name` set to `'initialize'`. We then call `this.parent()` inside the initialize method, and it gets the superclass by accessing `$caller.$owner.parent`, which points to `Animal`. Finally, `this.parent()` checks for the existence of the initialize method in the `Animal` class and invokes it, using `apply` to rebind it to the current instance. The result is that we were able to invoke an overridden method from our superclass.

It might be hard to wrap you head around at first, but once you understand how `parent` works, you'll realize how elegantly MooTools solves complex problems to provide a nice API.

Mixins

JavaScript's inheritance model allows for only *single direct inheritance*. An object directly inherits only from a single prototype, although it can indirectly inherit from multiple prototypes via the prototype chain.

Using the prototype chain for multiple inheritance, though, has its limitations. Take, for example, the following snippet:

```
var Phone = new Class({

    sound: 'phone.ogg',

    initialize: function(number){
        this.number = number;
    },

    call: function(from){
```

```
            this.ring();
            new Notification('New call!');
        },

        ring: function(sound){
            sound = sound || this.sound;
            new Sound(sound).play();
        }

});

var AlarmClock = new Class({

    sound: 'alarm.ogg',

    initialize: function(alarmTime){
        this.time = alarmTime;
    },

    alarm: function(time){
        if (time == this.time) {
            this.ring();
            new Notification('Wake up sleepy head!');
        }
    },

    ring: function(sound){
        sound = sound || this.sound;
        new Sound(sound).play();
    }

});
```

Here we have two classes, Phone and AlarmClock, and both have the same method called ring that plays a sound. This is considered bad design because we repeat the code for the ring method in both classes. When developing applications, we want to reuse code as much as possible.

We can, of course, simply make a new superclass that will be inherited by Phone and AlarmClock. But direct inheritance isn't a good design choice here: a phone and an alarm clock aren't really variations of the same object, so a RingingObject class is out of the question.

The MooTools class system supplies a very good system for code reuse:

```
var Ringer = new Class({

    sound: 'ring.ogg',

    ring: function(sound){
        sound = sound || this.sound;
        new Sound(sound).play();
    }

});

var Phone = new Class({
```

```
    Implements: Ringer,

    initialize: function(number){
        this.number = number;
        this.sound = 'phone.ogg';
    },

    call: function(from){
        this.ring();
        new Notification('New call!');
    }

});

var AlarmClock = new Class({

    Implements: Ringer,

    initialize: function(alarmTime){
        this.time = alarmTime;
        this.sound = 'alarm.ogg';
    },

    alarm: function(time){
        if (time == this.time) {
            this.ring();
            new Notification('Wake up sleepy head!');
        }
    }

});
```

Here, we declare a new class called Ringer, and we transfer the sound and ring members to this new class. But instead of declaring them to be subclasses of this new class, we use the Implements keyword to declare that the Phone and AlarmClock classes should take the properties and methods of the Ringer class and use them.

The Ringer class is an example of a **mixin**. As its name implies, a mixin is a class that's "mixed in" or combined with another class. Mixins present a form of multiple inheritance, and the MooTools class system makes it easy to create and implement your own mixin.

The Implements keyword is used to add mixins to your class. It can either take a single value, which is a name of the class you'd like to combine, or an array of class names:

```
var Ringer = new Class({

    sound: 'ring.ogg',

    ring: function(sound){
        sound = sound || this.sound;
        new Sound(sound).play();
    }

});

var Charger = new Class({
```

```
        charge: function(){
            new ElectricalSocket().connect(this);
        }

});

var Phone = new Class({

    Implements: [Ringer, Charger],

    initialize: function(number){
        this.number = number;
        this.sound = 'phone.ogg';
    },

    call: function(from){
        this.ring();
        new Notification('New call!');
    }

});

var phone = new Phone(0000);
console.log(typeof phone.ring); // 'function'
console.log(typeof phone.charge); // 'function'
```

Mixins are actual classes, but they're usually written without an initialize method since they're not meant to be used like regular classes. Rather, mixins are considered to be collections of properties and methods that will be added to other classes, and they provide a simple way to share and reuse code among many classes.

The Implements keyword should give you a clue as to how mixins are added to classes. When the implement method sees this keyword, it creates new instances of these classes that are then fed to another implement call. This process adds the members of the instance that are inherited from the mixin class to the class itself. Without using the Implements keyword, we could mimic this process by using implement directly:

```
var Ringer = new Class({

    sound: 'ring.ogg',

    ring: function(sound){
        sound = sound || this.sound;
        new Sound(sound).play();
    }

});

var Phone = new Class({

    initialize: function(number){
        this.number = number;
        this.sound = 'phone.ogg';
    },
```

```
    call: function(from){
        this.ring();
        new Notification('New call!' + this.from);
    }

});

Phone.implement(new Ringer);
```

This snippet shows exactly how mixins were done in older versions of MooTools. You shouldn't do this with the current versions, though, since it's verbose and hard to read. You should declare your mixins using Implements in your class declaration for readability.

One cool thing about mixins, though, is that the parent method respects their previous prototype chain rather than their new one. What this means is that when the parent method is called from within a method in a mixin that has been added to a class, the method will call the corresponding overriden method in the mixin's original prototype chain:

```
var MixinSuper = new Class({

    log: function(){
        console.log('MixinSuper');
    }

});

var Mixin = new Class({

    Extends: MixinSuper

    log: function(){
        this.parent();
    }

});

var Super = new Class({

    log: function(){
        console.log('Super');
    }

});

var Sub = new Class({

    Extends: Super,

    Implements: Mixin

});

new Sub().log(); // 'MixinSuper'
```

Unlike direct inheritance using Extends, mixins aren't linked to the prototype chain. Instead, their members are added directly to the prototype of your class. This means that changes to a mixin after it's been implemented into your class aren't inherited:

```
var Ringer = new Class({

    sound: 'ring.ogg',

    ring: function(sound){
        sound = sound || this.sound;
        new Sound(sound).play();
    }

});

var Phone = new Class({

    Implements: Ringer,

    initialize: function(number){
        this.number = number;
        this.sound = 'phone.ogg';
    },

    call: function(from){
        this.ring();
        new Notification('New call!');
    }

});

var phone = new Phone(0000);
console.log(typeof phone.ring); // 'function'

Ringer.implement('ringLoudly', function(sound){
    sound = sound || this.sound;
    new Sound(sound).playLoudly()
});

console.log(typeof phone.ringLoudly); // 'undefined'
```

Moreover, you can't call overridden methods via the parent method. The only way to call overridden mixin methods is to call them directly from your mixin's prototype, as we did in an example earlier.

The Wrap Up

In this chapter, we learned a lot about classical programming and how it differs from the prototypal model. We learned about classes, their similarities to prototypes, and the differences between the two. We also learned about the MooTools class system and how it provides a classical interface to JavaScript's object implementation. We found out how MooTools separates constructors from initializers, and how it encapsulates working with prototypes via the implement method. We dived into the internals of inheritance with classes, the parent method, and how to do multiple inheritance with mixins.

If you think we're done talking about classes, though, you're in for a surprise. The MooTools class system is as elegant as it is complex, and we've only touched the base of it in this chapter. In the next chapter, we'll learn more about the secrets of MooTools classes, as well as how to do complex programming using them.

So if you're ready, strap on your backpack and tie your shoelaces—it's time to trek deeper into the MooTools class system.

CHAPTER 5

■■■

Classes: The Extras

The things we've learned about the MooTools class system in the previous chapter fall under the category of "essential knowledge." While they form the foundation of what we need to know about classes, there are several other topics related to the classes that we need to discuss. Instead of cramming them all together, we set aside a separate chapter for these additional topics.

In this chapter, we'll learn about the "extras" that are part of the MooTools class system and how we can use them to create better and more flexible classes.

Mutators

In a class declaration, adding the `Extends` and `Implements` keys changes the class itself: the first one makes a class inherit from a superclass, while the second adds properties and prototypes from mixins into the class. In the last chapter, we called these two as "special keywords," but they're really functions. In MooTools, we call these special functions as `mutators`.

As the name implies, a mutator is a function that changes or "mutates" the class. In some programming languages, such functions are called `class macros` because they transform classes according to various user-defined rules.

In MooTools, all mutators are stored in the `Class.Mutators` object. The `Extends` keyword in a class declaration corresponds to the mutator function `Class.Mutators.Extends`, and the same goes for `Implements`, which corresponds to `Class.Mutators.Implements`.

■ **Note** Don't confuse the use of the word mutator in MooTools with its use in some classical languages. A *mutator* in classical terms is what we usually refer to as a "setter" method, which is a method that changes the value of an instance's property, in contrast to an *accessor* or "getter" method, which returns the property. As noted above, MooTools' mutators are actually class macros or functions that transform a class.

Invoking the mutator that corresponds to a key is the job of the `implement` method. For every key passed to it, the `implement` method checks `Class.Mutators` to see if there's a mutator function that corresponds to the key. If a mutator is found, `implement` invokes the function and passes the value of the key as an argument. To illustrate, let's look at this class declaration:

```
var Duck = new Class({

    Extends: Bird,
```

```
    Implements: [Events, Options],

    options: {
        name: '',
        color: ''
    },

    initialize: function(name){
        this.setOptions(name);
  }

});
```

In this example, we're declaring the Duck class by passing an object literal containing our members to the Class constructor. The Class constructor, after doing some preliminary processing, then calls the implement method to add the members to our new class. The implement method goes through each item in the object literal, starting with Extends, and checks whether there's a mutator named Extends in Class.Mutators. Since there is one, it calls Class.Mutators.Extends using the call method, binding the Duck class as the this keyword value and passing in the Bird class as an argument. It then does the same thing for Implements, which is also a mutator, but this time passing the array [Events, Options] as an argument. The initialize method, on the other hand, isn't a mutator and there's no Class.Mutators.implements, so it's added to the class just like a regular method.

Most class transformations are done via mutators, and they can be used to implement features from classical language easily. Take the two built-in mutators, Extends and Implements, for instance. They may be doing complex transformations to facilitate inheritance, but they're actually pretty simple functions. Extends, for example, which is the mutator that handles subclassing, does its job using only four lines:

```
Class.Mutators.Extends = function(parent){
    this.parent = parent;
    this.prototype = getInstance(parent);
};
```

The Extends mutator has its this keyword bound to the current class and accepts one parameter, parent, which refers to the superclass. When the mutator is called, it first adds a parent property to the current class and assigns the superclass as its value. It then creates a new, uninitialized instance of the superclass using the private getInstance function and sets the prototype of the current class to this instance.

Applying this to our previous Duck class example, the Extends mutator is called and passed the Bird superclass as an argument. The mutator then sets the value of Duck.parent to point to the Bird class. Finally, a new, uninstantiated instance of Bird is created and set as the value of Duck.prototype.

In contrast, the Implements mutator looks a bit more complex:

```
Class.Mutators.Implements = function(items){
    Array.from(items).each(function(item){
        var instance = new item;
        for (var key in instance) implement.call(this, key, instance[key], true);
    }, this);
};
```

As with the Extends mutator (or any other mutator for that matter), the this keyword of the Implements mutator is also bound to the current class. It receives a single argument, items, which could be a single mixin class or an array of mixin classes. The first thing it does is to make sure that the items argument is an array by passing it to Array.from. It does this so that it can use the same code for either a single mixin or an array of mixins. It then loops though each of the mixins using the each array method, which takes as an argument a callback function that will be invoked for each item in the array, and a second optional argument that will be used as the this value of the callback function. In this example, we set the this value of the callback function to the current class by passing the this keyword as the second argument to the each method.

The callback function itself receives a single argument item, which is a reference to the mixin, and it then creates an instance of the mixin. It then loops through the instance and adds each member to the current class using the implement function, which is a private version of the implement class method.

Applying this to our previous example, the Implements mutator is called and passed an array of mixins, [Events, Options], which becomes the value of the items variable. Because items is already an array, Array.from returns the same array and the mutator function loops through each item in the array. For each item, the callback function is called and is first passed the Events class. The callback function then creates an instance of the Events class and goes through each of its members and adds them to the Duck class using the implement function. The each method then moves to the next item in the array, Options, and the callback function is called once more and the process is repeated.

Amazingly, it only takes those two simple functions to form the core of MooTools' implementation of classical inheritance. When used with the class system, mutators enable us to create complex transformations using simple functions. But to fully understand the power of mutators, we'll need to implement our own mutator function.

Implementing Your Own Mutators

The mutator we'll implement is an easy one: a mutator for creating getter and setter methods. Take a look at the following class definition:

```
var Person = new Class({

    $name: '',
    $age: 0,
    $occupation: '',

    setName: function(name){
        this.$name = name;
        return this;
    },

    getName: function(){
        return this.$name;
    },

    setAge: function(age){
        this.$age = age;
        return this;
    },

    getAge: function(){
        return this.$age;
    },

    setOccupation: function(occupation){
        this.$occupation = occupation;
        return this;
    },
```

```
        getOccupation: function(){
            return this.$occupation;
        }

});

var mark = new Person();
mark.setName('Mark');
mark.setAge(23);
mark.setOccupation('JavaScript Developer');

console.log(mark.getName() + ', ' + mark.getAge() + ': ' + mark.getOccupation());
// 'Mark, 23: JavaScript Developer'
```

A few things about this class: first, you'll see that we prefixed all our properties with the dollar ($) character. JavaScript allows identifiers to begin with the dollar character, and it's MooTools style to mark "internal" properties—properties that should not be accessed directly outside the object—by prefixing them with the dollar character (more on this later). So in this example, $name, $age, and $occupation are considered internal properties and they shouldn't be accessed directly outside the object, which is why we have three pairs of getter and setter methods to modify them.

Another thing you'll notice is that we have a lot of repetition: the bodies of our three pairs of getters and setter are similar—the only difference among them is the name of the property they're accessing.

If we need to add another property, we'll have to write another set of those methods. This leads to unnecessary work. Wouldn't it be easier if we could automate this? We should, in fact, and we're going to implement a mutator to automatically create the getter and setter methods.

Creating a mutator is as simple as augmenting Class.Mutators. Mutator names should always be capitalized in order to differentiate them from normal class members: it's easier to see which keys correspond to mutators if the keys are visually different. Here, we'll choose an appropriate name for our mutator, GetterSetter, since it creates getter and setter methods.

Let's see how we can create this mutator. First, we'll need the mutator function to know the names of the properties for which methods will be created. These names will be the arguments to our function. As with the Implements mutator, we want to be able to receive a single property name or an array of property names. Then, we'll need to implement the getter method for that property using the implement method. We'll also have to do the same for the setter method.

With these specifications, we'll end up with something like this:

```
Class.Mutators.GetterSetter = function(properties){
    var klass = this;
    Array.from(properties).each(function(property){
        var captProp = property.capitalize(),   // changes 'prop' to 'Prop'
            $prop     = '$' + property;          // changes 'prop' to '$prop'

        // setter method
        klass.implement('set' + captProp, function(value){
            this[$prop] = value;
            return this;
        });

        // getter method
        klass.implement('get' + captProp, function(value){
            return this[$prop];
        });
    });
};
```

Before I explain how this works, though, let's see how it's used:

```
var Person = new Class({

    GetterSetter: ['name', 'age', 'occupation']

});

var mark = new Person();
mark.setName('Mark');
mark.setAge(23);
mark.setOccupation('JavaScript Developer');

console.log(mark.getName() + ', ' + mark.getAge() + ': ' + mark.getOccupation());
// 'Mark, 23: JavaScript Developer'
```

Nifty, isn't it? We turned that complex class declaration into a simple one that uses only a single mutator. This and the previous examples generate the same class, but this one is simpler to write since it's automated.

Our GetterSetter mutator might look more complicated than the built-in mutators we've seen so far, but they work using the same principles. Like the Implements mutator, GetterSetter accepts a single string or an array of strings as an argument. These strings will be used for the name of the property and the name of the methods. We also use the same Array.from function to turn the arguments into an array, and we use the each array method to loop through each item in the array.

In the first line of our GetterSetter mutator, you'll see a weird declaration: var klass = this;. This is a MooTools *idiom* that solves the issue of object referencing within functions. Remember that inside our mutator, the this keyword points to the class itself. However, within the callback function for the each array method, the this keyword points to the array and not the class. In the Implements mutator, we bound the callback function to the class by passing a second argument to each. However, in our GetterSetter mutator, we forgo the binding by declaring a local variable klass instead. Since the klass variable is available to our callback function due to lexical scoping, we will still be able to reference the class itself without having to rebind. Another reason we did this is to avoid confusion: since we'll need to use the this keyword inside the getter and setter methods themselves, it'll be easier to track which object we're talking about if the class itself is given a different identifier.

■ **Note** We used the identifier klass in this example because class is a reserved word—it can't be used as an identifier. In MooTools Core, the idiom is usually written as var self = this;.

The actual implementation of the getter and setter methods to the class happens inside the callback function. The first thing the callback function does is to transform the string property name into two forms: one capitalized using the string-capitalize method, and the other prefixed with the $ character. The capitalized version of the name is stored in the captProp variable and then used for the method names, while the $ prefixed version is stored in $prop and used inside the methods themselves to access the property. We then called the implement method of the class to add our methods.

When applied to our Person class, the mutator assigns the Person class as the value of the klass variable, and it receives the argument ['name', 'age', 'occupation']. This array is then passed to Array.from, which returns it without modification. Using the each method to loop through the array, the callback function is called and it first receives the property 'name' and transforms it into two forms: 'Name' and '$name'. The implement method of the Person class is then called, passing in getName and the function that will become the actual getName method. The same is then done for the remaining properties.

When getName or any other method added by the mutator is called, it accesses the property using this[$prop]. For getName, $prop has the value '$name', so this[$prop] is the same as accessing this.$name. Because of closures, the getName method retains the value of these variables outside of the GetterSetter mutator. The result is a very easy way to implement getter and setter methods using only a mutator.

Mutator Gotchas

While mutators themselves are easy to understand, their use can sometimes lead to weird behavior. One important thing to remember is that mutators are applied according to the order they're declared. As each mutator is processed, it can affect the already implemented members of the class and this leads to unexpected results.

Let's take a look at some tricky behavior you might encounter:

```
var Super = new Class({

    log: function(){
        console.log('Super');
    }

});

var Mixin = new Class({

    log: function(){
        console.log('Mixin');
    }

});

var Sub = new Class({

    Extends: Super,

    Implements: Mixin

});

var obj = new Sub();
obj.log(); // ?
```

What do you think is the value that will appear when we call obj.log()? If you answered 'Mixin', you are right. First, Extends: Super makes the Sub class inherit from Super, which means that Sub will inherit the log method from Super via its prototype chain. But because the Implements mutator adds the methods from the Mixin class directly into the current class, the Sub class gets its own log method that overrides the original log method from Super. The result is that we get Mixin instead of Super when we call obj.log(). So, how about the next example?

```
var Super = new Class({
```

```
    log: function(){
        console.log('Super');
    }

});

var Mixin = new Class({

    log: function(){
        console.log('Mixin');
    }

});

var Sub = new Class({

    Implements: Mixin,

    Extends: Super

});

var obj = new Sub();
obj.log(
```

Here, we flipped the declarations: Implements now comes before Extends, so what's the value of obj.log()? This is a tricky snippet and even I got confused when I first encountered it. Without knowing the internals of the MooTools class system, we'd probably say that the value would still be Mixin, like our previous snippet, since the prototype chain is still in effect. Implements will add the log member of the Mixin class to the Sub class, and then Extends will make Sub inherit from Super. Because Implements adds the log method directly, it will override the log method of Super, which is what we'd expect from how the prototype chain works. So it's Mixin, right? Actually, the answer is that obj.log() will output Super.

You're probably asking, "Huh? That's unexpected!" First, recall what I said about how the order of declaration affects the behavior of mutators: because each mutator is called according to the order in which it was declared, mutators can affect any members already implemented in the class. At the start of the declaration, we first used Implements to add the log method from the Mixin class to Sub, so now Sub has its own log method. And then we used Extends to make Sub inherit from Super. But now, remember how the Extends mutator actually works: first, it assigns the superclass to the parent property of the subclass and then it creates an instance of the superclass and *assigns it as the prototype of the subclass*.

And that explains the weird behavior. Because Extends assigns a new value to the prototype property of the subclass, the old prototype object is destroyed—as well as any properties or methods it already contains. This means that when we did Extends: Super in our example, a new instance of Super was created and it replaced the old Sub.prototype object that contained our log method from Mixin. Thus, obj.log() outputs Super rather than Mixin. Essentially, declaring Extends in your class effectively destroys all properties and methods you've already added prior to the Extends declaration.

An Implements declaration also affects previously implemented members:

```
var Mixin = new Class({

    log: function(){
        console.log('Mixin');
    }
```

```
});

var Sub = new Class({

    log: function(){
        console.log('Sub');
    },

    Implements: Mixin

});

var obj = new Sub();
obj.log(); // 'Mixin'
```

In this snippet, we declared the `log` method of the Sub class first before we declared `Implements`. When the `implement` class method parses this, it first adds the `log` method from our Sub declaration to `Sub.prototype`. But when we get to the `Implements` declaration, the methods of `Mixin` are then added to the class, and because the `Mixin` class has its own `log` method, it overwrites the original `log` method that has already been implemented. Therefore, we get `Mixin` in our `obj.log()` invocation rather than Sub.

But even though these quirky behaviors are present in the MooTools class system, they're easy to dodge if you know how the system works and if you follow the recommend style. Good MooTools developers always write their mutator declarations at the start of their class declarations, with `Extends` coming first since it's the most "destructive" mutator. `Implements` then comes next, since it also overrides any previous methods, and then any other mutator you might use. If you use proper MooTools style, gotchas such as these won't ever be a problem.

The Built-in Mixins

In the previous chapter, we learned that mixins provide a way to implement multiple inheritance in classes. We learned that mixins are reusable classes whose properties and methods are added to a class directly, which is different from prototypal inheritance where members are inherited using the prototype chain.

MooTools includes three built-in mixins: `Chain`, `Events`, and `Options`. These mixins are used throughout MooTools, and their behavior affects the way most MooTools classes work.

The Chain Mixin

The `Chain` mixin is a simple class that enables us to add chainable **call queues** to classes. This has very special applications for asynchronous programming, as we'll see in later chapters, but right now we'll present a simple example to show how this mixin can be used.

Suppose we have the following class:

```
var Phone = new Class({

    busy: false,

    call: function(name){
        console.log('Calling ' + name);
        this.busy = true;
```

```
        (function(){
            console.log('End call to ' + name);
            this.busy = false;
        }).delay(5000, this);

        return this;
    }

});

var phone = new Phone();
phone.call('Tim');
```

Here we have a simple class called Phone with a single method called call. When we invoke this method, it sets the busy property of the instance to true, indicating that the instance is currently occupied with an operation. It then creates a timer function that is automatically invoked after 5000 milliseconds (or five seconds) that will then change the busy status of the instance to false.

Now suppose we want the class to accept calls only when it's not busy. We could do this by adding an if statement at the start of our method that will check the busy property of the instance.

```
var Phone = new Class({

    busy: false,

    call: function(name){
        if (this.busy) return this;

        console.log('Calling ' + name);
        this.busy = true;

        (function(){
            console.log('End call to ' + name);
            this.busy = false;
        }).delay(5000, this);

        return this;
    }

});

var phone = new Phone();
phone.call('Tim');
phone.call('Chris');
```

In this snippet we invoke the call method twice. For the first invocation, the busy property is false, so the function continues execution. For the second invocation, though, the busy property will be true because it was just set by the first invocation, and the delayed function that resets the busy property won't have been fired yet because it takes five seconds before a call is ended. Thus, the second invocation will be ignored.

But what if we want to keep that second invocation? Instead of completely ignoring it, can we somehow store this second invocation and simply call it after the first call is done? That's where the Chain mixin comes in.

The Chain mixin adds a special method called chain to classes that implement it. This method accepts a single argument, fn, which should be a function, and then stores this function in an internal call queue that can be accessed later.

```
var Phone = new Class({

    Implements: Chain,

    busy: false,

    call: function(name){
        if (this.busy){
            var bound = this.call.bind(this, name);
            this.chain(bound);
            return this;
        }

        console.log('Calling ' + name);
        this.busy = true;

        (function(){
            console.log('End call to ' + name);
            this.busy = false;
        }).delay(5000, this);

        return this;
    }

});

var phone = new Phone();
phone.call('Tim');
phone.call('Chris');
```

Here we added the Chain mixin to our Phone class and we modified our call method. Instead of simply returning the instance if the busy property is true, we also created a bound version of the call method that keeps the current argument. What happens now is that when we invoke call while the instance is busy, the instance uses the chain method to store this invocation into the call queue, and we can then use it later. The second invocation to call is no longer ignored, but is kept for later use.

This brings us to the second part of the equation: the callChain method. This method is used to invoke the first function on the call queue. It accepts a variable number of arguments, all of which will be passed to the function from the queue that's being invoked.

```
var Phone = new Class({

    Implements: Chain,

    busy: false,

    call: function(name){
        if (this.busy){
            var bound = this.call.bind(this, name);
            this.chain(bound);
            return this;
        }
```

```
        console.log('Calling ' + name);
        this.busy = true;

        (function(){
            console.log('End call to ' + name);
            this.busy = false;
            this.callChain();
        }).delay(5000, this);

        return this;
    }

});

var phone = new Phone();
phone.call('Tim');
phone.call('Chris');
```

In this snippet we modified our delayed function to invoke callChain after it has set the busy property back to false. What happens now is that when callChain is invoked, it checks whether there were previous calls saved in the queue, and calls the first of these saved calls. The result is that all our function calls are now queued.

As I mentioned, the Chain mixin is used prominently in asynchronous MooTools classes, like Request and Fx. We'll take a look at how these classes use the Chain mixin later, but now we'll move on to another class that's used heavily in MooTools.

The Events Mixin

The Events mixin is used to add callback functionality to classes. An **event**, to define it very generally, is something interesting that happens, and classes can use the Events mixin to tell other parts of a program that something interesting has happened.

Reusing our previous Phone example, let's say we want to make our class more flexible by separating the logical and presentational parts of it. The logical part of the class deals with how the class actually works in terms of changes in state and data, while the presentational parts deal with how these changes are shown to the user. The toggling of the busy status of the class is logical, while the logging of the name is presentational. With this in mind, let's split up our class into several parts:

```
var Caller = new Class({

    busy: false,

    call: function(name){
        this.busy = true;

        (function(){
            this.busy = false;
        }).delay(5000, this);

        return this;
    }

});
```

```
var Display = new Class({

    callStart: function(name){
        console.log('Calling ' + name);
    },

    callEnd: function(){
        console.log('End call to ' + name);
    }

});

var Phone = new Class({

    initialize: function(){
        this.caller = new Caller();
        this.display = new Display();
    },

    call: function(name){
        this.caller.call(name);
    }

});
```

We divided the main components of the Phone class into two separate classes: the Caller class, which deals with toggling the busy status of the instance, and the Display class, which is used to log the call data. We then created a new Phone class that wraps these two classes together.

However, we now run into a problem: because our Caller and Display classes are now separate, there's no way to glue them together. In particular, the Display class no longer has a way to determine when to display the information using console.log. What we need then is a way for the Caller and Display classes to communicate—even though they're now separate classes.

This brings us to the Events mixin. Using this built-in mixin, we can turn our Caller class into an **event dispatcher**, which is simply an object that can produce events. We then use the fireEvent method from the Events mixin, which is the method used to broadcast that an event has happened. This method takes one main argument, type, which is a string denoting the type of event that will be dispatched, and an optional argument, args, which should be a value or array of values to be passed to the event handlers.

```
var Caller = new Class({

    Implements: Events,

    busy: false,

    call: function(name){
        this.busy = true;
        this.fireEvent('callStart', name);

        (function(){
            this.busy = false;
            this.fireEvent('callEnd', name);
        }).delay(5000, this);
```

```
        return this;
    }

});
```

In this snippet we modified our Caller class to use the Events mixin via Implements. We then added two calls to fireEvent, the first right after setting the busy property to true to dispatch the callStart event, and the second inside our delayed function to dispatch the callEnd event. In both invocations we passed the name variable as the second argument, which in turn will be passed to the event handlers.

Dispatching the events, though, is only half of the story. Even if our Caller class now has the ability to broadcast events, those events are useless unless they're heard. And that's where event handlers come in. An **event handler** is a function that listens to a class, waiting for a particular event to happen. When an event is dispatched, the event handlers associated with the event are invoked. This is how the classes communicate.

Event handlers are "attached" to the event dispatcher object. In our case, we need to attach our event handlers to the Caller instance. We can do this using the Events mixin's addEvent method, which takes two arguments: type, which is a string denoting the event name, and fn, which is the event handler function.

```
var Caller = new Class({

    Implements: Events,

    busy: false,

    call: function(name){
        this.busy = true;
        this.fireEvent('callStart', name);

        (function(){
            this.busy = false;
            this.fireEvent('callEnd', name);
        }).delay(5000, this);

        return this;
    }

});

var Display = new Class({

    callStart: function(name){
        console.log('Calling ' + name);
    },

    callEnd: function(){
        console.log('End call to ' + name);
    }

});

var Phone = new Class({
```

```
    initialize: function(){
        this.caller = new Caller();
        this.display = new Display();

        this.caller.addEvent('callStart', this.display.callStart);
        this.caller.addEvent('callEnd', this.display.callEnd);
    },

    call: function(name){
        this.caller.call(name);
    }

});
```

Here we updated our Phone class's initialize method with two calls to the caller object's addEvent method. In the first invocation we attached the callStart method of the display object as the callStart event handler, and the second object does the same with the callEnd method, but for the callEnd event. The result is that our two separate classes can now communicate using events.

Events are useful not only for classes but also for a host of other programming purposes. We'll learn more about events and event-based programming in Chapter 10.

The Options Mixin

A common MooTools idiom is the use of special option object arguments to class constructors as a way of customizing class instances. As its name implies, the Options mixin makes it easy to implement this idiom in your classes.

The Options mixin adds a single method called setOptions that takes a variable number of option object arguments and adds them to the options object property of the class.

```
var Person = new Class({

    Implements: Options,

    initialize: function(options){
        this.setOptions(options);
    },

    log: function(){
        console.log(this.options.name + ', ' + this.options.age);
    }

});
```

```
var mark = new Person({name: 'Mark', age: 23});
mark.log(); // 'Mark, 23'
```

Here we created a new Person class that implements the Options mixin. We then created an initialize method for the class that accepts an options argument, which we then pass to the setOptions method of the class. The setOptions method will then take this object and add its properties to the options property of the instance. We're able to access this options property in all other parts of the class, which is how we were able to get options.name and options.age in our log method.

A more powerful use of the `Options` mixin, though, is for setting default options for our classes. We can do this by declaring an explicit `options` property in our class that contains the default values for our options.

```
var Person = new Class({

    Implements: Options,

    options: {
        name: 'Blah',
        age: 0
    },

    initialize: function(options){
        this.setOptions(options);
    },

    log: function(){
        console.log(this.options.name + ', ' + this.options.age);
    }

});

new Person({name: 'Tim', age: 21}).log(); // 'Tim, 21'
new Person({name: 'Chris'}).log(); // 'Chris, 0'
new Person().log(); // 'Blah, 0'
```

In this example we defined an explicit `options` property in our class declaration. What happens now is that when `setOptions` is called, it merges the values of the explicit `options` property together with the passed values from the `options` argument. This gives us the ability to define default values for our options—an idiom that's used widely in MooTools itself.

Finally, we close this section with a special feature of the `setOptions` method. If the current class implements the `Events` mixin together with the `Options` mixin, all properties passed to `setOptions` in the form on<Name> will be added as event handlers:

```
var Person = new Class({

    Implements: [Events, Options],

    initialize: function(options){
        this.setOptions(options);
    }

});

var sleep = function(){
    console.log('Sleeping');
};

new Person({
    onSleep: sleep
});

new Person().addEvent('sleep', sleep);
```

Here, the two last operations are equivalent: passing an option with the name onSleep is the same as attaching an event handler for the sleep event using addEvent.

Static Members

One feature of some classical programming languages is the existence of *static members*. A static member is a property or method that is accessible via the class itself, but not from its instances. Revising our ooc example from Chapter 4:

```
Person: class {

    // Properties
    name := ""
    age  := 0


    // Methods
    init: func (name: String, age: Int) {
        this name = name
        this age = age
    }

    log: func {
        printf("%s, %d", this name, this age)
    }

    // Static Property
    count := static 0

    // Static Methods
    addPerson: static func {
        Person count += 1
    }

    getCount: static func {
        printf("Person count: %d", Person count)
    }

}

// Creating a new Person instance
mark := Person new("Mark", 23)
mark log() // "Mark, 23"

// Accessing the static method
Person addPerson()
Person getCount() // "Person count: 1"
```

In this example, we added three new static members to our original ooc Person class: a static property count and the static methods addPerson and getCount. Because these members are static, we can't call them using our mark instance. Instead, we called them directly from the class itself, as seen in the last lines. You'll also notice that in our addPerson and getCount methods, we didn't use the this keyword. Instead, we accessed the count property through the class identifier itself.

Because static members seem more like members of the class rather than members of the instance, they're often called `class members`. In fact, that is exactly what they are in languages where classes are objects, like JavaScript: they're properties and methods of the class itself. The `implement` method, for instance, is an example of a class member since it's called from the class itself and not through instances of the class.

Here's a reimplementation of the ooc example in JavaScript using a class:

```
var Person = new Class({

    // Properties
    name: '',
    age: 0,

    // Methods
    initialize: function(name, age){
        this.name = name;
        this.age = age;
    },

    log: function(){
        console.log(this.name + ', ' + this.age);
    }

});

// Static Property
Person.count = 0;

// Static Method
Person.addPerson = function(){
    this.count += 1;
};

Person.getCount = function(){
    console.log('Person count: ' + this.count);
};

// Creating a new Person instance
var mark = new Person('Mark', 23);
mark.log();

// Accessing the static method
Person.addPerson();
Person.getCount(); // 'Person count: 1'
```

As in the ooc example, the `count` property and `addPerson` and `getCount` methods become members of the `Person` class itself. Because the `Person` class is an object, creating static members is as simple as augmenting the `Person` object itself. So instead of declaring our static members inside the class, we just added them to our `Person` class directly. You'll also notice that in the `addPerson` and `getCount` methods, we used the `this` keyword instead of `Person` to access the count property. Since the methods are added to the class itself, they becomes methods of the class—and the value of the `this` keyword inside the method bodies is set to the class itself.

MooTools provides a function method called `extend` that we could use to easily add class members:

```
var Person = new Class({

    // Properties
    name: '',
    age: 0,

    // Methods
    initialize: function(name, age){
        this.name = name;
        this.age = age;
    },

    log: function(){
        console.log(this.name + ', ' + this.age);
    }

});

Person.extend({

    // Static Property
    count: 0,

    // Static Method
    addPerson: function(){
        this.count += 1;
    },

    getCount: function(){
        console.log('Person count: ' + this.count);
    }

});

// Creating a new Person instance
var mark = new Person('Mark', 23);
mark.log();

// Accessing the static method
Person.addPerson();
Person.getCount(); // 'Person count: 1'
```

The extend method is declared via `Function.prototype` and is inherited by all functions. Because a MooTools class is in essence a function, we could use the extend method for classes too. The method is similar to the `implement` method in that it takes an object argument with keys and values referring to members that will be added. Unlike `implement`, though, extend does not add the members to the prototype of the class, but to the class object itself.

▦ **Note** Don't confuse the `extend` method with the `Extends` mutator. Unlike `Implements` and `implement`, which are similar in how they work, `Extends` and `extend` perform different operations. And as I mentioned, `extend` is a function method inherited from `Function.prototype`, not `Class.prototype`.

Taking it one step further, we could combine what we learned from the previous sections to implement a Static mutator, so we could combine the declarations inside the class itself:

```
Class.Mutators.Static = function(members){
    this.extend(members);
};

var Person = new Class({

    Static: {

        // Static Property
        count: 0,

        // Static Method
        addPerson: function(){
            this.count += 1;
        },

        getCount: function(){
            console.log('Person count: ' + this.count);
        }

    },

    // Properties
    name: '',
    age: 0,

    // Methods
    initialize: function(name, age){
        this.name = name;
        this.age = age;
    },

    log: function(){
        console.log(this.name + ', ' + this.age);
    }

});

// Creating a new Person instance
var mark = new Person('Mark', 23);
mark.log();

// Accessing the static method
```

```
Person.addPerson();
Person.getCount() // 'Person count: 1'
```

The Static mutator is a very simple mutator that receives an object argument containing the members that will be added to the class and invokes the extend method of the class. To use it, we simply declared a Static key inside our class with an object value containing the static members we'd like to add. The result is a cleaner and tighter class declaration.

One last thing to remember before we move on is that static or class members aren't inherited. Because they are added to the class itself rather than the class's prototype, class members are not inherited by subclasses. This is different from how real classical languages with static members work, although we can mimic the behavior by overriding the original Extends mutator:

```
(function() {

    var origExtends = Class.Mutators.Extends;

    Class.Mutators.Extends = function(parent){
        origExtends.call(this, parent);

        var members = {};
        for (var key in parent){
            if (parent.hasOwnProperty(key) && !this.hasOwnProperty(key)) members[key] =
parent[key];
        }
        this.extend(members);
    };

})();
```

We first stored the original Extends mutator function in the origExtends variable so that we can call it later. We then overrode our Class.Mutators.Extends mutator with a new function. The first line of the new mutator function calls the original mutator function in order to set the prototype chain of the class. We then loop through the members of the superclass and check for class members that we should copy into the new class. We used hasOwnProperty to check the members so that we will copy only the members that were added directly to the class and not the ones inherited from Function.prototype or from Class.prototype. Finally, we use the extend method to add the members from our superclass to our new class.

Encapsulation and Visibility

Looking back at all the classes we've created so far, you'll notice that all of them are self-contained: we defined our classes so that they have all the properties and methods they'll need. We didn't store the information about our objects in a separate location, nor did we define external functions to perform operations on our objects. Instead, we defined the properties and methods of our classes so that each instance of our class—each object—is usable on its own.

The idea of having each object contain all data (properties) and behavior (methods) it needs is an important principle in object-oriented programming called *encapsulation*. Encapsulation dictates that each object should be self-contained: classes should declare the properties and methods needed so that everything is contained within the object.

Related to the principle of encapsulation is the idea that while you should include all of the properties and methods needed to make your object self-contained, you should also limit what you expose of your object. In other words, you should only expose the properties and methods of your object that need to be exposed to enable other objects to effectively use your object. This principle is called *visibility* and it's an important part of class design.

Take, for example, the following class:

```
var Person = new Class({

    // Properties
    name: '',
    age: 0,

    // Methods
    initialize: function(name, age){
        this.name = name;
        this.age = age;
        this.format();
    },

    log: function(){
        console.log(this.name + ', ' + this.age);
    },

    format: function(){
        this.name = this.name.capitalize();
        this.age = parseInt(this.age);
    }

});

// Creating a new Person instance
var mark = new Person('mark', '23');
mark.log(); // 'Mark, 23'

mark.format(); // returns nothing
```

Here we have the same `Person` class from the previous examples but with a new method called `format`. This new method does two things: first, it ensures that our `name` property is capitalized and second, it ensures that our `age` property is an integer. It's called automatically from our initializer and it doesn't return anything. In other words, it's an internal method: it's used by our class to perform a necessary action, but it's not meant to be called outside of the class.

The principle of visibility tells us that since it's not needed to make the class work, our `format` method should not be visible outside of our object. However, we could still invoke the function as in the last line of the snippet.

Internal methods such as `format` that are necessary but aren't meant to be called outside the object itself must have their visibility limited so that only the object itself can access them. Most classical languages allow you to set the visibility of your members to one of three levels:

- **Public members** are members that are accessible from within and from without the instance. In the example above, all our members are public.

- **Private members**, on the other hand, are accessible only from within the instances of the class. Private properties can be accessed only by methods of the instance and private methods can be invoked only by other methods of the instance. Also, if a subclass inherits from a superclass with private members, instances of this subclass won't be able to access the private members of the superclass.

- Finally, **protected members** are like private members: protected properties and methods can be accessed and invoked only from within the instance. However, unlike private members, protected members are also available to subclasses that inherit them.

Most popular classical languages support these three visibility levels. One notable exception, though, is the Python programming language, which supports only public members. To circumvent this "limitation," Python programmers use a generally accepted naming convention: any member that's prefixed by an underscore (e.g., _format) is considered protected. By accepting a common idiom, Python programmers are able to implement a form of style-guided visibility system.

The use of naming conventions to denote visibility can also be applied to JavaScript. Like Python, all members in JavaScript are public and it's usually the naming conventions that enable us to determine which methods are protected and which are public. In fact, you already saw one MooTools convention: the use of $ to prefix protected properties.

However, there are ways to actually mimic the behavior of private and protected methods in JavaScript. One involves using closures and the other is a nifty feature implemented by the MooTools' class system.

Private Methods

The easiest way to mimic private methods in JavaScript is to wrap your class declaration in a function and create a local function that will become your "private method":

```
var Person = (function(){

    // Our "private" method
    var format = function(){
        this.name = this.name.capitalize();
        this.age = parseInt(this.age);
    };

    // Our class
    return new Class({

        // Properties
        name: '',
        age: 0,

        // Methods
        initialize: function(name, age){
            this.name = name;
            this.age = age;
            format.call(this);
        },

        log: function(){
            console.log(this.name + ', ' + this.age);
        }

    });

})();
```

```
// Creating a new Person instance
var mark = new Person('mark', '23');
mark.log(); // 'Mark, 23'
```

```
console.log(typeof mark.format); // 'undefined'
```

First, we used a single-execution function as an *enclosure* for our class declaration. Inside our enclosure, we moved our original `format` method to a local function of the same name. Our class declaration is also inside our enclosure, so it has access to the local function. We then changed the function invocation inside the `initialize` method from `this.format()` to `format.call(this)`, since `format` is no longer a class method but a separate function. We used the `call` method to bind the `this` keyword inside our `format` function to the current instance. Because the `format` function is localized, it can't be called outside the body of the enclosure. However, when we returned the class object at the end of the function, we created a closure that retains references in our methods to the local `format` function. The result is that we get the same behavior as private methods: we're able to call the function from within our class, but it can't be called from outside it.

While this technique effectively mimics how private methods work, there are some drawbacks. The first is that unlike true private methods, our "private methods" aren't actually methods of the class, but external functions that are accessible only to the class because of closures. This means that we can't override them, nor can we change their implementation dynamically like real private methods.

Another drawback is that all methods that need to use the private method will have to be declared within the scope of the enclosing function. Because we employed an enclosure to localize the private function, methods that are declared from outside the enclosure also won't be able to access the function. This limits the extensibility of our class.

But perhaps the biggest drawback comes from the nature of private methods. Since they can't be accessed by inheriting classes, private methods have far too limited use. If a subclass needs the functionality of a private method from its superclass, it needs to either call a public or protected method from its superclass that has access to the method, or implement its own copy of the private method—both of which aren't appealing solutions.

Protected Methods

A better solution would be to use protected methods instead of private methods. A protected method also has limited visibility, but unlike a private method, it's accessible to inheriting subclasses. While there are times when you'd actually need to use private methods, there are more uses for protected methods in most programs you'll be building.

Unlike private methods, though, there's no simple way to implement protected methods in JavaScript. Fortunately, MooTools solves this for us by implementing its own version of protected methods:

```
var Person = new Class({

    // Properties
    name: '',
    age: 0,

    // Methods
    initialize: function(name, age){
        this.name = name;
        this.age = age;
        this.format();
    },
```

```
    log: function(){
        console.log(this.name + ', ' + this.age);
    },

    format: function(){
        this.name = this.name.capitalize();
        this.age = parseInt(this.age);
    }.protect()

});

// Creating a new Person instance
var mark = new Person('mark', '23');
mark.log(); // 'Mark, 23'

mark.format(); // 'Error: The method "format" cannot be called.'
```

This snippet is similar to our original example where all the members are public, but you'll see that in our declaration for format, we called on the protect method of the function. When called from inside the initialize method, our format method works normally. However, when called from outside the object like we did in the last line, the format method throws an error. This effectively mimics the behavior of a protected method.

The implementation of protected methods in MooTools is divided into two parts: first is the protect method itself and the second comes from the wrapper function. The protect method is declared through Function.prototype and is inherited by all functions, but its power only becomes apparent when the method is used in conjunction with the wrapper function provided by the class system.

If you'll recall, all class methods are wrapped in a special wrapper function. If you'll look back at the code for the wrapper function in the previous chapter, you'll see that much of it involves setting the values of the current and caller variables. As we saw from the previous chapter, these variables are used to track down the currently running method for the this.parent method that's used to invoke overridden methods from the superclass.

But aside from tracking overridden methods, the wrapper function also tracks the running method (aka, the "current" method) and which method invoked the running method (aka, the "caller" method). It is also the job of the wrapper function to ensure that protected methods are callable only from within the class by checking whether the protected method was invoked by another method inside the class or whether it was invoked directly from outside the class.

To illustrate how this works, let's apply it to our previous example. When we called new Person('mark', '23'), the constructor calls our initialize method. The wrapper function for this method sets initialize as the current method. Since initialize was called directly, the value of the caller method is set to null. The initialize method then invokes the protected method format and the wrapper function for format reconfigures the variables: it sets format as the current method and initialize as the caller method. Because format is protected, the wrapper function checks whether format was called from another method inside the object. It does this by checking the value of the caller method. If the method was invoked by another method inside the object, caller will never be null. In this example, the wrapper will see that the caller is initialize, and it will execute the format method as expected.

When we call the format method directly, the same sequence of operations is performed. The wrapper function first sets format as the current method and the value of the caller method will be null, since format was called directly. Since a protected method like format can only be called by another method of the object, the wrapper function will throw an error when it sees that the value of the caller method is null.

You'll fully understand how this all works when you look at the wrapper function that we saw in the previous chapter. Right before and just after the invocation of the actual method are a set of declarations that set the values of the current and the caller methods. It is these values that enable the class system to determine not only overridden methods from the superclass but also the chain of calls leading to the current method call—which is how the class system knows whether to invoke the function or throw an error.

Like real protected methods, MooTools' protected methods are also available to inheriting classes:

```
var Person = new Class({

    // Properties
    name: '',
    age: 0,

    // Methods
    initialize: function(name, age){
        this.name = name;
        this.age = age;
        this.format();
    },

    log: function(){
        console.log(this.name + ', ' + this.age);
    },

    format: function(){
        this.name = this.name.capitalize();
        this.age = parseInt(this.age);
    }.protect()

});

var Mark = new Class({

    Extends: Person,

    initialize: function(){
        this.name = 'mark';
        this.age = '23';
        this.format();
    }

});

// Creating a new Person instance
var mark = new Mark();
mark.log(); // 'Mark, 23'

mark.format(); // 'Error: The method "format" cannot be called.'
```

Even though our `format` method is protected, our `Mark` class still has access to it since the class inherits from our original `Person` object. The `format` method still works as expected, and still throws an error if called directly.

The implementation of protected methods in MooTools—while perfect for most use cases—can be a bit weird unless you know the internals. One particular gotcha is when protected methods are used in closures:

```
var Thing = new Class({

    test: function(){
        var self = this;
        (function(){
            self.log();
        })();
    },

    generate: function(){
        var self = this;
        return function(){
            self.log();
        };
    },

    log: function(){
        console.log('Yes');
    }.protect()

});

var obj = new Thing();
obj.test(); // 'Yes'

var fn = obj.generate();
fn(); // "Error: The method "log" cannot be called.'
```

Our class Thing has one protected method called log and two public methods: test and generate. When we call the test method, it creates a single-execution function that calls the log method. Because the single-execution function is created, invoked, and destroyed within the context of the test function, the call to the log method succeeds, since the whole procedure happens from inside the context of the method. On the other hand, generate returns a function that calls log inside its body, creating a closure. Because the procedure moves the invocation of the log method outside of the context of the generate method, the invocation fails and an error is thrown. This is because by the time that log is finally called, the generate function would have finished its execution. The call to log then would be just like directly calling log from the outside.

Because of how they're implemented, protected methods can only be called in the immediate body of other methods. This means that protected methods can't be used in callback function, event handlers, or any other function that uses closures, because the invocation gets removed from the current context. So if you need to use a method for any of these things, it's better to use a public method instead of a protected one.

Finally, we end this section with another mutator. In the section on static members, we implemented a Static mutator to simplify the process of declaring static members. To make the process of declaring protected methods easier, let's implement a corresponding Protected mutator:

```
Class.Mutators.Protected = function(methods){
    for (var key in methods){
        if (methods[key] instanceof Function) this.implement(key, methods[key].protect());
    }
};
```

As an exercise, I'll leave it to you to explain how our Protected mutator works and how to use it. This is a very easy exercise, since it's very similar to our Static mutator.

MooTools and Classes

MooTools is a class-based framework not only because it provides the best JavaScript class system currently available, but because it uses this class system itself. While other JavaScript frameworks provide some form of plug-in or extension system to add extra functionality to the framework, MooTools expects developers to use the built-in class system to do this.

Since the class system is central to MooTools, every developer who uses the framework is expected to know at least the basics of creating and extending classes. After reading this and the previous chapter, I expect that you already understand the MooTools class system deeply and I won't be surprised if you're well on your way to mastering the system.

However, knowing how to *create* classes and knowing how to *properly design* classes are wholly separate things. The first involves syntax and technique, which is easy enough to master. The second, on the other hand, involves a firm understanding of the principles and concepts of object-oriented programming, and it's a bit harder to master these.

These principles and concepts are, of course, outside the scope of this book, though we have touched on some of them, like code reuse, inheritance, encapsulation, and visibility. The only way to learn them is by reading books on object-oriented programming and design, and by using what you've learned in experimentation and in building complex JavaScript programs.

I will, however, provide you with some pointers that should come in handy:

- *Follow the MooTools style and code conventions.* While coding style is mostly a personal preference, the MooTools project keeps its own set of conventions that is followed for all code that's part of the framework. All snippets from this book are written according to this convention, and a guide is included at the end of this book for reference. I suggest that you follow the official conventions even if you're writing code for personal use. Having a common style makes it easier to share and reuse code, and enables us to have a common set of idioms that we can all understand.

- *Encapsulate.* Remember to make your classes self-contained. Make sure that instances of your classes can be used on their own, and be mindful of the visibility of your members.

- *If it's too big, split it.* Sometimes your methods will get too complex and sometimes your classes will seem too big. If this is the case, you might be putting a lot of stuff in one place. It's better to split these items into multiple methods or multiple classes. Don't be afraid to rewrite your code and divide it into smaller logical parts.

- *Reusability is important.* We create classes because we want to reuse code: instead of writing a function for each object, we create a blueprint and reuse the properties and members of that blueprint. When you see yourself doing the same thing over and over again, find a way to share a piece of code across all items that use it, like a mixin or a superclass. This is often called the DRY Principle (Don't Repeat Yourself).

- *Plan for extensibility.* As your project grows, you might need to add a behavior to your classes or modify members that already exist. Plan your classes in a way that permits extensibility and change. This ensures that your classes are flexible enough to handle anything new that might come up.

- *Learn how to use design patterns.* A **design pattern** is a particular idiom that dictates how to create common types of classes. While design patterns in general are beyond the scope of this book, you'll see several patterns used throughout the framework and I'll call your attention to them. As part of your study, read up on the common design patterns that you can use for your programs.

But perhaps the best advice I can give is to *never stop learning*. Read books about object-oriented programming and classical languages. Check out the code for the classes included in MooTools Core. The best way to learn the MooTools class system is to experiment and observe how MooTools does things. In fact, that's exactly what we'll do in the chapters ahead: we're going to look at the internals of core MooTools classes.

I can assure you that a lot more amazing things can be done using the features that MooTools—and the JavaScript language itself—provides.

The Wrap-Up

In this chapter, we learned more about the MooTools class system. We found out about mutators, which are class macros that enable us to transform the behavior and composition of our classes. We learned about static members and how to implement them, as well as the concepts of encapsulation and visibility and how we can use them to improve our classes.

The MooTools class system is actually part of a tandem. Its partner, called the type system, is very similar to the class system, but its use and purpose is different. In the next chapter, we'll learn all about types and native augmentation and how MooTools uses the type system to improve the features that JavaScript already provides, as well as how it adds new features of its own.

So if you're ready, put on your favorite swimwear and let's dive into the MooTools type system.

CHAPTER 6

■■■

Types

The class system we've been studying is one half of a pair of systems that MooTools implements. The other half, the MooTools type system, is very similar to the class system, but it focuses more on data as values and the various forms that values take.

Unlike the native object implementation and classes we discussed in separate chapters, the native JavaScript type system and the MooTools type system will both be tackled in this chapter. The two type systems are deeply intertwined, and discussing them separately wouldn't really aid our understanding of their similarities and differences.

With that in mind, let's talk about types.

Values and Type Systems

At the heart of programming is the manipulation of data. Whether we're writing a spreadsheet program to process numbers, a complex algorithm to animate images on a web page, or a backend system to keep track of user information, we're still working with data and its representations.

In our programs, we express our data in terms of **values**. The following, for example, are all valid JavaScript values:

```
42
true
'hello'
function square(x){ return x * x; };
{name: 'mark'}
```

The first value is a number, the second is the boolean value true, the third, a string spelling the word "hello", the fourth, a function named square, and, finally, a simple object. While all of these values represent data, they don't represent the same kind of data. Each value can be differentiated from the others by the kind of data it represents.

We distinguish the values in terms of their **types**. We can use the JavaScript typeof operator to determine the type of a value:

```
console.log(typeof 42);             // 'number'
console.log(typeof true);           // 'boolean'
console.log(typeof 'hello');        // 'string'
console.log(typeof function(){});   // 'function'
console.log(typeof {name: 'mark'}); // 'object'
```

The type of a value determines not only what kind of data it represents, but also what operations can be performed on it. Two Number values, for instance, can be added together to obtain their sum. However, you can't directly add a Number value to an Object value. In the same sense, you can't invoke a String or get the substring of a Function.

127

■ **Note** We're going to adopt the ECMAScript specification's standard of using capitalized type names. Thus, when you see "Object," we are referring to the Object type, in contrast to "object," which could mean any object. In the same way, we have Function versus function, Number versus number, and String versus string.

The types that values can take, as well as the operations that can be performed on particular types, are determined by the language's **type system**. The type system also provides ways to determine the type of a value and ways to convert a value from one type to another.

JavaScript uses a **type-by-specification system**: the type of a particular value is defined directly by the language specification. The result of the application of the typeof operator to a value is governed by specific rules defined by the ECMAScript specification, and the interpreter uses these rules to determine the type of any value.

JavaScript's type system is, unfortunately, quirky. It might appear fine from the example above, but it's skewed at best when used in practical situations. To illustrate, let's use the typeof operator to determine the types of some other values:

```
console.log(typeof {name: 'mark'}); // 'object'
console.log(typeof [1, 2, 3]);      // 'object'
console.log(typeof new Date());     // 'object'
```

Here we have three values: a basic object, an array, and a date object. These three values have different structures and uses, so we'd expect them to be different types. However, this is not the case; all these values are considered to be of the Object type in JavaScript.

JavaScript, at its core, is an object-based language. Most values in JavaScript are objects—and even the values that are not objects—like strings and numbers—are turned into objects when needed (more on this later). Weirdly enough, JavaScript's type system thinks that since all values are objects, they should all be grouped under the same type: Object. So an array or a date object, for example, is of the Object type in JavaScript, even if it's a special kind of object.

This is technically "logical," of course: since arrays and dates are objects, their type would be Object. But while this is okay from a semantic point of view, it becomes totally useless—and, often, counterproductive—for practical purposes. For us to be able to properly manipulate values, we need to be able to differentiate between the values we're working with. It's okay to think of everything as an object, but we also need a way to determine what kind of object it is exactly.

JavaScript's type system doesn't help in this area. All objects in JavaScript are of the Object type. The only exception is functions, which JavaScript distinguishes as the Function type, but that's just because these objects have the unique ability to be invoked. Any other object—regardless of its structure, use, or mode of creation—is of the Object type.

There is, however, an alternative. In the previous chapter we saw how objects are created using classes. We learned that a class is a special language construct that serves as a blueprint for creating objects by defining the structure of these objects in terms of properties and methods. When we instantiate a class, we create a new object that's structured according to the definition we put in our class.

Classes can actually be used as an alternative type system: a **type-by-class system**. Classes define the structure of objects and what operations can be done on these objects, effectively differentiating objects in terms of structure and use. An instance of the Car class, for example, is a different kind of object when compared to an instance of the Animal class. This is analogous to how types are determined: a Car value (or object) is different from an Animal value and it's their types (or classes) that determine what kind of value they are and what operations can be performed on them.

In fact, this type-by-class system is used as the native type system in many classical languages, like Ruby. As with JavaScript, every value in Ruby is an object instance of a class. The class and the type of an object are therefore the same thing in Ruby, and classes themselves are treated as types.

Interestingly, JavaScript also has an internal facility for a type-by-class system. Though there is no native class construct in JavaScript, the term "class" is used internally by the language to signify the type of an object. All JavaScript objects have an internal `class` property, which is a string containing the name of the object's type. Unfortunately, this property is only used internally by the interpreter for its type-based operations, and is not actually used in the language-accessible type system, which makes it unusable for our current purpose. To really implement a proper type system, we must do it ourselves by extending the language.

An Alternative Type System

Let's recall what we know about JavaScript objects. We know that all objects are created using a constructor function and these inherit from the `prototype` properties of these constructors. Like classes, constructor functions and their prototypes define the structure of objects through properties and methods. Since every possible JavaScript value (with the exception of `null` and `undefined`) has its own constructor, constructors can be used to implement a type-by-class system in JavaScript. Native constructors like `Object`, `Array`, or `Date` would become "classes" in this system, and the instances of these constructors would be typed properly according to the particular constructor.

MooTools classes seem like good candidates to use in a type-by-class system, since they're just abstractions on the native constructor-prototype pair. We could simply turn native constructors like `Object` into classes and use the same type-by-class system implemented in languages like Ruby. Unfortunately, this is impossible to do because of how the MooTools class system is implemented.

To illustrate, let's say we want to create a new `Animal` class. To do this, we pass an object that defines the structure of the class as an argument to the `Class` constructor. The `Class` constructor then returns a new `Animal` class. This `Animal` class is actually an abstracted constructor function created internally and returned by the `Class` constructor. It is the job of the `Class` constructor to create the constructor function that will become the class object. Therefore, *a particular constructor function can only be considered a class object if it was created using `Class`.*

The problem is that constructors like `Object` or `Array` are *built-in objects*; they're implemented directly by the JavaScript engine using another language, usually C or C++, and their implementation details aren't available via the JavaScript interface. Because only the `Class` constructor can create the abstracted constructor function that would become our class object, we'll have to replace the native implementation of these built-in constructors with our own if we want to turn them into classes. In other words, to turn built-in constructors into classes, we have to destroy them first.

Because of this limitation, MooTools doesn't use classes to implement its type system. Instead, it introduces a new class-like construct called a **type object**, which is created using the `Type` constructor.

Like a class, a type object is an abstracted constructor function that has additional properties and methods that make it easier to manipulate the underlying `prototype` object. But unlike a class, the actual constructor function that becomes the type object isn't created inside the `Type` constructor. Rather, type objects are simply existing constructor functions that are transformed by the `Type` constructor into type objects. Any existing constructor can therefore be turned into a type object—which makes it possible to use built-in constructors without replacing them.

The native `Array` constructor, for example, is turned into a type object simply by passing it to the `Type` constructor. The `Type` constructor doesn't create a new constructor function to replace the native `Array` constructor. Instead, it turns the original `Array` constructor function into a type object by augmenting it with new properties and methods. Thus, the built-in `Array` constructor and the MooTools `Array` type object are one and the same. Nothing was replaced or destroyed. In fact, most built-in constructor functions are turned into type objects automatically when MooTools loads.

Type objects perform two main functions. First, a type object is a representation of the actual kind of value in terms of what makes it different from all other values. For example, the `Array` type object represents all values that are ordered lists of data, while the `Function` type object represents all values that are separate units of code that can be invoked.

Second, a type object also functions as a "class" (in the object-oriented sense of the word) for the particular type, which means that the structure and behavior of the values of that type are controlled by the type object. Because the type object is a constructor function, all instances of this type inherit from its prototype property. The type object can therefore be used to modify or augment the structure of all values under that type.

The MooTools type system abstracts part of the native type system in the same way that the class system abstracts the native constructor-prototype model. But unlike the class system, the MooTools type system is meant to be a direct replacement—not just a simple alternative. The easiest way to see the type system in action is by using the typeOf function:

```
console.log( typeOf(42) );              // 'number'
console.log( typeOf(true) );            // 'boolean'
console.log( typeOf('hello') );         // 'string'
console.log( typeOf(function (){}) );   // 'function'
console.log( typeOf({name: 'mark'}) );  // 'object'
console.log( typeOf([1, 2, 3]) );       // 'array'
console.log( typeOf(new Date()) );      // 'date'
console.log( typeOf(new Class()) );     // 'class'
```

The typeOf function mimics the native typeof operator in the MooTools type system. Like its native typeof counterpart, the typeOf function gives us the type of a value as a string. Unlike the typeof operator, though, the typeOf function knows how to properly differentiate among objects. You'll see that arrays, dates, and classes don't return 'object' as their type, but rather their types as defined by their type objects.

■ **Note** typeof is a JavaScript operator, like the addition operator + or the instanceof operator, so you don't need parentheses when using it. The typeOf function, however, is a true function, so you have to invoke it using the invocation operator (aka, parentheses). Also, take note of the "camelCase" name: typeOf(), not typeof().

An important point to note is that since MooTools introduces a separate construct for its type system, classes are not used to determine the type of an object. The separation of classes and types means that objects created using classes will have both a class and a type:

```
// a class
var Person = new Class();

// an instance
var mark = new Person();

console.log(mark instanceof Person); // true
console.log(typeOf(mark));   // 'object'
```

In this example, mark isn't of the Person type but rather of the Object type, even if its class is Person. In the MooTools system, objects created from MooTools classes always have Object as their type and only objects created from the actual MooTools type constructors are given a different type.

While this is indeed a limitation, it's not such a big problem compared to the limitations of the native type system. Take, for instance, arrays and regular expressions: both of these are vastly different kinds of objects, but the native type system marks both as Object types—and in the case of regular expressions, they could even be typed as Functions in some implementations! We might not be able to distinguish among the class-defined object types with the MooTools type system, but at least we're able to tell whether an object is really a regular expression or a function.

Besides, the MooTools type system is able to distinguish among all native object types, which means that the only objects that will return 'object' when passed to the typeOf function are plain objects and objects created using classes. So it becomes much easier to guess what kind of object we're dealing with. Combined with our knowledge of the actual classes we use in our programs, the limitation of the class system becomes almost nonexistent.

Native Types and Values

Before we actually discuss the internals of the MooTools type system, we need to familiarize ourselves with the native types and the values they take. If you're one of those people who have already memorized the ECMAScript language specification, feel free to skip this part. But if you only know the basics of JavaScript types, keep on reading because much of what follows discusses the internals of the types themselves, rather than their basic use.

The ECMAScript specification defines six main types: Undefined, Null, Boolean, String, Number, and Object. We could further classify these types into three groups:

- **Existence Types** are special types whose values represent the condition of not having values. Null and Undefined are both existence types.

- **Primitive Types** (or "primitives" for short) represent the simplest immutable (or unchangeable) values. Strings, numbers, and booleans are all primitives.

- **Composite Types** represent compound values whose structures and behavior can be changed. All objects (including functions) are composite types in JavaScript.

All JavaScript values are typed as one of these native types, and we'll examine these native types and values as well as their corresponding MooTools type objects in the following sections. We'll also learn the value a particular type takes when it's converted to another value through the process of **type casting**.

Null and Undefined

The **Null** and **Undefined** types are the only **existence types** in JavaScript. These types and their values are special because they don't represent data, but instead stand for the absence of data.

▓ **Note** The ECMAScript language specification categorizes the Null and Undefined types as primitive types. However, I put them in their own group since they behave differently from other primitive values.

The Null type has only one value, which is represented by the null keyword. The null value denotes the *absence of a value*: assigning null to a variable means that the variable does not have an actual value. Thus, the Null value is like a placeholder value in cases where there's no value to use.

Like the Null type, the Undefined type has only one value, which is represented by the undefined variable. The undefined value is used to represent the value of any variable that has been declared but not defined:

```
// declare a variable
var thing;

console.log(typeof thing); // 'undefined'
console.log(thing === undefined); // true

// define the value
thing = 1;

console.log(typeof thing); // 'number'
console.log(thing === undefined); // false
```

Remember that in Chapter 2 we learned that variable *declaration* and variable *definition* are executed by JavaScript as two distinct steps. When a variable is declared but not given a value, its value is automatically set to undefined. The undefined value is also used as the value of object members that don't exist, as well as the value of a function's formal parameters with no corresponding argument passed during invocation.

One important thing to consider with the Undefined type is that its only representation—the undefined variable—is a variable, not a keyword. This means that the actual value of the undefined variable can be changed:

```
// declare a variable
var thing;

// change the value of undefined
undefined = 'nooo!';

console.log(thing === undefined); // false
```

The ECMAScript committee's decision to make undefined a variable was an unfortunate choice that's been resolved in ECMAScript 5 by making the variable read-only. However, you should still be careful not to change the value of the undefined variable since ECMAScript 3 is still widely used, and doing so would create havoc in your programs.

The null and undefined values can be transformed into primitives through type casting—and we'll see how this is done in a later section. For now, let's just remember that the null value is cast into the number value 0, the string value 'null' and the boolean value false. Meanwhile, the undefined value is cast into the number value NaN, the string value 'undefined' and the boolean value false.

Null and Undefined also have the distinction of being the only native types with no constructor functions. Therefore, they have no corresponding MooTools type object. Any variable that has null or undefined for its value will have no properties or methods, and trying to access a member of a null or undefined value will result in an error.

One important thing to note here is that MooTools treats the Undefined value the same as the Null value, which means that typeOf(undefined) will return 'null' instead of 'undefined'. This is a simplification on the part of MooTools, since both values represent the same state of not having an actual value. Therefore, in order to check for undefined in MooTools, you'll have to use strict comparison, such as value === undefined.

Primitive Types

The three **primitive types**—Number, String, and Boolean—represent the simplest of all possible values in JavaScript. They're the most basic types of data in terms of structure, containing only actual values without any properties or methods.

■ **Note** That last statement might be a bit surprising. In JavaScript, only objects have properties and methods, while primitives like strings and numbers don't—although they sometimes appear as if they do. We'll get around to that in a bit.

Primitive values are *immutable*, which means that they can't be modified. When a primitive value is stored in a variable or passed as an argument to a function, a new copy of the value is created—giving them their other name, **value types**.

Booleans

The simplest primitive type is the **Boolean** type, which has only two possible values: *true* and *false*; these are represented in code by the `true` and `false` **literals**. Booleans represent the *truth value* of an expression. For instance, `4 == 4` yields `true` because the number 4 is indeed equal to itself, while `(2 + 2) == 5` yields `false` since the correct answer should be 4. When cast to number values, `true` and `false` yield 1 and 0, respectively, and when cast to strings, they become `'true'` and `'false'`.

Numbers

The **Number** type, on the other hand, represents *numeric values*. A number value is represented in code using **number literals**, which are simply numeric characters written directly in the JavaScript program. Also within the Number type are two special values represented by the variables `Infinity` and `NaN`.

The `Infinity` variable represents the value of *numeric infinity*—in other words, a really, really large number (mindblowing, in fact). The `NaN`, meanwhile, represents the special *not-a-number value*, which is the result of an impossible mathematical operation—like squaring a negative number. `NaN` also represents any non-numeric value cast into the Number type. You can check whether a number value is `NaN` using the built-in `isNaN` function, and whether a value is not `Infinity` using the `isFinite` function.

■ **Note** Like undefined, `Infinity` and `NaN` are variables, so you'll also have to be careful not to overwrite their default values. These variables have also been declared as read-only in ECMAScript 5.

All number values are cast to the boolean `true` except for 0 and `NaN`, which are cast to the boolean `false`. When cast to strings, number literals are simply turned into their string literal representation—like 42 to `'42'`—while `NaN` and `Infinity` are cast to `'NaN'` and `'Infinity'`.

String

Finally, the **String** type represents values that are *sequences of characters*—or, to put it simply, string values are representations of textual data. Strings are created using **string literals**, which are pairs of single or double quotes (i.e., '' or "") surrounding one or more characters. Each character in a string is given a numeric index that starts with 0, and strings with no characters are called **empty strings**.

Empty strings are cast to the boolean value `false`, non-empty strings to `true`. Casting strings to number values is a little more complex. An empty string is always cast to the number value 0, while non-empty strings are checked first before being cast. If the characters in the string represent a valid number value, then the string is cast to the actual number value of the characters, otherwise the string is cast to the number value NaN. So the string `'24.50'` is cast to the number value `24.50`, but the string `'hello'` will be cast to NaN.

Primitives as Objects

A unique thing about JavaScript's primitive types is that they can behave like objects. To give you an example, let's take a look at how the substring of a string value can be retrieved:

```
console.log('Hello World!'.substring(0, 4)); // 'Hello'
```

Here, we have a string value "Hello World!" created through a literal. We then invoked the `substring` method, which takes two arguments—from and to—that represent the numeric indices for the beginning and the end of the substring. We passed 0 and 4, telling the `substring` method to take the first up to the fifth character in the string and return it. The result is a new string, `'Hello'`.

Remember the object method called `hasOwnProperty`? We said that all objects inherit a `hasOwnProperty` method from `Object.prototype`, and strangely enough, even primitives have them:

```
console.log( typeOf('M!'.hasOwnProperty) ); // 'function'
console.log( typeOf((42).hasOwnProperty) ); // 'function'
console.log( typeOf(true.hasOwnProperty) ); // 'function'
```

So strings, numbers, and booleans all inherit the `hasOwnProperty` method. But inheriting properties and method from `Object.prototype` is a characteristic of objects, not primitives. Does this mean that strings, numbers, and booleans aren't really primitive values but are objects?

That's not the case, of course. Earlier in the chapter, we saw that the `typeof` operator returns the proper types for primitive values. If these values were objects, `typeof` would have returned `'object'` and not `'string'`, `'number'`, and `'boolean'`. This was clearly not the case.

But if they're truly primitive values, why do they behave like objects? The answer lies in JavaScript's use of **wrapper objects**. For each primitive type, JavaScript has a corresponding "object version" of that type, which is simply an object representation of a primitive value. Thus, we have three constructors that represent primitive types: `String`, `Number`, and `Boolean`.

The instances of these three constructors are objects, not primitive values, and we can confirm this using the native `typeof` operator:

```
console.log( typeof 'hello' ); // 'string'
console.log( typeof new String('hello') ); // 'object'

console.log( typeof 42 ); // 'number'
console.log( typeof new Number(42) ); // 'object'

console.log( typeof false ); // 'boolean'
console.log( typeof new Boolean(false) ); // 'object'
```

The name "wrapper object" comes from the use of these constructors. When the JavaScript interpreter sees a primitive value in an expression that requires an object, it creates a wrapper object that is used as an object representation of the primitive value. The following is what actually happens to the string example above:

```
console.log(new String('Hello World').substring(0, 4)); // 'Hello'
```

The string literal "Hello World" is first turned into a string object by passing the original value to the String constructor. The substring method of String.prototype is then invoked, and a new string primitive is returned as a result of the method call.

The process of turning primitives into objects is done automatically by the JavaScript interpreter, and the process is repeated for every operation. When the operation is done, the wrapper object is discarded and the original primitive value is restored. Since the wrapper object is created and destroyed for each property access operation, any property added to the wrapper object isn't persisted, and this preserves the immutability of the primitive value:

```
var str = 'Hello World';
str.type = 'greeting';

console.log(str.type); // undefined
```

Here we stored the string value "Hello World" to our variable str. When the second line is executed, a new string object wrapper is created to wrap the value of str, before adding a new property called type to the object. Because this wrapper object is destroyed right after the operation, accessing str.type on the last line produces undefined. Thus, the original string value remains unchanged.

You can, however, persist changes by explicitly converting a primitive into an object:

```
var str = new String('Hello World');
str.type = 'greeting';

console.log(str.type); // 'greeting'
```

■ **Note** You don't have to worry about the performance implications of this wrapping process. Even if wrapper objects are created and destroyed for each property access, all modern JavaScript implementations handle the process efficiently.

Because of this automated wrapping process, primitive types can be used just like normal objects. The existence of constructor functions for primitive types also makes it possible to add new properties and methods that will be "inherited" by primitive values. Primitive types are represented in the MooTools type system by the type objects Boolean, Number, and String.

As a final note before we move on, be reminded that numeric literals need to be enclosed in a pair of parentheses when they are used in property-access operations, like (42).hasOwnProperty(). Forgetting to do so—like 42.hasOwnProperty()—results in a syntax error because the parser will think you're declaring a floating point literal.

Composite Types

JavaScript has only one **composite type**: the **Object** type. However, it can be divided into subtypes that define the special kinds of objects, such as arrays or dates. Unlike the native type system, the MooTools type system differentiates between objects according to these subtypes.

We already talked about objects in detail before, so we won't go into the internals of JavaScript's object implementation here. We know that objects are aggregate values composed of an unordered collection of key-value pairs. We also know that all objects are associated with a constructor function and they inherit from the prototype property of their respective constructor.

Unlike primitives, objects are *mutable*: their structure and their behavior can be changed. When stored in variables or passed as arguments, new copies of the object aren't created. Instead, a reference to the original object is passed, effectively "sharing" the same object in all operations. Because of this behavior, objects are also called **reference types**.

The ECMAScript specification divides objects into two kinds:

- **Native objects** (also called **built-in objects**) are objects provided by the language and defined directly by the ECMAScript specification. All complying ECMAScript implementations provide the same set of native objects. Built-in constructor functions and their prototypes, the Math object, and native functions like eval are all examples of native objects.

- **Host objects** are objects provided by the host environment (i.e., the interpreter) for the purpose of correctly executing an ECMAScript program. They are independently defined by a particular JavaScript implementation and are therefore "non-standard" when viewed against the ECMAScript specification. The DOM objects of a browser, the Module functions of a CommonJS engine, and the additional objects created by a JavaScript implementation are examples of host objects. By virtue of their being a language extension rather than a simple framework or library, we'll consider the objects provided by MooTools as host objects.

▧ **Note** As an aside, the language we know as "JavaScript" is technically the ECMAScript language plus a standard set of browser-specific host objects. Thus, all JavaScript implementations are ECMAScript implementations—but not all ECMAScript implementations are JavaScript implementations.

We have already seen some of these native and host objects, like functions, objects, and classes, in the previous chapters. We'll discuss most of the browser-specific host objects in the second part of this book, and the CommonJS host objects in part three.

Object-to-Primitive Casting

Casting objects to primitive types follows different rules depending on the kind of object being converted.

The easiest rule is object-to-boolean value casting: all objects are cast to the boolean value true. You should take note of this since even a boolean object created using new Boolean(false) is cast to true. Its internal value might be false, but it's still cast to true since all objects are *truthy*.

When casting objects to strings, the toString method of the object is called. All objects inherit a basic toString method from Object.prototype, which returns a string in the form '[object <Class>]'. <Class> in this form refers to the internal class property of the object, so a basic object will return '[object Object]' while an array will return '[object Array]'.

However, most native objects override the toString method with their own implementation that usually returns a more appropriate string value. The primitive wrapper objects, for instance, have toString methods that return the string representations of their primitive values as described above.

To cast objects to numbers, JavaScript uses another object method called valueOf. If the return value of this method is a number, or if it can be cast into any number that is not NaN, then this value is used as the numeric value of the object. Otherwise, the toString method of the object is called and the return value of that method is again cast into a number. If the return value of toString is still not a number value, the object is cast to NaN.

The default valueOf method inherited from Object.prototype returns the object itself, which means that all objects are cast to NaN by default. Primitive wrapper objects, however, return their primitive values with the valueOf method, and return their string-cast values for toString. The primitive values inside object wrappers are then cast according to the rules we saw in the previous section.

Not all built-in objects provide their own valueOf method, so it's safe to assume that most objects will be cast to NaN. We'll take note of how a particular native object type implements the valueOf and the toString methods as we discuss them.

The Base Object

At the top of the object hierarchy is the **basic object**, created using an **object literal** or via the Object constructor. The Object constructor represents the base object, and all objects inherit from Object.prototype.

The Object constructor, unlike other built-in constructors, is not turned into a type object by MooTools in order to prevent extension of its prototype. This is because Object.prototype is considered off-limits: no new properties or methods should be added to it. To understand why, let's examine a basic JavaScript program:

```
// a basic object
var obj = new Object();

console.log(typeOf(obj.constructor));    // 'function'
console.log(typeOf(obj.hasOwnProperty)); // 'function'

for (var key in obj) console.log(key);
```

Using the typeOf function, we confirm that a base object inherits properties and methods like constructor and hasOwnProperty from Object.prototype. We then use the for-in statement, which loops through all the members of an object, to print out the names of our objects members. If we execute this program using a JavaScript interpreter, though, the console.log(key) in the for-in statement will never be executed—and it will appear as though our object has no members.

The reason for this behavior is that JavaScript differentiates between enumerable and non-enumerable properties. An **enumerable property** is any property that will be listed by a for-in loop, while a non-enumerable property is the opposite. All non-enumerable properties are thus considered to be "invisible" in a for-in loop.

All default properties and methods of Object.prototype are non-enumerable to ensure that new objects appear "blank." This is a way to avoid confusion among new developers: unless you know the internals of the prototypal system, you might be surprised to see new objects already having properties and methods. Therefore, the properties and methods that are defined by the language itself are marked as non-enumerable by default to prevent novices from thinking that these methods were added directly to the object.

On the other hand, all properties and method that we define in code are enumerable by default. If we augment a native object or replace its existing member with our own value, the new value we add will appear in for-in statements. In the case of Object.prototype, this makes things go awry because all objects inherit from this prototype. New objects no longer appear "blank" and you no longer have a way of knowing whether a member was implemented natively or if it was added directly to the object without having to call the hasOwnProperty method.

Because it is currently impossible to implement non-enumerable properties in most JavaScript interpreters, the JavaScript community has decided that Object.prototype should never be augmented. As one JavaScript saying goes: "Object.prototype is *verboten*." The MooTools developers agree with this statement, and it was decided that the Object constructor itself should not be turned into a type object to prevent misuse.

■ **Note** I stated that it's currently impossible to implement non-enumerable properties in most interpreters because, at the time of writing, most of these implementations still adhere to ECMAScript 3. ECMAScript 5, on the other hand, allows setting properties that are non-enumerables through descriptors.

Functions

Functions represent *distinct, standalone chunks of executable code.* They are the only native object type that has the distinction of being given a different "type" by the typeof operator. This is because functions are the only objects that have associated executable code that is run when the function is invoked.

A function object's executable code is stored in a special internal property called call (not to be confused with the call method). When either the invocation operator, (), or the apply and call methods of a function object are invoked, the executable code of the internal call property is executed by the interpreter. This internal call property is also the distinguishing property by which the typeof operator differentiates a function from any other object: the ECMAScript specification explicitly defines that only functions have this internal call property.

We've already discussed the internal details of functions in Chapter 2, so we won't go too deep here. The Function constructor, which can be used to create function objects, is the main constructor for functions, and all functions inherit from Function.prototype. The MooTools type system automatically turns Function into a type object.

Function.prototype doesn't implement its own valueOf method, which means calling fn.valueOf() will return the function itself. The default toString method, on the other hand, is overridden, and it returns the source code of the function. Take note, however, that the output of the toString method is implementation-dependent: not all JavaScript engines will output the same string source.

One other distinctive feature of functions is that they are the only other object type—along with regular expressions—that can't be implemented using a basic object. You can implement a JavaScript version of any other native object type using a basic object literal, but you can't make a function by simply using an object literal. Because of this, functions can't be subclassed using normal inheritance patterns, and this presents a very unique problem for both classes and type objects that we'll see later on.

Arrays

An **array** is an object representing *an arbitrary-length, ordered collection of values.* JavaScript arrays can store any valid value, including objects, functions, and other arrays. And unlike its counterparts in some programming languages, a JavaScript array doesn't expect all values to be of the same type, which means you can store values with different types in one array. All arrays inherit from the prototype property of the Array constructor.

Each value in an array is called a **member** and each member is associated with a numeric index that signifies its position in the collection. Arrays have a special dynamic property called length, which represents the number of members in an array. Arrays are usually created using the **array literal**, which is a pair of square brackets enclosing a set of values separated by commas, like [1, 2, 3].

Arrays inherit the default valueOf method from Object.prototype, and calling this method simply returns the array itself. Meanwhile, the toString method is overridden in Array.prototype: it returns the string representation of each member of the array separated by a comma, like '1,2,3'. Notably, this string value is the same as the result of calling the join method of arrays:

```
[1, 2, 3].join(','); // '1,2,3'
```

JavaScript arrays are implemented differently from the "real" arrays of other programming languages. A JavaScript array is nothing more than an object with numeric indices as keys and with a dynamic property length—plus additional methods inherited from Array.prototype. In fact, the array above could have very well been written as:

```
{
    '0': 1,
    '1': 2,
    '2': 3,
    length: 3
}
```

This is the basic structure of a JavaScript array. The numeric indices for this example—as well as for regular array—are strings, not numbers, since object keys need to be valid JavaScript identifiers. When numeric values are used to access the members of an array or an object using the bracket notation like in our example, the interpreter automatically converts these numbers to strings—something we can verify by using our two examples in a similar way:

```
// real array
var arr = [1, 2, 3];

for (var i = 0, l = arr.length; i < l; i++){
    console.log(arr[i]);
}

/* output:
    1
    2
    3
*/

// "object" array
var objArr = {
    '0': 1,
    '1': 2,
    '2': 3,
    length: 3
};

for (var i = 0, l = objArr.length; i < l; i++){
    console.log(objArr[i]);
}

/* output:
    1
    2
    3
*/
```

Both the real array and the dummy array created using a basic object behaved the same in this snippet because the implementation of JavaScript arrays is based on regular objects with a few minor differences. First, real arrays inherit from `Array.prototype`, which enables us to use nice array methods like forEach, and second, the `length` properties of real arrays are dynamically updated. The `length` property also behaves differently from other properties because changing its value by assignment actually changes the number of members in an array.

Our dummy array actually represents another set of objects in JavaScript called **array-like objects**. As its name implies, an array-like object is an object that looks similar to an array: it has numeric indices for keys and it has a `length` property that reflects the number of members it contains. The `arguments` object of functions, DOM collections, and nodelists are examples of array-like objects.

Because these objects aren't true arrays, they don't inherit from `Array.prototype` and you can't call array methods through them. However, you can invoke the methods of `Array.prototype` and bind the `this` keyword to these array-like objects to perform array operations using them. For example, we could turn our dummy array-like object into a true array using the `Array.prototype.slice` technique we used in the chapter on functions:

```
var objArr = {
    '0': 1,
    '1': 2,
    '2': 3,
    length: 3
};

console.log(typeOf(objArr)); // 'object'

// turn it into a true array
objArr = Array.prototype.slice.call(objArr);

console.log(typeOf(objArr)); // 'array'
```

All array methods can be used for array-like objects with this technique, not just `slice`. This is possible because the methods of Array.prototype are implemented as *generics*, which means they can be used on any object.

Arrays, for example, have the methods `unshift` and `push`, which add members to the beginning and the end of the array, respectively. We can use these two methods to augment our array-like object using the same approach as with `slice`:

```
var objArr = {
    '0': 1,
    '1': 2,
    '2': 3,
    length: 3
};

console.log(objArr.length); // 3

// the first member of the array
console.log(objArr[0]); // 1

// add a member to the front
Array.prototype.unshift.call(objArr, 0);

console.log(objArr[0]); // 0
console.log(objArr.length); // 4

// add a member to the back
```

```
Array.prototype.push.call(objArr, 4);

console.log(objArr[4]); // 4
console.log(objArr.length); // 5

// check that it's still an object
console.log(typeOf(objArr)); // 'object'
```

The array methods not only modified our object as if it were a real array, they also automatically adjusted the length property of the object. This proves that JavaScript arrays are truly implemented using simple objects, and it also gives us a very useful technique we can use for building our own array-like objects.

Regular Expressions

Regular expression objects or **regexps** are used for the *string pattern-matching* feature of JavaScript. Regular expressions are created using the RegExp constructor or using a **regular expression literal**, and they inherit from RegExp.prototype. Like arrays, JavaScript doesn't consider regexp objects as separate object types, but rather as special versions of the basic object type.

The toString method of RegExp.prototype will return the string version of a regular expression literal. This string representation is implementation-specific, and is sometimes parsable by the RegExp constructor. Meanwhile, the valueOf method of regexps is inherited from Object.prototype, so it returns the object itself.

■ **Note** In ECMAScript 5, the toString() method of a regexp object is required to return a string that's parsable by the RegExp constructor.

Curiously, some JavaScript implementations will output 'function' when the typeof operator is applied to a regexp object. While it is true that both functions and regular expressions share the same trait of not being implementable using a basic object, this behavior is actually a byproduct of a buggy feature addition that was wrongly copied by other implementations.

Mozilla implemented a special feature for its **SpiderMonkey** JavaScript engine that allowed direct calls to regexp objects as though they were functions. For example, this feature allowed the expression /string/.exec('string') to be shortened to /string/('string'). Mozilla added the ability to use the invocation operator on regular expressions—just like functions—and doing so would automatically call the exec method of the regexp object.

To implement this feature, Mozilla added an internal call property to the regexp object—a property that should be available only to functions, according to ECMAScript standards. This internal call property of the regexp object exploits the same technique of binding executable code to an object as in the case of functions, but here the executable code is actually the regexp's exec method. And this is where everything went haywire.

The typeof operator only checks a single property to determine whether an object is a function: the internal call property. However, because of this new feature added by Mozilla, the typeof operator gets tricked when it encounters regular expression objects, and it mistakenly outputs 'function' rather than 'object'.

This might not have been such a big deal if not for the fact that this feature—along with its bug—was copied by other implementations. **JavaScriptCore**, the JavaScript engine of the Webkit project and the Safari browser, implemented this same feature. Google, in developing its Chrome browser, also used

Webkit, but replaced JavaScriptCore with its own JavaScript implementation called **v8**. Unfortunately, this new engine was implemented to remain compatible with the JavaScriptCore engine it replaced, so the same feature and the same bug persisted.

Because of this bug, it's impossible to actually differentiate between real functions and regexp objects through the typeof operator alone in some browsers. Mozilla has fixed this bug in the version of SpiderMonkey that shipped with Firefox 3, but it still persists in the current versions (at the time of writing) of Chrome and Safari. Fortunately for us, the MooTools typeOf function is immune from this bug.

Regexps are a powerful feature of any programming languages, and they allow us to retrieve parts of a string using patterns. We won't be discussing them in detail in this book, but we'll see much of their use in the chapters that follow.

Dates

Date objects represent *calendrical values*. They are created using the Date constructor and they inherit from Date.prototype. Unlike other built-in types, dates don't have a corresponding literal form: all date objects need to be created using the Date constructor function.

Essentially, a date object is a collection of numeric values that represent a specific date value. Stored inside a date object are values for the year, month, day, hour, minute, second, and millisecond that represent a specific calendrical value. However, date objects are fully encapsulated: these values are accessible only through getter and setter methods defined by Date.prototype.

The toString method of a date object returns a string representation of the date value in the form <weekday> <month> <day> <year> <hours>:<minutes>:<seconds> <timezone>, like 'Wed Jun 03 1987 19:30:00 GMT+0800 (PHT)'. This string representation is parsable by the Date constructor, so you can use it to build a similar date object.

■ **Note** As with the regexp object, the return value of the date toString method is implementation-specific. However, all major JavaScript engines follow the format presented above.

Similarly, the valueOf method from Date.prototype also returns the value of the date object, but as a numeric timestamp. This timestamp is a representation of the number of milliseconds since January 1, 1970 00:00:00 GMT (often called *the Epoch*). Calling the valueOf method for the date object above therefore yields 549718200000. This numeric value is also the same value returned by the getTime date method.

■ **Note** The epoch timestamp in most programming languages is a 10-digit number, plus additional decimal places to denote offsets. JavaScript, in contrast, uses a 12-digit timestamp.

Date objects are the only native objects that can be cast to their proper strings and number values.

Error Objects

ECMAScript designates a group of objects called **error objects** that are used for *error-handling operations*. When the JavaScript interpreter encounters problematic code, it "throws" an error object that can then be handled by the program through the try-catch statement.

The main error constructor, Error, represents the most basic type of error object. It has a name property, the default value of which is "Error", and a message property, which contains the specific human-readable error message. Some JavaScript implementations also add other non-standard properties, like the line number of the error or the stack trace for the execution context where the error occurred.

JavaScript itself doesn't use the base Error constructor, though. Instead, it uses special error subclasses:

- EvalError—for errors involving the eval function.

- RangeError—for errors when numeric values exceed the defined bounds of possible numeric values.

- ReferenceError—for errors that happen when performing operations on invalid references, such as accessing the properties of an undefined variable.

- SyntaxError—for errors that arise from being unable to parse improperly written code.

- TypeError—for errors involving passing incorrect value types to operations.

- URIError—for errors involving the URI encoding and decoding functions.

The name properties of these error subclasses are the same as the identifiers of their constructor functions.

The valueOf method of error objects is inherited from Object.prototype. Thus, they return the objects themselves. Meanwhile, the toString method of error objects is implementation-specific, and weirdly enough, the return value of this method isn't required by the specification to be the actual error message—which means that implementations can simply output anything they want. Thankfully, most JavaScript implementations do return the value of the message property of the error object when the toString method is invoked.

▓ **Note** In ECMAScript 5, the toString method of error objects is required to return strings in the form
'<ErrorType>: <message>'.

The MooTools framework has a unique policy of handling errors gracefully and silently, so errors are rarely used. Thus, Error and the other built-in error subtypes are not turned into type objects.

Type Casting

We've seen the rules on how values are cast from one type to the other, but we didn't actually find out how to convert objects from one type to another. Type casting can be tricky in some cases, so we need to discuss how values of one type can actually be converted to another type.

Like other dynamic languages, JavaScript actually performs automatic, or implicit, type casting. **Implicit type casting** is when values are cast from one type to another by the interpreter in order to properly execute an operation. These transformations are usually silent and aren't noticeable unless they're carefully observed.

The best example of implicit type casting is the automatic wrapping of primitives with object wrappers when the primitive values are used in operations that require objects. The interpreter silently wraps the primitive value with an object wrapper, and we don't really need to do anything to make this happen.

Similarly, the values null and undefined, as well as all object values, are turned into primitives when they are used in operations that require primitives. For instance, using an object in a division or multiplication operation automatically casts the object into a number value. Similarly, statements that require boolean values, like the if statement, as well as the property access operator [ ], also do implicit boolean and string casting. And wrapper objects for primitives are automatically cast to their primitive values if needed.

■ **Note** JavaScript has numerous implicit casting rules, and we can't cover all of them in this section. Instead, I advise you to read one of the recommended books on JavaScript noted in the Resources section at the end of this book.

In contrast to implicit casting, **explicit type casting** is the process of directly transforming one value into another using special operations. There are several ways to explicitly cast a value from one type to another, and we'll explore each one in turn.

Casting Using Constructors

The first and easiest way to explicitly cast a value to another type is to use the built-in constructors. Most native JavaScript constructors can actually be invoked as regular functions, and they perform type conversions when used this way.

The constructor objects for primitive wrappers, for instance, can be used to convert values to primitive types:

```
// boolean
console.log(Boolean(0));      // false
console.log(Boolean(''));     // false
console.log(Boolean('24'));   // true
console.log(Boolean({}));     // true

// number
console.log(Number(false));   // 0
console.log(Number(''));      // 0
console.log(Number('24'));    // 24
console.log(Number({}));      // NaN

// string
console.log(String(false));      // 'false'
console.log(String(24));         // '24'
console.log(String({}));         // '[object Object]'
console.log(String([1, 2, 3]));  // '1,2,3'
```

The casting operations here follow the same rules we described earlier: primitives are converted using the rules for converting one primitive type to another, while objects are converted using their valueOf and toString methods.

An important thing to remember is that the return values of these primitive conversions are actual primitive values and not objects—only when used in conjunction with the new operator do they return objects. Thus, String(1) will return the primitive string value '1', while new String(1) will return a new string object.

Native object constructors, on the other hand, behave differently when used as regular functions. The Function, Array, RegExp, and Error constructors, when invoked as regular functions, operate the same as if they were used with the new keyword. Thus, they don't actually perform type casting, but rather, they perform object instantiation. It is therefore advisable not to invoke them as regular functions.

The Date constructor's behavior, in contrast, is unique when it's invoked as a function: it doesn't perform type casting nor does it create a new date object. Instead, it returns the current date as a string.

Finally, the Object constructor performs type casting according to the actual type of value passed. If you pass in a primitive value, it will return a wrapped object version of that value—so you'll receive either an instance of String, Number, or Boolean. But if you pass in an object value, the constructor will simply return the same object, with no modification. And if you pass in null or undefined, it will return a new plain object—just like doing new Object().

Casting Using Native Functions and Idioms

There are two special functions defined in JavaScript that handle string-to-number conversions: parseFloat and parseInt. Unlike the Number constructor, these functions are more lenient when used for parsing strings, as they allow non-numeric trailing characters in the strings.

The parseFloat function converts both integer and floating point numbers, while parseInt can only convert to integers:

```
console.log(Number('42 is the answer.'));       // NaN
console.log(parseInt('42 is the answer.'));     // 42
console.log(parseFloat('42 is the answer.'));   // 42

console.log(parseInt('3.14'));      // 3
console.log(parseFloat('3.14'));    // 3.14

console.log(parseInt('024'));       // 20
console.log(parseInt('024', 10));   // 24
```

The last two lines feature a quirk with the parseInt implementation. The parseInt function has a special "feature" that treats strings that begin with 0 as octal values. Thus, parseInt('024') returns the value 20 instead of 24. This creates a problem when parsing non-octal strings that start with 0, although you can solve it by passing a second argument, radix, which tells the function what base to use for the conversion. This "feature" has been removed in ECMAScript 5.

One idiom that's used to convert any value to a number is JavaScript's implicit type conversion for mathematical operations. By using numeric identity operations (such as subtracting 0 from a value or dividing or multiplying a value by 1), you can convert a value to a number:

```
console.log('42' / 1); // 42
console.log('42' - 0); // 42
console.log('42' * 1); // 42

console.log(true - 0); // 1
console.log(false * 1); // 0

console.log({} - 0); // NaN
```

But don't use the addition identity operation (x + 0) because the + operator is both the addition and concatenation operator in JavaScript. You can, however, use + as a unary operator for the purpose of numeric casting:

```
console.log(+'42'); // 42
console.log(+true); // 1
console.log(+{}); // NaN
```

To convert any value (except for null and undefined) to a string, we can simply use the toString method. This works with primitives as well because of the automatic object wrapping mechanisms:

```
console.log(true.toString());       // 'true'
console.log((42).toString());       // '42'
console.log([1,2,3].toString());    // '1,2,3'
```

▓ **Note** Number.prototype.toString() is a special case, because it allows you to specify an argument, radix, that will be used as the base for conversion. By default, the radix value is 10.

Another way to convert values to strings is to exploit the concatenation operator, +. This operator is used for both addition of numbers and concatenation of strings, but it gives special priority to string values: if one of the operands in the expression is a string, it also casts the other value into a string. We can therefore turn any value into a string by concatenating it with an empty string:

```
console.log(true + '');      // 'true'
console.log(42 + '');        // '42'
console.log([1,2,3] + '');   // '1,2,3'
```

Finally, casting values to booleans is rarely done since JavaScript allows any value to be used in place of an actual boolean value when needed. If you do want to convert a particular value into its boolean representation quickly, though, you can use the *double-negation* trick:

```
console.log(!!''); // false
console.log(!!'M'); // true

console.log(!!0); // false
console.log(!!42); // true

console.log(!!{}); // true
console.log(!![]); // true
```

The negation operator, !, automatically casts a value into a boolean and it reverses a boolean true value to false and vice versa. Using the negation operator twice yields the same boolean value that was negated at the start of the expression. For example, the number value 0 is cast to the boolean value false. When negating this value, we get !false == true. The true value is then negated again, and the final value goes back to false. Thus, we get a proper conversion from 0 to false.

The MooTools Type System

Now that we've familiarized ourselves with the native type system and its components, let's turn our attention to its MooTools counterpart. The most important component of the MooTools type system is the Type constructor, and it is this simple constructor function that enables us to streamline the process of working with native types.

The Type Constructor and Function Subclassing

The Type constructor accepts two arguments: a required name argument, which should be a string representation of the capitalized type name, and an optional object argument, which is the constructor function to be transformed. If an object argument is passed, the Type constructor returns the same object after it adds additional properties and methods to it. Otherwise, it returns null.

As I mentioned earlier, the Type constructor doesn't create new constructor functions but rather transforms already existing constructors into type objects by augmenting new properties and methods to it. To illustrate, here's how the native Array constructor is turned into a type object:

```
new Type('Array', Array);
```

And that's all it takes to turn a native constructor into a type object. We simply instantiated a Type object using the new keyword and passed the name of the type, 'Array', and the native Array constructor function. You'll notice that we didn't even need to store the results in a variable. Because the Array constructor is transformed directly, there was no need to store the result of the expression in a new identifier. The process is both simple and elegant—and certainly says a lot about the MooTools type system implementation

One question that continually pops up when developers see that example is whether the new keyword is actually needed. If we're not really creating a new object but simply transforming an existing constructor function into a type object, why not just make Type a simple function? Does it really have to be a constructor?

The question is even more valid once you consider the fact that instances of Type are not really "instances" of Type:

```
new Type('Array', Array);

// make sure that Array is a type object
console.log(typeOf(Array)); // 'type'

// is Array an instance of Type?
console.log(Array instanceof Type); // false
```

We do know that Type transforms the constructor directly, so it really doesn't create a new object. The type object returned by the Type constructor isn't really an instance of Type since it's a function that already existed before we passed it to the constructor. So does this mean we could really do away with using new?

To answer this question, we must first examine the same question but with regard to classes, which are similar to type objects. Unlike the Type constructor, the Class constructor actually creates a new constructor function for the class, so using the new operator with Class seems like a logical thing to do. What's surprising is that the same behavior can be observed in classes as well:

```
var Person = new Class();

// make sure that Person is a class
```

```
console.log(typeOf(Person)); // 'class'

// is Person an instance of Class?
console.log(Person instanceof Class); // false
```

This seems a little counter-intuitive: the Class constructor creates the new constructor for the class, so we'd expect that the result of instantiating the Class constructor would be a class instance. But when the instanceof operator is used to check, classes exhibit the same behavior of not being instances of the Class constructor—just like type objects with Type.

Recall something I mentioned earlier in this chapter about functions: they are one of the two types of objects in JavaScript that can't be created using a basic object (the other being regular expressions)—which means they can't be subclassed. The reason for this is simple: functions depend on an internal call property that references the executable code that's called when the function is used in conjunction with the invocation operator. Since we have no way of setting this internal property in regular objects, we can't create subclasses of the Function type because we'll end up referencing the same executable code.

The Type and Class constructors both deal with constructor-prototype pairs, with emphasis on constructors. In essence, type objects and classes are "subclassed" functions: they're constructor functions that have special properties and methods. But because JavaScript places no distinction between regular functions and constructors (except for their behavior when used with new), both Type and Class need to circumvent the limitation of function subclassing using direct augmentation of functions, rather than simple prototypal inheritance.

Here's how it works. For the type definition new Type('Array', Array), a new object inheriting from Type.prototype is created by the new operator and then used as the this value inside the Type constructor. Type then takes all the properties and methods of this new instance and adds them to the Array constructor function, thereby making sure that the resulting Array type object will "inherit" the members in Type.prototype. The operation involves direct augmentation of members to the type object, and not inheritance via the prototype chain. The new keyword is essential because it creates the template object that will be used for augmentation. The same thing is applicable to the Class constructor, with the minor difference of the resulting class object being created inside the Class constructor itself.

Of course, direct augmentation has its limitations, which we already saw in the Chapter 3. The main issue would be dynamic modification: since type objects and classes are augmented directly, any changes to Type.prototype and Class.prototype aren't propagated to existing type objects and classes. This isn't a big issue in practice, though, since the number of type objects and predefined classes in the MooTools-Core library are small enough to modify directly.

The snippets above don't just show why we need something like the new operator when we're creating new type objects, they also shows us some limitations encountered when trying to implement a new type system on top of the existing one. In order for the replacement MooTools type system to be fully usable, it needs to cover not only the creation and management of types but also things like instance checking and type detection.

Interestingly, the core mechanisms for adding these two features to the MooTools type system are implemented by the Type constructor itself, as we'll see in the next two sections.

Instance Checking

Native JavaScript instance checking is done using the instanceof operator. We've already seen it in action several times in this and earlier chapters, so it hardly needs any introduction.

The instanceof operator works by comparing the constructor of the object on the left-hand side of the expression to the constructor function on the right-hand side. In the expression myCar instanceof Car, for example, the constructor function that created the myCar object is compared to the Car constructor to see if they're the same function. If they are, the expression evaluates to true.

However, if the constructor function for the `myCar` object and the `Car` constructor aren't the same, the expression doesn't immediately evaluate to `false`. Instead, the prototype chain of the `myCar` object is traversed, and the constructor function of each object in the prototype chain is compared with the `Car` constructor. Only when the last constructor function has failed comparison will the expression evaluate to `false`.

This "deep" comparison is why the `instanceof` operator evaluates to true not only for the immediate constructor of the object, but also the ancestral constructors of the object. All objects are therefore seen as instances of the `Object` constructor, since all objects inherit from `Object` at one point in their prototype chain.

As you've probably guessed by now, the `constructor` property of objects plays a central part in native instance checking. All objects are linked to their corresponding constructor functions via their `constructor` property, and it's the value of this property that gets compared to the constructor function on the right-hand side of the expression.

In our examples in the previous section, both type objects and classes fail the `instanceof` test because they don't have links to the `Type` and `Class` constructors directly. Both type objects and classes are abstracted constructor functions, so their prototype chain consists only of instances of `Object` and `Function`. Because the `Type` and `Class` constructors augment these constructor functions directly rather than through prototypal inheritance, their constructor functions never get "linked" to the object. Thus, type objects and classes are not seen as true instances of their respective constructors by the `instanceof` operator.

To circumvent this limitation, a link has to be made by the MooTools type system between these objects and their constructors. This is done by adding a new property to these objects called `$constructor`. Like its native constructor counterpart, the `$constructor` property is a reference to the object's original constructor function. Type objects therefore have their `$constructor` properties pointing to `Type`, while classes have theirs pointing to `Class`.

Of course, just because MooTools added a new property that resembles the native `constructor` property doesn't mean that `instanceof` will respect it. The MooTools type system works on a separate level from the native one, so we can't expect a simple solution like that to take care of the issue altogether. Instead, MooTools adds the second part of the equation by creating a new function to replace the `instanceof` operator: the `instanceOf` function.

The `instanceOf` function takes in two arguments: `item`, which is the object being checked, and `object`, which should be a constructor function to check against. Unlike the `instanceof` operator it replaces, though, the `instanceOf` function properly handles cases like type objects and classes:

```
// Type Object
new Type('Array', Array);

// make sure that Array is a type object
console.log(typeOf(Array)); // 'type'

// is Array a native instance of Type?
console.log(Array instanceof Type); // false

// is Array an instance of Type in MooTools?
console.log( instanceOf(Array, Type) ); // true


// Class
var Personn = new Class();

// make sure that Person is a class
console.log(typeOf(Person)); // 'class'

// is Person a native instance of Class?
```

```
console.log(Person instanceof Class); // false

// is Person an instance of Class in MooTools?
console.log( instanceOf(Person, Class) ); // true
```

Revamping our examples from the previous section, you'll notice that instanceOf(Array, Type) and instanceOf(Person, Class) now both return true. This tells us that Array and Person are instances of Type and Class respectively—which is exactly what we would want to know.

■ **Note** Like typeOf, the instanceOf function isn't an operator like its native instanceof counterpart but a real function. Therefore, the use of the invocation operator is essential, as well as proper casing (it's instanceOf(), not instanceof()).

Like its native counterpart, the instanceOf function works by comparing the constructor of the item argument with the constructor function that's the value of the object argument. Unlike the native instanceof operator, though, instanceOf is aware of the $constructor property and uses this property instead of the regular constructor property as much as possible. The comparison process involves a direct equality test, which means that instanceOf(Array, Type) is somewhat equivalent to Array.$constructor == Type.

I said "somewhat equivalent" because the comparison isn't a one-off process. Like the native instanceof operator, the instanceOf function also does "deep" comparison, so checking whether an object is an instance of some ancestral constructor also works:

```
new Type('Array', Array);

console.log(instanceOf(Array, Type)); // true
console.log(instanceOf(Array, Function)); // true
console.log(instanceOf(Array, Object)); // true
```

The creation of the $constructor property is done by the Type constructor (and by the Class constructor for classes). When the constructor function argument is processed by Type, it adds a $constructor property to the constructor function that's used for the instanceOf function. The $constructor property of the constructor function passed to Type is always set to the Type function itself, so that instanceOf will be able to determine that the type object is an instance of the Type constructor.

However, the Type constructor doesn't just add a $constructor property to the constructor argument, but also to the prototype of the constructor argument. In the snippet above, for instance, Type doesn't just set Array.$constructor to Type, but also adds the property Array.prototype.$constructor. The $constructor property of the prototype is then set to the constructor itself, so in our example, Array.prototype.$constructor == Array. This additional prototype property creates one big difference between the instanceof operator and the instanceOf function: the ability to check primitive values.

The instanceof operator, by design, only works if the left-hand side of the expression is an object, not a primitive. If you use a primitive as the value of the left-hand side, it won't work: 'hello' instanceof String evaluates to false. The instanceof operator does not perform type-casting, so primitive values are treated as true primitives and not objects.

However, the instanceOf function doesn't have the same limitation. Because it depends on the $constructor property rather than the true native type of the value, the instanceOf function is able to determine types even for primitive values. In the process of accessing the $constructor property of the value passed, primitives are automatically turned into objects within the instanceOf function, and therefore inherit the $constructor property from their respective type objects. Thus, instanceOf('hello', String) evaluates to true.

Before we move on, though, it's important to note that the instanceOf function also uses instanceof internally as a fallback mechanism in case regular $constructor checking doesn't work. This is an important thing to remember because of a special group of types that don't have type objects, which we'll encounter in a bit.

Type Detection

JavaScript gives us the typeof operator for detecting the types of our values. But as we saw earlier in this chapter, the native typeof operator leaves a lot to be desired. Its replacement from the MooTools type system, the typeOf function, does a better job at detecting the types of values as well as differentiating among the actual types of objects.

Unlike the instanceOf function, though, which only depends on the constructor and $constructor properties of the value passed, the typeOf operator uses a couple of different ways to properly detect the type of a value. At the top of the list is the use of type objects to pass special functions to their instances, which are called **family methods**.

A family method is a special private method that's added by the Type constructor to the prototype of the type object that's used to return the type of the object. It is a very simple function that simply returns the lowercase name of the type as a string. When creating new Type('Array', Array), for example, the Type constructor adds a new method called $family to Array.prototype, and this new method simply returns the lowercase equivalent of the name passed to the Type constructor. Thus, Array.prototype.$family returns 'array' when invoked.

This family method is then invoked by the typeOf function to return the type of the value. Because the family method is added to the prototype of the type object directly, all instances of the type will therefore inherit the same family method. So detecting the type of an object is as simple as calling its $family method. In the case of arrays, for instance, doing [].$family() or typeOf([]) returns 'array' for both cases—which is the actual type of the object. The typeOf operator simplifies this process of calling the $family function of the object by doing it automatically.

You might be asking then, "What's the use of calling typeOf then, when I could just invoke the $family method directly?" Well, the first answer is because typeOf is part of the private API—and like many things in the private MooTools API, it's bound to change eventually. Making direct calls to this method makes your code prone to breakage when new versions of the library come out—especially ones that change the internal API dramatically (and it happens!).

But even if we're absolutely sure that it will never break—and that's highly unlikely—there's an even bigger reason why you should not call the $family method directly:

```
// regular object
var obj = {};

// typeOf
console.log(typeOf(obj)); // 'object'

// obj.$family
console.log(obj.$family()); // this will throw an error
```

In this snippet, passing the obj variable to typeOf works as expected, and we get the proper type—'object'—as the return value. However, if we try to do obj.$family(), we'll get an error—because obj has no method named $family.

Remember that the $family method is inherited by objects from their type objects, and it is added directly to the prototype of the type object via the Type constructor. However, some objects don't have a $family method because they don't inherit the method from their type objects. In fact, it's just not the case of not inheriting the method; it's a case of not having actual type objects in the first place!

151

Some native constructors, Object being the most notable, are not turned into type objects by the MooTools type system. A few of them aren't turned into type objects because they're not used in common programming tasks, while some aren't converted to impose restrictions. The Object constructor is the chief example of that second reason: it isn't turned into a type object to prevent extension of Object.prototype.

One other important set of types are those with no real constructors. For instance, argument objects, which are created for use inside functions, don't have a corresponding constructor—there's no Argument constructor in JavaScript. Other notable examples are DOM objects like textnodes and whitespaces, which also don't have constructor functions.

The MooTools type system recognizes these types even though they don't have corresponding type objects. However, it presents a little challenge to using $family directly. Because not all values inherit a $family method, we can't depend on this function alone to detect the type of a value. So, as in the case of our example above, we can't call the $family method directly because there's a risk that the object might not have the method to begin with.

This is the prime reason why the $family method should not be used as a replacement for typeOf. The typeOf function is smart enough to know whether the value in question has a $family method that can be called and does so if that's the case. If there's no $family method present, though, it uses another technique to detect the type.

So what's this other technique? It's called *duck typing*, and its name comes from the common saying: "*If it walks like a duck and talks like a duck, then it must be a duck.*"

Duck typing bases its assumption of an object's type according to the structure of the object. As long as the object's properties and methods match the declared properties and methods for a type (walks like a duck and talks like a duck), it's considered to be of that type (it must be a duck). Duck typing is commonly used in dynamically typed languages to support substitutability. Because of the loose requirements of duck typing, you can design your code in such a way that it accepts objects of any type as long as they have a particular method or property.

However, very loose duck typing can't be applied to a type system directly, since we'd risk having false positives. For example, you can check for the existence of a length property to find out whether an object is an array, and it'll work for the most part, but it'll also think that string objects, argument objects, and element collections are arrays, since all of those appear to be array-like.

For duck typing to be really useful, the criteria for considering an object to be a type need to be very strict. The typeOf function uses several strict criteria to determine the type for values that have no type objects. Argument objects, for example, are tested not only for the presence of the length property, but for the existence of a callee property as well.

This, of course, isn't perfect and is easily bypassed by cunning manipulation of code. The code typeOf({length: 1, callee: 1}), for example, will return "arguments" even if what you have is not really an argument object. Unfortunately, there's nothing we can do about this, since duck typing is the only other solution we can use for values with no corresponding type objects. Thankfully, though, we can use the idea of duck typing to craft code that doesn't rely entirely on the specificity of type to do its job.

Take note that family methods take precedence in the typing process for typeOf. Duck typing is a fallback technique used only for objects with no corresponding type objects. And if these two techniques don't work, the typeof operator is used by the typeOf function as a last resort.

Working with Type Objects

Up to this point we've been talking about type objects in the context of type detection. But as I said earlier in this chapter, a type object also acts as the representative for its instances. Like classes, type objects are abstracted constructor-prototype pairs that can be used to change the structure and behavior of the items of that type. In fact, both classes and type object share very similar methods to accomplish this, as we'll see later on. And just like classes, type objects also have a special set of methods available only to them that can be used to streamline the process of working with types.

Implementing New Members

When working with native JavaScript, adding new properties or methods to existing types is done by augmenting the prototype object of their respective constructor. If we want to add a new repeat method for strings, for instance, we have to do something like this:

```
var str = 'hello';

console.log(typeOf(str.repeat)); // 'null'

String.prototype.repeat = function(times){
        var arr = [];
        while (times--) arr.push(this);
        return arr.join('');
};

console.log(typeOf(str.repeat)); // 'function'
console.log(str.repeat(3)); // 'hellohellohello'
```

At the start of the code, the repeat method doesn't exist yet, so str.repeat is typed as 'null'. We then declare this new method by assigning a function to String.prototype.repeat. Afterwards, we check whether the repeat method is now available for strings, and we use it to repeat the string 'hello' three times.

We looked at this technique of augmenting the prototype property of a class in a previous chapter, and we saw how it's not the best way to add new members to a class. Adding new members directly to the prototype limits the additional features MooTools can offer, and the verbosity of the code could mean having to manage really complex declarations in the future. Instead of doing it that way, we learned that it's better to use the implement class method, which replaces the need for direct augmentation and streamlines the process of implementing new members.

Like classes, type objects also have an implement method, and we can use this method to rewrite the previous snippet:

```
var str = 'hello';

console.log(typeOf(str.repeat)); // 'null'

String.implement({

    repeat: function(times){
        var arr = [];
        while (times--) arr.push(this);
        return arr.join('');
    }

});

console.log(typeOf(str.repeat)); // 'function'
console.log(str.repeat(3)); // 'hellohellohello'
```

The implement methods of classes and type objects are used similarly: implement accepts as an argument an object literal that describes the properties and methods you want to add and it loops through each of these members and adds them to the prototype.

While they appear to be the same function from the outside, the implement method of objects is not the exact same method as the one for classes. In the chapter on classes, we discovered the various internal features of the class implement method, including dereferencing, code wrapping, and mutator management. The type `implement` method also has some powerful internal features, although overall, it is much simpler than its class counterpart.

One of the more noticeable differences is that the type `implement` method does not do wrapping:

```
var myFn = function(){
    console.log('fn');
};

// class
var Person = new Class();

Person.implement({
    method: myFn
});

var shiela = new Person();

console.log(shiela.method == myFn); // false

// type
String.implement({
    method: myFn
});

var str = 'hello world';

console.log(str.method == myFn); // true
```

In the first part of this snippet, we compare the `method` method of the `Person` class with the original `myFn` function using the line `shiela.method == myFn`. The result is false, which is expected because the `implement` method of classes wraps the original function in order to add additional class features. In the case of types, however, the methods added through `implement` are not wrapped but are added directly to the type's prototype object. Thus, when we do `str.method == myFn`, we get true—and this tells us that the methods are indeed the same function.

Newly added methods are not wrapped by the type `implement` method because the wrapper is no longer needed. Classes need method wrappers in order to implement protected methods and `this.parent`, but type objects don't support (or need) either of these features. Moreover, type objects are created using existing constructors that often already have existing members in their prototypes, and wrapping these existing methods might break them.

In the previous chapter, we learned about the `protect` method, which is used to implement protected methods in classes. The `protect` method has another use, in fact, and that is to protect a native method from being overridden. Consider the following example:

```
// original method
String.implement('method', function(){
        console.log('Original');
}.protect());

'hello'.method(); // 'Original'

// override original
String.implement('method', function(){
        console.log('Override');
});
```

```
'hello'.method(); // 'Original'
```

Here we first implemented a new String method called method which simply logs 'Original' in our console. However, we also called the protect method of the function value we're passing to implement, making our new method protected. When we tried to override this original method by calling implement again with a new method definition, our original function wasn't overridden, which is why we still get the same string in our logs.

The protect method is therefore very handy for making sure that native methods that browsers already implement aren't overridden by the user. By default, all the native methods for native objects defined by the ECMAScript specification are protected by MooTools, and therefore cannot be overridden by the user.

Aliases and Mirroring

Type objects support a special feature called **aliasing**, which is simply reimplementing an existing method using another name. It is done using the alias method, which takes two string arguments: the name for the new method and the name of the old method to be aliased.

```
var str = 'howdy';

// implement the original
String.implement({

    repeat: function(times){
        var arr = [];
        while (times--) arr.push(this);
        return arr.join('');
    }

});

console.log(str.repeat(2)); // 'howdyhowdy'

// alias repeat
String.alias('again', 'repeat');
console.log(str.again == str.repeat); // true

console.log(str.again(2)); // 'howdyhowdy'
```

In this example, we aliased the original repeat method of the String type simply by calling String.alias('again', 'repeat'). The alias method then takes the original function value of String.prototype.repeat and copies it to String.prototype.again. The result is that the two methods now point to the same function, making it possible to substitute calls to one for the other.

Aliasing is a very useful feature for creating shortcuts for commonly used methods with very long names. The Array method forEach, for example, is automatically aliased by MooTools into the each method, which is shorter and easier to type. You can do the same for other methods in any type objects to shorten your code and make it cleaner.

An important thing to note, though, is that aliasing uses implement internally, and all aliases methods are true references. Therefore, if you override the original method, your alias will not be updated:

```
var str = 'hi';

// implement original
String.implement({

    original: function(){
        console.log('hello');
    }

});

String.alias('copy', 'original');
console.log(str.copy == str.original); // true

str.original(); // 'hello'
str.copy(); // 'hello'

// override original
String.implement({

    original: function(){
        console.log('woot!');
    }

});

console.log(str.copy == str.original); // false

str.original(); // 'woot!'
str.copy(); // 'hello'
```

In the first part of the snippet, both the original method and its aliased copy method point to the same function, and therefore act as the same method. However, when we reimplement the original method, the aliased copy method doesn't get updated.

Another useful feature that's related to aliasing is called **mirroring**. While aliasing allows you to reimplement a method on a type, mirroring allows you to copy any implemented method from one type to another. To perform mirroring, we use the mirror method of a type, which accepts a single argument that is a type object. Take a look at the following snippet:

```
var arr = [], str = 'hello';

console.log(arr.log); // undefined
console.log(str.log); // undefined

// make String "mirror" Array
Array.mirror(String);

// implement log on array
Array.implement({

    log: function(){
        console.log('log called.');
    }
```

```
});

console.log(arr.log == str.log); // true

arr.log(); // method called.
str.log(); // method called.
```

The important line in this snippet is `Array.mirror(String)`. This tells the type system that `String` is a "mirror" of `Array`, and any methods implemented on `Array` from then on should also be implemented on `String`. Because of this mirroring, the `log` method we implemented on the `Array` type is also implemented on `String`.

Mirroring makes it possible to automatically implement methods across multiple types. A single type can have multiple mirrors, which makes implementing the same method among many types easier and cleaner. The `Array` type, for instance, could have mirrors for other array-like objects, so that any method that's implemented for arrays would also be available to these objects.

It's the job of the `implement` method to manage mirrors. When the `implement` method of a type is called, it not only adds the properties and methods to the type object's prototype, but also checks whether the type has mirrors. The `implement` method then adds the properties and methods to these mirrors, making sure that the members are available to these types as well.

Because mirroring is managed by `implement`, only those members that are added after the mirror was declared would be automatically added. Existing properties and methods aren't copied, so we have to do that manually if we want to copy them. For instance, even though `String` was added as a mirror of `Array`, only the methods that were added via `implement` after the declaration would be copied—like the `log` method. Existing array methods, like `splice` or `push`, aren't copied automatically.

Another thing to consider is that mirrors aren't reciprocal: implemented methods on a type will be implemented on all its mirrors, but implemented methods for the mirrors aren't added for the type. In the example above, any method implemented on `Array` after the `mirror` declaration would be copied to `String`, but any method implemented on `String` won't be copied to `Array`. If you want reciprocal mirrors, you'll have to declare mirrors for both types.

The `mirror` method of type objects isn't actually limited just to type object arguments. We can also pass a callback function that will be invoked for every item that's implemented:

```
var callback = function(name, method){
    console.log(name);
};

Array.mirror(callback);

Array.implement({

    logA: function(){},

    logB: function(){}

});
```

In this example, we declared the `callback` function to be a mirror for `Array`. For every item processed by implement, the `callback` function will be invoked and passed two arguments. The first argument, `name`, is the key of the item being implemented and the second argument, `method`, is the actual function. For this code, the `callback` function will be invoked first with the arguments 'logA' and a function, and then with 'logB' and another function.

Function mirrors are especially useful in cases when you want to process the method first before implementing it on another type. For example, the MooTools `Elements` type uses a function mirror to transform methods from `Element` into methods that work on an array-like object. We'll learn more about this particular trick in Chapter 8 on the `Element` type.

The extend Method and Generics

We first saw the use of the extend method in the chapter on class extras. This method is inherited from `Function.prototype`, and allows us to augment function objects directly:

```
var fn = function(){};

console.log(fn.prop); // undefined
console.log(fn.item); // undefined

fn.extend({

    prop: 'property',

    item: 'item'

});

console.log(fn.prop); // 'property'
console.log(fn.item); // 'item'
```

Instead of declaring the properties `prop` and `item` directly using an assignment statement, we passed an object to the extend method of `fn` containing these new properties. The result of using extend is the same as a normal assignment, but it's cleaner and more organized.

Classes, being abstracted constructor functions, also inherit the extend method from `Function.prototype`. Type objects, on the other hand, also have an extend method, but it's an overriding method that's inherited from `Type.prototype`. The original extend method from `Function.prototype` and the one from `Type.prototype` have the same external API—they both accept an object argument and they both perform the same extension operation using direct augmentation. `Type.prototype.extend` has an additional feature that's not present in its `Function.prototype` counterpart—but we'll talk about this in the next section.

One important use of the extend method that we saw before was to add static methods to classes. We can also do this with type objects:

```
Array.extend({

    identity: function(){
        console.log(this === Array);
    },

    log: function(){
        console.log('Hello');
    }

});

Array.identity(); // true
Array.log(); // 'Hello'
```

Here we added two static methods to `Array`, identity, and log. The `identity` method is used to show that the this keyword in the static method is bound to the type object, while the log method is a simple method that logs the string 'Hello'. Though these two are very trivial examples, they tell us that static methods work the same for type objects as they do for classes: they're actually methods of the type object itself rather than its instances.

There's a special group of static methods, though, that are particularly important in MooTools and they're called generics. A generic is a static version of an instance method that can be applied to any object. Generics are handy for using methods from one type on another type without having to directly call the method from the prototype.

The best way to explain generics is with an example. In the section on array objects in this chapter, I mentioned that array methods are intentionally generic in the sense that they can be used on any object. For example, we can use the push method of arrays to add a new item to an array-like object:

```
var obj = {0: 'pizza', length: 1};

console.log(obj.length); // 1

// invoke the push method of arrays
Array.prototype.push.call(obj, 'soda');

console.log(obj.length); // 2
```

In order to access the push method, we had to access the method via Array.prototype. We then used the function method call, passing in the arguments obj and 'soda'. The first argument becomes the value of the this keyword inside the push method, while the second is the actual item that will be pushed into the object. The result is that the string 'soda' is pushed into our array-like object, and its length property is automatically incremented.

Now imagine that you need to use the push method on that particular object several times through your code. Accessing it via Array.prototype is unnecessarily verbose, and doing it multiple times leads to unnecessary repetition—not to mention having to use the call method, too. To really make these methods useful, we need an easier way to access them.

This is where generic methods come in. Take a look at this version of the previous example:

```
var obj = {0: 'pizza', length: 1};

console.log(obj.length); // 1

// invoke the push method of arrays
Array.push(obj, 'soda');

console.log(obj.length); // 2
```

We replaced the original call to Array.prototype.push.call(obj, 'soda') to Array.push(obj, 'soda'). Array.push is a generic method. Using this method is the same as calling Array.prototype.push.call, and it expects the same arguments. The first argument is always the this keyword value for the method, and the arguments after that are the actual arguments for the method. The result is the same, but the actual invocation pattern is shorter than our original example.

MooTools automatically creates the generic versions of the methods of all native types. The string instance method split, for example, is available via String.split generic, while the regexp method test is accessible via RegExp.test. All generic methods have the same invocation signature: the first argument is always the this keyword value, and the arguments after that will be the actual arguments passed to the method.

The implement method also creates generic methods automatically. Any method you add using the implement method would have a corresponding generic method:

```
console.log(typeOf(Array.log)); // 'null'
```

```
Array.implement({

    log: function(){
        console.log('Hello');
    }

});

console.log(typeOf(Array.log)); // 'function'

Array.log(); // 'Hello'
```

Generic methods are used heavily in the MooTools framework. In fact, MooTools forgoes extending `Object.prototype` by implementing all additional `Object` methods as generics. We've already encountered some generics used inside MooTools in the previous chapters, like `Array.slice` and `Object.merge`, and we'll encounter more of them as we go along.

Another set of important static methods are the `from` methods, and there are four of them:

`String.from` takes any argument and returns the string value of the argument. The call `String.from([1, 2, 3])`, for example, returns '1,2,3'.

`Number.from` takes any argument and uses `parseFloat` to change the argument to a number value. It then returns that value as a number, or null if it can't be turned into a proper number.

`Array.from` takes any argument and returns an array. If the argument passed is already an array, it returns the argument without modification. If the argument passed is an array-like object, array.from turns it into a true array before returning it. If the argument is neither an array nor an array-like object, it returns a new array containing the argument. For example, `Array.from('hello')` will return ['hello'].

`Function.from` takes any argument and returns a function. If the argument passed is already a function, `function.from` returns it without modification. Otherwise, it returns a new function that returns the passed argument: `Function.from('hello')` will return `function(){ return 'hello' }`.

We already saw `Array.from` in Chapter 5, and we'll see it—and the other `from` methods—again throughout this book.

Creating New Types

One of the best things about the MooTools type system is its extensibility and openness. Not only are developers allowed to use the type system to implement new methods for native types, but we're also encouraged to make use of the publicly available `Type` constructor to implement our own set of custom types.

This was not always the case, of course. Prior to version 1.3 of MooTools, the inner workings of the MooTools type system were considered off-limits to developers. In older versions of the framework, the type system was implemented through the private `Native` constructor, which was a more complex forerunner of the `Type` constructor. It was one of those APIs that the experts knew about and used, but was not discussed in the documentation nor divulged to regular developers because of its private status.

However, times have changed and the `Native` constructor has been replaced with the simpler `Type` API—which is considered part of the public API. It's great that we can take full advantage of the type system now, and we'll do just that by implementing our own custom type.

A Table Type

As an example, we'll create a new type called a table. A table is a wrapper for the basic JavaScript object that supports getters and setters, as well as other utility methods. Before we actually implement it, let's see an example of its usage:

```
var table = new Table();

// setting values
table.set('item', 'pencil');
table.set({'fruit': 'banana', 'person': 'shiela'});

// accessing objects
table.get('item'); // returns 'pencil'
table.get('item', 'fruit'); // returns {item: 'pencil', fruit: 'banana'}
table.get('event'); // returns undefined

// removal
table.set('event', 'birthday');
table.get('event'); // returns 'birthday'

table.remove('event');
table.get('event'); // returns undefined

// membership
table.hasKey('item'); // returns true
table.hasValue('banana'); // returns true
table.keyOf('pencil'); // returns 'item'

// keys and values
table.keys(); // returns ['item', 'fruit', 'person']
table.values(); // returns ['pencil', 'banana', 'shiela']
table.length(); // returns 3

// traversal
table.each(function(item, key){
    console.log(key + ': ' + item);
});

/*
    item: pencil
    fruit: banana
    person: shiela
*/
```

Unlike a basic object, the items in a table aren't accessible from the table object directly via dot notation, but are accessible only using the get and set methods. We'll also have a remove method for removing items from the table, and three membership methods, hasKey, hasValue, and keyOf, to check whether specific keys or values are present in the table. Finally, we have the utility methods keys, values, and length to give us more information regarding the table itself, and an each method for table traversal.

This sounds like a very complex type, but it's actually pretty simple to implement as we'll see through this section. All the utility functions we need to implement this are already available through native JavaScript functions and MooTools language additions, and creating this new type will be quite easy.

The Table Constructor

The first thing we need to consider, though, is the constructor. Unlike classes, type objects make no distinction between constructors and initializers. In fact, there are no initializers for type objects: the constructor function acts both as object constructor and initializer.

There are two main reasons why this design was implemented for the type system. First is that native type constructors don't separate constructors and initializers, so it was deemed necessary to follow this standard in the MooTools type system. The second reason is more important: it is because type constructors were created for the purpose of initializing basic data types, which should be much simpler and more lightweight than classes. If you want a full-featured object system, use a class; otherwise, use a type. (We'll talk more about these distinctions in the last part of this section).

Since the special constructor features like automatic dereferencing available to classes aren't implemented for type objects, we need to make sure we're mindful of these issues. Dereferencing is the biggest of these issues, and we have to make sure that we create any object-based property inside the constructor itself, rather than declare them in our prototype.

In our table type, we'll need one of these object properties called $storage. Since it's an object property, we need to set it inside our Table constructor:

```
function Table(){
    this.$storage = {};
};
```

This is the foundation of our table type: the Table constructor. We used a function definition rather than a declaration since we want our constructor to have a proper name property—and also since this is recommended MooTools style. Inside the constructor, we have a line that creates a $storage property for the instance, which will then be used to store the items for our table. Because $storage is an object, we set it inside the constructor rather than in Table.prototype so that each table instance will have a unique storage object.

In order to make our Table constructor similar to native types, we need to give it the ability to be called as a regular function. If you recall from earlier in this chapter, we found out that native constructors could be called as regular functions, and they either perform type casting or create new instances. We'll follow the latter: if our Table constructor is called in conjunction with the new keyword, it'll act as a regular object constructor; otherwise, it'll return a new Table instance.

```
function Table(){
    if (instanceOf(this, Table)){
        this.$storage = {};
    } else {
        return new Table();
    }
};
```

We modified our constructor by adding an instanceOf check to see if the new keyword was used. If our Table constructor was called with the new keyword, the value of this inside the function will be an instance of the Table type. On the other hand, calling Table as a regular function sets the this keyword differently, so we'll need to instantiate and return a true instance of the Table type.

Now that the constructor is ready, all we need to do is turn it into a type object, and that's as simple as passing it to the Type constructor:

```
function Table(){
    if (instanceOf(this, Table)){
        this.$storage = {};
    } else {
        return new Table();
    }
```

```
};

new Type('Table', Table);

var table = new Table();

console.log(typeOf(table)); // 'table'
```

Setter, Getter, and Removal

With the constructor done, it's now time to implement our getter and setter methods. Instead of adding these methods directly to Table.prototype, we'll use the implement method so that our code is more organized.

The methods themselves are very simple:

```
Table.implement({

    set: function(key, value){
        this.$storage[key] = value;
        return this;
    },

    get: function(key){
        return this.$storage[key];
    }

});
```

The first method is set, and it takes two arguments: a string key, which is the identifier for the item, and value, which can be any value associated with the key. Storing the value in the $storage itself is as simple as assigning the particular key to the value. The get method, on the other hand, requires only one argument, key, which is the key of the item being accessed, and returning the value from the storage is also done using the simple access expression.

However, if you look back at the example use, you'll notice that the set and get methods have two forms. In the first form, they're used like the simple declaration above: set requires two arguments, while get requires a single one. In the second form, they're used to perform multiple operations. The set method in this form requires only one argument, an object literal, and it adds all the items from this object to the storage. Meanwhile, the get method in the second form accepts multiple key arguments, and returns an object containing the results.

To implement these new forms, we can modify our methods so they'll accept different argument types. The set method would have to be modified to check the first argument: if the argument is a string, it's used as a key and the second argument is used as the value, and if it's an object, the method should loop through the object and add each item to the internal storage. The get method, on the other hand, will have to check for the number of arguments and return either a single value or an object containing multiple key-value pairs depending on the number of key arguments passed.

It sounds like a very complicated task to add these additional features. Fortunately, MooTools already has it covered with two function decorators we can use to transform our set and get methods. The first is the overloadSetter decorator, which takes a function with the signature fn(key, value) and gives it the ability to accept object literal arguments, such as fn({key: value}). The second decorator, overloadGetter, takes a function with the signature fn(key) -> value, and turns it into a function that can accept the signature fn(key1, key2, ...) -> {key1: value1, key2: value2, ...}.

These two decorators are implemented as function methods, and using them for our functions is as simple as invoking them in our declaration:

```
Table.implement({

    set: function(key, value){
        this.$storage[key] = value;
        return this;
    }.overloadSetter(),

    get: function(key){
        return this.$storage[key];
    }.overloadGetter()

});
```

Just by adding these invocations, we've transformed our set and get methods into methods that take different argument types. With this declaration, our methods are now usable in the two forms we saw in the initial example.

Finally, we add the remove method, which deletes items from the storage:

```
Table.implement({

    remove: function(){
        var storage = this.$storage;
        Array.from(arguments).each(function(key){
            delete storage[key];
        });
    }

});
```

Like our decorated get method, the remove method can take multiple key arguments. Unlike get, though, we didn't decorate remove but instead used very simple code to implement the method. First, we created a local variable storage so we could access the internal storage object from inside our callback function. We then used the Array.from generic to transform the arguments object into a true array, and finally we looped through each of the arguments using the each method and deleted them from the storage. The result is a cleanly implemented remove method that accepts multiple arguments.

Membership Methods

Next on our list of methods are the three membership methods: keyOf, hasValue, and hasKey. The keyOf method takes a single argument, value, and returns the key associated with that particular value, while the hasValue and hasKey methods check whether a particular value or key exists in the table.

Let's implement the easiest one first: hasKey. If you recall our discussion on objects, we learned that if we try to access a nonexistent property of an object, we'll get the undefined value. We can therefore implement hasKey simply by checking whether a particular key in our storage object is equal to the undefined value:

```
Table.implement({

    hasKey: function(key){
        return this.$storage[key] !== undefined;
    }

});
```

The next two methods, keyOf and hasValue, are trickier. Since they operate on values rather than keys, we have no way to directly access them through our storage object. What we need to do is to use a traversal loop to go through each of the items in our storage and compare their value with the argument.

The hasValue method is easier to implement, since we'll simply have to check if the particular value exists in our storage object, regardless of which key is associated with it:

```
Table.implement({

    hasValue: function(value){
        var storage = this.$storage;
        for (var key in storage){
            if (storage[key] === value) return true;
        }
        return false;
    }

});
```

Inside our hasValue method, we loop through each item in the storage object using a for-in loop. For every item we go through, we compare the value of the item with the value argument passed to our method. If we get a match, we immediately halt execution of the function by returning true. If the loop finishes without finding any matches, we fall back to a return value of false.

The keyOf method is similar to the hasValue method, but instead of returning a boolean, we return the actual key associated with the object, or null if there's no such key:

```
Table.implement({

    keyOf: function(value){
        var storage = this.$storage;
        for (var key in storage){
            if (storage[key] === value) return key;
        }
        return null;
    }

});
```

Keys, Values and Traversals

We're almost done with our Table type, but we need to implement a couple more methods. Thankfully, they're all similar to our previous item-traversing functions, so it will be very easy to implement them.

Two of the methods we still need to implement are keys and values, which deal with the keys and the values as groups. The keys method returns all the keys of the items in a table, while the values method returns the values of these items:

```
Table.implement({

    keys: function(){
        var storage = this.$storage;
        var results = [];
        for (var key in storage) results.push(key);
        return results;
    },
```

```
    values: function(){
        var storage = this.$storage;
        var results = [];
        for (var key in storage) results.push(storage[key]);
        return results;
    }

});
```

We introduce a new variable in these methods called results, which is an array the keys and values are pushed into. Like hasValue or keyOf, both methods require a traversal loop to iterate through the items in the storage object. For each pass of the traversal loop, the methods push the current key or value into the results array. At the end of the methods, we return the results array, which then contains the needed values.

For the length method, we need to create a method that returns the number of items in the table. One way to do this is through another traversal loop, with an accumulator variable that is incremented with each pass through the loop. But a much simpler way is to reuse the keys (or values) method:

```
Table.implement({

    length: function(){
        return this.keys().length;
    }

});
```

Instead of writing another traversal loop for length, we simply invoked the keys method to retrieve an array of keys and then return the length of the array. This shortcut is possible since the number of keys in the internal storage would be equal to the number of items it contains.

Finally, we need to implement the last method: each. Like the array method of the same name, the each method of our Table type accepts a callback function that will be invoked for every item in the table as well as an optional bind argument that will be the this keyword value for the callback function. The callback function will receive three arguments when invoked: the current value, the current key, and the table itself.

```
Table.implement({

    each: function(fn, bind){
        var storage = this.$storage;
        for (var key in storage) fn.call(bind, storage[key], key, this);
        return this;
    }

});
```

```
Table.alias('forEach', 'each');
```

As with our previous methods, we use a for-in loop to traverse our storage object. For each item in our storage, we invoke the callback function fn using the call method, binding the object value of our bind argument and passing in the current value, the current key, and the table itself. Since we don't need to return any special value for this method, we simply return the table itself at the end of the function. We also add an alias, for the each method called forEach in order to conform to the native name of the method.

Our Final Type

Now that we've implemented all the necessary methods for our `Table` type, let's combine all our snippets into our final code:

```
function Table(){
    if (instanceOf(this, Table)){
        this.$storage = {};
    } else {
        return new Table();
    }
};

new Type('Table', Table);

Table.implement({

    set: function(key, value){
        this.$storage[key] = value;
        return this;
    }.overloadSetter(),

    get: function(key){
        return this.$storage[key];
    }.overloadGetter(),

    remove: function(){
        var storage = this.$storage;
        Array.from(arguments).each(function(key){
            delete storage[key];
        });
    },

    hasKey: function(key){
        return this.$storage[key] !== undefined;
    },

    hasValue: function(value){
        var storage = this.$storage;
        for (var key in storage){
            if (storage[key] === value) return true;
        }
        return false;
    },

    keyOf: function(value){
        var storage = this.$storage;
        for (var key in storage){
            if (storage[key] === value) return key;
        }
        return null;
    },

    keys: function(){
```

```
        var storage = this.$storage;
        var results = [];
        for (var key in storage) results.push(key);
        return results;
    },

    values: function(){
        var storage = this.$storage;
        var results = [];
        for (var key in storage) results.push(storage[key]);
        return results;
    },

    length: function(){
        return this.keys().length;
    },

    each: function(fn, bind){
        var storage = this.$storage;
        for (var key in storage) fn.call(bind, storage[key], key, this);
        return this;
    }

});

Table.alias('forEach', 'each');
```

It looks good, right? Using what we've learned about the Type constructor and type objects, we were able to implement a totally new object type. The simplicity of the MooTools type system is apparent in this sample code: our code is clean and organized, the API itself is easy to follow and understand, and the results are awesome enough to warrant real-life usage.

There is, of course, room for improvement. Our Table type is fine as it is, but still has some issues that need fixing. A particular improvement that I want you to figure out is how to limit items to only those that are directly defined through set. For example, calling table.get('constructor') will always return a value, even if we never set a 'constructor' item. This is because our internal storage object inherits several properties and methods from Object.prototype, and these members are also accessible to our methods. The easiest way to solve this would be to add checks using hasOwnProperty in our methods—and I'll leave it to you to fix the code accordingly.

The Wrap-Up

In this chapter, we learned about the native JavaScript type system and its MooTools counterpart. We learned what a type is exactly, as well as how JavaScript handles native types. We went through the various native types that JavaScript implements, and the rules that govern their transformation from one type to the other.

We also learned about the components of the MooTools type system and type objects in particular, which are class-like objects that are used to manage and enhance native types. We discovered how we can easily extend native types, and we topped it off by implementing our own custom type

This chapter certainly discusses quite a handful of topics, and I hope it is a fitting finale for part one of this book. We've gone through a lot of stuff in the past six chapters, from functions and objects to classes and types, and I expect that, at this point, you've already acquired the knowledge you'll need to understand much more complicated JavaScript code.

If your understanding is still a bit shaky, though, I advise you to reread this and the previous chapters. We're going to start exploring more complicated terrain in the next chapters, and unless you're comfortable with what we've already studied, you might have a hard time understanding parts two and three of this book.

But if you think that you're ready to trek onward, better put on your hiking boots because we're about to explore exotic lands crafted outside the ECMAScript specification.

Ready? Then turn the page so we can begin our exploration of JavaScript in the browser.

PART II

Conquering the Client Side

CHAPTER 7

■ ■ ■

JavaScript in a Window

In the previous chapters, we explored JavaScript as ECMAScript, a powerful object-oriented language, and we saw how MooTools uses the native features of the language to enhance it by adding features like a class system and a better type system.

But while the JavaScript language itself is a very interesting topic, the application of JavaScript for practical use is important as well. From its inception, JavaScript has always been a practical language, specifically for creating applications that run on a web browser. Of course, this is no longer the case. JavaScript has ceased to be a browser-bound language and has moved into the realm of the server, as we'll see in the last part of this book. However, we must first focus on JavaScript as it was envisioned: a language for building browser-based programs.

This chapter begins our journey through browser-based JavaScript. First, we'll learn a little about the browser itself, and then we'll take a look at the APIs the browser provides for working with web documents. Finally, we'll discuss the issue of cross-browser development, and how MooTools makes working with multiple-browsers possible.

A Language for Every Computer

JavaScript can be considered the most popular scripting language in the world. Most personal computers today, from big desktop machines to tiny handhelds and smartphones, have full JavaScript interpreters installed on them—usually as part of the default software package. And JavaScript owes this ubiquity to being the default scripting language of the humble web browser.

Well, maybe not so humble anymore. In the early days of the Internet, web browsers were very simple applications for displaying content. Web pages back then were simple: some text, a few images, and not much graphical style. Basic stuff compared to what we regularly see online these days.

But things got a little more complex when Netscape introduced JavaScript in 1996, which led to the new idea of the *scripted browser*. Suddenly, simple web pages became much more interactive, and the browser became far more than an application to display web pages. And it was this ability to add dynamic behavior to web sites that gradually evolved over the years into the complex JavaScript ecosystem we have today.

These days, browsers are much more powerful, more efficient, and more flexible. The competition among browser developers to create the best web browser can be brutal at times, but it does have the benefit of bringing about innovations in web technologies. And for a programming language like JavaScript, whose fate is irreversibly tied to the web browser, such innovations are beneficial to its future.

But what role does the browser really play in the JavaScript ecosystem? To put it simply, the browser is the platform for developing JavaScript applications: our programs are not only built around it, our users also access our programs via the browser. And while the browser is no longer the only JavaScript platform (more on this in Part Three), its availability and pervasiveness in modern computing is enough to warrant our full attention.

The subject of browsers is quite complex—after all, it's both an application and a platform. It's not possible to really get into a deep discussion on the internal architecture of a browser in this chapter, especially since there's no "one true browser," so instead we'll focus on the browser as part of the JavaScript ecosystem, particularly on the additional APIs it provides for our use. But before any of that, we need to understand a very basic subject that seems to be glossed over by most JavaScript books: how does a browser actually display a page?

Life Cycle of a Page

At its core, the web browser is an application that displays web pages. The main component of a web page is the HTML markup that describes the nature and content of the page and defines the external resources that are associated with the page, like style sheets and images. It is the job of the browser to turn this markup from text-based code into a graphical representation that will be displayed to the user.

Each browser uses different methods to achieve this, and how one browser does it may or may not be the same as how others do it. Still, there is a general flow that's applicable to all browsers, as Figure 7.1 illustrates.

The first thing a browser does is download the particular page for processing. When we enter a **Uniform Resource Identifier** (or URI) in a browser, the browser's **fetch engine** uses this identifier to locate and download the page and store it in its resource cache, where downloaded resources are kept for a specific amount of time to avoid having to download them each time they're accessed. In fact, if the page or resource we're accessing is already in the cache, the fetch engine often skips the downloading process, and uses this cached version instead.

When the fetch engine finishes downloading the page, the browser does a quick parsing of the markup to detect external resources—things like images, CSS stylesheets, or embedded media. The fetch engine then downloads these external resources while the browser starts the next step in the process.

As the fetch engine downloads the resources, the browser starts parsing the HTML markup of the page to build a **DOM Tree**. We'll discuss this in more depth later and in the next chapter, but for now it's enough to say that this DOM Tree is the HTML markup transformed into a hierarchical, tree-structured object. At this point, the text-based HTML markup becomes a usable object that can be manipulated by the browser.

The browser then starts parsing the CSS style sheets and the style definitions associated with the page to create a **style object**. This style object is used to determine how the browser will display the page, and it consolidates the final styles that will be applied to items in the DOM Tree based on the rules of CSS.

When both the DOM Tree and the style object have been prepared, the browser builds the **render tree** by applying the rules from the style object to the DOM Tree. The resulting render tree is sometimes different from the DOM tree: since some items won't be displayed because of style rules, they won't be present in the render tree and won't be processed in the next step.

Now the browser proceeds to do what is called a **reflow**, a process by which the browser's layout engine calculates the size and position of individual items in the render tree in relation to the whole page. By the time this process is done, all items in the page are properly positioned, and the final layout of the page is finished.

The last step in displaying the page is handing over the work to the browser's **paint engine**, which renders or "paints" the graphical representation of the page by combining the data from the render tree with the calculations done by the reflow. The page is then displayed by the browser in its window, and the user will be able to view it.

However, that's not the end of the story. After the page has been rendered, the browser will go into an **event loop**—and this is when things start getting interesting. Basically, the browser waits for something to happen, and that something is loosely termed an "event." An event can be anything from a user clicking a link or resizing the browser window to scripts performing manipulations on the page. When the browser detects an event that affects the layout of the page, it goes through the reflow and painting steps once again in order to update the displayed page.

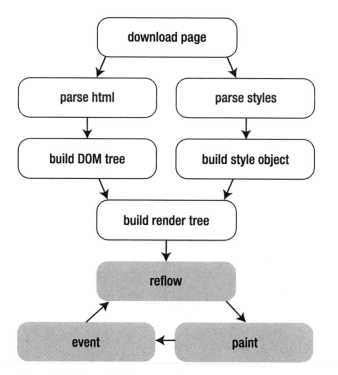

Figure 7–1. A typical browser flow

This "reflow, paint, wait for event" process is repeated by the browser for as long as necessary. In fact, this looping process plays a central role in visual animation as well as in browser events, which we will talk about in Chapters 12 and 9 respectively.

Pause, Script

One element that has to be taken into account in this rendering process is <script> tags. We know that <script> tags are the containers that enable us to program a web page, and whatever we put inside these tags is executed by the JavaScript interpreter that's built into the browser. This execution complicates the rendering process.

JavaScript is a single-threaded language—there can be only one process working at a time. Take a look at this example:

```
function B(){
    console.log('B');
};

console.log('A'); // 'A'
B(); // 'B'
console.log('C'); // 'C'
```

The output of this snippet is `'A'`, `'B'` and `'C'`, in that order. After we logged the first string `'A'`, we called the function `B()` and it logs the second string `'B'`. The execution is sequential: the JavaScript interpreter waits for the function to finish before executing the next line.

This single-threaded nature also affects the rendering process. When the browser's parsing engine encounters a `<script>` tag, it halts its parsing to let the JavaScript interpreter execute the contents of the `<script>` first. It is only after the interpreter finishes executing the script that the parsing (and rendering) process continues. In the case of scripts that have a `src` attribute, the browser first fetches the external script and then executes the contents of the script before continuing—which could make your web pages unresponsive for a time.

There are two reasons for this behavior. The first is because of the scripted nature of the browser: JavaScript, through browser-exposed APIs, can manipulate items on the page, which leads to a difference between the original content of the page and the new, modified version. Since JavaScript can affect the page's layout, the browser needs to make sure that all these layout-modifying processes are executed before rendering the page so that the final layout that will be displayed remains consistent with the modification.

The second reason is so that all scripts in the page are executed sequentially. Because all scripts on a web page share the same global environment, it is common for programs to be divided across multiple scripts, which then share data through the global environment. If scripts weren't executed sequentially, a script that depends on some variables being set by a script declared prior to it might not get access to these variables. Scripts are therefore executed according to the order they appear on the page to make sure any dependencies are properly resolved.

This blocking process and sequential execution, though, presents a very distinctive problem in terms of DOM manipulation. We'll look at it in detail in the next chapter. Right now, we'll focus our attention on the APIs that intersect the browser and JavaScript.

The Scripted Browser

If we are being truly technical, the things we've discussed in the previous chapters were about ECMAScript—not JavaScript. In fact, almost all of the snippets we presented could be executed by any compliant ECMAScript 3 interpreter—whether or not that interpreter is a JavaScript interpreter.

JavaScript is really a different beast from ECMAScript, though. While JavaScript is based on ECMAScript, it adds other host objects to the language that make it possible to execute complex programs in the browser. It is these additional APIs that turn ECMAScript into JavaScript, and enable the language to transform the browser from an application for displaying static web pages into a fully scriptable application platform.

Unfortunately, things are not really that simple: there is no definitive specification of what actually constitutes JavaScript, or what makes it different from ECMAScript—except for the idea that JavaScript has additional features. What these additional features are exactly, we can't precisely say. To quote Allen Wirfs-Brock, implementer of Tektronix Smalltalk and current JavaScript Language Architect for Microsoft:

In an ideal world, a standards specification is the complete story. A JavaScript implementation would just include everything in the ECMAScript specification and nothing more. [..] In the real world of the web, things are not so clear-cut. Specifications are seldom perfect and sometimes they are intentionally incomplete or ambiguous. [..] The result is that there are widely implemented and used features that are not defined by any standard specification.

The problem is rooted in how JavaScript—and ECMAScript—came to be. After Netscape introduced JavaScript and the idea of the scripted browser in 1995, Microsoft decided to implement the same features for its Internet Explorer browser. To do this, Microsoft reverse-engineered JavaScript to create JScript, a seemingly compatible language implementation. Standardization of the language into ECMAScript came later, after both Netscape and Microsoft had already shipped their own implementations.

Standardization didn't help in defining all of JavaScript either. ECMAScript was created to standardize the core of the language itself, in terms of language syntax, semantics, and execution. But the true core of JavaScript during those times—the API that enabled developers to use the language for web pages—was left out of the specification, along with the all the additional features each browser maker implemented to attract more developers to use their respective browsers.

And as the years passed, more features were added by browser developers that were not in the specification. Some of these innovations were later absorbed into the official language, some became **consensus features** that were adopted by all browsers even though they were not in the specs, and the rest became browser-specific features that are incompatible or missing from other implementations. The result is a rich and powerful language with a long list of features that may or may not work in all implementations—and more unfortunate, a language whose entire scope we can never define.

Thankfully, all is not lost. We may never really know what JavaScript is, but we don't have to in order to use it. The core language—ECMAScript—is well-defined, and the most important APIs for browser-based development have been standardized, or at least considered "stable enough" consensus features to guarantee they'll work in all browsers. And the two most important APIs, the Browser Object Model and the Document Object Model, are our next topics.

The Document Object Model

The **Document Object Model**, or **DOM**, is a set of technologies that define the API for interacting with and manipulating documents—particularly XML documents and its cognate variants. At its center is the idea of the document as an object composed of smaller interconnected objects, which can be manipulated to control the structure of the document itself. While the DOM specification isn't bound to one programming language, the DOM and JavaScript have become almost synonymous with client-side scripting.

Like JavaScript and other web technologies, the DOM came into existence long before it became a specification. When Netscape released its first JavaScript-enabled version of the Netscape Navigator browser, it included a very basic API for manipulating the page consisting of the global `document` object and array-like properties referencing document elements, such as `document.forms`, `document.images`, and `document.anchors`. Microsoft, in creating its JavaScript-compatible JScript, implemented the same API in order to make its Internet Explorer browser compatible with web pages developed in Netscape Navigator.

Those early APIs form the first cross-browser implementation of a DOM-like ancestor, which we now call *DOM Level 0*. This "level 0" designation indicates that these APIs are non-standard, but they formed the basis of further standardization efforts. Much of DOM Level 0 is still implemented in most browsers, and some of the parts that were not standardized became important consensus features as we'll see later.

After their initial scurry to release the first versions of JavaScript and JScript, Netscape and Microsoft eventually diverged by adding two new, different DOM implementations. Netscape developed a model that revolved around *layers*, which are special scriptable elements representing individual documents. Microsoft, on the other hand, developed a special object called `document.all`, which is an array-like object representing all elements in the document.

These two models are called the *Intermediate DOMs* and they gave web developers more powerful document-manipulation features, at the expense of cross-browser compatibility. Developers then had to either target individual browsers or create two versions of the code to support both. Suddenly, DOM scripting became much more cumbersome and complicated, and it is perhaps this complexity that fostered the initial animosity towards the JavaScript language—even though the DOM itself was technically separate from JavaScript.

Fortunately, the standardization of the JavaScript language as ECMAScript triggered the eventual standardization of the DOM. The World Wide Web Consortium (W3C) spearheaded the effort in 1997, and the first specification for the DOM, named *DOM Level 1*, was released four years later. The DOM Level 1 specification was initially targeted toward XML documents, but because XML and HTML are cognate languages, the DOM model was deemed appropriate for HTML use as well. This specification came in two parts: Core and HTML. The Core specification detailed the structure and API of the document as an object composed of other objects, while the HTML specification added features specifically for HTML documents.

Eventually, Netscape and Microsoft adopted this new standard, which brought cross-browser compatibility back for both browsers. When Netscape passed its development torch to the Mozilla foundation, Mozilla decided to drop the previous layer-model from Netscape's intermediate DOM and instead focused on DOM Level 1 exclusively for its Firefox browser. Meanwhile, Microsoft—for the sole purpose of backward compatibility—still includes legacy DOM support in Internet Explorer.

The next DOM specification to arrive was *DOM Level 2*, which brought new DOM features. This specification is composed of six parts, the two most important of which are the **DOM Events** and the **DOM Styles** specifications. DOM Events added a new event model to the DOM—a very important feature that we'll discuss in length in Chapter 9, while **DOM Styles** added further CSS and style sheet capabilities to the model, which are important for visual animations, as we'll see in Chapter 11. After DOM Level 2 came *DOM Level 3*, which builds on DOM Level 2 and adds new features to the Core and Events specification, as well as new specifications such as XML loading and saving and document validation.

One thing to bear in mind is that even if the DOM specifications are considered standards, browser support for these specifications isn't as well-defined as you might think. DOM Level 1 is highly supported in most browsers, but DOM Levels 2 and 3 are a different matter. Browsers generally implement only subsets of these specifications, which means that not all features are available in all browsers. This creates problems when using these APIs for cross-browser scripting.

Thankfully, the subset of important APIs—such as the ones dealing with document manipulation—is available in all browsers. This doesn't mean that they're perfect, of course. In fact, a lot of these APIs have implementation-specific bugs that make the DOM a very hard thing to work with—and these issues are the reason frameworks like MooTools exist. Frameworks were specifically built to make working with multiple browsers easier by abstracting the native APIs to implement cross-browser solutions. MooTools uses several techniques to do this, which we'll discuss later in this chapter.

Because the DOM itself is a complex set of APIs and interrelated ideas, we can't cover all of it in this chapter. Therefore, we'll divide our discussion across several chapters, starting with the core of the DOM model in the next chapter, then events and styles, and ending with some specific DOM manipulation tasks connected to the whole "Ajax" movement. Right now, though, we'll focus on an important part of the legacy DOM.

The Browser Object Model

The **Browser Object Model**, or **BOM**, is a set of related APIs that deal with the browser itself. At its heart is the idea of representing the browser window as a JavaScript object. The BOM API is represented by the top-level window object, which acts not only as the main interface for accessing the BOM but also as the representation of the actual browser window and as the global JavaScript object in the browser.

Technically, the BOM is part of the DOM, specifically the Level 0 DOM, and it's one of the consensus features in browser-based JavaScript: there is no specification that describes the BOM, which means that it's pretty much implementation-dependent. However, most browsers do implement a "standard" set of useful objects for the BOM:

- navigator—represents the browser application itself.

- location—represents the current resource being displayed.

- history—represents the browser's history timeline.

- document—represents the current HTML page.

All of these objects are properties of the `window` object and, since the `window` object also serves as the global object in the browser, these objects are also available as top-level objects in JavaScript. There are some other BOM APIs, like `screen` or `frames`, which we won't cover here since they aren't relevant to our current discussion.

Since the BOM itself is not that complex an object, we'll simply go through these important members in the next sections. One exception is the `document` object, which we'll discuss in the next chapter because of its importance in the DOM Element model. And we'll cover the actual use of these objects in practice later on as we go through this chapter and the next ones, so we'll limit our discussion here to the basics.

■ **Note** Some parts of the BOM might not retain their status as consensus features for long. HTML5, the newest version of the HTML language currently under development, includes specifications for most parts of the BOM, like window, location, and history. This means that future browsers will no longer have to depend on an API based on what we loosely describe as DOM Level 0, but on a better specification.

The navigator Object

The name of the `navigator` object is of course a reference to the first scripted browser, Netscape Navigator. When Microsoft reverse-engineered the original JavaScript implementation to create its own JScript engine for Internet Explorer, the name of the object was retained—probably for the purpose of cross-platform compatibility. Because the BOM is not part of the ECMAScript standard, the object identifier `navigator` was never replaced, and all major browsers still support this BOM object.

The `navigator` object acts as the representation of the current browser, and the properties of this object are used to describe the browser. In an ideal world, the `navigator` object would be the prime candidate for browser detection: we'd simply detect the browser by examining the properties of the `navigator` object, and then work around the various bugs in the browser using platform-targeted code. Of course, we live in a far from ideal world, and the `navigator` object and its properties are almost useless for browser detection.

Early developers saw the same potential for the `navigator` object as a useful way to perform browser detection. Unfortunately, those early days of browser development were truly competitive: not only were browser vendors trying to lure more developers to their products by adding new features, they were also trying to win market share by ensuring that web pages developed in other browsers would work with theirs. Specifically, early browser vendors made sure that their implementations appeared as if they were Netscape Navigator (the leading browser at the time), and a big part of this involved spoofing the properties of the `navigator` object.

This practice hasn't died out, and we still see browsers with `navigator.appName` properties with the value `'Netscape'`, even though Netscape Navigator is no longer widely used. Thus, a lot of the properties of the `navigator` object are useless for the purpose of browser detection, and we won't talk about the `navigator` object in detail for the same reason.

One property, though, `navigator.userAgent`, is still important and is still used for browser detection, despite traces of legacy spoofing being present in its value. We'll talk about this later in the section on browser detection.

The location Object

The location object represents the current location of the browser. In particular, it represents the current page from which the specific JavaScript code is executed.

The most important property of the location object is href, a string that denotes the current URL of the page. If we access a page with the URL
http://www.foobaz.com:80/_files/test.html?name=mark#index, for example, that entire URL will be the location.href value. The href property therefore denotes the full URL of the current page and is useful for getting the location of the currently running script.

Aside from the href property, the location object also has properties that refer to each part of the URL:

- protocol represents the particular protocol used to access the page, usually with the value http: or https:. Note that the value of this property also includes the colon, not just the protocol name. In our example above, the value of location.protocol is 'http:'.

- hostname represents the host section of the page's URL, including any subdomains. In our example, location.host has the value 'www.foobaz.com'.

- port represents the port section of the URL as a string—if available. If no port is specified in the URL, location.port will be equal to an empty string. In our example URL, the value of this property is '80'.

- host is a shortcut property that combines both the hostname and port values of the page's URL with proper delimiters. The value of location.host in our URL, for example, is 'www.foobaz.com:80'.

- pathname represents the specific resource location as defined by the URL. The value of this property always starts with /, and for URLs with no specific paths, the value will only be '/' to denote the root resource. In our example URL, location.pathname is equal to '/_files/test.html'.

- search represents the query string portion of the URL. The *query string* is a string that's used to pass data to the server. Usually it contains a collection of key-value pairs in the format key=value, with each pair delimited by an ampersand (&). The whole string—as represented by location.search—follows the same URL format by being prefixed with a question mark. The value of location.search for our example is '?name=mark'.

- hash represents the anchor part of the URL, and its value is an empty string if not present in the URL. Like the search property, hash also follows the URL format by being prefixed with a hash sign, #. In our example, location.hash is '#index'.

As you've probably noticed, the href property combines all of these properties together to produce the final URL. You can get the same value as location.href by concatenating the other properties with the proper delimiters:

```
var url = [
    location.protocol,
    '//',
    location.host,
    location.pathname,
    location.search,
    location.hash
].join('');

console.log(url === location.href); // true
```

The location object also has methods for working with the browser's location. The three most important ones are reload, assign, and replace.

- The reload method reloads the current page and is equivalent to refreshing the page using the browser. It takes a single optional boolean argument, force, which determines whether to bypass the browser's cache and reload the page directly from the server.

- The assign method takes a single argument, url, and loads that URL in the current window. Take note that the url value is interpreted as a relative URL unless you specify a protocol. For example, if we are on http://foobaz.com/ and we do location.assign('mootools.net'), the URL http://foobaz.com/mootools.net will be loaded. However, if we do location.assign('http://mootools.net') instead, the proper location will be loaded in the browser.

- The replace method works just like assign with one big difference: it does not register the URL in the browser's history. If we do location.assign('http://mootools.net'), for example, a new entry in the browser's history will be created and the user can go back to the previous page using the back button. However, if we do location.replace('http://mootools.net'), no new entry is created in the history. Instead, the current entry in the history will be modified to point to the loaded location.

The reload and assign methods are the two most-used methods of the location object, although replace can be handy in some cases.

One nifty feature of the location object is related to the assign method: the properties of the location object are dynamically tied to the actual location, and changing the value of a property changes the location of the page as well. For example, setting location.href = 'http://mootools.net' will load the URL in the current window—the same behavior we get with location.assign('http://mootools.net').

The really interesting use of this feature, though, is when we work with the properties of location that relate to parts of the URL. When we assign a new value to a property that references only a section of the URL, it changes only that section of the URL. Going back to our original URL example, http://www.foobaz.com:80/_files/test.html?name=mark#index, if we do location.hostname = 'mootools.net', it loads http://mootools.net:80/_files/test.html?name=mark#index in the current window. As you can see, only the original hostname is changed—from www.foobaz.com to mootools.net—and all the other parts of the URL remain the same. The same thing goes for all other sectional properties, such as search or port.

One really important use of this feature is with *history management* via location.hash. Unlike other URL parts, changing the anchor of a URL doesn't reload the page. Together with the history object, this makes it possible to implement some kind of history management for Ajax applications, as we'll see in Chapter 11.

The history Object

The most basic model of the web is of documents connected through hyperlinks. Users go to one document and navigate by clicking a link in the document that points to another document. Because of this linked nature, browsers had to find a way to present a linear progression of changes from one location to another, as well to provide a way to help users navigate through this linear progression. Thus, the concept of *browser history* was born.

The `history` object represents the linear history of the current browser window. In earlier browsers, the actual locations that were visited were available through the history object as URL strings. This, however, presented a large privacy hole in the browser, and was thus scrapped.

The `history` object today is a very simple object containing one property, `length`, which represents the number of items in the current window's history stack. It also has two simple methods, `back` and `forward`, which respectively load the previous and next locations in the browser history relative to the current location.

Another method, `go`, takes a numeric argument and loads the particular location relative to the current location, which is given the index 0. For instance, `history.go(-1)` will load the previous page in the history, which therefore makes it similar to doing `history.back()`, while `history.go(2)` will load the page after the next page in the history, just like hitting the browser's forward button twice.

■ **Note** The new HTML5 specification adds two new methods to the history object: `pushState` and `replaceState`. These are considered history-modifying features, and they are important features that can be used to manage history states for Ajax applications. We'll talk more about them in Chapter 11.

Frameworks, Libraries, and Toolkits

If you recall Mr. Wirfs-Brock's words earlier in this chapter, you'll notice they refer in particular to specifications and how the lack of standards for a lot of browser features make it hard for browser developers to create truly compatible products. However, specifications only refer to one side of the story. If we happen to suddenly find ourselves in an ideal world where all features are standardized with proper specifications, we still have to grapple with one big problem: implementation inconsistencies. Or to put it more succinctly, bugs.

We could have perfect standards, and for the most part we have a very good set of them in our less-than-ideal world, but we can't escape the fact that the software industry is one that makes mistakes. We have clear, solid specifications for ECMAScript, the DOM, and the HTML language, yet our browsers are far from perfect in their implementations. Standards are therefore only part of the equation: getting browsers to properly implement these specifications is just as important.

And this is a real problem we face in cross-browser development. Not only are we dealing with the fact that not all features are available in all browsers, we also have to work around the various bugs in the features that are present. Fortunately, this problem isn't crippling and most inconsistencies and bugs can be solved using JavaScript itself. This brings us to the topic of frameworks, libraries, and toolkits.

Most of the popular JavaScript code collections these days would call themselves a library, a framework, or a toolkit. These terms have very different meaning in software development, so for the purpose of our discussion, we'll use the most generic term—library—to denote all of them. All current JavaScript libraries—despite how they may categorize themselves—were built with at least one of these three goals in mind:

- Make cross-browser DOM development easier by providing abstractions that work around the inconsistencies and incompatibilities of the browser.

- Make cross-browser JavaScript development better by fixing inconsistencies among different implementations.

- Add additional features that make working with both the DOM and JavaScript easier.

The first goal is perhaps the most important one, because JavaScript's main stage has always been the browser. All major JavaScript libraries, including MooTools, will have some facility that makes writing cross-browser DOM scripts easier using simpler APIs. These APIs include stuff for element creation and manipulation, style management, an events system, and animation systems.

The last two goals are sometimes seen as much less important, depending on the library. While most JavaScript libraries add features that make working with the DOM easier, not all of them are concerned with adding new features to the JavaScript language. We do know that's not the case with MooTools: the framework implements several non-DOM related features, such as the class system and the type system, which makes MooTools a true JavaScript framework and not just a DOM scripting library. But it is important to note that not all libraries give the same amount of focus to the language as MooTools.

We've already examined how MooTools adds new language-level features to JavaScript in the previous chapter on Class and Type, and we'll examine the specifics of MooTools' DOM-related features in the next chapters.

MooTools and the Browser

As I mentioned, a big problem with cross-browser development is the fact that browsers are often inconsistent. While we do have full specifications for ECMAScript and the DOM, it doesn't necessarily follow that the browser implementations follow these specifications properly. Whether the inconsistencies are the consequences of bugs or a vague misinterpretation of the spec is of no big concern for us; what matters is that the cross-browser development is often a buggy affair.

And because browser vendors are largely concerned with making their own products better rather than maintaining compatibility with their competitors, the burden of making cross-browser development easier therefore gets passed to frameworks and libraries like MooTools.

Fixing Browsers with MooTools

At a general level, the MooTools approach is based on the idea of *abstraction versus fabrication*. What this means is that instead of creating an entirely new system to replace the native one, MooTools creates a new system by providing a new API that abstracts the native system. We've already seen this approach at work in the class and the type systems, and we'll see the same philosophy applied to DOM-related APIs as well.

This approach provides a big benefit when it comes to dealing with browser-specific issues. Because the native system is abstracted, MooTools is able to apply fixes internally, without the user's knowledge. This makes it possible to apply additional fixes in the future without changing APIs. It also makes it possible to apply fixes in a fine-grained manner, targeting only specific items without affecting the whole system.

MooTools has two main ways of dealing with implementation fixes. The first is *test-based fixes*, and this technique is easier to implement in most cases. Basically, MooTools tests for inconsistencies in the current browser by running a piece of code and then deciding whether or not to apply a fix based on the results of the test.

One example is `Array.prototype.splice`. In certain versions of Firefox and Internet Explorer, the `splice` method does not work properly with array-like objects. As we found out in Chapter 6 when we discussed Type, array methods should be generic according to the specs and they should work not only on real arrays but on array-like objects, too. Unfortunately, this is not the case with some versions of the aforementioned browsers, which becomes a problem for MooTools' `Elements` type that relies on this method.

To overcome this issue, MooTools uses a simple test-based fix. First, it performs a basic operation on an array-like object using `splice`, and then it checks the result. If the result is correct, MooTools does nothing. However, if the result is incorrect, MooTools implements its own version of `splice` for the

Elements type that works properly. The result is a proper splice method for Elements regardless of browser. And because the fix is applied on an *as-needed* basis, only browsers with improper implementations are targeted, and browsers that are already conformant are left alone.

But while test-based fixes are handy, not all issues can be resolved using this method. The limitation of this technique is imposed by how the technique itself works: to successfully apply the fix, you must be able to run a test that detects the need for a fix. Unfortunately, some issues aren't testable, like memory and rendering issues. These problems can be detected and observed with the proper external tools, but they can't be tested using JavaScript alone due to the lack of proper APIs.

Therefore, another technique must be used. These issues, more often than not, are browser-specific, which means that only a single browser is affected. This therefore limits the scope of the fix: if we know that the current browser is buggy, we can apply the fix. Finding out whether there are problems with the current browser and what code needs to be applied to fix them is a whole other topic, but applying the fix itself is easy—all we have to do is detect the current browser and run the fix-related code as necessary.

MooTools provides a single global object, Browser, that forms the center of MooTools' browser-related APIs. Some of its properties like Document, Element, and Event, are actually references to the native browser objects of the same identifiers, which are used further on for MooTools' reimplementation of the element and event systems. The Browser object itself, though, has a much more important use: it's the basis for browser-specific decisions in the MooTools framework.

The Browser object has two main properties that relate to the browser itself: name, which is the string name of the current browser, and version, which denotes the version of the current browser as a number. For example, if MooTools is run on a page in Google Chrome 7, Browser.name will be 'chrome' and Browser.version will be 7.

Additionally, the Browser object has dynamic properties that act as shortcuts for these two properties. The first one is the *dynamic name property*, which is added via Browser[Browser.name] = true;. In Chrome, for example, Browser.chrome will be equal to true and Browser.ie will be undefined. On the other hand, Browser.ie will be true in Internet Explorer, while Browser.chrome will be undefined. The other dynamic property is the *dynamic name-version property*, which combines the name and version of browser, such as Browser.chrome7 or Browser.ie8.

■ **Note** The dynamic name-version property has a limitation that makes the property name only register major versions. For example, Firefox 3.5 will register Browser.firefox3, and not Browser.firefox3.5, because the period—which is used in version numbers as a delimiter—is used for property access in JavaScript.

These Browser properties are used throughout MooTools, and they're essential to fixing browser-specific issues. Suppose we find an issue with Apple Safari that affects version 5 of the browser, and we need to apply some code to fix the issue. Using the Browser object, we simply have to do something like this:

```
if (Browser.safari5){
    // code
}
```

If we run this code on Safari 5, the code inside the if block will be executed, thereby targeting the browser properly. However, other browsers will ignore this code because Browser.safari5 will be undefined in them and the if condition will fail.

Browser Detection

The Browser object raises an interesting question: how does MooTools actually know what browser is currently running? This brings us to the topic of **browser detection**.

There are two main techniques for browser detection and the first is called **user agent sniffing**. **User agent** is another term for client software in a client-server system, such as a browser. In the web architecture, user agents identify themselves to servers using a special string called the **user agent string**, which follows the format <Product Name>/<Product Version> <Comments>.

The current browser's user agent string is accessible via the navigator object's userAgent property, and user agent sniffing relies on this property for detecting the current browser. The core of the operation involves running some regexp-based tests on the userAgent property value, then extracting parts of the string for use.

The user agent string is easily parsable, even if the structure of user agent strings among browsers varies widely. The problem with this technique, though, is that user agent strings are easily changed, and therefore can't be relied on. This is especially problematic when *user agent spoofing* is involved, where user agents "pretend" to be other user agents by passing the user agent string of another user agent to the server.

A second technique is much less prone to spoofing, and it's called **feature sniffing**. This technique involves checking for the existence of several special features in the current environment: if the environment has the both features X and feature Y, then it's probably browser Z. Feature sniffing therefore relies on the existence of certain objects to perform inference, and is therefore related to the concept of duck typing as we saw in the previous chapter.

But while feature sniffing is much more reliable than user agent sniffing, it's more brittle. Because we're checking for the existence of certain objects, adding or removing these objects from the current environment will result in wrong inferences. It's even more problematic when we take into account the pace of browser development: new versions of browsers are released more often these days, and a feature we use for feature sniffing could be gone instantly.

In versions of MooTools prior to 1.3, feature sniffing was the choice for browser detection. For example, MooTools relied on the existence of window.opera to check if the current browser is Opera, while it used window.ActiveXObject to check for Internet Explorer. This worked well for the framework—until the release of Firefox 3.6, which removed the getBoxObjectFor method of the document object, thereby breaking the MooTools feature-sniffing tests. This affected all versions of MooTools, making it necessary to call for an upgrade for all MooTools users.

Because of the magnitude of this incident, it was decided to move away from feature sniffing to user agent parsing for future versions of the framework, which of course included MooTools 1.3. In preparing the name and version properties of the Browser object, MooTools first parses navigator.userAgent using a regular expression, and then uses this parsed version to fill up the values of the properties. The properties are then used to create the dynamic name and name-version properties.

Feature Detection

But because user agent sniffing is easily breakable using spoofing, MooTools does not rely entirely on the name and version properties of the Browser object. As I mentioned earlier, test-based fixes are normal in MooTools and are used as much as possible. Another technique, related to both test-based fixes and feature sniffing, is called **feature detection**, and is employed as well.

Feature detection, like feature sniffing, relies on the existence of certain features in the current environment. However, like test-based fixes, feature detection is used mainly for fine-grained fixes and feature-based decision-making rather than true browser detection like feature sniffing.

A good example of this involves the events system, which we will discuss in detail in Chapter 9. There are two main event models: the standard DOM Level 2 Events model, which is supported by all major browsers, and the proprietary Internet Explorer model. In attaching events to elements, MooTools uses feature detection by checking the existence of the addEventListener method, which is the native method of the DOM Level 2 model. If it doesn't exist, MooTools then checks for the Internet Explorer model's counterpart for that method, called attachEvent. MooTools doesn't rely on the value of Browser.name, but rather, it uses feature detection to decide which event model to use.

The Wrap-Up

This chapter gave us some insight into the browser, as well as the issues involved in browser-based JavaScript. We learned how the browser renders a page, as well as the special exception given to scripts. We then found out about the two main APIs that are used for browser-based scripting, the DOM and the BOM, and we discussed a bit about their use and their structures. Finally, we learned about cross-browser issues and how MooTools performs user-agent sniffing and feature detection to make cross-browser scripting possible.

In the next chapter, we'll continue investigating browser-based JavaScript by exploring the most important API for browser-based development: the DOM Element API. We'll learn about DOM scripting and how MooTools abstracts the native DOM Element API to provide a sane and more consistent API that works across all supported browsers.

So if you're ready, turn off your mobile phone, take a seat, and applaud as we focus the spotlight on Elements.

CHAPTER 8

■ ■ ■

Elements

When working with JavaScript in the browser, the first and most important subject to learn is the DOM and its relationship to the JavaScript language. In fact, the bulk of the work done with browser-based JavaScript belongs to the category of *DOM Scripting*, a fancy term that basically means programming the DOM.

In this chapter, we'll learn about the DOM Tree, which is the representation of the HTML document as an object, and how to manipulate it through MooTools' DOM API. We'll also learn about the Element and Elements types, the two main type objects MooTools uses to add functionality to elements in the DOM Tree.

This chapter will guide you through the basics of DOM Scripting, and the concepts you learn here will be applied throughout the rest of the book. So if you're ready, let's start our exploration of the DOM.

Families and Trees

We learned in the previous chapter that after it downloads an HTML resource, the browser starts parsing the HTML markup to turn it into a **DOM Tree**. This special data structure is used for some internal preprocessing involving calculations related to how the page will eventually be rendered, but it's used for other things as well. In particular, the DOM Tree is also eventually used to create an object that will be exposed to JavaScript as part of an API, which we refer to as the DOM.

At the heart of the DOM is the idea of an HTML page as an object. Because JavaScript was originally intended as a language for working with web pages, it needed an appropriate API for manipulating the contents of a web page. And since, at heart, it's an object-oriented language, it's only fitting that JavaScript be given an API that represents an HTML page as an object.

A web page's representation in the DOM is called a **document**, which is not just an object but a special structural object called a **tree**. As its name implies, the tree structure is taken from the real world concept of a tree—although in reality it doesn't look anything like a tree. The name is actually a metaphor for a tree's hierarchical and branching structure, as we'll see.

A tree is composed of several linked items called **nodes**. At the starting point in the tree is a special node called the **root node**, from which all other nodes branch. A node that branches off from another node is called a **child node**, and the node from which that node branches is called a **parent node**. A parent can have multiple child nodes, as in the case of the root node, but a node can only have one parent node—or no parent node if it's the root node. If nodes have the same parent, they're said to be **sibling nodes**, while a node with no children is called a **leaf node**.

Take a look at Figure 8–1:

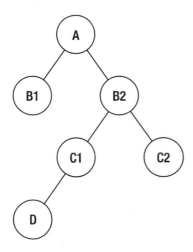

Figure 8–1. *A basic tree structure*

Here we have a basic tree with six nodes. The node named A is the root node and it is the parent node of two child nodes, B1 and B2. B1 is a leaf node, but B2 has two children of its own, C1 and C2. C1 has a single child, a leaf node called D, while C2 has none. The nodes B1 and B2 are sibling nodes, as are the two nodes C1 and C2.

To apply this idea of a tree structure to an HTML document, we need to examine the source markup of the page and see how it is turned into object. Let's look at the following example:

```
<html>
    <head>
        <title>Greeter</title>
    </head>

    <body>
        <img src="helloworld.png">
        <p>Hello <em>World!</em></p>
    </body>
</html>
```

Since I expect that you already understand this HTML document, I won't go into detail about tags and attributes. The first thing you'll notice is that the HTML source is already hierarchical, but in a container sense. For example, the <html> is the container for all the items: everything in the source is within the <html> tag and its corresponding </html> end tag. You'll also notice that some tags, like <html>, <body> and <p> can contain other tags as well as text, while other tags like <img> don't contain anything (and <img>doesn't have an end tag, either).

When transforming the markup to a tree structure, the <html> tag becomes our root node since it's the tag that contains everything else. The <head> and <body> tags then become the child nodes for <html> and the tags within these tags become child nodes themselves. An interesting case is the <img> tag, which is always a leaf node, since it can't contain any other tags.

Transforming this into a diagram, we have Figure 8–2:

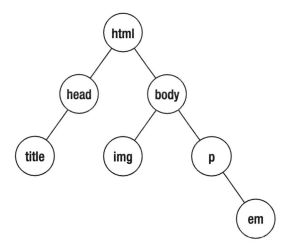

Figure 8–2. *HTML source as a tree*

However, we have something missing. How about the text inside some of those tags? How is that represented? We could actually represent it as nodes too, but we'd have to designate those nodes as a special type called a **text node** to differentiate them from normal tags. Figure 8–3 shows the text nodes in place.

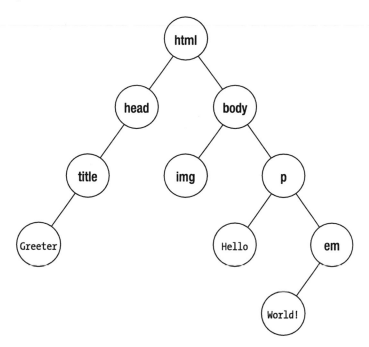

Figure 8–3. *HTML source as a tree, with text nodes*

Now that our HTML source is ordered in a tree structure, we can easily transform it into a JavaScript object. As I said, the DOM's main object representation is the document object, which is an object of type Document and represents the whole tree. Each of the nodes we saw in Figure 8–3 is transformed into an object that inherits from the Node type, which represents a single node in the document structure. A page's document will have a single node object representing the root <html> node, a single node object representing the <head> node, and a single node object that represents the <body> node. Within the <head> and <body> nodes go all the other nodes from the tree.

The Node type, though, isn't itself used, but it is further subtyped into the Element and CharacterData types.

The Element node represents actual HTML tags, which are called elements when they are transformed into objects. Element is then further subtyped to HTMLElement, which represents element objects from HTML documents (as opposed to other documents that use the DOM model). Furthermore, HTMLElement is subtyped into particular elements, like HTMLHtmlElement for the <html> node, HTMLParagraphElement for <p> nodes and so forth.

The CharacterData type, on the other hand, only has two main subtypes: Comment and Text. Comment represents HTML comments in the document, while Text represents the text nodes that are contained within tags.

These subtypes enable nodes to have specialized properties and methods that aren't available from the top Node type. However, the properties that associate a particular node to the tree itself are inherited by node objects directly from the Node type:

- The parentNode property is a reference to the node object that is the parent of the current node or null if it has no parent. In our original example, the parentNode property of the <p> node object is the <body> node object, while the <html> node object—being the root node—has a parentNode property of null.

- The childNodes property is an array-like object containing a list of all the children of a node. Accessing the length property of this object will give you the total number of children for a node. In our example, the <html> element has a childNodes property with the length of 2, and this property contains two objects: the <head> node object and the <body> node object.

- Related to the childNodes property are two properties named firstChild and lastChild, which are references to the first and last children of a node. If a node has no children, both properties will be null. If a node has only one child, both properties will point to the same node object.

- The previousSibling and nextSibling properties reference the sibling nodes of a node object. If a node is the only child of its parent, both properties will be null. In the same vein, the previousSibling property of the first child node and the nextSibling of the last child node will always be null.

All nodes regardless of type have these properties and it is these properties that make it possible to find a particular node within the document tree using JavaScript, which will be discussed in depth in Chapter 9 when we talk about the Selector Engine.

The document object itself is actually a node, but it's important to note that it's not actually the root node—although it may seem as such—but rather the object representation of the html page itself as an object tree of nodes. The true root node of a document is the <html> node, although it is rarely used. The more commonly accessed nodes are the <head> and <body> nodes, since these are the nodes that contain the data relevant to the page. In the native DOM API, the <body> node is accessible through document.body, but no such shortcut is available for <head>. MooTools, though, adds a feature to make the <head> node available via document.head.

When working with nodes in MooTools, you can use the typeOf function to distinguish between elements and textnodes. The typeOf function will return 'element' for element nodes and 'textnode' for text nodes. In practice, you won't have to distinguish between them that much, since MooTools puts much more focus on elements, as we'll see. But before we do, we have to look back at <script> tags.

Is My DOM Ready Yet?

In the previous chapter, we learned that the HTML source is parsed sequentially to create the DOM tree. The browser goes through the HTML source and "interprets" each of the tags it encounters, creating new nodes and elements for the DOM tree. We also learned that <script> tags are executed sequentially by the browser. When the browser encounters a <script> tag, it executes the code contained between the tags before moving on to parse the next tag in the HTML source. In the case of external scripts, the browser downloads the external code first and then executes it, and only after that will the parsing start again.

This sequential parsing of the DOM, together with the blocking nature of script execution, presents a gotcha when it comes to DOM scripting. To truly understand this issue, let's suppose we're browsers trying to parse the following HTML source sequentially:

```
<html>
    <head>
        <title>Test</title>
    </head>

    <body>
        <img src="hello.png">
    </body>
</html>
```

Let's do it step by step:

1. First, we see the <html> tag and create a new node. Since the <html> tag has a corresponding closing tag, we know it can contain other tags as well, so we'll mark it as our current parent. Our DOM Tree currently has one node.

2. We parse the next tag, <head>, and create a new node that becomes the child of our current parent, <html>. Because <head> also has a corresponding closing tag, it can be a parent as well, so we set this new node as our current parent. Our DOM Tree now has two nodes.

3. The next tag we encounter is <title> and we create a new node for this. The current parent is <head>, so our <title> node becomes a child of the <head> node. As with <html> and <head>, we'll mark the <title> node as our current parent since it can contain other tags. We now have three nodes.

4. Within the <title> tag we encounter our first text, so we create a new textnode that will be a child node of our current parent, <title>. Because text nodes can't have child nodes, we won't set this node as our current parent, so <title> is still the current parent node. The DOM Tree now has four nodes.

191

5. We now encounter </title>, a closing tag that tells us that the <title> node is complete and has no other children. We set our current parent back to the parent of <title>, which is <head>. Since we didn't add any new nodes, we still have four nodes in our DOM Tree.

6. Another end tag comes into our view, </head>, which marks the end of the <head> node. We set the current parent to the parent node of <head> so our current parent is <html> again. Our DOM tree is unchanged with four nodes.

7. We see a new tag, <body>, so we create a new child node for our current parent, <html>. Since <body> has an end tag, we set <body> as our current parent. We now have five nodes in our tree.

8. The next tag is an <img> tag, so we create a new child node for the current parent <body>. The <img> tag is one of the few tags that doesn't have a closing tag, and is therefore seen as "self-closing." It can't have any child nodes, so we won't set it as the current parent. Our DOM Tree now has six nodes.

9. We then encounter an end tag, </body>, signaling the end of the <body> tag, so we set the current parent back to the parent node of the <body> tag, <html>. Our DOM Tree remains unchanged, so we still have six nodes.

10. Finally, we get to the last tag, </html>, signaling the end of the <html> tag and the end of our HTML source. The final DOM Tree has been built and it contains six nodes in total.

Now if you've been paying attention to the steps, you'll notice that the DOM Tree grows as each tag is parsed. We started with a single node and ended up having six nodes. The number of nodes in each step can be different from the number of nodes before or after that step, and only after everything has been parsed will we know how many nodes there actually are in the DOM Tree.

With this in mind, we can say that our DOM tree only becomes final after we've parsed the HTML source completely. We call the final DOM Tree—with all tags parsed and turned into nodes—the **completed DOM Tree**. From the start of parsing right up to the step before we finally parse the </html> end tag, we don't have a completed DOM Tree, only part of it—and we call this a **partial DOM Tree**. The interesting thing about the partial DOM Tree is that each step of the parsing process can potentially change the DOM Tree, and so the partial DOM Tree in one step can be different from the partial DOM Tree in another step.

Now suppose we add a <script> tag into our HTML source, like so:

```
<html>
    <head>
        <title>Test</title>
        <script src="mootools.js"></script>
        <script>
            console.log(typeOf(document.body));
        </script>
    </head>

    <body>
        <img src="hello.png">
    </body>
</html>
```

We won't parse this step by step again, since we can just think of the extra step we'll add to the parsing we did above: after step 5, we now have to parse the two <script> tags and then create new child nodes for the current parent <head>. However, we also have to execute the code contained within the

`<script>` tag before we move on to the next step. Only after `console.log(typeOf(document.body));` finishes can we move to the next step of parsing the `</head>` tag and closing the `<head>` node.

Okay, so what's the gotcha I was talking about then? The best way to see the issue is to run the example HTML page in your browser. Remember that `document.body` points to the `<body>` node, so you'll probably expect `typeOf(document.body)` to return `'element'`. However, if you try to run it in your browser, you'll see that `typeOf(document.body)` doesn't return `'element'`—it returns `'null'`.

And that's the gotcha. Our main interface for manipulating the DOM is the document object, and we use this object to access the nodes in our DOM Tree. But an important thing to remember is that the document is a true mirror of the DOM Tree: whatever the state of the DOM Tree is, it will be reflected in the document object.

This goes back to the idea of a partial DOM Tree. In our example, `typeOf(document.body)` returns `'null'` instead of `'element'` because at the point that the script is executed, we only have a partial DOM Tree. This partial DOM Tree already contains the `<html>`, `<head>`, and `<title>` nodes, but the `<body>` node is yet to be parsed, so `document.body` is truly `null` at that point. And because executing the script is a blocking process, the browser can't just continue parsing the rest of the HTML source: it has to wait until the JavaScript interpreter finishes before it can parse the rest of the HTML source.

Because browser-based JavaScript is largely concerned with manipulating elements in the DOM tree, we need to make sure they're accessible when we start working with them. If we start working on elements before they're created—like we did in the preceding example—we'll run into errors and other weird behavior.

There are several ways around this. The first is to move your script to right after the element you're working on to make sure that the element is already in the DOM tree when you need it:

```
<html>
    <head>
        <title>Test</title>
        <script src="mootools.js"></script>
    </head>

    <body>
        <script>
            console.log(typeOf(document.body));
        </script>
        <img src="hello.png">
    </body>
</html>
```

In this example, `typeOf(document.body)` will return `'element'` as expected since the `<body>` node will be available by the time our script is executed.

While this technique works, it gets hard to manage as your script grows. For example, if we add some new function to our script that modifies the `<img>` element in our page, we have to move the script again. If our script changes yet again after that, we'll have to move our script to reflect the change.

Moving scripts around could get taxing after a while, especially if you have many of them. So a better technique is to move the scripts to the bottom of the page, right before the `</body>` tag:

```
<html>
    <head>
        <title>Test</title>
        <script src="mootools.js"></script>
    </head>

    <body>
        <img src="hello.png">
        <script>
```

```
            console.log(typeOf(document.body));
        </script>
    </body>
</html>
```

Placing scripts right before the </body> is a good way to ensure that the elements you'll need to access are already available. Since the </body> tag is almost always the second to the last tag in the page (the last always being the </html> tag), it is safe to assume that all tags would have been parsed and turned into proper nodes in the DOM tree by the time this closing tag is reached. Therefore, the partial DOM Tree right before the </body> tag—even though it's not yet truly complete—will be close to being a complete DOM Tree. Scripts executed at this point will therefore have access to an almost complete DOM Tree with the necessary nodes accessible and ready for manipulation.

Placing scripts right before </body> also yields an additional benefit: pages appear to load faster. Since executing scripts halt the parsing of the DOM tree, they also block the rendering steps. While a script is executing, the browser can't render anything on the page. If you have a script in the <head> of your page that takes too long to execute or one that takes too long to download, it will take quite some time before the browser can start the reflow and painting processes that will output the page in the window.

If the scripts are at the bottom of the page, however, the browser can start the reflow and painting process earlier. Since there are no scripts to block the rendering process, the browser can output the page faster and the user will be able to see it immediately. By the time the browser reaches the scripts at the bottom of the page, most of your site would already be visible, so there's no blocking behavior apparent to the viewer.

Unfortunately, this technique has one flaw. Say we have the following HTML source:

```
<html>
    <head>
        <title>Test</title>
        <script src="mootools.js"></script>
    </head>

    <body>
        <img id="hello" src="hello.png">
        <p>Some text.</p>
        <p>Another text.</p>
        <div>
            <p>More Text Here</p>
        </div>
        <script src="change_content.js"></script>
    </body>
</html>
```

Here we have an external script called change_content.js instead of an embedded one. The script is huge, several hundred kilobytes, and includes the following snippet:

```
...

// Remove the hello image..
var img = $('hello');
img.destroy();

...
```

The snippet says to retrieve the element with the id "hello" and remove it from the DOM. Easy enough, right? However, consider the rendering flow: the browser first renders the image; then when it gets to the script tag, it has to download the script first before executing the code that removes the image from the page. The result is that the user will see the image appear and then disappear—which could get pretty confusing.

While the example might sound contrived, this is actually a very common phenomenon called **Flash of Unstyled Content** or **FOUC** for short. Originally an issue with Cascading Style Sheets, FOUCs have now entered the JavaScript domain because of the numerous style and behavioral modifications added via scripts. What happens is that users see the page's initial "unstyled" content, which then suddenly changes because of modifications done via JavaScript.

But while FOUCs are more annoying than truly problematic, a similar issue—which I'll dub as a **Moment of Behaviorless Interaction** or **MOBI**—is worse. Instead of styles, MOBIs are concerned with behavior. Let's change the code above:

```
<html>
    <head>
        <title>Test</title>
        <script src="mootools.js"></script>
    </head>

    <body>
        <p><a id="greeter" href="#">Click Me!</a></p>
        <script src="add_events.js"></script>
    </body>
</html>
```

And here's the corresponding add_events.js script:

```
...

// Say hello
var greeter = $('greeter');
greeter.addEvent('click', function(event){
    event.preventDefault();
    alert('Hey There Mister!');
});

...
```

The scenario remains the same: add_events.js is a large script file that has to be downloaded and executed by the browser at the end of the page. Unlike the previous example, though, add_events.js doesn't change the style of an element in the page; instead it adds behavior to an element. In particular, it defines an event handler (we'll discuss these in Chapter 10) that will be fired when the link with the id "greeter" is clicked.

However, the same FOUC issue rears its head here: the link will be rendered by the browser first, and then the browser will download and execute the external script. Because the script will be executed a bit later, there will be a few moments when users will be able to click the link and nothing will happen. The behavior hasn't been added at that point, and your page will seem interactionless—and thus you'll get a "Moment of Behaviorless Interaction."

Both FOUCs and MOBIs present an interesting issue for DOM scripting. On the one hand, this is where the blocking behavior of script tags comes in handy: by placing script tags in the <head> of the document, you'll be sure that they're executed and ready before any of the actual content in the <body> is displayed—so styles and behavior will already be defined by the JavaScript interpreter. On the other, however, this brings us back to our original problem: if our script is in the <head> of our document, we'll only have access to a partial DOM tree.

The solution then has to be two-fold: first, the script must be placed early on the page (preferably in the <head>) so that it will be downloaded and ready beforehand, and second, the execution of the script must somehow be delayed until after we have a complete enough DOM tree to work with. The solutions we've seen so far can't meet these requirements, so we'll have to look in another place: JavaScript events.

An event in the broadest sense is something that happens within the lifetime of a page. In our previous add_events.js snippet, for instance, we added an event handler—which is basically a function—that will be executed as an effect of an event happening (in that case, a link being clicked). For our particular issue right now, we'll also make use of an event, one that tells us when there is a complete enough DOM tree to work with.

That event is called the DOMReady event, and it's a special event that MooTools provides. Changing our FOUC example to use this event, we end up with this:

```
<html>
    <head>
        <title>Test</title>
        <script src="mootools.js"></script>
        <script src="change_content.js"></script>
    </head>

    <body>
        <img id="hello" src="hello.png">
        <p>Some text.</p>
        <p>Another text.</p>
        <div>
            <p>More Text Here</p>
        </div>
    </body>
</html>
```

Now for the change_content.js:

```
...

window.addEvent('domready', function(){
    // Remove the hello image..
    var img = $('hello');
    img.destroy();
});

...
```

We do two things here: first we move our script to the top of the HTML source so that we'll get the blocking behavior. This ensures that our event handlers and other necessary boilerplate code are executed and prepared before any content is rendered. Next, we wrap the original image-destroying code inside a function and register that function as an event handler for the DOMReady event. If we run this on the browser, we'll get our desired result.

We'll talk more about how the DOMReady event works in Chapter 10, but right now it suffices to say that by using DOMReady, we're telling the browser to defer the execution of the event handler function until the DOM tree is complete enough.

Applying the same to our second example, we get the following:

```
<html>
    <head>
        <title>Test</title>
        <script src="mootools.js"></script>
        <script src="add_events.js"></script>
    </head>
```

```
<body>
    <p><a id="greeter" href="#">Click Me!</a></p>
</body>
</html>
```

As for the add_events.js script:

```
...

window.addEvent('domready', function(){
    // Say hello
    var greeter = $('greeter');
    greeter.addEvent('click', function(event){
        event.preventDefault();
        alert('Hey There Mister!');
    });
});

...
```

As in our previous example, we move the script to the <head> of the page to ensure that it's executed before any content rendering happens. We again use the DOMReady event to defer execution of the code until the DOM Tree is in a complete enough state for manipulation. The result is that we get rid of the MOBI, and users will be able to interact with our page without seeing any undefined behavior.

▨ **Note** There is another way to achieve the same results in browsers, one that involves using a special <script> tag attribute called defer. When a <script> is declared with a defer attribute, the browser delays execution of the script until the DOM is ready—just like the DOMReady event. Unfortunately, support for defer isn't available in all major browsers, so we'll stick to DOMReady for the time being.

The obvious question then is whether it's better to entirely replace the technique of adding scripts at the bottom with DOMReady handlers. The answer to this question, of course, is "it depends." Using DOMReady handlers has the benefit of making sure that style and behavioral changes are declared before any content is rendered, but putting all scripts on the top of your page will slow rendering time. On the other hand, putting scripts in the bottom enables the browser to render the page quicker, but at the expense of getting FOUCs and MOBIs.

Personally, I find that the sweet spot lies in using both techniques at the same time. The best way to do this is to divide your JavaScript programs into small logical parts. Scripts that declare important style and behavioral changes should be placed at the top, while scripts that aren't particularly important should be placed at the bottom. With this scheme, FOUCs and MOBIs are eliminated, and the blocking time before rendering is minimized.

Since we won't be creating complex programs in this chapter, we'll be using both techniques separately. For examples that use only the native DOM APIs, we'll place scripts at the bottom of the page, while examples that work with MooTools will use a DOMReady handler.

DOM Scripting with MooTools

DOM scripting is the common term for using JavaScript to program a web page, and much of it involves manipulating elements on a page: selecting elements, creating new elements, moving elements around, changing their attributes and styles, and destroying them when necessary.

To script the DOM, you'll need to use the API provided by the DOM itself. Unfortunately, it's not a perfect API. In fact, a common saying in the JavaScript world is that when people say they hate JavaScript, what they're really saying is that they hate the DOM. I find this somewhat true, but unfortunate: the DOM API is one of the harder APIs to work with, but not because it was designed that way. The problem lies with the browsers that implement the specs: somehow, browsers always find a way to add bugs and deviations from the specs. As such, the DOM API is inconsistent, and what works for one browser may not work for another.

The developers of MooTools know this, and the bulk of the framework was created just for the purpose of taming the mess that is the DOM. In fact, the MooTools API effectively replaces the DOM API, making it almost unnecessary to use native DOM methods for most tasks.

With this in mind, we won't go through the native DOM API in detail. Aside from the fact that MooTools abstracts this API so we don't have to worry about it, the subject has already been covered in numerous JavaScript books—and is therefore not worth repeating. If you want to learn more about it, you can refer to any of the DOM Scripting books in the References section at the end of this book.

What follows is an overview of how basic DOM manipulation is done through the MooTools-provided API. Be sure to pay attention to what follows, since we'll be discussing what forms the core of DOM scripting with MooTools.

Selecting Elements

The most basic task in DOM scripting is selecting a particular element from the DOM Tree. In order to manipulate a particular element in the DOM Tree, we must first find it using special functions called **selector functions**.

The ID Selector

The most commonly used selector function is the **ID Selector**, document.id, which takes a single string argument id and returns the element from the DOM Tree with the corresponding id:

```
<html>
    <head>
        <title>test</title>
        <script src="mootools.js"></script>
        <script>
            window.addEvent('domready', function(){
                console.log(document.id('hello').get('tag')); // 'img'
            });
        </script>
    </head>

    <body>
        <img id="hello" src="hello.png">
        <p>some text.</p>
        <p>another text.</p>
        <div>
```

```
            <p>more text here</p>
        </div>
    </body>
</html>
```

Here we use `document.id` to fetch the element with the id "hello", which is an image element. We then confirm that we got the proper element by calling the get method of the element to determine the element's tag name. This call returns `'img'`, which confirms that we got the proper method.

The semantics of HTML require id attributes to be unique: a particular id should be used only once for a single element. Because `document.id` selects an element based on its id attribute, it will always return a single element if an appropriate one is found. If there is no element in the DOM Tree with the id passed to `document.id`, it returns `null`:

```
<html>
    <head>
        <title>test</title>
        <script src="mootools.js"></script>
        <script>
            window.addEvent('domready', function(){
                console.log(document.id('hi')); // null
            });
        </script>
    </head>

    <body>
        <img id="hello" src="hello.png">
        <p>some text.</p>
        <p>another text.</p>
        <div>
            <p>more text here</p>
        </div>
    </body>
</html>
```

The `document.id` method is *idempotent*: applying the function to a result of the function returns the same result:

```
<html>
    <head>
        <title>test</title>
        <script src="mootools.js"></script>
        <script>
            window.addEvent('domready', function(){
                var result = document.id('hello');

                // pass result to document.id again
                console.log(document.id(result) === result); // true

                // result's tag
                console.log(result.get('tag')); // 'img'
            });
        </script>
    </head>

    <body>
```

```
        <img id="hello" src="hello.png">
        <p>some text.</p>
        <p>another text.</p>
        <div>
            <p>more text here</p>
        </div>
    </body>
</html>
```

We first invoke document.id to fetch our element with the id hello, and then store the returned image element in our variable result. We then invoke document.id again, but this time pass the image element using the result variable. Comparing the result of this new call to the original result, we see that they are indeed the same objects. This is because document.id returns the passed argument immediately if it's already an element—which makes it safe to apply the function on an element object more than once. In the same vein, document.id('hello') === document.id('hello') will be true, because document.id will always return the same element when called with the same argument.

The document.id method is similar to the native document.getElementById function. The difference is that the native document.getElementById function returns a native HTMLElement, while document.id returns an instance of the MooTools Element type—which we'll discuss in depth later. However, MooTools overrides the native getElementById function with its own variant that's more or less like the document.id function, which we can confirm by comparing the results of both:

```
<html>
    <head>
        <title>test</title>
        <script src="mootools.js"></script>
        <script>
            window.addEvent('domready', function(){
                console.log(document.id('hello') === document.getElementById('hello')); //
true
            });
        </script>
    </head>

    <body>
        <img id="hello" src="hello.png">
        <p>some text.</p>
        <p>another text.</p>
        <div>
            <p>more text here</p>
        </div>
    </body>
</html>
```

In this example we see that the return value of document.id('Hello') and document.getElementById('hello') are the same element objects. This is because of MooTools' overriding of the native getElementById function. If MooTools didn't override this function, the results would not be the same objects: document.id would return a MooTools Element instance, while getElementsById would return a native HTMLImageElement object.

As I mentioned, document.id is a very popular function, and it's not uncommon to use it more than once in a single program. Because of this, MooTools provides a shortcut, called **the dollar selector function: $:**

```
<html>
    <head>
```

```
        <title>test</title>
        <script src="mootools.js"></script>
        <script>
            window.addEvent('domready', function(){
                console.log($('hello').get('tag')); // 'img'
                console.log(document.id('hello') === $('hello')); // true
            });
        </script>
    </head>

    <body>
        <img id="hello" src="hello.png">
        <p>some text.</p>
        <p>another text.</p>
        <div>
            <p>more text here</p>
        </div>
    </body>
</html>
```

Both $ and `document.id` return the same element in this example, and you can use $ as a replacement for `document.id` in most instances.

The use of the dollar symbol ($) as a function shortcut is a popular practice, and most JavaScript frameworks include a similar function. In fact, some libraries—JQuery being the most notable example—actually depend on $ by default. Unfortunately, this creates issues with library interoperability: loading two different libraries in a single page would lead to one library overriding the $ function of the other library.

In order to add some interoperability, MooTools includes a feature called **dollar-safe mode**: MooTools automatically checks whether a $ function has already been declared, and if so, it won't declare its own $ function. This way, MooTools won't override the $ function of other libraries.

Of course, this might not be the behavior you want. Because `document.id` is used often, you might want to have the $ shortcut ready for use all the time. Some older MooTools scripts also depend on the MooTools $ function and it will lead to errors if they get another library's $ function instead. You can force the MooTools $ function by adding a declaration as a prelude to your scripts:

```
<html>
    <head>
        <title>test</title>
        <script src="mootools.js"></script>
        <script>
            // ensure that $ is MooTools'..
            window.$ = document.id;

            window.addEvent('domready', function(){
                console.log($('hello').get('tag')); // 'img'
            });
        </script>
    </head>

    <body>
        <img id="hello" src="hello.png">
        <p>some text.</p>
        <p>another text.</p>
        <div>
```

```
            <p>more text here</p>
        </div>
    </body>
</html>
```

By declaring `window.$ = document.id`, you'll be able to force the use of the MooTools `document.id` function as the $ function.

By doing this however, you'll override the $ function of any other library loaded along with MooTools, which may affect interoperability with other scripts. If you simply want to use the $ function for your own scripts, you can use a single-execution function to localize $:

```
<html>
    <head>
        <title>test</title>
        <script src="mootools.js"></script>
        <script>
            // localize the $ function
            (function($){

                window.addEvent('domready', function(){
                    console.log($('hello').get('tag')); // 'img'
                });

            })(document.id);
        </script>
    </head>

    <body>
        <img id="hello" src="hello.png">
        <p>some text.</p>
        <p>another text.</p>
        <div>
            <p>more text here</p>
        </div>
    </body>
</html>
```

■ **Note** Most JavaScript developers agree, though, that using multiple JavaScript frameworks in a single page is a recipe for disaster. In general, JavaScript frameworks were designed to be used separately, and MooTools is no exception. Because it's strongly recommended to avoid using MooTools with another framework on a single page, most of the issues with the dollar-safe mode will likely never pop up. However, if you're developing scripts that you'll be distributing to other users, you should use `document.id` instead of the dollar function since you can't be sure your end users will be using MooTools alone.

CSS-Based Selectors

The MooTools `document.id` function and the native DOM API `document.getElementById` function are considered *simple selector functions*: you pass them a string id and they return the element with that particular id. However, the native DOM API provides two simpler selector functions: `document.getElementsByTagName` and `document.getElementsByClassName`:

```html
<html>
    <head>
        <title>test</title>
    </head>

    <body>
        <img class="viewable" src="hello.png">
        <p>some text.</p>
        <p>another text.</p>
        <div class="viewable">
            <p>more text here</p>
        </div>
        <script>
            console.log(document.getElementsByTagName('p').length); // 3
            console.log(document.getElementsByClassName('viewable').length); // 2
        </script>
    </body>
</html>
```

The `document.getElementsByTagName` function takes one argument, `tag`, and returns all elements of the corresponding tag, while `document.getElementsByClassName` also takes a single argument, `class`, and returns all elements with the corresponding class. In our example, we used `getElementsByTagName` to get all paragraph elements and we used `getElementsByClassName` to get all elements that have the class `viewable`.

HTML semantics allow multiple instances of a tag type in a single document, as well as using a single `class` attribute value for multiple elements. Because of this, `getElementsByTagName` and `getElementsByClassName` don't return single elements—they return instances of `NodeList`. A `NodeList` is a read-only array-like object containing the elements that were gathered by the selector function. As we saw in the example above, our code received two `NodeList` instances, and we were able to determine the number of elements in the `NodeList` by the `length` method.

MooTools doesn't override these two functions, but instead unifies them in a single function: **the double-dollar function**, or $$. This function takes a single argument, `selector`, and returns all the elements that correspond to the selector. For example, we can use $$ to replace `document.getElementsByTagName`:

```html
<html>
    <head>
        <title>test</title>
        <script src="mootools.js"></script>
        <script>
            window.addEvent('domready', function(){
                console.log($$('p').length); // 3
            });
        </script>
    </head>

    <body>
```

```
        <img class="viewable" src="hello.png">
        <p>some text.</p>
        <p>another text.</p>
        <div class="viewable">
            <p>more text here</p>
        </div>
    </body>
</html>
```

Instead of calling document.getElementsByTagName('p') in this example, we simply used $$('p') and it returns similar results. Checking the length property of the returned value, we see that the number of elements returned is 3, which is consistent with our previous getElementsByTagName example.

Replacing getElementsByClassName though, is a bit different because you can't just pass the class name:

```
<html>
    <head>
        <title>test</title>
        <script src="mootools.js"></script>
        <script>
            window.addEvent('domready', function(){
                console.log($$('viewable').length); // 0
            });
        </script>
    </head>

    <body>
        <img class="viewable" src="hello.png">
        <p>some text.</p>
        <p>another text.</p>
        <div class="viewable">
            <p>more text here</p>
        </div>
    </body>
</html>
```

Calling $$('viewable') gives back a return value with a length property of 0—which means that no elements were selected. This is because the $$ function's argument, the string selector, is expected to be a *CSS Selector*.

The semantics of CSS selectors is a complex subject in itself, and we'll learn more about them in Chapter 9 when we discuss the selector engine. For now, it is enough to understand that an identifier such as p or viewable is interpreted in CSS selector semantics as a type selector. Type selectors correspond to particular HTML tags. When we use $$('p'), it returned all elements with the tag p. In the same way, $$('viewable') will return all elements with the tag viewable—which, in the case of our example, corresponds to no elements.

In order to use $$ to select elements with the particular classname, you must prefix your classname with a period:

```
<html>
    <head>
        <title>test</title>
        <script src="mootools.js"></script>
        <script>
            window.addEvent('domready', function(){
                console.log($$('.viewable').length); // 2
```

```
            });
        </script>
    </head>

    <body>
        <img class="viewable" src="hello.png">
        <p>some text.</p>
        <p>another text.</p>
        <div class="viewable">
            <p>more text here</p>
        </div>
    </body>
</html>
```

Notice that we used the argument '.viewable' instead of 'viewable' like in the previous example. By prepending a period to the identifier, we tell $$ that we're looking for a class and not an element. The result is that $$('.viewable') returns a value with the length property of 2, which is what we'd expect.

The $$ function can also be used to retrieve elements using their ids by prepending the selector id with a hash symbol:

```
<html>
    <head>
        <title>test</title>
        <script src="mootools.js"></script>
        <script>
            window.addEvent('domready', function(){
                console.log($$('#hello').length); // 1
            });
        </script>
    </head>

    <body>
        <img id="hello" class="viewable" src="hello.png">
        <p>some text.</p>
        <p>another text.</p>
        <div class="viewable">
            <p>more text here</p>
        </div>
    </body>
</html>
```

Here we called $$ with the argument '#hello', which means we want to select all elements with the id "hello". Take note, though, that while they do the same thing here, document.id and $$ are not interchangeable: the former always returns a single element, while the latter always returns a collection of elements—a collection that contains a single element in this case.

While getElementsByTagName and getElementsByClassName return NodeList instances, the $$ function returns another array-like object called Elements. As its name implies, Elements is a collection of MooTools Element objects. We'll learn more about Elements later, but right now it's important to keep in mind that the selector functions in MooTools that return a collection of elements will return an Elements instance and not a NodeList.

Unlike document.id, which is idempotent, the $$ function will always return a new instance of Elements, even when called with the same arguments:

```html
<html>
    <head>
        <title>test</title>
        <script src="mootools.js"></script>
        <script>
            window.addEvent('domready', function(){
                console.log($$('.viewable') === $$('.viewable')); // false
            });
        </script>
    </head>

    <body>
        <img class="viewable" src="hello.png">
        <p>some text.</p>
        <p>another text.</p>
        <div class="viewable">
            <p>more text here</p>
        </div>
    </body>
</html>
```

Our snippet $$('.viewable') === $$('.viewable') is false here because the result of a $$ call will always return a new Elements instance, and therefore these two calls produce different objects. In the same vein, passing the result of a previous $$ call to another, like $$($$('.viewable')), won't return the same Elements instance, unlike document.id, which returns the same element no matter how many times it's applied.

Passing a single element—such as the result of document.id or $—to $$ will produce a new Elements instance with a single item, but passing an Elements instance—such as the result of $$—to document.id or $ will produce null:

```html
<html>
    <head>
        <title>test</title>
        <script src="mootools.js"></script>
        <script>
            window.addEvent('domready', function(){
                var img = $('hello');
                var viewable = $$('viewable');

                console.log($$(img).length); // 1
                console.log($$(img)[0] === img); // true

                console.log($(viewable)); // null
            });
        </script>
    </head>

    <body>
        <img id="hello" class="viewable" src="hello.png">
        <p>some text.</p>
        <p>another text.</p>
        <div class="viewable">
            <p>more text here</p>
        </div>
```

```
    </body>
</html>
```

So far we've used the id, the tag, and the class selectors, but not together. The $$ function also allows for the use of combined CSS selectors, which use combinations of all of these as well as more complex CSS selectors:

```
<html>
    <head>
        <title>test</title>
        <script src="mootools.js"></script>
        <script>
            window.addEvent('domready', function(){

                // all images with the class viewable..
                console.log($$('img.viewable').length); // 1

                // all images that have the src attribute
                console.log($$('img[src]').length); // 2

                // all images with the src attribute 'hi.png'
                console.log($$('img[src="hi.png"]').length); // 1

                // all elements that have class attributes
                console.log($$('[class]').length); // 2

                // all paragraphs and images
                console.log($$('p, img').length); // 5

            });
        </script>
    </head>

    <body>
        <img id="hello" class="viewable" src="hello.png">
        <img src="hi.png">
        <p>some text.</p>
        <p>another text.</p>
        <div class="viewable">
            <p>more text here</p>
        </div>
    </body>
</html>
```

We'll learn more about complex CSS selectors in Chapter 9 when we discuss Slick, the selector engine that MooTools uses. For now, it's enough to remember that $$ accepts not only simple selectors but complex selectors as well.

Aside from $$, MooTools also provides two other selector functions that accept CSS selector strings as arguments. The first one is getElements, which is actually an Element method. When invoked from an element, getElements returns the elements inside the element that match the selector string. To illustrate, let's look at this snippet:

```
<html>
    <head>
        <title>test</title>
```

```
        <script src="mootools.js"></script>
        <script>
            window.addEvent('domready', function(){
                console.log($('wrapper').getElements('p').length); // 2
            });
        </script>
    </head>

    <body>
        <img id="hello" class="viewable" src="hello.png">
        <img src="hi.png">
        <p>some text.</p>
        <div id="wrapper" class="viewable">
            <p>more text here</p>
            <p>another text.</p>
        </div>
    </body>
</html>
```

First we use $('wrapper') to select the element with the id wrapper, which is our div element. Next, we call the getElements method of our div element and pass the argument 'p', and we get back an Elements instance that contains the two paragraph elements inside our div element. To translate this to English, our code says, "From the element with the id 'wrapper', get all elements with the tag 'p'."

The great thing about getElements is that it's an Element method: you can use it to limit the search to only a part of the DOM Tree. In our example, the search is limited to only the contents of our div, which means that the search will be faster.

You can actually use getElements to replace $$ by calling document.getElements, which searches the whole document:

```
<html>
    <head>
        <title>test</title>
        <script src="mootools.js"></script>
        <script>
            window.addEvent('domready', function(){
                console.log($$('p').length); // 3
                console.log(document.getElements('p').length); // 3
            });
        </script>
    </head>

    <body>
        <img id="hello" class="viewable" src="hello.png">
        <img src="hi.png">
        <p>some text.</p>
        <div id="wrapper" class="viewable">
            <p>more text here</p>
            <p>another text.</p>
        </div>
    </body>
</html>
```

Another element method, getElement, works like getElements—but instead of returning an Elements instance, it returns a single Element that matches the selector string.

```
<html>
    <head>
        <title>test</title>
        <script src="mootools.js"></script>
        <script>
            window.addEvent('domready', function(){
                console.log($('wrapper').getElement('p').get('text')); // 'more text here'
            });
        </script>
    </head>

    <body>
        <img id="hello" class="viewable" src="hello.png">
        <img src="hi.png">
        <p>some text.</p>
        <div id="wrapper" class="viewable">
            <p>more text here</p>
            <p>another text.</p>
        </div>
    </body>
</html>
```

Like our getElements example, we pass the argument 'p' as our selector string. This time, though, we use the method getElement, which returns only the first matching element. In this case, we confirm this by getting the text contained by our paragraph, which is 'more text here' as expected.

▓ **Note** It is worth noting that the getElement and getElements functions act like the MooTools counterparts of the native querySelector and querySelectorAll functions, respectively. However, these two native methods have limited browser support, unlike the MooTools methods that work across all supported browsers. Keep in mind, though, that they are not interchangeable within MooTools.

Both getElements and getElement have a trick up their sleeves: they understand CSS combinators as prefixes. **Combinators** are special markers that join two simple selectors, and we'll learn more about them in Chapter 9. By default, getElement and getElements use the **descendant combinator** when no combinator-prefix is present in the argument passed to them. The descendant selector is marked by a space in between two simple selectors, and it's used to select elements within a particular element. Doing $('wrapper').getElements('p'), for example, is the same as doing $$('#wrapper p').

But to illustrate how combinator-prefixes work with these two functions, we need a more complex combinator as an example. The **adjacent sibling combinator**, denoted by +, is used to select an element that is an adjacent sibling of an element. Let's take a look at how we can use it:

```
<html>
    <head>
        <title>test</title>
        <script src="mootools.js"></script>
        <script>
            window.addEvent('domready', function(){
                console.log($('hello').getElement('+').get('src')); // 'hi.png'
            });
```

```
        </script>
    </head>

    <body>
        <img id="hello" class="viewable" src="hello.png">
        <img src="hi.png">
        <p>some text.</p>
        <div id="wrapper" class="viewable">
            <p>more text here</p>
            <p>another text.</p>
        </div>
    </body>
</html>
```

First we select the element with an id "hello", which is the first image element in our DOM Tree. We then call the getElement method of this element, passing the adjacent sibling selector '+' as an argument. This returns the first adjacent sibling of our element, which is the second image element in this example. We confirm this by calling the get method of the element returned by getElement to retrieve the value of its src attribute.

Relation-Based Selectors

The last set of selector functions select elements based on their relation to a particular element. These selector functions are methods of the Element type, and are therefore available to all element objects.

The first ones are the **sibling selectors**, getPrevious and getNext, which return the previous and next sibling element of an element. Both functions take an optional selector argument, which is used to match the sibling. When invoked without an argument, they return the adjacent sibling of the element.

```
<html>
    <head>
        <title>test</title>
        <script src="mootools.js"></script>
        <script>
            window.addEvent('domready', function(){
                var el = $('img2');

                // without arguments
                console.log(el.getPrevious().get('id')); // 'img1'
                console.log(el.getNext().get('id')); // 'div2'

                // with selector arguments
                console.log(el.getPrevious('div').get('id')); // 'div1'
                console.log(el.getNext('.textual').get('id')); // 'p2'
            });
        </script>
    </head>

    <body>
        <p id="p1" class="textual">Hello!</p>
        <div id="div1"></div>
        <img id="img1" class="viewable" src="hello.png">
        <img id="img2" src="hi.png">
        <div id="div2"></div>
```

```
        <p id="p2" class="textual">Hi!</p>
    </body>
</html>
```

The getPrevious and getNext methods have "greedy" versions, getAllPrevious and getAllNext, which return an Elements instance instead of a single element. Like their non-greedy counterparts, these two methods also accept an optional selector argument that is used to match the elements.

```
<html>
    <head>
        <title>test</title>
        <script src="mootools.js"></script>
        <script>
            window.addEvent('domready', function(){
                var el = $('img2');

                // without arguments
                console.log(el.getAllPrevious().length); // 3
                console.log(el.getAllNext().length); // 2

                // with selector arguments
                console.log(el.getAllPrevious('div').length); // 1
                console.log(el.getAllNext('.textual').length); // 1
            });
        </script>
    </head>

    <body>
        <p id="p1" class="textual">Hello!</p>
        <div id="div1"></div>
        <img id="img1" class="viewable" src="hello.png">
        <img id="img2" src="hi.png">
        <div id="div2"></div>
        <p id="p2" class="textual">Hi!</p>
    </body>
</html>
```

The getPrevious and getNext methods return either a single element or null if there is no sibling found, while getAllPrevious and getAllNext always return an Elements instance.

The getSiblings method is like a combination of both getAllPrevious and getAllNext methods, and returns all siblings regardless of position:

```
<html>
    <head>
        <title>test</title>
        <script src="mootools.js"></script>
        <script>
            window.addEvent('domready', function(){
                var el = $('img2');

                // without arguments
                console.log(el.getSiblings().length); // 5

                // with selector arguments
                console.log(el.getSiblings('.textual').length); // 2
```

```
            });
        </script>
    </head>

    <body>
        <p id="p1" class="textual">Hello!</p>
        <div id="div1"></div>
        <img id="img1" class="viewable" src="hello.png">
        <img id="img2" src="hi.png">
        <div id="div2"></div>
        <p id="p2" class="textual">Hi!</p>
    </body>
</html>
```

The next set of relation-based selector functions comprises the **children selectors**, the first of which is the getChildren method of Element instances. Like the previous relation-based selector functions, getChildren can take an optional selector string argument to limit the return value. When invoked without an argument, it returns all child elements regardless of type.

```
<html>
    <head>
        <title>test</title>
        <script src="mootools.js"></script>
        <script>
            window.addEvent('domready', function(){
                var el = $('wrapper');

                // without arguments
                console.log(el.getChildren().length); // 4

                // with selector argument
                console.log(el.getChildren('img').length); // 2

                // getChildren versus getElements
                console.log(el.getElements('*').length); // 6
            });
        </script>
    </head>

    <body>
        <div id="wrapper">
            <div id="hello">
                <p>Hello World!</p>
            </div>
            <img src="img1.png">
            <div id="hi">
                <p>Hi Universe!</p>
            </div>
            <img src="img2.png">
        </div>
    </body>
</html>
```

Notice the last line in our code where we used the getElements method instead of the getChildren method. Calling getElements with the universal selector returns an Elements collection with six items, but getChildren only returns four items. This is because getChildren selects child nodes while getElements selects descendant nodes by default: getChildren does not count the two paragraph elements inside the divs since they're descendants of wrapper and not direct child nodes.

The last two children selector functions are getFirst and getLast, which respectively return the first and last child of an element. Like the other functions so far, you can pass an optional selector string argument to limit the selection.

```html
<html>
    <head>
        <title>test</title>
        <script src="mootools.js"></script>
        <script>
            window.addEvent('domready', function(){
                var el = $('wrapper');

                // without arguments
                console.log(el.getFirst().get('id')); // 'hello'
                console.log(el.getLast().get('id')); // 'img2'

                // with selector argument
                console.log(el.getFirst('img').get('id')); // 'img1'
                console.log(el.getLast('div').get('id')); // 'hi'
            });
        </script>
    </head>

    <body>
        <div id="wrapper">
            <div id="hello">
                <p>Hello World!</p>
            </div>
            <img id="img1" src="img1.png">
            <div id="hi">
                <p>Hi Universe!</p>
            </div>
            <img id="img2" src="img2.png">
        </div>
    </body>
</html>
```

And finally, we have the **parent selector function**, getParent, which returns the parent element of a particular element. When called without an argument, getParent returns the direct parent of the element, while calling it with a selector argument returns the first parent (direct or indirect) that satisfies the selector matcher.

```html
<html>
    <head>
        <title>test</title>
        <script src="mootools.js"></script>
        <script>
            window.addEvent('domready', function(){
                var el = $('world');

                // without an argument
                console.log(el.getParent().get('tag')); // 'p'
```

```
                    // with selector arguments
                    console.log(el.getParent('section').get('id')); // 'greeting'
                    console.log(el.getParent('div').get('id')); // 'wrapper'
                });
            </script>
        </head>

        <body>
            <div id="wrapper">
                <section id="greeting">
                    <p>
                        Hello <em id="world">World</em>!
                    </p>
                </section>
            </div>
        </body>
    </html>
```

The getParent selector function also has a greedy version, getAllParents, which works like the getParent method but returns all parents of an element as an Elements collection.

```
<html>
    <head>
        <title>test</title>
        <script src="mootools.js"></script>
        <script>
            window.addEvent('domready', function(){
                var el = $('world');

                // without an argument
                console.log(el.getParents().length); // 6

                // with selector arguments
                console.log(el.getParents('div, p').length); // 3
                console.log(el.getParents('div').length); // 2
            });
        </script>
    </head>

    <body>
        <div>
            <div id="wrapper">
                <section id="greeting">
                    <p>
                        Hello <em id="world">World</em>!
                    </p>
                </section>
            </div>
        </div>
    </body>
</html>
```

You'll notice that the getParent method, when called without an argument, returned an Elements collection with six members. We get six and not five because the root element, <html> is also counted as a parent.

An Elemental Segue

Before we move on, we need to clear up some things about Element objects and Elements objects. As I've mentioned in passing, an Element object refers to a single element node in the DOM Tree, while an Elements object is an array-like collection that represents a group of Element objects. We'll have an in-depth look at these types in a later section, so right now we'll discuss some important details regarding their usage.

The first one involves the use of Element and Elements for **existence checks**. All MooTools selector functions that return a single element—like document.id or getElement—will return either an Element instance, or null. This makes it easy to check for the existence of an element:

```
<html>
    <head>
        <title>test</title>
        <script src="mootools.js"></script>
        <script>
            window.addEvent('domready', function(){
                var el1 = document.getElement('div');
                console.log( el1 ? 'el1 exists!' : 'el1 does not exist!'); // 'el1 exists!'

                var el2 - document.getElement('section');
                console.log( el2 ? 'el2 exists!' : 'el2 does not
exist!'
            });
        </script>
    </head>

    <body>
        <p id="para1">some text.</p>
        <p>another text.</p>
        <div class="viewable">
            <p>more text here</p>
        </div>
    </body>
</html>
```

For our first existence check, we use document.getElement to return the first div in our document. Because this div element exists, the function returns an element object and our console.log call outputs 'el1 exists!'. Our second check, on the other hand, tries to select the first section element in the document. Since there are no section elements in our document, the function returns null and console.log outputs "el2 does not exist!". So for functions that return single elements or null, checking the existence of an element is simply a matter of a falsy comparison.

Functions that return Elements objects, in contrast, aren't as straightforward. These functions—like $$ and getElements—always return an Elements collection, regardless of whether it did or did not find elements. This means that if no elements are found, you won't get back a null value, but simply an Elements instance containing no elements. Now if you recall our previous discussion on types, we learned that all array-like objects—empty or not—are truthy values, which means that a simple truth check like we did above won't suffice.

Instead, of using Boolean comparison, we need to access the `length` property of `Elements` objects to determine whether the object is empty. Thus, we could do the following:

```html
<html>
    <head>
        <title>test</title>
        <script src="mootools.js"></script>
        <script>
            window.addEvent('domready', function(){
                var els1 = document.getElements('div');
                console.log( els1.length > 0 ? 'els1 has members!' : 'els1 is empty!'); //
'els1 has members!'

                var els2 = document.getElements('section');
                console.log( els2.length > 0 ? 'els2 has members!' : 'els2 is empty!'); //
'els2 is empty!'
            });
        </script>
    </head>

    <body>
        <p id="para1">some text.</p>
        <p>another text.</p>
        <div class="viewable">
            <p>more text here</p>
        </div>
    </body>
</html>
```

Here we compared the `length` property of the returned `Elements` objects to see if they're greater than 0. If the length is greater than 0, it implies that our collection isn't empty, and the opposite if it's not greater than 0.

`Elements` also has a very interesting interface. We've seen that a single element object has its own set of special methods, like get or destroy. These methods are inherited by element objects from `Element.prototype`. The interesting thing about these methods is that they can be used with an `Elements` instance as you would in a single element object.

To illustrate, we'll use one of the basic element methods, get, to return the text of an element:

```html
<html>
    <head>
        <title>test</title>
        <script src="mootools.js"></script>
        <script>
            window.addEvent('domready', function(){
                console.log($('para1').get('text')); // 'some text.'
            });
        </script>
    </head>

    <body>
        <p id="para1">some text.</p>
        <p>another text.</p>
        <div class="viewable">
            <p>more text here</p>
        </div>
```

```
    </body>
</html>
```

First we select our paragraph element using the $ function, as in $('para1'). This returns the paragraph element, whose get method we invoke with the argument 'text' to retrieve the text inside the element. This method returns a string, 'some text' which corresponds to the text of our paragraph.

Nothing surprising so far. But what happens if instead of a single element, we invoke the get method of an Elements collection?

```
<html>
    <head>
        <title>test</title>
        <script src="mootools.js"></script>
        <script>
            window.addEvent('domready', function(){
                var result = $$('p').get('text');
                console.log(result); // ['some text.', 'another text.', 'more text here']
                console.log(typeOf(result)); // 'array'
            });
        </script>
    </head>

    <body>
        <p id="para1">some text.</p>
        <p>another text.</p>
        <div class="viewable">
            <p>more text here</p>
        </div>
    </body>
</html>
```

We select all the paragraphs in the document using the $$ function, and then we call the get method of the returned Elements object, storing it in our result variable. When we log the result variable, it shows us that the get method doesn't return a string like our previous example. Instead, it returns an array of strings.

The basic rule is that when an Element method is called on an Elements instance, it will return an array of results instead of a single return value. The code above could be done like so:

```
<html>
    <head>
        <title>test</title>
        <script src="mootools.js"></script>
        <script>
            window.addEvent('domready', function(){
                var result = [];

                $$('p').each(function(element){
                    result.push(element.get('text'));
                });

                console.log(result); // ['some text.', 'another text.', 'more text here']
                console.log(typeOf(result)); // 'array'
            });
        </script>
    </head>
```

```
        <body>
            <p id="para1">some text.</p>
            <p>another text.</p>
            <div class="viewable">
                <p>more text here</p>
            </div>
        </body>
    </html>
```

Calling an `Element` method on an `Elements` instance will iterate over each element in the `Elements` collection and then invoke that particular method on each element. Therefore, doing `$$('p').get('text')` is technically the same as invoking the get method of each element in the collection and storing the value in an array.

A tricky thing to consider is when calling an `Element` method that returns a collection object on an `Elements` instance. If we do `$('id').getParents()`, for example, the method will return an `Elements` collection containing all the parent element objects of the element with the id "id". If we call `$$('a').getParents()`, on the other hand, it will return an array containing several `Elements` object, each representing the parent elements of each anchor element in the document. This could get confusing really fast.

To avoid the complexity of nested collections, it is recommended you perform operations like this by iterating over each element in the `Elements` object. You can easily do this using the each method of `Elements`. So instead of doing `$$('a').getParents()`, you could do:

```
$$('a').each(function(element){
    element.getParents();
});
```

The each function of an `Elements` object is similar to the each function of arrays: it takes a single argument, `callback`, which is a function with the signature: `function(item, index, collection)`. It then iterates over each element in the collection and invokes the `callback` function, passing in the appropriate arguments.

Interestingly, MooTools uses the each method internally to transform `Element` methods into methods that can be used on `Elements`. We'll see how MooTools does this when we look at these types later in this chapter.

Moving Elements Around

Now that we know how to select elements from the DOM Tree, the next thing we need to learn is how to move them around. However, since we're moving away from simply selecting elements to actually changing them, it is important that we first consider the DOM Tree's relationship to the rendered page.

The DOM Tree that's accessible for our use via the JavaScript DOM API isn't just an abstraction of the page, it is a true representation of the document. Any changes we make in the DOM Tree are reflected immediately and will be apparent to the user interacting with your page. For instance, changing the src attribute of an image element or changing the styles of a paragraph will immediately trigger a reflow and a repaint, which then updates the displayed page. Changing the property of an element doesn't just affect the DOM Tree, it also affects what your users will see on their screen.

It's important to keep this idea in mind when working with the DOM Tree and elements in general. Some operations performed on elements will be silent and will not show any visible change on the page, but most actions will trigger a noticeable change. Remembering this helps us make informed decisions as to how to craft our code, and will make our programs better.

inject

MooTools provides several Element methods for moving elements in and around the DOM Tree, the most popular being inject. It has two forms, the simpler of which involves passing the id of the element to where the subject element will be moved as an argument. For example, suppose we have this section in our DOM Tree:

```
<div id="items"></div>
<a id="home-link" href="home.html">Home Page</a>
```

Now we want to move the link inside the empty div. We can use the inject method like so:

```
var link = $('home-link');
link.inject('items');
```

First we select our link element using $('home-link') and store it in a variable link. We then call the inject method of the element, passing in the id of our div, 'items', as a string. As a result, the DOM Tree now looks like this:

```
<div id="items">
    <a id="home-link" href="home.html">Home Page</a>
</div>
```

By calling the inject method, we turn our link object—which was originally a sibling of the div—into a child of the div object. The inject method therefore takes the subject (i.e., the element from which the method was called) and moves it into the target (i.e., the element passed as an argument to inject).

▓ **Note** We'll be using the previous form for our examples from now on. Instead of showing the whole HTML source, we'll only show snippets that represent sections in our DOM Tree. All of the HTML source code in our examples should go into the <body> tag, while all our JavaScript source code is supposed to go into a <script> tag in the head, wrapped in a DOMReady handler. We're using this form for two reasons: to keep our examples shorter and to work around the fact that the actions modify the DOM Tree as an object and not the actual HTML source. That final reason is important: modifying the DOM Tree does not actually change the HTML source code, only the object representation of it (i.e., the DOM Tree itself).

The inject method uses document.id internally, which is why we can simply pass a string id as an argument. But one thing we learned about document.id is that it's idempotent: passing an element object to document.id will return the same element object. This means that we can also do the following to achieve the same results:

```
var link = $('home-link'),
    div = $('items');

link.inject(div);
```

Instead of passing a string argument, we simply pass an actual element object that will be the new parent of our link object. The resulting DOM Tree will be the same:

```
<div id="items">
    <a id="home-link" href="home.html">Home Page</a>
</div>
```

The second form of the inject method involves passing a second argument called where. This is a string argument that tells inject exactly where to place the element. Suppose we have the following section in our DOM Tree:

```
<div id="items">
    <a href="profile.html">Profile</a>
    <a href="contact.html">Contact</a>
</div>
<a id="home-link" href="home.html">Home Page</a>
```

We want to move our "home-link" link element into the "items" div, but we want it to go on the top before any other element. If we do a simple inject:

```
var link = $('home-link');
link.inject('items');
```

We'll get this:

```
<div id="items">
    <a href="profile.html">Profile</a>
    <a href="contact.html">Contact</a>
    <a id="home-link" href="home.html">Home Page</a>
</div>
```

Our home-link element is injected into the bottom of the items div, which is not what we wanted. However, we can use the second form of the inject method by passing a second argument, where:

```
var link = $('home-link');
link.inject('items', 'top');
```

This will produce a result like this:

```
<div id="items">
    <a id="home-link" href="home.html">Home Page</a>
    <a href="profile.html">Profile</a>
    <a href="contact.html">Contact</a>
</div>
```

By specifying the where argument as 'top', we're able to control the inject method's positioning of the element. By default, the inject method uses the where option 'bottom' when no argument is specified, which is why it usually inserts the subject element as the last child of the target.

Aside from 'top' and 'bottom', you can also use two other values as arguments to where: 'before' and 'after'. These two options alter the behavior of inject such that the method no longer moves the subject element to inside the target, but moves the subject around the target as a sibling.

To illustrate, let's take the original DOM Tree section:

```
<div id="items">
    <a href="profile.html">Profile</a>
    <a href="contact.html">Contact</a>
</div>
<a id="home-link" href="home.html">Home Page</a>
```

Now let's use 'before' as the argument:

```
var link = $('home-link');
link.inject('items', 'before');
```

Our resulting DOM Tree section will now look like this:

```
<a id="home-link" href="home.html">Home Page</a>
<div id="items">
    <a href="profile.html">Profile</a>
    <a href="contact.html">Contact</a>
</div>
```

Instead of moving the link inside the items div, the inject method moved the link object so that it comes before the items div. On the other hand, if we use the 'after' option:

```
var link = $('home-link');
link.inject('items', 'after');
```

Our resulting DOM Tree section will remain the same:

```
<div id="items">
    <a href="profile.html">Profile</a>
    <a href="contact.html">Contact</a>
</div>
<a id="home-link" href="home.html">Home Page</a>
```

Because the link object is already after the items div, calling link.inject('items', 'after') has no effect.

The 'before' and 'after' options may not seem that useful in these examples, but they can actually help in fine-tuning your inserts. Suppose we have the following section:

```
<div id="items">
    <a href="home.html">Home Page</a>
    <a href="profile.html">Profile</a>
    <a href="contact.html">Contact</a>
</div>
<a id="projects-link" href="projects.html">Projects</a>
```

Now we want to move the projects-link element into the items div, but we want it to be the second element inside items. We can't use 'top' or 'bottom' because they insert elements at the topmost and bottommost area of the target, but we can use 'after':

```
var link = $('projects-link');
var links = $('items').getElements('a');

link.inject(links[0], 'after');
```

Right after we select our projects-link element, we use the getElements method to select all the links inside out items div. Now instead of injecting projects-link right inside our items div, we tell the inject function to insert the subject element after the first link element inside items—which we reference by accessing the element via its numeric index (collections are array-like, remember?). The resulting section looks like this:

```
<div id="items">
    <a href="home.html">Home Page</a>
    <a id="projects-link" href="projects.html">Projects</a>
    <a href="profile.html">Profile</a>
    <a href="contact.html">Contact</a>
</div>
```

Aside from showing us a great way to use the 'after' option, this example also gives us a new insight about moving elements: it's not just about parents and children. For the most part, a lot of DOM element movement is concerned with inserting elements into other elements but there are also times when you'll want to do sibling-based insertions, as we did above.

Like all Element methods, inject can also be used with an Elements instance. Suppose we have these two lists:

```
<ul id="first">
    <li>Item A</li>
    <li>Item B</li>
    <li>Item C</li>
</ul>

<ul id="second">
</ul>
```

To transfer all the list items from the first list to the second list, all we have to do is to select those items and use inject:

```
var items = $('first').getElements('li');
items.inject('second');
```

This will move items between lists, producing the following DOM Tree section:

```
<ul id="first">
</ul>

<ul id="second">
    <li>Item A</li>
    <li>Item B</li>
    <li>Item C</li>
</ul>
```

An important thing to note, though is that you can't use an Elements instance as the target for inject. Because inject uses document.id internally, passing an Elements instance to will result in a null value as the target and will therefore throw an error.

replaces

The next movement method is called replaces, and it's used to replace one element with another.

```
<div>
    <a id="home-link" href="home.html">Home</a>
</div>

<a id="profile-link" href="profile.html">Profile</a>
```

Now we want to replace the home-link element with the profile-link element, so we use replaces:

```
var link = $('profile-link');
link.replaces('home-link');
```

Like the inject method, the replaces method also uses document.id internally, which means we can pass it either a string id or an actual element—but not an Elements instance. Running the script above, our DOM Tree will now look like this:

```
<div>
    <a id="profile-link" href="profile.html">Profile</a>
</div>
```

The profile-link element was moved to the original position of the home-link element, thereby replacing that element. But what happens to the home-link element? The short answer is that it gets destroyed and removed from the DOM Tree. This is an important thing to remember when using replaces: the target element that's replaced by the subject will be removed and destroyed—and that includes any elements inside that target element.

It might seem that using replaces isn't a good idea, especially because it tends to destroy elements. However, when we use it with the element creation techniques we'll discuss in the next section, it'll make a lot more sense: you'll see that you can use replaces to update elements in the DOM Tree with new ones.

One more caveat with replaces, though: don't use it for an Elements collection with more than one item or you'll get errors. This is because replaces removes the original element from the DOM, thereby turning it into a null value. For example, if we do $$('section').replaces('main-div'), the first section element will be used to replace the main-div element and main-div will be destroyed. The same process will be called for the next section element, but since main-div is now destroyed, it will try to replace a null value with an element—resulting in an error. My advice is to use replaces for single element-with-element replacements.

wraps

Next on our list is another element method called wraps. As its name implies, wraps takes the subject element and wraps the target element with it:

```
<a id="home-link" href="home.html">Home</a>
<div id="items"></div>
```

Now we'll use wraps to make the items div enclose the home-link element:

```
var items = $('items');
items.wraps('home-link');
```

Our resulting section will now look like this:

```
<div id="items">
    <a id="home-link" href="home.html">Home</a>
</div>
```

Like inject and replaces, wraps also uses document.id internally so you can pass string ids or element objects (but again, not Elements instances). And, like inject, wraps can also take a second argument so you can specify where the target element will be inserted. This is useful when your wrapping element already has children, like so:

```
<a id="home-link" href="home.html">Home</a>
<div id="items">
    <a href="profile.html">Profile</a>
</div>
```

By default, wraps uses 'bottom' as the value for the second argument, but you can also pass the other option values such as 'top':

```
var items = $('items');
items.wraps('home-link', 'top');
```

This produces the following DOM Tree section as a result:

```
<div id="items">
    <a id="home-link" href="home.html">Home</a>
    <a href="profile.html">Profile</a>
</div>
```

What's interesting with the `wraps` method is that it is similar to `replaces`: the subject element replaces the target element by taking its position in the DOM Tree. Unlike `replaces` however, `wraps` does not discard the target element but turns it into a child node of the subject. In the examples above, the items div element was moved to the original position of the home-link element, but home-link wasn't removed from the DOM Tree. Instead, it was moved inside the items div.

This behavior has weird consequences when `wraps` is used on an `Elements` instance. Take, for example, the following section:

```
<a id="home-link" href="home.html">Home</a>

<div id="div1"></div>
<div id="div2"></div>
<div id="div3"></div>
```

Now let's call `wraps` on a collection of divs:

```
var divs = $$('div');
divs.wraps('home-link');
```

The resulting DOM Tree section will look like this:

```
<div id="div1">
    <div id="div2">
        <div id="div3">
            <a id="home-link" href="home.html">Home</a>
        </div>
    </div>
</div>
```

To understand why we get this result, we need to remember that the `Elements` versions of `Element` methods are modified so they can be used with collections. This modification involves adding an internal loop that applies the method to each item of the collection. Our `wraps` code above can therefore be rewritten like this:

```
var divs = $$('div');
divs.each(function(div){
    div.wraps('home-link');
});
```

In the first iteration of the loop, the first div object, div1, is inserted in the original position of the home-link element, thereby replacing it. The home-link element is then inserted inside div1, turning it into a child node of the div. The loop then continues, and the second div, div2, is used to replace home-link. Because home-link is now inside div1, div2 is also injected inside div1 first so that it can take the new position of home-link and then home-link is again injected into div2. The process is repeated a third time for div3, and the final result is what we see in the DOM Tree section above. Because of this cascading behavior, it is advised not to use `wraps` for Elements instances.

grab

The three movement methods we've seen so far—inject, replaces, and wraps—all follow the same pattern: the element from where the methods were called (the subject) is the element that's going to be moved to another location (the target). These methods are therefore *nominative* methods because the element becomes the subject of the method. However, MooTools has two other methods that are *accusative*. In this case, the element from where the methods are called becomes the target and the arguments passed to the methods are the ones that become the subject of the movement. That sounds more complicated than it is, so let's look at a few examples to make it clear.

The first of these two accusative methods is grab, which works like inject but instead of moving the subject, it moves the target.

```
<div id="items"></div>
<a id="home-link" href="home.html">Home Page</a>
```

With this example, we can move home-link to within items using grab:

```
var items = $('items');
items.grab('home-link');
```

This produces the following section in the DOM Tree:

```
<div id="items">
    <a id="home-link" href="home.html">Home Page</a>
</div>
```

The grab method moved the home-link element inside the items div. This illustrates why we call grab accusative: the subject of our code, items, isn't the one being moved. Instead, the target—which in our example is home-link—is the one that's inserted into the subject. This is the reverse of how nominative methods work. With a nominative method like inject, if we do $('items').inject('home-link'), the items div will be inserted inside home-link. However, this grab code would be equivalent to a reversed form of inject: $('home-link').inject('items').

Like inject, grab uses document.id internally, so you can pass a string id or an element object as an argument (but not an Elements instance). The grab method also accepts where arguments, such as 'bottom' and 'top'.

The second accusative method, and the last movement method, is called adopt. It is similar to grab, but it allows for multiple arguments: you can pass string ids, element objects, or even Elements instances. Revisiting our earlier two-list example:

```
<ul id="first">
    <li>Item A</li>
    <li>Item B</li>
    <li>Item C</li>
</ul>

<ul id="second">
</ul>
```

We can move the items from the first list to the second using adopt:

```
var listItems = $('first').getElements('li');
$('second').adopt(listItems);
```

The result is as we'd expect:

```
<ul id="first">
</ul>
```

```
<ul id="second">
    <li>Item A</li>
    <li>Item B</li>
    <li>Item C</li>
</ul>
```

Unlike all other methods so far, adopt allows for several elements at once, so passing an `Elements` instance will not result in an error. It does not support where arguments, but it can take more than one argument. This allows us, for example, to move items from several places instantly:

```
<ul id="first">
    <li>Item A</li>
    <li>Item B</li>
    <li>Item C</li>
</ul>

<ul id="second">
    <li>Item D</li>
    <li id="itemE">Item E</li>
</ul>

<ul id="third">
    <li>Item F</li>
    <li>Item G</li>
</ul>

<ul id="final">
</ul>
```

We want to move all list items from the first and third lists into the final list and we also want to move the list item with the id "itemE" to the final list. We can do this quickly using adopt:

```
var firstItems = $('first').getElements('li');
var thirdItems = $('third').getElements('li');

$('final').adopt(firstItems, thirdItems, $('itemE'));
```

And here's the result:

```
<ul id="first">
</ul>

<ul id="second">
    <li>Item D</li>
</ul>

<ul id="third">
</ul>

<ul id="final">
    <li>Item A</li>
    <li>Item B</li>
    <li>Item C</li>
    <li>Item F</li>
    <li>Item G</li>
```

```
        <li id="itemE">Item E</li>
</ul>
```

With a single adopt call, we were able to move several elements from different sources at once. This makes adopt ideal for multiple transfers between elements.

▦ **Note** The adopt method isn't just fast in terms of code: it's also fast internally because it uses a special DOM feature called **document fragments**. A document fragment is like a mini DOM Tree that can be used to store elements prior to inserting them into the DOM. The amazing thing about this feature is that a fragment can be inserted directly into the DOM without having to loop through its contents. This makes for very fast inserts—something that's important for large element collections.

Modifying Element Objects

Aside from moving them around, another common operation on elements is modifying their attributes and styles. MooTools provides both separate and unified APIs for these processes, and we'll look at the methods from these APIs one by one.

Working with Attributes

The first attribute method is setProperty, which is used to add or modify element attributes. It takes two arguments: attribute and value, which are the attribute being set and the value it will be set to.

```
<a id="home-link" href="home.html">Home</a>
```

Here we have a simple link element. We want this link to open in a new page, so we decide to add a target attribute to it and point it to _blank. We can do this using setProperty:

```
var link = $('home-link');
link.setProperty('target', '_blank');
```

This will add a new target attribute to our element, like so:

```
<a id="home-link" href="home.html" target="_blank">Home</a>
```

When the attribute argument is an attribute that does not exist yet on the element, setProperty will add this new attribute to the element. However, if the element already has that attribute defined, setProperty will update the value of the attribute. This means we can change the href of our original link like so:

```
var link = $('home-link');
link.setProperty('href', 'otherhome.html');
```

This updates our link's href property:

```
<a id="home-link" href="otherhome.html">Home</a>
```

The setProperty method is not limited to attributes that are considered "valid" in the sense that they're included in the HTML specs. You can use any attribute you'd like, even weird ones. The snippet

`$('home-link').setProperty('super-weird-attrib', 'wow')`, for example, is just as "valid" as our other example with setProperty.

You can define multiple properties using the setProperties method, which takes a single object argument instead of two string arguments:

```
var link = $('home-link');
link.setProperties({
    'href': 'otherhome.html',
    'target': '_blank',
    'super-weird-attrib': 'wow'
});
```

This will update our original example to produce this:

```
<a id="home-link" href="otherhome.html" target="_blank" super-weird-attrib="wow">Home</a>
```

The getProperty method is the accessor equivalent of setProperty. It takes a single string argument, attribute, and returns the corresponding value of the attribute as a string for existing attributes and null for nonexistent attributes.

```
var link = $('home-link');
console.log(link.getProperty('target')); // '_blank'
console.log(link.getProperty('silliness')); // null
```

It also has a multiple-argument equivalent, getProperties, that accepts several attribute arguments and returns a map of the values:

```
var link = $('home-link');
console.log(link.getProperties('target', 'silliness')); // {target: '_blank', silliness: null}
```

The final attribute method is removeProperty, which is used to remove an attribute from an element. It takes a single argument, attribute, which is the name of the attribute to remove:

```
var link = $('home-link');
console.log(link.getProperty('target')); // '_blank'

// remove the target attribute
link.removeProperty('target');

console.log(link.getProperty('target')); // null
```

An interesting thing to note is that if you pass null as the value argument for the setProperty method, setProperty will behave like removeProperty:

```
var link = $('home-link');
console.log(link.getProperty('target')); // '_blank'

// remove the target attribute
link.setProperty('target', null);

console.log(link.getProperty('target')); // null
```

This works because setProperty checks the value argument and if it is null, it calls removeProperty automatically. The check is actually a non-existence check, which means simply that calling setProperty('target') will trigger removeProperty('target'), because the value argument is undefined (and therefore equal to null).

Working with Styles

While attributes are a straightforward topic, element styles are much more complicated because they involve a discussion of browser style rendering and CSS styles. In order to keep our focus, we'll defer the deep discussion on styles to Chapter 12, when we talk about animation and the Fx classes. For now, we'll talk about the simple style-related methods: setStyle and getStyle.

The setStyle method takes two arguments, property and value. The property argument is a string that corresponds to the specific style property that will be set, while the value argument is the value that will be used for the property.

```
<div id="wrapper"></div>
```

Suppose we have a div element with the id "wrapper" in our DOM Tree and we want to set its background color to black. We can do this using setStyle, like so:

```
var div = $('wrapper');
div.setStyle('background-color', '#000');
```

We called setStyle and passed two arguments: first is the string 'background-color' and the second is another string '#000'. The first argument tells setStyle that we want to change the background-color style property of our div, and the second tells it that we want to change this particular style property to black (#000 is the HEX color code for black).

Internally, the setStyle method works by modifying the element's style property, which is a CSSStyleDeclaration object. An element's style property represents the particular styles defined via the element's style attribute. After we called the code above, the div's style attribute will be updated to reflect the changes in the style property:

```
<div id="wrapper" style="background-color: #000;"></div>
```

This change of the style property will be reflected in the rendered page, and your users will see it in their browser window immediately.

You can set several styles at once using a variant of the setStyle method called setStyles. This variant takes a single object as an argument, each key-value pair of which represents a single style declaration. Suppose we want to update our wrapper div to have a white background and a height of 200px:

```
var div = $('wrapper');
div.setStyles({
    'background-color': '#FFF',
    'height': '200px'
});
```

This results in an update of the div element:

```
<div id="wrapper" style="background-color: #FFF; height: 200px;"></div>
```

The accessor equivalent of setStyle is getStyle. It takes a single argument, property, and returns the value of the style property with that name. Continuing with our example, we can find out the value of our wrapper div's background-color using getStyle:

```
var div = $('wrapper');
console.log(div.getStyle('background-color')); // '#FFF'
```

Finally, like setStyle, getStyle also has a multi-argument method: getStyles. It takes multiple property arguments and returns an object containing the values for those properties.

Get, Set, and Erase

Undoubtedly the most useful set of element modification methods is composed of three simple functions: set, get, and erase. These three methods can be used to do the work of all the modification methods we've seen so far—which gives them their nickname *universal modificators*—and their use extends to areas we haven't covered yet.

These three methods are dynamic: their behavior changes depending on the argument passed to them. In particular, they get their behaviors using a special object called Element.Properties, which defines the rules—called dynamic property objects—for how they behave according to how they were called and the arguments passed to them. We'll learn more about how this all works in a later section, but right now we'll focus on how they're used.

The set method is called the universal setter because it can be used to set the value of almost any element property. It takes two arguments: property, which tells the method which property we'd like to set, and value, which is the value to set that property to.

The set method understands several property values by default. For example, passing 'html' as the property argument, like $('myEl').set('html', '<p>Hello!</p>'), will turn set into an innerHTML setter that changes the HTML source of the element. Other default properties include 'text', which sets the inner text of an element, and 'class', which changes the element's class attribute.

But that's only the simple property options. Remember our setStyle method? The set method also understands the 'style' option, which means we can do something like this:

```
$('wrapper').set('style', 'background-color: #000');
```

And how about setStyles, which uses an object argument? No problem, it's supported via the 'styles' option, too:

```
$('wrapper').set('styles', {'background-color': '#000', 'height': '200px'});
```

For attributes, it gets even simpler: if set receives a property argument that it doesn't understand, it automatically uses setProperty:

```
$('home-link').set('target', '_blank');
```

Because set doesn't understand the 'target' option by default, it will invoke setProperty to handle the setting. The code above is in fact conceptually the same as doing setProperty('target', '_blank')—but it's much terser.

One great thing about set is that it can be used to set multiple properties at once. Instead of calling set multiple times, you can simply pass it an object argument with the things you want to set:

```
$('wrapper').set({
    'html': '<p>Hello!</p>',
    'class': 'greeting',
    'styles': {
        'background-color': '#000',
        'color': '#FFF'
    },
    'fancy-attrib': 'magical'
});
```

The resulting update will be similar to this:

```
<div id="wrapper" class="greeting" style="background-color: #000; color: #FFF;"
    fancy-attrib="magical">
    <p>Hello!</p>
</div>
```

The get method, in a similar manner, is the universal getter method. This method takes a single argument, property, and returns the value associated with that property. Like set, get understands the default property options, like 'html' or 'text', as well as special options like 'style', and it also defaults to getProperty when it doesn't understand the passed property option.

```
var div = $('wrapper');
console.log(div.get('html')); // '<p>Hello!</p>'
console.log(div.get('class')); // 'greeting'
console.log(div.get('style')); // 'background-color: #000; color: #FFF;'
console.log(div.get('fancy-attrib')); // 'magical'
```

You can also use a single get call to retrieve multiple properties. To do this, you have to pass it an array containing the properties you want to access. It then returns an object containing the results, like so:

```
var div = $('wrapper');
var result = div.get(['html', 'class', 'style', 'fancy-attrib']);

console.log(result);
/*
{
    'html': '<p>Hello!</p>',
    'class': 'greeting',
    'style': 'background-color: #000; color: #FFF;',
    'fancy-attrib': 'magical'
}
*/
```

The final universal modificator, erase, is the universal remover method. It is invoked in the same fashion as get, but it removes properties instead of returning them. Since erase is pretty much self-explanatory, we won't go into detail—although I do have to mention that erase is rarely used because you can achieve the same results by passing a null value with set.

These three universal modificators are the swiss-army knives of element modification, and their use is much broader that what we see here. We'll take a look at how they're implemented in a later section, and we'll see more of their use in the next chapters.

Creating Elements

While moving elements around the DOM Tree and modifying their properties is enough for some scripting tasks, some programs involve creating new elements and inserting them into the DOM Tree. MooTools provides several ways to do this, each with its own pros and cons.

The easiest way to add new elements to the page is by adding new HTML source to the document. You can do this by setting the HTML source of an element using the set method.

Suppose we have an empty list like so:

```
<ul id="list">
</ul>
```

We can add an item to the list by inserting some new HTML source:

```
var list = $('list');
var htmlString = '<li>Item A</li>';

list.set('html', htmlString);
```

We called the set method of the list element, passing in 'html' to tell it that we want to modify the HTML source of the element. We also passed a second argument, htmlString, which contains the actual HTML source string we want to insert. This code will produce a DOM Tree section like this:

```
<ul id="list">
    <li>Item A</li>
</ul>
```

Setting the HTML source of the element will create new elements, and we can then use the selector functions to select the new elements and manipulate them as we would with elements that are already in the tree.

This technique is the fastest way to create new elements, and it is the preferred method to use for really large element insertions—such as updating the document using HTML responses from XMLHttpRequest. Internally, set('html') works by setting the innerHTML property of the element, which is fast because it's a simple assignment statement.

However, this method is not the holy grail of element creation. For one, it changes the actual structure of your element by replacing its internal HTML source: any child nodes inside the element will be destroyed and replaced with the new HTML. While this is fine in some cases, most of the time you'll want to keep structure, so simply replacing the HTML source of an element won't suffice.

The second technique involves cloning an already existing element using the clone method. Take, for instance, the following section:

```
<ul id="list">
    <li>Item A</li>
    <li>Item B</li>
</ul>
```

Now we simply want to add a new list item to the list, without destroying the original list items. We can do this by cloning one of the list items:

```
var newItem = $('list').getElement('li').clone();
```

We use the getElement method to select a single list item from the list, then we use clone to create a new element that copies the element. However, if we look at the result of this snippet, we'll see that nothing changed:

```
<ul id="list">
    <li>Item A</li>
    <li>Item B</li>
</ul>
```

The clone was created, but it didn't appear in the DOM Tree. What gives?

What happened is that the new element was indeed created, but it's not yet in the DOM Tree. This is an important point that you have to understand: when you create new elements, they exist outside the DOM Tree. They are not yet part of the DOM Tree, and you have to explicitly insert them using one of the movement methods we saw in the previous section. Until then, they are simply element objects that are inside the JavaScript environment but outside the DOM.

With this in mind, we can modify our original snippet:

```
var newItem = $('list').getElement('li').clone();
newItem.inject('list');
```

And this will update the list element like so:

```
<ul id="list">
    <li>Item A</li>
```

```
    <li>Item B</li>
    <li>Item A</li>
</ul>
```

As you can see, the new element is exactly like the element it was cloned from. In fact, almost every property from the original element will be copied to the clone. One exception is event handlers, which are not cloned by default—but you can clone event handlers from one element to another using the cloneEvents method, which we'll talk about in Chapter 10.

You can update your newly cloned object using the methods we saw in the previous section. For example, we can use set to change the text of our new element:

```
var newItem = $('list').getElement('li').clone();
newItem.set('text', 'Item C').inject('list');
```

This will yield the following result:

```
<ul id="list">
    <li>Item A</li>
    <li>Item B</li>
    <li>Item C</li>
</ul>
```

Like using set('html') however, cloning elements using the clone method is a very limited technique. Because cloning involves copying elements, the kinds of elements you can create are limited to the ones already in your DOM Tree. In order to have true flexibility, we need a proper element constructor—and that constructor is, of course, Element.

Like other type constructors, the Element constructor is used in conjunction with the new keyword. It takes a single required argument, tag, which corresponds to the type of element you want to create. Going back to our list example:

```
<ul id="list">
    <li>Item A</li>
    <li>Item B</li>
</ul>
```

We can add a new list item by creating a new element object via the Element constructor and then injecting it into our list:

```
 var newItem = new Element('li');
 newItem.inject('list');
```

This will update our list with the new element:

```
<ul id="list">
    <li>Item A</li>
    <li>Item B</li>
    <li></li>
</ul>
```

The new element we created has no inner text, nor does it have any attributes attached because the Element constructor creates blank element objects by default. Like in the example for clone, we can update our newly created element using the modification methods we saw in the previous section.

```
 var newItem = new Element('li');
 newItem.set('text', 'Item C').inject('list');
```

We use the set method to change the inner text of our new list item, and this will update the result like this:

```
<ul id="list">
    <li>Item A</li>
    <li>Item B</li>
    <li>Item C</li>
</ul>
```

While this works, there's an even easier way to do it. The Element constructor actually allows a second argument, properties, which is an object that will automatically be passed to set. We can remove the extra call to set in our example above and move the text setting to the Elements constructor:

```
var newItem = new Element('li', {'text': 'Item C'});
newItem.inject('list');
```

This internal use of the set method makes it easy to define really complex elements:

```
new Element('div', {
    'id': 'wrapper',
    'class': 'container',
    'html': '<p>Hello!</p>',
    'styles': {
        'background': '#000',
        'color': '#FFF',
        'font-size': '12px'
    },
    'data-name': 'wrapper div'
});
```

This snippet creates a new div element and automatically sets both its attributes and styles, as well as its innerHTML value. Using the Element constructor this way makes it easy to create elements on the fly and decreases additional calls to the element modification methods.

Before we close this section, though, there's one more nifty trick with Element: you aren't limited to passing just an HTML tag for the first argument—you can also use a full CSS selector.

Suppose you want to create a new link that looks like this:

```
<a id="home-link" class="internal" href="home.html" target="_blank">Home Page</a>
```

The common way would be to specify all those properties using the second argument, like so:

```
new Element('a', {
    'id': 'home-link',
    'class': 'internal',
    'href': 'home.html',
    'target': '_blank',
    'text': 'Home Page'
});
```

This is the preferred way of doing it. However, a nifty feature is that you can move all those declarations (except text) into the first argument by passing a CSS selector instead:

```
new Element('a#home-link.internal[href="home.html"][target="_blank"]', {text: 'Home Page'});
```

This will produce the same results as the previous example. Unfortunately, it doesn't look as pretty, but it does showcase the selector-parsing abilities built into the Element constructor.

Destroying Elements

Finally, we end with the methods for destroying elements. Let's say we have the following DOM Tree section:

```
<div id="nav">
    <a id="home-link" href="home.html">Home</a>
</div>
```

We can destroy the element in several ways. The first is with the destroy method, which removes an element from the DOM Tree and destroys the object completely:

```
var homelink = $('home-link').destroy();
console.log(typeOf(homelink)); // 'null'
```

In this snippet we call the destroy method of the home-link element, which removes the element from the DOM Tree and then deletes the actual node object, making it completely unusable from thereon. The resulting HTML section will look like this:

```
<div id="nav"></div>
```

Another way to remove elements is through the dispose method. Like the destroy method, the dispose method also removes an element from the DOM Tree. However, it does not completely destroy the element, which makes it possible to reuse the element later:

```
var homelink = $('home-link').dispose();
console.log(typeOf(homelink)); // 'element'
```

Like the previous example, this snippet also results in the following DOM Tree section:

```
<div id="nav"></div>
```

However, the dispose method does not destroy our element completely, but instead only removes it from the DOM Tree. This is why we get 'element' instead of 'null' when we pass the argument to typeOf. The dispose method thus makes it possible for us to remove an element from the DOM Tree and reinject it later if needed.

Finally, we have the empty method. Unlike the previous two methods, the empty method does not remove the element from where it was called, but instead destroys the children of the element.

```
$('nav').empty();
```

In this snippet we called the empty method of the nav element. This will remove all the elements inside the nav element, producing the same DOM Tree section as above:

```
<div id="nav"></div>
```

Internally, the empty element uses destroy, which means that all the child elements are completely obliterated. We can achieve the same thing by calling destroy on all child nodes:

```
$('nav').getChildren().destroy();
```

The Element Type

The Element type is unarguably the most important MooTools type object when it comes to DOM scripting. All element objects—both inside and outside the DOM Tree—inherit from Element.prototype and with this type object, MooTools is able to extend all elements in the page to create a better API for working with the DOM.

In the native DOM API, the `Element` constructor is a placeholder constructor: you can access it using its identifier, but you can't invoke it as a constructor using the new keyword. This is because the `Element` constructor isn't actually used for creating elements. Instead, the `Element` constructor is used to implement a proper prototype chain between `Node` and `HTMLElement`, which means it's used for nothing else aside from inheriting properties from `Element.prototype`. In fact, Internet Explorer versions prior to version 9 go the extra mile and hide the `Element` constructor from the DOM API, making it inaccessible from JavaScript.

MooTools, on the other hand, gives good use to the `Element` constructor by turning it into a proper constructor. MooTools does this by storing the browser's native Element constructor (if available) in `Browser.Element` and then overriding this native constructor with a new global type object. This involves declaring a new constructor function called `Element` in the global scope to override the native constructor. The prototype of this new constructor is then pointed to the prototype of the original using `Browser.Element.prototype`, which effectively turns the new `Element` type into a full replacement for the native one—prototype included.

On the inside, `Element` is a very simple constructor. As we saw in the previous section, it can take two arguments: tag, which is the element to be created, and properties, which are properties passed to the set method of the newly created element.

When the value of the tag argument is a string and is a simple HTML tag like `'a'` or `'section'`, the `Element` constructor simply passes the arguments to a special function called `document.newElement`. This function first calls on the `document.createElement` function, which is a function from the native DOM API, to create a new element with that particular tag. It then passes the new element to `document.id`, which will return the element immediately, and then the `set` method is invoked using the `properties` object as an argument. The resulting element is then be returned by the `Element` constructor.

If the value of the tag argument is a complex string selector like our last example in the previous section, an extra step is added to the process. The `Element` constructor first parses the string selector using the selector engine so it can separate the actual tag from the attributes, and then adds these attributes to the `properties` object. It then goes through the same process as above, producing an element as a result.

However, if the tag argument isn't a string to begin with, all these steps are skipped and the tag argument is passed directly to `document.id` for processing. The result then is whatever `document.id` returns.

You'll notice that the return value of the `Element` constructor is never the instance created through the new keyword. This is intentional: for the most part, we want our elements to be instances of their true types, like `HTMLAnchorElement` for links or `HTMLDivElement` for divs. The `Element` constructor, on the other hand, creates generic elements. We therefore discard this generic element and use `document.createElement` to create a proper instance.

In any case, the results are the same: `document.createElement` returns an element that inherits from `Element`, so our `Element` methods are still present in the new elements even if they weren't constructed directly via the `Element` constructor.

Revisiting document.id

The `document.id` function, which we first encountered as a means to select elements from the DOM, is a very interesting function. As we found out, this function is used throughout the `Element` constructor, as well as inside the `document.newElement` function. So what exactly does it do?

Like the universal modificator methods, `document.id` is a dynamic method: its behavior changes depending on the arguments passed to it. The function can understand three kinds of arguments: strings, elements, and objects. Each of these argument types has its own special operation stored in a special function named after that type.

When you pass a string argument to `document.id`, it performs the string operation. This operation starts with an id search using the selector engine. The selector engine called Slick (which we'll learn more about in Chapter 9), is the one responsible for actually selecting elements from the DOM Tree.

MooTools only wraps the Slick API to provide its own variants, but all element selection still happens using the selector engine.

The selector engine will search for the element using the string id argument passed to document.id. If it doesn't find a match, document.id will simply return null. If it finds a match, however, a second operation is done.

This second operation is called the element operation. It involves turning the element returned by the selector engine into a unique MooTools element by providing it with a special property called uid. This uid property is used internally by MooTools, and is therefore not of concern right now. The element operation also does object extension for elements that do not inherit methods automatically from Element. When this operation is done, the final element object is returned by document.id.

If the argument to document.id is an element object, something else happens. The function will first check this element instance if it's already a proper MooTools element by checking its $family and uid property. If these properties exist in the element object, document.id simply returns the object immediately. However, if one of the properties is missing, it means that the element hasn't been properly extended yet, and document.id will perform the element operation on this object to turn it into a proper element before returning it.

When document.id receives an object argument that's not an element, though, it performs an object operation. This is one of the more interesting operations because it involves a special feature of objects (and classes). In particular, the object operation involves checking whether the object argument has a special method called toElement. If it doesn't, the object operation will exit and document.id will return null. If it does, however, the object operation will invoke this method to retrieve the element value of object, and then use the returned value for the element operation.

To understand how the object operation works, let's look at these examples:

```
console.log(document.id({})); // null
```

Here we passed an empty object to document.id, which then performs the object operation on the argument. The object operation checks whether the object has a toElement method, and since it doesn't, it simply terminates and document.id returns null.

However, suppose we pass an object with a toElement method:

```
var obj = {
    toElement: function(){
        return new Element('div');
    }
};
```

```
console.log(document.id(obj)); // <div></div>
```

Here we define a new object called obj with a toElement method that returns a new div element. When we pass this object to document.id, we no longer get null. Instead, document.id performs the object operation, which calls the toElement method of the obj. The div element returned by the method is then processed through the element operation to turn it into a proper element, before returning it from document.id.

This special feature makes it possible for us to create types and classes that can be used with document.id:

```
var Widget = new Class({

    initialize: function(element){
        this.element = element;
    },

    toElement: function(){
        return this.element;
```

```
    }

});
```

Instances of this `Widget` class can now be simply passed to `document.id` to retrieve an actual element. When the instance of a class with a `toElement` method is passed to it, `document.id` will call the `toElement` method in order to get the element value of the class. We can therefore treat `toElement` like the `valueOf` method, but for exporting the element value of an object instead of its primitive value.

Extending Element

Because the `Element` constructor is a type object, we can use the same type object methods we saw in Chapter 6 to add new methods to element objects.

As with other types, we use the `implement` method to add new methods to `Element`:

```
Element.implement({

    switchClass: function(first, second){
        var hasSecond = this.hasClass(second);
        this.removeClass(hasSecond ? second : first);
        this.addClass(hasSecond ? first : second);
        return this;
    }

});
```

This adds a new method to `Element.prototype` that's used for switching between two classes:

```
var myDiv = new Element('div', { 'class': 'yes' });

console.log(myDiv.get('class')); // 'yes'

myDiv.switchClass('yes', 'no');
console.log(myDiv.get('class')); // 'no'

myDiv.switchClass('yes', 'no');
console.log(myDiv.get('class')); // 'yes'
```

One thing you'll notice in our `switchClass` method is that we end the function by returning the element itself, via `return this`. This is deliberate: almost all `Element` methods—with the exception of selector and getter methods—will return the element itself. This is to provide for a chaining pattern, which allows us to call multiple methods in a single chain.

```
new Element('div').set({
    'class': 'yes'
}).switchClass('yes', 'no').inject(document.body);
```

This chaining pattern is popular, and it's especially useful for instances where you don't want to keep references to the element using a variable. However, method chaining should be used moderately: very long chains make your code very unreadable and can sometimes lead to errors if a part of your chain returns a value other than an element. Because this problem plagues new MooTools users who come from other libraries that heavily use chaining, I will give you just a single piece of advice regarding it: variables are cheap in JavaScript—use them.

As with other types, the methods of Element can also be used as generics. They follow the same rule as other generic functions: the first argument needs to be the object that will be the this keyword value, followed by the actual arguments to the method:

```
Element.set(document.id('wrapper'), 'class', 'container');
```

The Elements Type

While the Element type is a native constructor that is turned into a type object by MooTools, the Elements type, in contrast, is a purely MooTools construct and it is a very interesting type to study because it showcases one of the real-world uses of custom types.

The Elements type is a special array-like type created by MooTools to represent collections made up of several Element instances. In older versions of MooTools, the Elements type was actually a real array instance with additional properties. However, its current implementation is no longer based on a true array but on an array-like object.

Being an array-like object, an Elements instance has a length property that denotes the number of elements in the collection, and an Elements instance with a length property of 0 is considered an empty collection. Each item inside the collection is referenced by a zero-based numeric index, which can be accessed using the bracket notation.

In itself, Elements is a boring type. Unlike the Element constructor that can be used to create new elements, the Elements constructor functions only as an aggregator. It takes a single optional argument, nodes, which must be an array or array-like object containing elements. The Elements constructor itself does not perform DOM Tree lookups nor create new elements, but only iterates through the arguments passed to it, checking whether the argument is an element and then pushing it into itself. In fact, functions that return Elements instances, like $$ or getElements, first search for the elements using the selector engine and then pass the results from the selector engine to a new Elements instance as a final step.

The basic methods that are available from Elements instances, like each or slice, are in fact methods that Elements copies directly from Array.prototype. Elements copies all Array methods for its use, and then hooks to Array.implement via Array.mirror(Elements) so that any newly implemented Array method will also be available to Elements. However, Elements does reimplement a few Array methods with its own variants that check whether the arguments passed are element objects.

But the really cool thing about Elements is how it receives Element methods. If you recall our earlier examples, we saw that Element methods can be called through Elements instances. This is possible because of a special hook attached to Element using the mirror. This hook automatically implements a looping version of the Element method that iterates over the collection and applies the function to each of the elements in the collection. The result is Element methods that are collection-aware that can be used on Elements instances.

Finally, as with other type objects, you can use the implement method of Elements to add new methods to its instances. However, it is rarely used, since most of the methods for Elements are better implemented through Array or Element instead.

The Universal Modificators

Earlier, when we were discussing element modification, we came across a set of element methods called the universal modificators. These three functions—set, get, and erase—are the three most useful modification functions in MooTools, and their dynamic behavior supports a wide array of uses.

As I mentioned earlier, the behavior of these modificator methods is controlled by a special object, Element.Properties. This object is reminiscent of the Class.Mutators object, because like Class.Mutators, Element.Properties is used to store special objects called property objects.

When a universal modificator function is called, the first thing it does is to take the passed property argument and use it to search for a property object in the `Element.Properties` object, like so: `Element.Properties[property]`. If a corresponding property object is found, the universal modificator method will then check if the property object has a method that corresponds to the name of the universal modificator, and if so, it will invoke this function, passing in the arguments it received. If no property object is found, or if the property object does not have a method that corresponds to the name of the modificator function, the modificator will default to using an attribute-modifying function.

Let's clear this up with some examples. Here, for instance, are property object definitions for the `'style'` option:

```
Element.Properties.style = {

    set: function(style){
        this.style.cssText = style;
    },

    get: function(){
        return this.style.cssText;
    },

    erase: function(){
        this.style.cssText = '';
    }

};
```

When we call `$('wrapper').set('style', 'background: #000')`, the first thing the set function does is to look for the property object `'style'` via `Element.Properties['style']`. Because a style property object is present, as we see above, the set function will proceed by checking if `Element.Properties.style` has a method called set—which it does. As a final step, it invokes the set method using `Element.Properties.style.set.apply(this, value)`, binding the this keyword of the method to the current element and passing `'background: #000'` to the method. The function then sets the style.cssText property of the element, thereby changing its style. If we invoked get(`'style'`) or erase(`'style'`) instead of set, the same lookup will occur, but the get or erase method of `Element.Properties.style` will be invoked instead of set.

However, if a corresponding property object is not found, the modificator method will default to an attribute method. For example, if we do set(`'magical'`, `'wand'`), the set method won't be able to find `Element.Properties['magical']`, so no property object will be used. This will force set to use setProperty instead, which adds the attribute "magical" to the element. In the same vein, get will default to getProperty, and erase will default to removeProperty.

The great thing about dynamic properties is that you can define your own property objects. The process is as simple as adding a new property object to `Element.Properties`. Here's an example that adds a dynamic property, "display":

```
Element.Properties.display = {

    set: function(type){
        return this.style['display'] = type || 'block';
    },

    get: function(){
        return this.getComputedStyle('display');
    },
```

```
    erase: function(){
        return this.style['display'] = 'none';
    }

};
```

After adding this property object, we can use it in conjunction with our modificator methods, like so:

```
var main = $('main');

main.erase('display');
console.log(main.get('display')); // 'none'

main.set('display', 'block');
console.log(main.get('display')); // 'block'
```

Dynamic properties like 'style' or 'html' are only a couple of the default properties included in MooTools that can be used with universal modificator methods. MooTools adds properties for other complex operations involving things like events, XMLHttpRequest functions, and even Fx animations. We'll see more uses for dynamic properties in the next chapters.

Element Storage

There are times when you want to associate certain data to elements. For most kinds of objects, we'd normally do this by augmenting the object itself with new properties. However, augmenting new properties to elements can sometimes have weird effects on some browsers that track the state of elements, so directly attaching this data to the element itself isn't recommended.

A commonly used technique is to attach such data to the element using attributes. We could, for example, use the get and set method to do this:

```
var element = $('item');

// store the data
element.set('price', 20);

// retrieve the data
console.log(element.get('price')); // '20'
```

Here we attach the price data to our item element using the set method, which adds a new attribute to our item element and stores the data as the value of that attribute. We then fetch the data back using the get method, which returns the value of this attribute.

While this technique works, it has some limitations. First, we need to make sure that we'll use keys for our data that don't conflict with the known element attributes. For instance, we used price in our example, but we can't use keys like id, name, or href because these are known attributes that have special meaning in HTML.

Second and most important, using attributes for storage limits us to string data. Since attribute values are stored and retrieved as strings, all our values will be typecast to strings:

```
var element = $('item');

// store the data
element.set('items', [1, 2, 3]);
```

```
// retrieve the data
console.log(element.get('items')); // '[1,2,3]'
```

Here we tried storing an array in our element object using an attribute. Because attributes need to be strings, our array was first cast to a string value before it was attached to our element. When we retrieve the data again using get, we get back a string and not the original array.

Because associating data with elements is a common operation, MooTools provides a special feature called **element storage** that enables us to attach data directly to an element. We can do this using two element methods, store and retrieve.

```
var element = $('item');

// store the data
element.store('price', 20);

// retrieve the data
console.log(element.retrieve('price')); // 20
```

In this snippet we modified our original example to use the store and retrieve methods from the element storage API. Like in our original example, the price data was attached to the element, which makes it possible for us to retrieve it later.

Unlike using attributes for data storage, the MooTools element storage API is much more flexible because it does not actually store anything on the element. Instead, the element storage API uses a private object store that's accessible only to store and retrieve. This private object store uses the uid property of an element to determine the data associated with the object, which it then exposes to store and retrieve for processing.

Because the element storage API uses a JavaScript object, it's possible to store any kind of data inside it without losing references.

```
var element = $('item');

var array = [1, 2, 3];

// store the data
element.store('items', array);

// retrieve the data
console.log(element.retrieve('items') === array); // true
```

In this snippet we use element storage to store an array in the element. When we retrieve this stored array and compare it with the original, we see that it's still the same array.

This flexibility of the element storage API makes it usable in many areas, and MooTools employs it for some of its most important features. We'll see these storage uses as we go through the next chapters.

The Wrap Up

Wow, we certainly covered quite a bit of ground in this chapter, didn't we? We learned about the DOM Tree and how the various objects inside it are connected through a hierarchy. We also learned about elements, and got a taste of DOM Scripting, MooTools style.

We found out the different ways to select elements, modify their position, and change their properties and styles. We learned about the various ways to create new elements and how the Element and Elements constructors work. Finally, we discussed the universal modificator functions and how they can be used for easier DOM Scripting.

I can't stress enough the importance of this chapter. The concepts you learned here are the basics of all DOM Scripting using MooTools, and the stuff we saw in this chapter will appear a lot in the next chapters. If you still haven't gotten a hang of how everything works, I suggest you reread this chapter once more. Go on—it will be worth it.

We'll continue talking about elements in the next chapter, but we'll focus on how they're selected from the DOM Tree. We won't talk about functions and methods to do these, though, since we already did that here. Instead, we'll explore the Deus behind the Machina: the thing that enables us to actually find that elemental needle in the DOM Tree haystack.

So line up at the concession stand and get yourself a soda and some popcorn because the show's about to begin: the supporting cast are CSS Selectors, and the star is the Selector Engine.

CHAPTER 9

■■■

Selector Engines

Selecting elements from the DOM is quite an easy affair these days. We simply use the element methods, put in a selector, and we're done. However, the technology that operates this selection process is actually quite complex. In fact, it's interesting enough that it warrants our attention for the next few pages.

In this chapter, we'll learn how selection is done in tree-based structures like the DOM. We'll also learn about the MooTools selector engine, called Slick, which makes the process easier for us.

What Node?

In Chapter 7, we learned about trees, which are special data structures composed of several linked nodes. We learned that all trees have one node from which all other nodes come, and we called that the root node. We also learned that nodes have parents, children, and even siblings—like one big, happy family. What we didn't discuss, however, is how we find a node in this family.

Let's look again at a simple tree structure (Figure 9–1).

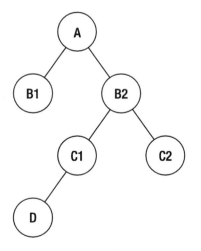

Figure 9–1. A simple tree with six nodes

This is the tree we first saw in Chapter 7. It has 6 nodes: A, B1, B2, C1, C2, and D. Now let's say we are tasked to find the node marked as C1. How do we find it?

Of course, this might sound silly. You can clearly see where C1 is in the diagram and you can just point at it with your finger, so this isn't much of a challenge. But what if there was no diagram and all we had was code:

```
var tree = {
    root: {
        name: 'A',
        children: [
            {
                name: 'B1',
                children: []
            },
            {
                name: 'B2',
                children: [
                    {
                        name: 'C1',
                        children: [
                            {
                                name: 'D',
                                children: []
                            }
                        ]
                    },
                    {
                        name: 'C2',
                        children: []
                    }
                ]
            }
        ]
    }
};
```

This snippet transforms our tree from a diagram into a JavaScript object. We kept everything fairly simple: each object—aside from the tree object itself—is a node. Nodes have two properties: name and children. The name property is a string and it's the representation of the node's actual name. The children property is an array that contains other nodes. Now we can go back to our original problem: how do we locate the node named C1?

There are two ways we can do this. One way is a bit like cheating: since we know exactly where the node is, we can use simple object access methods to get the node directly. We know that C1 is the first child of B2, and we know that B2 is the second child of A, so we can simply take that information and use it to access the node:

```
var C1 = tree.root.children[1].children[0];
console.log(C1.name === 'C1'); // true
```

Here's what happens when we run that code: we first access node A using tree.root, because A is the root node of the tree. We then access B2 by taking the second child of A, or children[1], before finally accessing C1 by taking the first child of B2 using children[0]. When we check the name property of the node, we find out we're right—we've located C1.

This location method, where nodes are found by accessing the absolute path from the root of the tree to the actual node being sought, is called **path selection**. Think of it like going from the front door of your house to a particular room, say your kitchen. The front door is your root node, while the kitchen is the node you're seeking. Because you already know how to get from your front door to your kitchen, you just need to follow a particular path to get there.

This location method is quite fast, since we're simply pinpointing a node in terms of the path you have to take to it from the root node. However, the speed of this method is hampered by its inflexibility. In order to do path selection, we need to know in advance where we're going, then plan a path that leads from the starting point to the final location. But what if we don't know the path?

Reusing our house example, let's say we're in a different house. We've never been there before, and we don't know the floorplan of the house or what rooms it contains. Now we're told that we need to find the room with the blue wallpaper. We aren't told which room that is, so it could be any room: it could be the living room; it could be the kitchen; it could even be a small walk-in closet. In this case, we can't use path selection since we don't know what path to take from the front door to the blue-wallpapered room. In fact, we don't really know where this room is. So how do we find it?

I'm sure we'd all probably do the same thing: check all the rooms until we find the one with the blue wallpaper. We'd start with the room closest to us and check the wallpaper. If the wallpaper is blue, we're done—we found our room. If not, we move on to the next room and check that, and so on until we find our blue-wallpapered room.

This same technique can be applied to solve our original problem. If we want to find the node named C1, we can check each node in the tree, starting from the top and working our way down until we find the node in question.

```
var find = function(node, name){
    if (node.name == name){
        return node;
    } else if (node.children && node.children.length){
        for (var i = 0, y = node.children.length; i < y; i++){
            var found = find(node.children[i], name);
            if (found) return found;
        }
    }
    return null;
};

var C1 = find(tree.root, 'C1');
console.log(C1.name === 'C1'); // true
```

Here we implemented a recursive function called find to locate a particular node. It accepts two arguments: node, which is the node object to search for first, and name, which is the name of the particular node we're looking for.

The function works like this: first, it checks the current node to see if its name property matches the name argument. If it does, it's the node we're looking for so the node is simply returned and the process ends. If it's not the same, the process continues, and the find function is applied to each of the current node's children until we find the node we're seeking. If we fail to find any node with that name, the function simply returns null.

This location method is called **traversal selection**. Unlike path selection where a predefined path is used to locate a particular node, traversal selection works by visiting each node in the tree and testing it against a criterion.

Because traversal goes through each of the nodes in the tree, it's considerably slower than path selection. The saving grace, though, is that we can speed up future searches by narrowing the search to a specific part of the tree: instead of beginning future searches at the root node, we can start at a lower point of the tree, thereby limiting the number of nodes that need to be traversed.

You can see that in our example we applied the same find function to each node, which means that a specific subset of the tree's nodes can be searched. And because this subtree is smaller, the search will be faster.

```
var find = function(node, name){
    if (node.name == name){
        return node;
    } else if (node.children && node.children.length){
        for (var i = 0, y = node.children.length; i < y; i++){
            var found = find(node.children[i], name);
            if (found) return found;
        }
    }
    return null;
};

var C1 = find(tree.root, 'C1');
console.log(C1.name === 'C1'); // true

var D = find(C1, 'D');
console.log(D.name === 'D'); // true
```

Here we did a further search for another node, D, which is a child of the C1 node. Instead of starting the search for the D node from the root of the tree, we used a specific subtree where the C1 node is the root. Since we're limiting our search to a smaller part of the tree, the operation is faster.

But the best thing about traversal selection is the flexibility. In our examples, we didn't need to know exactly where the node was in order to find it. We simply invoked our function, passing in the tree and the name of the node, and it searched the tree for us. The only real requirement is that we know the name of the node we want to locate; after that everything's done automatically.

Selecting in Style

Tree traversal is actually the process that powers DOM APIs such as getElementById, getElementsByTagName, and getElementByClassName. These functions all take a single argument that is used as the criterion to match the node's id, tag, or classname, respectively. Then they traverse the DOM using the node where they were invoked as the starting point for the search. They then return the node (or nodes) that match the criterion, just like our find function.

The flexibility of tree traversal becomes more apparent as soon as we start working with more than one selection criterion. In our examples above, we searched a node using its name property. However, real DOM nodes rarely have just one property, and you may well want to pass several criteria, such as both a tag name and a class name, in order to match a node.

A good example of this use case is the browser's style engine, which uses *CSS selectors*. A CSS selector is a special notation that describes the criteria for matching nodes in the DOM tree. In preparing the page for rendering, the browser will read the style declarations on the page's style sheets and select each element that matches the declarations' selectors so it can apply the style rules.

```
div.colored {
    color: blue;
}
```

Here is an example CSS declaration. The part that reads div.colored is the selector, while the item surrounded by curly braces is the style rule. In this case, the browser searches all div elements in the page with the class "colored" and then applies the rule to all of them, giving their text a blue color.

Because of its close ties with HTML, the CSS selector notation is very expressive in defining the search criteria for DOM tree traversal. Using very simple pieces, we can build complex criteria sets that can be used to select elements from the DOM Tree in order to apply styles to them.

Selector Engines

The simplicity and expressiveness of the CSS selector notation didn't escape early JavaScript developers. They realized that the same notation could be useful for DOM scripting with JavaScript. If we could somehow use CSS selectors for selecting elements from the DOM Tree in JavaScript, it would make scripts much easier to write. CSS selectors would let us quickly select all the elements we need for an operation without having to perform long-winded path selection. Thus, JavaScript-based CSS selector engines were born.

A **selector engine** is a fancy term for a special mechanism that's used to select nodes from a DOM Tree using traversal. Our find function, for instance, is an example of a simple selector engine. A browser has several internal selector engines, too, including one used for the style engine and another for DOM functions such as getElementById.

A JavaScript selector engine, in contrast, is one that's implemented dynamically using JavaScript. There are several JavaScript selector engines available today, and each major library or framework uses one. MooTools uses its own selector engine called *Slick* to power all DOM selector functions, such as $$ or getElements.

A Whirlwind Tour of CSS Selector Notation

JavaScript selector engines are usually tied to a specific selector notation, and in most cases, it's the *CSS selector notation*. Because the notation itself is important in understanding how selector engines work, we need to become familiar with the selector notation before we move on.

Simple Selectors

A **simple selector** as defined by the CSS3 specs is composed of "either a type or universal selector followed by zero or more attribute selectors, ID selectors, or pseudo-classes, in any order."

A **type selector** is used to select elements based on their tag name, such as div or span. A related selector, called a **universal selector**, is denoted by the asterisk symbol (*), and is used to select elements regardless of their tag. The type and the universal selectors are the simplest selectors available.

An **id selector** is used to select an element based on the value of its id attribute. Each id attribute in a given document must be unique, so the id attribute can only be used to match a single element. In CSS selector notation, an id selector is prefixed by the hash symbol, #, like #item or #wrapper.

A **class selector** is used to select elements based on the value of their class attribute. An element can have several CSS classes, and a CSS class can be used for more than one element. In CSS selector notation, a class selector must be prefixed by a period, such as .notification or .colored.

An **attribute selector** is used to select elements based on the value of their attributes. The syntax of an attribute selector is [<Attribute Name><Operator>"<Value>"]. The <Attribute Name> refers to an attribute of the element to select, such as name or href, and this is the only required part of an attribute selector. The <Operator> can be one of the following:

- = (equal to)
- ~= (includes in space list)
- |= (includes in pipe list)
- ^= (starts with)
- $= (ends with)
- *= (contains)

This `<Operator>` is used to compare the actual value of the node's attribute with the `<Value>` specified in the selector. The first three are *full matchers*, which compare the exact values of the node attributes with the `<Value>`.For example:

```
[name]
[name="item"]
[name~="item"]
[name|="item"]
```

The first selector selects all elements with a name attribute, regardless of value. The second selects all elements with a name attribute with the exact value of item, while the third selects all elements that have the value item in a space-separated list. Finally, the last selector selects all elements that have the value item in a hyphen-separated list in their name attribute, such as `<div name="item-a">`.

The last three `<Operator>` values are *substring matchers*, which compare only a part of the node's attribute value to the `<Value>`.

```
[name^="item"]
[name$="item"]
[name*="item"]
```

The first selector selects all elements with a name attribute that starts with item, such as `<div name="itemPrice">` or `<div name="itemQuantity">`. The second selector selects all elements with a name attribute that ends with item, like `<div name="sale_item">`. The last selector selects all elements that contain item, regardless of its position, like `<div name="excitement">` or `<div name="parasitemia">`.

Each of these pieces can be used on its own, but they're usually combined to form more specific selectors. For example:

```
form[target="iframe"][method="POST"]
*[href="http://keetology.com"].navigation
#wrapper.ie
[name*="password"].error
```

You'll notice that the spec said that each simple selector must begin with either a type or a universal selector, but our last two selectors don't begin with either. In these cases, the universal selector is implied: #wrapper.ie is therefore the same as saying *#wrapper.ie.

Pseudo-Selectors

Simple selectors are used to match elements based on their definition and structure. The properties matched by these selectors are defined in the HTML source and can therefore be easily inspected. There are special selectors, though, that don't deal with properties, but rather with states, and they're called **pseudo-selectors**.

A pseudo-selector is a special selector that selects an element based on its particular state at a particular period of time. A very simple example of this involves a elements. In most browsers, hovering over an a element changes the element's color to tell the user that it's clickable. When the user mouses over the a element, it changes state and this state can be detected using the :hover pseudo-selector to change the color of the element.

In CSS selector notation, a pseudo-selector is prefixed by a colon, as in :hover or :first-child. Some pseudo-selectors, such as :lang, also require an argument like a function, which can be added using parentheses:lang(de) or :lang(tl).

Because some pseudo-selectors signify fleeting states, not all of them are supported by selector engines. Here are the ones most commonly supported:

- :empty—matches a node with no child nodes.

- :first-child—matches a node if it's the first child of its parent.

- :last-child—matches a node if it's the last child of its parent.

- :only-child—matches a node if it has no sibling nodes.

- :contains(<text>)—matches a node that contains the string value passed as the argument to <text>

- :not(<selector>)—matches a node if it doesn't match the simple selector passed as the argument to <selector>

- :first-of-type—matches a node if it's the first element of its type (i.e., a tag).

- :last-of-type—matches a node if it's the last element of its type.

- :only-of-type—matches a node if it's the only element of its type.

Combined Selectors

While simple selectors are enough in most cases, sometimes we need to be more specific. For example, say we want to select all a elements that are the children of a div element. This criterion can't be expressed using a simple selector, so we need another way to express this: combined selectors.

A **combined selector** is composed of two or more simple selectors that are connected using a combinator. A **combinator** is a special symbol that denotes the relationship of one simple selector to another.

```
div a
div > a
div ~ a
div + a
```

Here we have four combined selectors, each composed of two simple selectors. The combinators here are the characters in between the combined selectors: a whitespace character, a greater than symbol, a tilde, and a plus sign.

The whitespace character is the **descendant combinator**. It is used to denote a descendant relationship between two nodes: the node that matches the selector on the right must be a descendant of the node that matches the selector on the left. In our example, it will match all a elements so long as they're inside a div.

The greater than symbol is the **child combinator**. It is used to denote a parent-child relationship between two nodes: the node that matches the selector on the right must be a child of the node that matches the selector on the left. In our case, it will match an a element only if its parent node is a div.

The tilde symbol is the **general sibling combinator**. It is used to denote a preceding sibling relationship between the two nodes: the node that matches the selector on the right must be preceded by a node that matches the selector on the left. In our example, the selector will match an a element that has a previous div element sibling.

Finally, the plus sign is the **adjacent sibling combinator**. It is used to denote a sibling relationship between two nodes: the node that matches the selector on the right must be a sibling of the node that matches the selector on the left. In our example, the a node must be a sibling of the div node in order to be selected. It's important to note with this combinator that the position is relevant: if the a comes before the div, it won't be matched—the position must be exactly as defined by the selector.

Selector Grouping

You can apply a specific CSS rule to multiple selectors by using a selector group. A **selector group** is composed of two or more simple or complex selectors separated by a comma:

```
h1, h2, h3, div.content > a:hover {
    color: red;
}
```

Here we have a selector group composed of four separate **sub-expressions**. We have three simple selectors—h1, h2, and h3—together with a complex selector, div.content > a:hover. This specific rule will therefore be applied to all these elements.

Slick: the MooTools Selector Engine

The release of MooTools 1.3 brought a new selector engine called **Slick** to the MooTools framework. This new selector engine is the brainchild of Thomas Aylott, one of the core developers, and it applies recent advances in selector engine development to create a powerful and flexible implementation that drives much of MooTools' DOM selection functionality.

In the previous chapter, we saw the multitude of selector functions and methods that MooTools provides for DOM scripting. All of these functions actually use Slick selection methods internally, and they're basically abstractions of the simple selector functions available with Slick.

Selecting Elements with Slick

Slick has two main selector functions for selecting elements from the DOM Tree. The first one, Slick.find, takes two arguments: context, which is the root node where the traversal will begin, and expression, which is a CSS selector string that will be used to match elements. It will then return the first node that matches the selector string, or null if none is found.

```
Slick.find(document, 'div');
```

Here we have a very simple invocation of the Slick.find function. For the context parameter, we pass in the document object, which tells Slick we want to search the whole document. We then pass 'div' as the value of the expression argument, which means we're looking for a div element. Slick will traverse the document object to look for a div. When it finds one, it returns this node immediately.

The MooTools document.id function is actually implemented using the Slick.find method. A very simple version of document.id using Slick.find would look something like this:

```
document.simpleID = function(id){
    return Slick.find(document, '#' + id);
};
```

Of course, this version is an oversimplification of the actual document.id function, which—as we learned in the previous chapter—performs several operations aside from simply selecting elements using their ids. However, it does illustrate how the MooTools document.id uses the Slick.find method.

The second Slick selector function is called Slick.search, and it takes the same two main arguments: context and expression. Like Slick.find, the Slick.search function uses the context argument as the starting point for the traversal process, and the expression argument to match the elements. Unlike Slick.find, though, Slick.search returns all elements that match the selector as an array.

```
Slick.search(document, 'div');
```

In this snippet, we use the same arguments as we did with the `Slick.find` example above. Here, however, we won't receive either a single node object or `null` as the return value. Instead we'll get an array that contains all the nodes that match the selector. If there are no matches, we'll receive an empty array.

As you've probably guessed, `Slick.search` is used to implement the MooTools $$ function.

```
var simple$$ = function(expression){
    return Slick.search(document, expression);
};
```

As with our `simpleID` example above, the implementation shown here is also a simplification of the real $$ function. Like `document.id`, the $$ function performs other processes aside from simply selecting the elements using `Slick.search`.

One important thing to know is that the `Slick.find` and `Slick.search` functions return native node objects and not MooTools `Element` or `Elements` instances. In some browsers that allow for extending the native `Element` type, the nodes returned by these functions might appear like normal MooTools `Element` instances, but this is a byproduct of extending the native `Element` type.

That's why `document.id`, $$, and the other MooTools selector functions don't simply return the values from the Slick functions like our `simpleID` and `simple$$` methods above. Instead, they process these nodes returned by Slick internally in order to turn them into real MooTools `Element` and `Elements` instances before returning them.

One great feature of Slick has to do with the `context` argument. Because `Slick.find` allows us to pass in any node as the value of this argument, we can greatly limit our searches to specific parts of the DOM Tree.

```
var post = Slick.find(document, 'div.post');
var author = Slick.find(post, 'div.author');
```

In this snippet, we initially select the first `div` element with the class `post` in our document object. Then, in the next line, we take the returned node from the previous call and use that as the new `context` for the next selection.

Being able to limit selection to only a part of the DOM Tree using the `context` argument speeds up the selection process, because the traversal only happens on a smaller portion of the tree. This is beneficial to DOM scripting, and it makes complex selection relatively cheap, which is important for large DOM Trees.

The `context` argument also makes it relatively easy for MooTools to implement the `Element` selector methods like `getElement` and `getElements`. When these selector methods of an `Element` instance are invoked, the instance will be used as the value of the context argument. Thus, the expression `div.getElement('a')` will be processed internally as `Slick.find(div, 'a')`, which means that the benefits of limited tree traversal will be available.

Combinator Prefixes

In normal CSS syntax, we place combinators between two simple selectors to combine them into a single selector expression. Slick, however, allows string selectors to start with combinators rather than selector expressions.

To understand how this works, we need to go back to the two arguments to `Slick.find` and `Slick.search`. Remember that `context` is used as the starting point for the traversal, while `expression` is used to match the nodes.

```
Slick.find(document, 'div');
```

Here we have `document` for the context and `'div'` for the expression. If we translate this to an English phrase, we could say that the operation is to "select all div elements from inside the document."

That phrase gives us a clue as to what kind of combinator might be in effect here. The phrase says to select all div elements, regardless of their position, as long as they're inside the document object. This sounds like the descendant combinator, which selects all nodes inside another node. If we were to write this in a CSS-syntax kind of way, we'd end up with something like this:

```
document div
```

There is, of course, no "document" type in CSS, so this selector won't work in actual CSS syntax. However, it does give us a glimpse of how Slick.find and Slick.search treat the arguments passed to it: the context argument becomes the leftmost expression in the CSS selector expression, and the expression argument is appended to the right of the context.

```
var wrapper = Slick.find(document, '#wrapper');      // document #wrapper
var links = Slick.search(wrapper, 'div.name > a');   // #wrapper div.name > a
```

Now we have a bigger example consisting of two expressions. In the first line we want to find the element with the id wrapper in the document, which translates to the CSS selector expression document #wrapper. In the next line, we use the node we selected in the first line as the new context, which translates to the CSS expression #wrapper div.name > a.

So by default, the expression argument is appended by Slick as though we're using the descendant combinator. However, the interesting thing is that we can change this default behavior by appending a combinator in front of our expression.

```
Slick.find(document, '> div'); // document > div
```

In this example, we added a child combinator prefix to our expression argument. When Slick interprets this expression, it no longer uses the default descendant combinator but instead honors the combinator prefix we used. So instead of selecting all div elements from inside the document context, Slick will now select only the div elements that are the direct children of the document.

Slick understands all CSS3 combinators, and therefore allows all of these combinators as prefixes in selector expressions. And because MooTools itself uses Slick internally, most MooTools Element methods can also take advantage of combinator prefixes, for example:

```
div.getElements('> a');
wrapper.getElement('+ div');
```

Reverse Combinators

One of the more impressive features of Slick is its support for **reverse combinators**. These combinators are used just like regular combinators, but they alter the selection behavior by flipping the relationship described by the combinator.

The default CSS combinators describe a top-down relationship between nodes: the nodes that match the selector on the left of the combinator always comes first in the DOM Tree before the nodes that match the selector on the right. For example, the expression div > a uses the child combinator to describe the relationship of the div elements to the a elements, and it means that we want to select all anchor elements that are the children of div elements. The relationship is therefore top-down in the sense that all div elements must be the parents of the anchor elements that will be selected. The same is true for the other combinators: the descendant combinator denotes a top-down ancestor-descendant relationship, while the adjacent sibling combinator denotes a relationship between an older child and its sibling.

The selection process for normal combinators is therefore from a higher part of the DOM Tree to a lower part. Reverse combinators, as their name implies, switch the relationship of the default combinators from top-down to bottom-up and reverse the selection process. To understand how this works, let's take a look at a simple reverse combinator expression:

```
a !> div
```

Here we took the original div > a expression and flipped it: the a selector now goes to the left of the combinator, and the div selector goes to the right. We also changed our original child combinator with a weird looking one that looks like a negated child combinator.

In the original example, the child combinator denoted that the nodes that match the selector on the right should be direct children of the nodes that match the selector on the left. In this flipped expression, however, everything is reversed: the nodes that match the selector on the left should be direct children of the nodes that match the selector on the right. We are therefore no longer selecting children in this case, but parents—which gives this !> combinator its name: parent combinator.

Reverse combinators therefore allow us to switch the traversal of the DOM Tree by giving us a way to select higher nodes from lower nodes—something we can't do with normal combinators. All Slick reverse combinators start with an exclamation point:

- ! is the ancestor combinator, which is the reverse of the descendant combinator.

- !> is the parent combinator, which is the reverse of the child combinator.

- !~ is the previous sibling combinator, which is the reverse of the general sibling combinatory.

- !+ is the previous adjacent sibling combinator, which is the reverse of the adjacent sibling combinator.

Like regular combinators, reverse combinators can also be used as prefixes in selector expressions.

```
div.getElement('! div');
```

Here we used the ancestor combinator as a prefix for the getElement expression. The result is similar to what we'd get if we use the MooTools method getParent, which actually uses reverse combinators internally.

Pseudo-Selector Functions

Slick supports all of the common pseudo-selectors we've seen so far, together with a few additional ones:

- :enabled—matches a node if its disabled property is false.

- :disabled—matches a node if its disabled property is true.

- :checked—matches a checkbox if it's currently checked.

- :focus—matches a node if it currently has user focus.

- :selected—matches a form element if it's currently selected.

The interesting thing about pseudo-selectors in Slick is that they're actually implemented as functions. We can think of pseudo-selectors as conditional functions that are applied to nodes in order to test whether they pass a certain condition.

For example, the :enabled pseudo-selector function is actually implemented like so:

```
function (node){
    return node.disabled === false;
}
```

This function can then be used to test the nodes during the selection process. For instance, when we pass the selector expression input:enabled to Slick, it first selects all input elements in the context, then it invokes the :enabled pseudo-selector function for each one of them. The function then checks the disabled property and returns a Boolean value. If the pseudo-selector function returns true, the node will be included in the results. Otherwise, it will be removed from the results.

Slick allows us to add our own pseudo-selectors using the Slick.definePseudo function. This function takes two arguments: name, which should be the name of the pseudo-selector without the colon prefix, and fn, which is the function associated with the selector.

```
Slick.definePseudo('input', function(node){
    var tag = node.tagName.toLowerCase();
    return (tag == 'input' || tag == 'select' || tag == 'textarea');
});
```

Here we defined a simple pseudo-selector that can be used to select all form elements. All pseudo-selector functions receive the current node being tested as their first argument. As you can see, we did a simple tagname comparison to check the tagname of the node. This function, like all other pseudo-selector functions, will return a Boolean result that will be used to filter out elements from the results.

Custom pseudo-selectors can also take in arguments from the selector string using a second parameter:

```
Slick.definePseudo('custom', function(node, arg){
    console.log(arg);
    return false;
});
```

In this snippet we defined a dummy pseudo-selector called custom that can accept string arguments. When this function is called by Slick, it will pass in the arguments to the selector along with the node itself. Thus, the expression :custom(something) will pass the string value 'something' to the function when it is invoked. Take note that Slick does not parse the actual value of the argument, and therefore only passes strings to all pseudo-selector functions.

Inside Slick

Slick is composed of two main parts: the *parsing engine* and the *selection engine*. The **parsing engine**, as its name implies, is concerned with taking string CSS selectors and turning them into objects that will be used for the selection process. The **selection engine**, on the other hand, does the gruntwork of taking the parsed selector object from the parsing engine and using it to traverse the DOM Tree and select the appropriate elements.

The Slick Parser Engine

The parser engine, Slick.Parser, is used to transform a string CSS selector into an **expression object**, which is used later for the actual selection process. Expression objects, to put it simply, are simple objects that define the structure of a particular CSS selector expression.

Slick uses a recursive regular expression-based parser function to transform string selectors into expression objects. This parser function is accessible through the Slick.parse method. It takes a single string argument, expression, and returns a selector object. For example:

```
Slick.parse('#wrapper > a.highlight, h1')
```

This will return an expression object that looks like this:

```
{
    // the raw expression string
    raw: '#wrapper > a.highlight, h1',

    // selector groups
    expressions: [

        // selector expression
        [
            {combinator: ' ', tag: '*', id: 'wrapper'},
            {combinator: '>', tag: 'a', classList: ['highlight'], classes: [{value:
'highlight', regexp: RegExp}]}
        ],

        // selector expression
        [
            {combinator: ' ', tag: 'h1'}
        ]
    ],

    // number of selector groups
    length: 2,

    // reversal function
    reverse: fn,

    // Slick flag
    Slick: true
}
```

You can see that the basic structure of an expression object is simple enough. Each expression object has a raw property that contains the actual selector string that was parsed. It also has an expressions array that contains each sub-expression from the selector string. Our example had two sub-expressions, #wrapper > a.highlight and h1, so the expressions array has two members.

Each sub-expression is turned into an expressions array composed of several objects. Each object represents a simple selector from the sub-expression. The first selector in our example, for instance, consists of two simple selectors, so its expressions array has two objects. Our second selector, however, has only a single simple type selector, so it has only one object in its corresponding expressions array.

Each object breaks down a simple selector according to its parts. There's a member that denotes the combinator used (which defaults to a descendant combinator) and then members that denote each specific part, like the class names or the id, or the tag. As we'll see later, the combinator is important in this object, because it will be used for traversal decisions by the selection engine later.

Finally, Slick adds three more properties to the expression object: length, which indicates the number of selector groups in the expression, reverse, which is a function used to reverse the expression, and Slick, which is a simple flag that helps the parser to avoid reprocessing an expression object. Because selector string parsing can be taxing on performance, Slick caches parsed selectors for later use. If the same string selector is passed to Slick twice, Slick will simply return the expression object from its cache that was previously parsed. This enables Slick to avoid recomputing selectors for each call to the Slick.parse function.

The Slick Selection Engine

Once a string CSS expression has been turned into a selector object, it is then turned over to the selection engine called `Slick.Finder`. It is up to this engine to parse the selector object and locate the node or nodes in question.

Both `Slick.find` and `Slick.search` use a single internal function called `search` to perform the selection. This function takes the context and expression arguments from the two functions, calls `Slick.parse` to turn the string expression into an expression object, and uses this expression object to traverse the context to find the nodes being selected.

I mentioned in the previous section that the combinator properties from the expressions are important for Slick's functionality. This is because Slick uses a combinatorial traversal mechanism, where the combinators of each expression are used to decide how to select the nodes being matched. Slick does this by assigning each supported combinator a function.

To illustrate how this works, let's say we're using the following expression:

```
Slick.search(document, 'div p > a');
```

Here we're trying to select all the anchor elements that are direct children of paragraph elements, which are in turn descendants of `div` elements. The context we're using here is the document object, which means that we'll start the search from the top-most level of the document.

Parsing this, we get an expression object with an `expressions` property like this:

```
'expressions':[
    [
        {'combinator':' ','tag':'div'},
        {'combinator':' ','tag':'p'},
        {'combinator':'>','tag':'a'}
    ]
]
```

Because we didn't have selector groups in our expression, we end up with a single expression group. This expression group divides our original expression into three objects: one for the `div` tag, one for the `p` tag, and one for the `a` tag.

Now that it has an expression object to work with, the `search` function will begin the selection process. First, it assigns the context argument as the initial context for the search. It then takes the first expression group from the `expressions` array and starts the actual traversal with that expression group.

The `search` function takes the first object in the group and looks at its `combinator` property. In our example, the first one is the descendant combinator, so `search` calls the internal `'combinator: '` function, which is the function associated with the descendant combinator. The internal `'combinator: '` function will then take the initial context, which is the document in our case, then search this context for all the elements that match the properties of the first object. In our case, we're matching all elements with the type `div`, so the `'combinator: '` function will take all the descendant elements of the document element and check whether they're of the `div` type before storing them in an array. In cases where there are other matchers present—such as class names, pseudo-selectors, or attribute selectors—the `search` function will also test the nodes against those criteria before storing the ones that pass into the array.

If there were no elements selected during the first selection process, the `search` function stops there and returns immediately. However, if there were elements matched, the process continues to the next object in the expression group. Before that happens, however, the `search` function first switches the context so that the next elements will be searched in relation to the results of the previous search. In our example, this means that after all the `div` elements from the document have been selected, `search` will switch the context so that the next selection will take place in the context of these new divs.

What happens next is that the `search` function will take the next object from the expression group and again check its `combinator` property. In our case, the combinator is once again the descendant combinator, which means that the `search` function will again call the `'combinator: '` function. This time, however, search will call this function for each node that was selected from the previous expression. So for each div that was selected in the previous round, the 'combinator: ' function will be invoked in order to fetch the paragraph elements. Like before, the function will also test the nodes using the criteria defined in the object before adding them into a new array.

All the paragraph elements selected from all div elements are combined into a single array, and search will once again switch the context to this new array. The process will then be repeated for the final object in the expression group, which uses the 'combinator:>' function to search for child nodes. The process is continued and repeated until all of the objects from the expression group have been selected. If there are other expression groups in the expression object, the process will be repeated for that as well.

If there are no matches at any point of the selection process for an expression group, the search function moves on to the next expression group until all groups have been examined. In cases where only single elements are needed—such as with Slick.find—the process is stopped as soon as one element is found.

The Wrap-Up

In this chapter, we learned more about trees and how nodes in a tree could be selected using traversal. We also learned about selector engines and the CSS selector notation that most of them use. Finally, we learned about Slick and its API. We found out about its special features that we can use with our MooTools code, and took a peek at the internals of this awesome selector engine.

In the next section, we'll explore another important topic in DOM Scripting, one that changes the way we write our code. So, if you're ready, hop on your elemental horse and turn the page so we can explore the crazy world of DOM events

CHAPTER 10

■■■

Events

Events are the lifeblood of the most powerful JavaScript applications. At its core, the browser is an event-based programming platform, and a very nice one at that. Without a firm grasp of JavaScript events, we won't be able to create sophisticated programs, so it's essential that we study how exactly event-based programming fits into the whole JavaScript ecosystem.

In this chapter, we'll talk about events and event-based programming, and we'll look at the two main models that are used for browser event systems. We'll also take a look at the MooTools event system, which unifies these two models and makes cross-browser event-based programming easier and more powerful.

A Loopy World

If you look back at the programs we've worked on so far, you'll notice that all of them are linear: the program is interpreted a piece at a time, jumping for function calls and ending when there is no more code to be interpreted. Take a look at the following code, for example:

```
var sum = function(num1, num2){
    return num1 + num2;
};

sum(2, 3);
```

The interpreter first executes our function expression, setting the value of the sum variable as a function that takes two arguments and adds them. Then, the interpreter executes the invocation sum(2, 3), calling the sum function to add the two values and then returning the result. After the last line, our program is done: there is no more code to be interpreted, and our program therefore "exits" and finishes execution.

While there are hundreds of simple programs like this, most programs aren't so linear. Most user applications, such as word processors or painting programs, never really exit. In fact, barring crashes or explicitly closing the program, most applications will run continuously. This behavior is different from the programs we've seen thus far, which exit as soon as they're done with all their instructions. Like that bunny on TV, those applications just keep going and going.

But how exactly do these applications keep themselves from exiting? We know that programs exit naturally when there are no more instructions to interpret. No matter how long our programs are, there still comes a point when the interpreter will run out of instructions and exit, so the length of code isn't what's keeping these applications alive. The only way to keep a program from exiting is to keep it from running out of instructions, and the simplest way to do that is to use a loop.

A loop is a block of code that is repeatedly executed. Some loops execute code over and over for a predefined amount of time, while some others run indefinitely until they're explicitly stopped. Compare the example above with this one:

```
var add5 = function(num){
    return num + 5;
};

while (true){
    var num = prompt('Please enter a number to add 5 to, or "quit" to exit.');
    if (num == 'quit'){
        break;
    } else {
        num = parseFloat(num);
        if (num !== NaN) alert(num + ' plus 5 is ' + add5(num));
    }
}
```

In this example, we're using a JavaScript while statement to create a loop. A while loop will repeat the block within its braces until the condition inside the parentheses evaluates to false. In our example, our condition is a literal true, which means that the loop will never exit on its own. Since our loop will keep on iterating indefinitely, the interpreter has to keep on executing the block inside the loop. The result is a program that never exits.

Examining the code further, the first thing we do inside the loop is ask the user for a number using the prompt function. prompt is a special browser-provided function that opens a small dialog window where users can type in their input. The interesting thing about prompt is that it blocks execution: the interpreter waits for the user to type in some input and hit OK before proceeding with the next line of code. In our example, the if statement won't be processed until the user inputs a value to the prompt dialog. And only after that can we proceed with processing the input.

If we boil it down to the basics, the whole process consists of three core steps: wait, process, repeat. The waiting step is done by a blocking construct that also listens to user input, which in the case of our example is the prompt function. The process step is then performed by the main logic part of the application. Finally, the repeat step is guaranteed by the looping structure we use to continuously perform the operations. Putting these three together, we get a very important programming construct called the *main loop*.

The main loop is the essential ingredient for long-running programs. All long-running programs—from low-level system programs to GUI applications like word processors—will implement some sort of main loop. Sometimes the main loop is implemented directly in the program itself, but it could also be provided by the environment where the program is running, like the operating system or the runtime interpreter.

In the case of browser-based JavaScript, the main loop is provided by the browser. When we discussed how the browser processes a web page in Chapter 7, we saw that the browser enters a looping phase at the end of the process, and that looping phase is controlled by none other than a main loop.

The browser-provided main loop is internal, and is automatically created for each window. Because the browser implicitly enters a main loop during the lifetime of a page, all scripts in a page don't necessarily terminate after they're executed by the interpreter. Instead, the variables and objects they've created remain alive along with the page. This is different from a true linear program where everything is destroyed after the program finishes execution.

Because the browser treats each document as a single program sharing a single environment, all scripts on a page also share the same main loop, which makes it possible to perform the process step from the wait-process-repeat flow in any part of your application.

The main loop provided by the browser isn't usually called as such, though. Rather, we use another name, one that reflects the event-based nature of the browser.

The Event Loop

The browser-provided main loop is more commonly called the event loop. To understand this term, let's first look back at our earlier looping example:

```
var add5 = function(num){
    return num + 5;
};

while (true){
    var num = prompt('Please enter a number to add 5 to, or "quit" to exit.');
    if (num == 'quit'){
        break;
    } else {
        num = parseFloat(num);
        if (num !== NaN) alert(num + ' plus 5 is ' + add5(num));
    }
}
```

If you recall, we found out that the `prompt` function performs the wait step of the three-step main loop process by blocking the execution until the user provides input for us to process. Here, the user input is a string we can then check using simple code. If the string is equal to 'quit', we step out of the loop and end execution; otherwise, we try turning it into a number value using `parseFloat,` and then use it for our `add5` function. Our wait step in this case is very limited, because we're only waiting for user input, and we're only concerned about the data the user provides us using the `prompt` dialog.

If we examine GUI-based applications, on the other hand, we'll see that a lot more things could happen. An application's interface may have complex controls, like data grids or file browsers, as well as interactive items like menus or input forms. The complexity of these applications can't be handled like our `prompt`-based example; otherwise, we'll end up with hundreds of blocking functions to handle each of the items in the interface—and that would be too complicated to work with.

To avoid the difficulty of having a separate blocking function to handle each control on a complex application, most applications employ a single "waiting" construct called an observer that monitors all of the controls in the application. The observer blocks execution and waits for something to happen in the application. When something happens, like when a user clicks a button or the window gets resized, the observer takes note of this and creates an object called an event. The event object encapsulates the details of the action, such as the type of action, the target of the action, and other information that can be used to respond to the action. The event object is then handed over to a dispatcher, which informs the program of the event so that it can react by performing some process.

With this model, the steps thus change from wait-process-repeat to a more specialized one: observe-dispatch-repeat. And because events are central to this model, the main loop is therefore given a more appropriate name: an event loop.

Because a web page is like a graphical application, browsers employ an event loop for the programming environment. In the browser, a global observer monitors all elements in a page—from the document element itself to small elements like <em> or <strong>—and waits for something to happen. When a user interacts with the page, the observer creates a new event object and passes it to the dispatcher, which then informs the JavaScript program that something has happened. This process is repeated over and over again until the page is closed, which then formally marks the termination of the program.

Event-Based Programming

The event loop, of course, has a more powerful use than just keeping applications alive for a long time. Because events are central to the event-loop model, we're given a flexible programming paradigm for handling graphical applications called event-based programming.

In the programs we've worked on so far, most of the code is explicitly executed. In our earlier prompt-based code, for example, we explicitly invoke the add5 function after processing the user's input. This explicit invocation works in our case because we know that at that point of our program, we would already have the user's data accessible to us in a variable.

In a graphical application like a web page, however, we don't really know when a user will interact with the controls. A user may click on a link two seconds after the page loads, or she may do so after ten minutes. We also don't know whether the user will click one link or another, or if she'll even click anything at all.

This is the reason for having a global observer in our event loop that waits for an event. The observer will wait until something happens, then it will create a new event object that represents what has happened and send it to the dispatcher, which then informs our program that an event has been fired.

This behavior leads to an interesting inversion of our original process. In our original approach, we explicitly invoke our function to perform an action. In the event-based model, however, we can no longer do that because anything can happen. What we have to do, rather, is to wait for the dispatcher to tell us that something has happened and then react accordingly.

Of course, the global observer and dispatcher are only one side of the equation. These things are provided in the browser environment and are present whether we want to use them or not. In order to make use of the event-based approach, we also have to craft our applications to be event-aware. As an example, let's say we have the following HTML markup:

```
<ul id="contacts">
    <li data-id="contact-001">Garrick Cheung</li>
    <li data-id="contact-002">Djamil Legato</li>
    <li data-id="contact-003">Christoph Pojer</li>
    <li data-id="contact-004">Jabis Sevon</li>
    <li data-id="contact-005">Tim Wienk</li>
</ul>
```

On the browser's side, the event loop's observer will be listening to all of the elements on the page automatically. The observer will be listening to the list element, as well as all the list item elements inside the list. Any actions performed on the elements will be noted by the observer. So if we click on one of the list items, for instance, the observer will take note of this and create a click event and then tell the dispatcher that a list item has been clicked.

Now let's say we want our application to be able to react to that click event. Every time a list item is clicked, we want to log the data-id attribute of the clicked item using console.log. This is where the second part of the event-based equation—the part that we have to implement ourselves through our code—comes into play.

To make our programs event-aware, we have to explicitly tell the environment—and the dispatcher in particular—that we'd like to react to events. We do this using a special API that focuses on event handlers. An event handler, also called an event listener, is a function that's called in response to an event.

In DOM scripting, event handlers are attached directly to each element. It is the job of the dispatcher to call these handler functions when an event happens. In our example, we have to attach a click event handler for each item in the list, which tells the dispatcher that we want to react to the click event of the list items. When an item is clicked, the observer creates an event object and passes it to the dispatcher, which then looks for the click event handlers of the clicked item and invokes them.

So now we have the two parts of the equation for event-based programming in the browser: the event loop, which is concerned with monitoring the items on a page and dispatching events, and the event handlers, which are functions we use to handle events. Together these form the browser's event system. But while the ideas seem straightforward enough, the actual implementation details of event-based programming in browsers is a little more complex than what we've seen so far.

The Event Models

There are two models currently used by browsers to implement their events systems. The first is the standard model that's from the DOM Level 2 spec, and the second is a proprietary model used by Microsoft for its Internet Explorer browser. While these two models share the flow we discussed, they both have specific quirks that we need to look at, and that's what we'll do right now.

■ **Note** There is a third model, the legacy event model, which is the original event model that comes with the legacy DOM. This model is still widely supported in browsers, but its use is now considered bad practice due to the availability of better event models, and no major JavaScript library still employs this model. Therefore, we won't discuss the legacy event model here.

The Internet Explorer Model

We'll start with the simpler model, the Internet Explorer model. This model is used in all major versions of IE up to the latest (version 9 as of this writing), and is specific only to this browser. It involves three methods of the Element type: attachEvent, removeEvent, and fireEvent.

Attaching Event Handlers

Looking back at our earlier problem, we had the following HTML markup:

```
<ul id="contacts">
    <li data-id="contact-001">Garrick Cheung</li>
    <li data-id="contact-002">Djamil Legato</li>
    <li data-id="contact-003">Christoph Pojer</li>
    <li data-id="contact-004">Jabis Sevon</li>
    <li data-id="contact-005">Tim Wienk</li>
</ul>
```

We said that we wanted to react to click events on the list items. Specifically, we wanted to output the value of the data-id attribute of the clicked element using console.log. We learned that to do that, we have to attach an event handler—a function—to each of the elements to tell the browser's event dispatcher that we'd like to handle the click events of the items.

In the Internet Explorer model, we use the attachEvent function to attach event handlers to an element. The function takes two arguments: type, which is a string denoting the event we'd like to handle, and handler, which is the handler function we're going to attach:

```
var handler = function(){
    console.log('Clicked.');
};
```

```
var contacts = $('contacts').getElements('li');
contacts.each(function(contact){
    contact.attachEvent('onclick', handler);
});
```

First, we declare a handler function, which is the event handler we'll use for all our elements. Next, we select all list items inside the contacts list and loop through them, calling on their attachEvent method. We pass two arguments: 'onclick', which tells the event system that the event handler we're attaching responds to the click event, and 'handler', which is the identifier of our actual function. If you run this code in an Internet Explorer browser and click one of the list items, you'll get the string 'Clicked.' on your console.

■ **Note** Notice the string we passed to attachEvent. We used 'onclick' rather than 'click', and this is an important thing to remember when working with the Internet Explorer model. Event names, when passed to the event methods of IE, need to be prefixed by "on". Forgetting to do this means IE will ignore your event handlers.

A specific event handler can be attached only once per event type. If you call attachEvent multiple times with the same arguments, the other calls will be ignored.

```
var handler = function(){
    console.log('Clicked.');
};

var item = $('item');
item.attachEvent('onclick', handler);
item.attachEvent('onclick', handler);
item.attachEvent('onclick', handler);
```

Here we try to attach the same event handler three times to the item element. When we run this in Internet Explorer and click on the item element, though, we only get a single 'Clicked' console output. This is because the second and third calls to attachEvent are ignored. This is a feature of all event models that prevents us from accidentally attaching the same event handler twice.

One of the more glaring problems with IE's event model, however, is the fact that multiple event handlers for an element aren't called in the order they were attached.

```
var handlerA = function(){
    console.log('Handler A.');
};

var handlerB = function(){
    console.log('Handler B.');
};

var item = $('item');
item.attachEvent('onclick', handlerA);
item.attachEvent('onclick', handlerB);
```

When we run this on Internet Explorer and click on the item element, the browser will invoke both event handlers, but the order will be random. For one click, they might be invoked in order. For another, handlerB might be invoked first.

This is intentional behavior, as noted on the MSDN website, which says that event handlers are fired randomly. Unfortunately, we can't do anything about it. The rule of thumb, therefore, is to write your event handlers so that the order of their invocation isn't dependent on the order they were attached.

The Global Event Object

So now our list items are clickable, but our coded event handler is still incomplete. We want the event handler to output the value of the clicked element's `data-id` property, but right now it only logs 'Clicked.' All of the items, when clicked, will output the same thing, so we need a way to differentiate among items inside our event handler. To be exact, we want a way for our event handler to know exactly which item was clicked.

One way to do this is to use different event handlers for each element, like so:

```
var contacts = $('contacts').getElements('li');
contacts.each(function(contact){
    contact.attachEvent('onclick', function(){
        console.log('Clicked on ' + contact.get('data-id'));
    });
});
```

Instead of declaring a single event handler for all our list items, we create a new event handler function for each element. When we run this example, each item will output a different string when clicked. If we click on the second list item, for example, it will output 'Clicked on contact-002'.

While this works, it's not as good as having a single event handler. For one, we're creating too many functions: if our list has a hundred elements, we'd have to create a hundred handler functions as well, and that could affect performance. And more importantly, we're using anonymous functions in our example that are created inside the scope of the each callback, which means that we can't access these functions—something we'll need to do if we want to detach the handlers, as we'll see later. So it's better if we have a single handler function to handle all these items, but we're back to our original problem: how do we know which element was clicked?

Let's recall how the event loopz works: first, the observer monitors all elements on the page and when something happens, it creates an event object that contains data about the event, which it hands off to the dispatcher, which then invokes the event handler. The key, therefore, is the event object, because that's where the observer puts all data about what happened—and one of those pieces of data is the element where the event happened.

In Internet Explorer, there is only one global event object that is accessible via `window.event`. The global event object is where the global observer puts the details of the event, and we can read the properties of this object to find out more about the event that we're handling.

An important property of the global event object is `srcElement`, which is a reference to the actual element where the event happened. We can use this property to pinpoint which element was actually clicked, and we can then edit our code to make use of this property:

```
var handler = function(){
    // get the clicked element using window.event
    var contact = $(window.event.srcElement);
    console.log('Clicked on ' + contact.get('data-id'));
};

var contacts = $('contacts').getElements('li');
contacts.each(function(contact){
    contact.attachEvent('onclick', handler);
});
```

We modified our handler function in this example to access the clicked list item using `window.event.srcElement`. We then output the value of the `data-id` attribute of the element as in our individual handler example. When we run this in the browser, we'll get properly differentiated output for each of our list items, just as we require.

■ **Note** In our example, we passed the value of `window.event.srcElement` to `$` instead of using it directly, in order to give it the MooTools Element methods. The value of `srcElement` isn't extended by default, due to Internet Explorer's DOM model, so we need to pass it first to `$` to be able to use `Element` methods like `get`.

Aside from `srcElement`, the IE event object also has some other properties that are useful for event handling:

- The `type` property is a string that contains the type of event that's currently being handled, without the "on" prefix. If the current event is a click event, for example, the value of `window.event.type` will be 'click'. If you're handling a mouseover event, the value of this property will be 'mouseover'.

- The `button` property is a number that's used to indicate which mouse button was used to perform a mouse-related action such as a click. The value of this property will be 1 if the left button was pressed, 2 if the right button was pressed, and 4 if it's the middle button. If more than two buttons were pressed, the value of this property will be the sum of the two button values, like 3 if both the left and right button were pressed or 7 if all buttons were pressed together. If no button was pressed during the event, the value of this property will be 0.

- `altKey`, `ctrlKey`, `metaKey,` and `shiftKey` are special Boolean properties that tell the state of the modifier keys during the event. If you click on an element while holding down the shift key on the keyboard, for example, the `shiftKey` property will have the value true.

- The `keyCode` property is used in conjunction with the keyboard events. For the keydown and keyup events, the value of this property will be a numeric value that represents the keycode value of the specific key pressed, such as 77 for the M key or 118 for the F7 key. Meanwhile, the value of the property when used in conjunction with the keypress event will be the Unicode value of the specific character, such as 77 for the uppercase M and 109 for the lowercase m.

- `clientX`, `clientY`, `offsetX`, and `offsetY` are coordinate properties used in conjunction with mouse events. The first two are used to determine the position of the mouse relative to the top-left corner of the window, while the last two are used to determine the position of the mouse relative to the top-left corner of the `srcElement`.

You won't need to use all these properties all the time when working with events, but there will be times you'll need this information to properly handle an event.

Cancelling Default Actions

There are two other properties of the event object we need to discuss. The first is `returnValue`, which is a special Boolean flag you can use to prevent the default action of an event. For example, let's say you have a set of links on your page:

```
<a href="home.html">Home</a>
<a href="about.html">About</a>
<a href="projects.html">Projects</a>
```

When clicking links on a page, the default action of the browser is to load the location specified in the `href` property of the link. However, let's say you don't want to perform this default action. Instead, you want to simply log the value of the `href` property. To do this in the Internet Explorer model, we have to write:

```
var handler = function(){
    window.event.returnValue = false;
    console.log($(window.event.srcElement).get('href'));
};

var links = $$('a');
links.each(function(link){
    link.attachEvent('onclick', handler);
});
```

By setting the value of `window.event.returnValue` to false inside our handler function, we tell the browser that we don't want to perform the default action for the event. In this case, we're preventing the browser from loading a new page when a link is clicked.

Event Propagation

The last important property of the event object that we'll talk about is called `cancelBubble`, and it's connected with the concept of event propagation. To understand this concept, we have to go back to the idea of the DOM Tree.

Suppose we have the following HTML markup:

```
<html>
    <body>
        <img src="hello.png">
    </body>
</html>
```

To simplify the markup, I didn't include the `<head>` portion, but this example will work for our purpose. In our discussion of the DOM Tree in the last chapter, we learned that each item in the page is turned into a node by the browser. In this case, we have four nodes: the `<html>` node, the `<body>` node, and the `<img>` node, and the document node, which is the representation of the page as a whole.

One thing you'll notice is that the relationship between parent nodes and child nodes is visible from the markup itself. The `<img>` element, for example, is visually enclosed by the start and closing tags of the

<body> element. From this view, the child element therefore lies inside the parent element, and this leads us back to the concept of event propagation.

Event propagation tells us that when an event happens on an element, it also happens on the elements that enclose that element. Because the element is enclosed by its parent, the events of a single element ripple and affect its parent as well. In other words, the events that happen on a child node are also propagated upwards to its parent node.

However, the propagation doesn't stop at the parent node of the element that received the event. Instead, the event continues upward until it reaches the last node. If we click on the <img> element, for example, we are not only clicking the element itself, we are also clicking all the elements that enclose it, which are the <body>, <html>, and document elements.

When we put the idea of the event propagation together with the other things we've learned, we get a very advanced event model. First the global observer monitors all elements on a page, waiting for something to happen. When something interesting occurs, the observer creates an event object to capture the details of what happened. It then passes this event object to the dispatcher, which invokes the appropriate event handlers for the target element, which is the element from where the event originated. It does not end there, however: the dispatcher then starts event propagation by looking for the parent elements of the source element and it will fire event handlers for these elements as well.

It's easy to observe this behavior. Let's take our example and modify it a bit:

```
<html>
    <head>
    <script src="mootools.js"></script>
    <script>
        window.addEvent('domready', function(){
            // the image
            $$('img').attachEvent('onclick', function(){
                console.log('img');
            });

            // the body element
            $$('body').attachEvent('onclick', function(){
                console.log('body');
            });

            // the html element
            $$('html').attachEvent('onclick', function(){
                console.log('html');
            });

            // the document element
            $$(document).attachEvent('onclick', function(){
                console.log('document');
            });
        });
    </script>
    </head>
    <body>
        <img src="hello.png">
    </body>
</html>
```

You can run this script in Internet Explorer, and you can click on the `<img>` element to test it. If you look at the console output, you'll see the following strings in order: 'img', 'body', 'html', 'document'. The order of the output is the same as the order of the elements in the DOM Tree. The dispatcher first calls the click handler for the target element, which is the `<img>` element, and then it calls the event handlers for the parent elements of `<img>`, starting from its immediate parent, `<body>`, and ending at its final parent, document.

This event propagation model is called a *bubbling* model, because the propagation of the event starts from the bottommost node in the DOM Tree and ends at the topmost node, like a bubble floating from the bottom to the top.

I mentioned earlier that there's a special property in the global event object called `cancelBubble`. This property is useful for controlling the dispatcher's propagation of the event. If we set this property to true, the propagation will be stopped, and the event handlers of the elements further up the tree will no longer be invoked.

Let's look at the following example to see how it works:

```
<html>
    <head>
    <script src="mootools.js"></script>
    <script>
        window.addEvent('domready', function(){
            // the image
            $$('img').attachEvent('onclick', function(){
                console.log('img');
            });

            // the body element
            $$('body').attachEvent('onclick', function(){
                console.log('body');
                window.event.cancelBubble = true;
            });

            // the html element
            $$('html').attachEvent('onclick', function(){
                console.log('html');
            });

            // the document element
            $$(document).attachEvent('onclick', function(){
                console.log('document');
            });
        });
    </script>
    </head>
    <body>
        <img src="hello.png">
    </body>
</html>
```

In this snippet, we set the `cancelBubble` property of the global event object to true inside the `<body>` event handler. When we run this in the browser and click on the image, we get the following console output: 'img', 'body'. Because we canceled the bubbling of the event in the click event handler of the

<body>, the dispatcher stopped further propagation of the event, and no longer called the click event handlers of the other elements.

Detaching Event Handlers

Just as with attaching event handlers, the Internet Explorer event model also gives us a method for detaching event handlers, called detachEvent. Like attachEvent, the detachEvent method is available on all elements, and takes two arguments: type, which is the type of event handler that we're detaching, and handler, which is the actual handler function we're removing.

For example, here's an event handler that detaches itself after the element has been clicked three times:

```
var counter = 0;
var handler = function(){
    if (counter < 3){
        console.log('Hello!');
    } else {
        window.event.srcElement.detachEvent('onclick', handler);
    }
    counter++;
};

var item = $('item');
item.attachEvent('onclick', handler);
```

When the element with the id "item" is clicked, the handler function will be invoked, which then checks how many times the function has been called. If it's been called less than three times, the function simply outputs 'Hello' via the console. However, if it's been called more than three times, the handler function detaches itself from the element.

Notice that we use the same function identifier, handler, for both the attachEvent and detachEvent methods. This is because the value of the handler method must be the exact same function you used with attachEvent. The event dispatcher will search through the event handlers for the element and compare each handler to the function; if it finds a match, that handler is detached. This is why I advised against using anonymous functions if you need to detach events later: if you don't have access to the original function you used for attachEvent, you won't be able to detach it via detachEvent.

Dispatching Events

Finally, we have the last important event method called fireEvent. This method is used to dispatch events from JavaScript, without any user intervention. To use this method, we have to create our own event object using a special IE function called document.createEventObject, which returns an event object we can use:

```
var handler = function(){
    console.log(window.event.type); // 'click'
    console.log(window.event.faked); // true
};

var link = $('main');
```

```
link.attachEvent('onclick', handler);

// dispatch a click event
setTimeout(function(){
    // create a new event object
    var e = document.createEventObject();
    e.faked = true;

    // dispatch
    link.fireEvent('onclick', e);
}, 5000);
```

In this example, we attach a basic event handler to the element with an id "main". We then use `setTimeout` to create a delayed function that will be called after five seconds. When this function is called, it creates a new event object using `document.createEventObject` that will be used as the value of `window.event` when we fire the click event of the element by calling `fireEvent('onclick', e)`. The result is that the click event of the element will be called after five seconds, even if we don't do anything.

Notice how we extended the event object with a property called `faked`. Because the event object is like any other JavaScript object, we can simply augment it directly with new properties. An important thing to take note of, though, is that the event generated by `document.createEventObject` is a blank event object: the values of its `type` and `srcElement` properties will automatically be filled based on the `fireEvent` call, but its other values, like `button` or `keyCode` will be blank. Therefore, you have to specifically augment the object with those properties to make it appear like a real event object generated by the global dispatcher.

The DOM Level 2 Model

One of the things that came out in the second version of the DOM standard is the DOM Events specification. This module was created to define a standard event model that can be used in all browsers. All major browsers, except Internet Explorer versions 8 and below, have adopted this event model, and it is therefore the standard model that should be used when working with DOM events.

Attaching Events

The implementation details of the standard Events model are very similar to the Internet Explorer model, with a few key differences. Like the Internet Explorer model, it starts with a method for attaching events: `addEventListener`. Like the IE equivalent, `attachEvent`, `addEventListener` takes three arguments: `type`, which is a string denoting the type of event to handle, `listener`, which is the event handler function to invoke in response to an event, and `useCapture`, which is used for the capturing mode. The last argument requires some more discussion, but for now let's assume it is always supposed to be false.

Rewriting our list item example from the previous section, we get the following snippet:

```
var handler = function(){
    console.log('Clicked.');
};

var contacts = $('contacts').getElements('li');
contacts.each(function(contact){
    contact.addEventListener('click', handler, false);
});
```

Here we declare our event handler function called handler, which logs the string 'Clicked.' when invoked. We then select all the list item elements inside our contacts element and loop through them using the Elements method, each. Inside our each callback, we call the addEventListener method of the element to attach our event handler.

You'll notice a key difference between attachEvent and addEventListener in our example: the type argument for addEventListener doesn't include the "on" prefix. This is a very important distinction. When using the IE model and attachEvent, the name of the event is always prefixed with "on". However, when using the standard DOM Events model and addEventListener, the name of the event should not be prefixed with "on".

When we run this example in a browser that supports the standard model (any browser aside from Internet Explorer 8 and below), you'll see that the result is the same as the Internet Explorer example: clicking on a list item will log the 'Clicked.' string.

Like in the IE model, the standard model does not allow the same event handler to be attached more than once.

```
var handler = function(){
    console.log('Clicked.');
};

var item = $('item');
item.addEventListener('click', handler, false);
item.addEventListener('click', handler, false);
item.addEventListener('click', handler, false);
```

Here we try attaching the handler function as the click event hander of the item element three times. When we run this on a browser and click the element, however, we get only a single console output because the second and third invocations of addEventListener are ignored since the handler function is already attached.

The standard model guarantees that the order of invocation for the event handlers is according to the order they were added.

```
var handlerA = function(){
    console.log('Handler A.');
};

var handlerB = function(){
    console.log('Handler B.');
};

var item = $('item');
item.addEventListener('click', handlerA, false);
item.addEventListener('click', handlerB, false);
```

When we run this example and click on the item element, we'll always get two console outputs in this order: 'Handler A.' and 'Handler B.'. The order of the handler invocation in the standard model always follows the order in which the event handlers were attached. This is different from the problematic IE model, which invokes event handlers randomly.

Event Objects

Remember that in our Internet Explorer example in the previous section, we accessed the event object generated by the global observer using the window.event identifier. We then used this object to access information regarding to the event by inspecting its properties.

In the standard model, however, there is no window.event. Instead, the event object is passed directly as an argument to our handler functions:

```
var handler = function(event){
    console.log(event.type); // 'click'
};

var contacts = $('contacts').getElements('li');
contacts.each(function(contact){
    contact.addEventListener('click', handler, false);
});
```

Here, we add a new formal parameter to our handler function called event. When a click event occurs on one of the list items, the dispatcher invokes the click event handlers of that element, passing an event object as an argument. The handler can then inspect this event object to learn more about the event. Here we log the type property of the event object to know what kind of event it is.

Like the global event object in the IE model, the event objects in the standard model also have properties that contain information about the event. All event objects in the standard model actually inherit from Event.prototype, which defines a handful of useful properties, such as type. Another important property, target, is equivalent to the srcElement property in the IE model. This property is a reference to the element from where the event occurred:

```
var handler = function(event){
    var contact = $(event.target);
    console.log('Clicked on ' + contact.get('data-id'));
};

var contacts = $('contacts').getElements('li');
contacts.each(function(contact){
    contact.addEventListener('click', handler, false);
});
```

In this snippet, we modified our example from the last section to use the event object argument to the handler function. We pass the value of event.target to the $ function to extend it, and then we retrieve the value of its data-id attribute before logging it via console.log.

The standard model, however, provides a very nice shortcut for event handlers. In the IE model, event handlers are fired from the global context, and the value of their this keyword is the window object. Meanwhile, the standard model fires the event handlers of an element as though they are element methods, which means that the this keyword inside the event handlers will point to the element.

We can therefore rewrite our previous example to use this instead of event.target:

```
var handler = function(event){
    var contact = $(this);
    console.log('Clicked on ' + contact.get('data-id'));
```

```
};

var contacts = $('contacts').getElements('li');
contacts.each(function(contact){
    contact.addEventListener('click', handler, false);
});
```

Aside from type and target, there are a few other properties that events inherit from Event.prototype:

- bubbles is a Boolean property that denotes whether the event can be propagated by bubbling. Most events, like click, mouseover, or keypress, are bubbling events, but there are some events, like the load and unload events of windows, that do not bubble. If an event supports propagation by event bubbling, this property will be true and false otherwise.

- cancelable is a Boolean property that denotes whether the default action for an event can be canceled. Remember when we used the returnValue property of the IE event object to cancel the default action of the page? This property of the standard model event object tells us whether cancelling the default action of an event is possible.

- currentTarget is a reference to the current element where the event is taking place during event propagation. This property is different from the target property, which always remains the same whether or not the currentTarget is the actual source of the event.

- eventPhase is a special property that can be compared with special browser-defined constants to check for the event propagation phase that's happening when the event handler was fired.

All these properties are read-only, which means we can't set their values. This is different from the IE model, where some properties can be set to perform a particular action. The last two properties, however, deserve some more discussion, so we'll examine each of them in turn.

The Current Target

To understand the currentTarget property, let's recall our discussion about event propagation. We said that DOM events are propagated: the event is first dispatched from the target element, which is the origin of the event, and then it's fired for each of the parent elements of the target.

One limitation of the IE event model is that we don't have a way to check whether our event handler was called directly, or whether it was called through propagation. The global event object contains a srcElement that points to the event target, but there aren't any properties that tell us the current element whose event is currently being dispatched. Recall our example:

```
<html>
    <head>
    <script src="mootools.js"></script>
    <script>
        window.addEvent('domready', function(){
            // the image
            $$('img').attachEvent('onclick', function(){
```

```
                console.log('img');
            });

            // the body element
            $$('body').attachEvent('onclick', function(){
                console.log('body');
            });

            // the html element
            $$('html').attachEvent('onclick', function(){
                console.log('html');
            });

            // the document element
            $$(document).attachEvent('onclick', function(){
                console.log('document');
            });
        });
    </head>
    <body>
        <img src="hello.png">
    </body>
</html>
```

Here if we click on the <img> element, we get the console output 'img', 'body', 'html', then 'document'. If we click anywhere inside the page, but outside the <img> element, we'll still get an output: 'body', 'html', 'document'. For these two cases, window.event.srcElement changes to reflect the target: for the first case, this property will point to the <img> element, while it will point to the <body> element for the second case. However, from inside our event handlers, we can't determine whether the event originated from the current element or another element, because all we have access to is the target element, not the current element whose handler is being fired.

The standards model solves this by providing the currentTarget property. This property is a reference to the current element whose handler is being fired. For the target element's event handlers, the target and currentTarget properties of the passed event object will be the same object. In contrast, elements whose event handlers are fired due to event propagation will have different currentTarget and target properties.

```
<html>
    <head>
    <script src="mootools.js"></script>
    <script>
        window.addEvent('domready', function(){

            var handler = function(event){
                if (event.currentTarget == event.target)
                    console.log('The source of the event is ' + $(this).get('tag'));
            };

            var items = $$('img, body, html').concat(document);
            items.each(function(item){
                item.addEventListener('click', handler, false);
            });
```

```
            });
        </script>
    </head>
    <body>
        <img src="hello.png">
    </body>
</html>
```

In this snippet, we create a generic event handler called "handler" that compares the values of the currentTarget and target properties of the event object argument. Next we take the <img>, <body>, <html>, and document elements and combine them in an Elements collection, then loop through each of them to attach a click event handler via addEventListener. When we run this script in a browser and click an element, we won't get console output for every item even though we're using propagation. Instead, the handler function will call console.log only if the clicked element is the true target of the event.

Interestingly, though, we don't need the currentTarget property at all, because the standard model calls the event handlers like element methods. The value of the this keyword inside our event handlers is the same as the value of the currentTarget property. We could have very well written the code above like this:

```
<html>
    <head>
        <script src="mootools.js"></script>
        <script>
            window.addEvent('domready', function(){

                var handler = function(event){
                    if (this == event.target)
                        console.log('The source of the event is ' + $(this).get('tag'));
                };

                var items = $$('img, body, html').concat(document);
                items.each(function(item){
                    item.addEventListener('click', handler, false);
                });

            });
        </script>
    </head>
    <body>
        <img src="hello.png">
    </body>
</html>
```

Three Phases of Event Propagation

The next property we need to discuss, eventPhase, is also related to event propagation, and it highlights the most important difference between the Internet Explorer event model and the DOM Level 2 Events model.

When we discussed event propagation in the IE model, we learned that it uses a bubbling model of propagation: the event is first fired for the target node, and then the event "bubbles" up to the parent nodes of the target until it reaches the last node in the tree.

Netscape implemented a similar event model, but used a reverse type of propagation. Instead of starting from the bottom, the Netscape model starts firing the event from the topmost node and then goes all the way down the DOM Tree until it reaches the target element. In this approach, the event flows from the topmost node to the last, target node like a drop of water, which gives it the name the *trickling* model.

In standardizing the event model, the W3C decided to combine both approaches: instead of simply supporting the bubbling method of propagation, the DOM Level 2 Events model was designed to support the trickling method as well. In order to support both types of propagation, the standard event model allots each one a phase.

When an event happens in the standard model, the dispatcher first uses the trickling approach in what's called the capturing phase. In this phase, the dispatcher invokes the event handlers for the event of the topmost node first, then it goes down the DOM tree and invokes the event handlers of the parents of the target element. When the dispatcher finally reaches the target element, it moves to the second phase, the "at target" phase and fires the event handler for the target element itself, starting with the trickling handlers for the target and then the bubbling handlers. Finally, the dispatcher moves to the last phase, the bubbling phase, where it will go back up the DOM Tree and fire events for each parent node, thus performing a bubble propagation.

The use of both the trickling and bubbling models does not mean that event handlers for each event will be fired twice. Instead, you are given the choice of attaching an event handler that will be invoked during the capturing phase or one that will be invoked during the bubbling phase.

All our examples above are called during the bubbling phase of the event dispatch. To make an event handler use the trickling phase instead, we need to use the third Boolean argument to addEventListener, called useCapture. Passing a truthy value to this argument makes the event handler use the trickling model, while passing a falsy value makes the event handler use the bubbling model:

```
<html>
    <head>
    <script src="mootools.js"></script>
    <script>
        window.addEvent('domready', function(){

            // trickling model
            document.getElement('html').addEventListener('click', function(e){
                console.log('Trickling Handler');
            }, true);

            // bubbling model
            document.getElement('html').addEventListener('click', function(e){
                console.log('Bubbling Handler');
            }, false);

        });
    </script>
    </head>
    <body>
    </body>
</html>
```

In this example, we attach two event handlers to the `<html>` element, one for the trickling phase and the other for the bubbling phase. When we run this in a browser and click anywhere, we get two log outputs: 'Trickling Handler' and then 'Bubbling Handler'.

The three event phases are represented by three property constants of the Event constructor: `Event.CAPTURING_PHASE`, `Event.AT_TARGET`, and `Event.BUBBLING_PHASE`. You can then compare the value of the eventPhase property of the event object to know the phase when your target was invoked. This is useful for creating event handlers that can be used for both the trickling model and the bubbling model:

```
<html>
    <head>
    <script src="mootools.js"></script>
    <script>
        window.addEvent('domready', function(){

            var handler = function(event){
                var phase = '';
                switch (event.eventPhase){
                    case Browser.Event.CAPTURING_PHASE:
                        phase = 'Capturing';
                        break;
                    case Browser.Event.AT_TARGET:
                        phase = 'Target';
                        break;
                    case Browser.Event.BUBBLING_PHASE:
                        phase = 'Bubbling';
                }
                console.log(phase + ': ' + $(this).get('tag'));
            };

            var items = $$('img, body, html');
            items.each(function(item){
                // capturing listener
                item.addEventListener('click', handler, true);

                // bubbling listener
                item.addEventListener('click', handler, false);
            });

        });
    </script>
    </head>
    <body>
        <img src="hello.png">
    </body>
</html>
```

In this example, we declare a single handler function that can be used for all phases in the standard event model. Inside the function, we compare the value of event.eventPhase to the phase constants. Note that we access the phase constants using `Browser.Event.<PHASE_NAME>` rather than via `Event.<PHASE_NAME>`. This is because the MooTools event system implements its own Event type, as we'll see later. The handler function will then log the phase, together with the tag of the current element. If we run this in a browser and click the image element, we get the following output:

```
Capturing: html
Capturing: body
Target: img
Target: img
Bubbling: body
Bubbling: html
```

The console output matches the order of the phases, as well as the order of the event dispatch for each of our phases. It starts with a capture phase on the topmost node, <html>, and then goes to <body>. It then moves to the "at target" phase and starts by firing the trickling handler of the target, then the bubbling handler. Finally, it goes back up to perform the bubbling phase starting with the immediate parent of the target, <body>, then moving up the DOM Tree to <html>.

While the trickling model of propagation is interesting and useful in some cases, it is almost never really used in cross-browser development. The biggest reason for this is the lack of support for a trickling model in the older IE versions. In fact, MooTools itself, as we'll see later in this chapter, relies entirely on the bubbling model, and for most development concerns, the bubbling model suffices entirely.

Stopping Event Propagation

In the IE model, we use the cancelBubble property of the global event object to stop further event propagation. In the standard model, we use the event method stopPropagation to do this.

The stopPropagation method is available in all error objects, inherited from Event.prototype. When called in any event handler, it will stop the event propagation no matter what phase it is in.

The last part is important: the stopPropagation method works in any phase and if called from earlier phases, it will stop the propagation for later phases. For example, if you call stopPropagation on a handler during the capturing phase, the event propagation stops there and does not enter the "at target" or bubbling phases.

```
<html>
    <head>
    <script src="mootools.js"></script>
    <script>
        window.addEvent('domready', function(){

            var handler = function(event){
                var phase = '';
                switch (event.eventPhase){
                    case Browser.Event.CAPTURING_PHASE:
                        phase = 'Capturing';
                        event.stopPropagation();
                        break;
                    case Browser.Event.AT_TARGET:
                        phase = 'Target';
                        break;
                    case Browser.Event.BUBBLING_PHASE:
                        phase = 'Bubbling';
                }
                console.log(phase + ': ' + $(this).get('tag'));
            };
```

```
                    var items = $$('img, body, html');
                    items.each(function(item){
                        // capturing listener
                        item.addEventListener('click', handler, true);

                        // bubbling listener
                        item.addEventListener('click', handler, false);
                    });

                });
            </script>
        </head>
        <body>
            <img src="hello.png">
        </body>
</html>
```

Here, we called event.stopPropagation() during the capturing phase. When we try clicking the <img> element, we get the following output:

```
Capturing: html
```

The event propagation stops at the trickling handler of the first element and no longer goes through any other handlers or phases.

However, remember that event propagation is concerned with broadcasting events from the target node to its parents, or the reverse for the trickling model. Stopping propagation, therefore, only stops the dispatcher from invoking the event handlers of other nodes, but not the other event handlers of the same node. Let's look at another example:

```
<html>
    <head>
    <script src="mootools.js"></script>
    <script>
        window.addEvent('domready', function(){

            var handler = function(event){
                var phase = '';
                switch (event.eventPhase){
                    case Browser.Event.CAPTURING_PHASE:
                        phase = 'Capturing';
                        break;
                    case Browser.Event.AT_TARGET:
                        phase = 'Target';
                        event.stopPropagation();
                        break;
                    case Browser.Event.BUBBLING_PHASE:
                        phase = 'Bubbling';
                }
                console.log(phase + ': ' + $(this).get('tag'));
            };
```

```
            var items = $$('img, body, html');
            items.each(function(item){
                // capturing listener
                item.addEventListener('click', handler, true);

                // bubbling listener
                item.addEventListener('click', handler, false);
            });

        });
      </script>
    </head>
    <body>
        <img src="hello.png">
    </body>
</html>
```

Here we stopped the propagation at the "at target" phase rather than the capturing phase. Clicking on the `<img>` element, we get the following console output:

```
Capturing: html
Capturing: body
Target: img
Target: img
```

All our elements in this example have two handlers: one for the capturing phase and one for the bubbling phase. We know that if the element is the target of the action, both handlers will be called successively. In the case of using `stopPropagation`, we only stopped the event from going to the next phase of the process: we didn't stop the dispatcher from invoking the other event handlers of the node that we're working with. Thus, we get two "Target: img" logs rather than one.

Preventing Default Action

We used the `returnValue` property of the global event object in the IE model to stop the browser from performing the default action associated with the event. In the standard model, we have method called `preventDefault` that's used for the same thing.

Going back to our links example:

```
<a href="home.html">Home</a>
<a href="about.html">About</a>
<a href="projects.html">Projects</a>
```

Here we have a set of links. When we click a link item, the default action of the browser is to navigate away from the page and load the URL of the link as defined by the `href` property. In the IE model, we used `window.event.returnValue = false` to prevent this from happening. In the standards model, we simply have to invoke the `preventDefault` method:

```
var handler = function(event){
```

```
    event.preventDefault();
    console.log($(this).get('href'));
};

var links = $$('a');
links.each(function(link){
    link.addEventListener('click', handler, false);
});
```

Inside our handler function, we invoke event.preventDefault(), which tells the browser that we don't want to perform the default action for the event. In this case, we don't want our links to navigate us away from the page.

Event Flavors

When we discussed the properties of Event.prototype above, you might have noticed that the event object doesn't have properties that relate to specific events. The IE model's global event object has properties like keyCode, button, and clientX, which are properties you'd use for more complex event handling. However, I never mentioned these properties for the event object. Does this mean they're omitted from the standard model?

This is not the case, of course. Instead of cramming all these properties into the Event type, as IE does with its global event object, the standard model defines subtypes for different kinds of events. The bulk of the common events—such as blur, change, and scroll—inherit directly from Event.prototype, while mouse events and keyboard events inherit from special subtypes.

The first subtype is UIEvent, which is directly subtyped from the Event type. This is a general type for all user-interface events, and is used as the constructor for three browser events: DOMActivate, DOMFocusIn, and DOMFocusOut. These events, as well as this event type, aren't used that much in browsers. Instead, UIEvent serves as a supertype for the other special user-interface events.

One of the special user-interface events is mouse events, which are under the MouseEvent type. The type is subtyped directly from UIEvent, and is used as the constructor for events like click, dblclick, mouseover, and mousemove. The MouseEvent.prototype object defines several properties that are used for working with mouse events:

- button is a numeric value that indicates the button pressed during a mouse event. It can take one of three values: 0 for the left button, 1 for the middle button, and 2 for the right button. Note that the values of this property are not compatible with the IE model's button property.

- altKey, ctrlKey, metaKey, and shiftKey are Boolean properties that indicate the state of their corresponding modifier keys during the event. These properties are compatible with the IE model's properties of the same name.

- clientX, clientY, screenX, and screenY are coordinate properties that indicate the position of the mouse pointer during the mouse event. The first two, clientX and clientY, determine the position of the mouse pointer relative to the top-left corner of the window, while the final two, screenX and screenY, determine the position of the mouse pointer relative to the top-left corner of the user's screen.

Like the properties of the IE model's global event object, the properties of MouseEvent instances are useful when we're working with complex event handlers. There are incompatibilities between the two models, but it's easy to work around these incompatibilities in the code, as we'll see later when we discuss the MooTools event system.

The other group of special user-interface events is keyboard events. The DOM Level 2 Events standard actually didn't include keyboard events, but they were later added in the DOM Level 3 specification. Keyboard events inherit from the `KeyboardEvent` type, which is subtyped from `UIEvent`.

■ **Note** An important exception is Opera, which has no `KeyboardEvent` type, but instead uses the main `Event` type to implement its keyboard events.

Like `MouseEvent.prototype`, `KeyboardEvent.prototype` contains special properties related to keyboard events:

- `keyCode` is a number representing the keycode value of the particular key pressed, like 77 for M and 118 for F7.

- `charCode` is a number representing the Unicode value of the particular key pressed, such as 77 for the uppercase M and 109 for the lowercase m.

- `altKey`, `ctrlKey`, `metaKey`, and `shiftKey` are Boolean properties that indicate the state of the modifier keys during the keypress event. These are equivalent to the properties of the same name from the `MouseEvent` type, as well as with the IE model's global event object.

You'll notice that the standard model separates the property for accessing the keycode and Unicode numbers of keyboard events, unlike in the IE model where there's only one property that changes depending on the event type. This means that these two keyboard event models are somewhat incompatible.

In practice, the existence of different event types in the standard model shouldn't make event handling much different from the IE model. One thing we have to do, though, is to be mindful of the event type and what kind of event object we might receive for that event type. A simple criteria for determining the kind of event object for a specific event is to look at how the event is triggered: if it's triggered by the mouse, we get a mouse event; if it's triggered by the keyboard, we get a keyboard event; and if it doesn't fall into these two categories, then chances are it's a basic event.

The last part is not that straightforward, though. The DOM Level 3 Events model introduces several other event types, like wheel events, text events, and mutation events. The proliferation of touch-capable devices also brings about a new type of events called touch events. All these event types would have different properties associated with them, which, unfortunately, we can't cover in this chapter. However, we'll find out later how these events can be handled easily through the MooTools system.

Detaching Event Handlers

Like its IE counterpart, the standard event model also provides a method to detach event handlers called `removeEventListener`.

This method is similar to the IE model's `detachEvent` method, and also takes three main arguments: `type`, which is a string denoting the type of event, `handler`, which should be a reference to the event handler to detach, and `useCapture`, which indicates whether we're removing a bubbling or trickling handler. Rewriting our old self-detaching handler example to the standard model, we get this:

```
var counter = 0;
var handler = function(event){
    if (counter < 3){
```

```
        console.log('Hello!');
    } else {
        event.target.removeEventListener('click', handler, false);
    }
    counter++;
};

var item = $('item');
item.addEventListener('click', handler, false);
```

Like the IE version of this example, the handler function automatically detaches itself after it has been called thrice. Also like detachEvent, the removeEventListener method's handler function needs to be the exact same function that was attached using addEventListener in order to work properly.

We learned a few sections ago that the standard model supports both the trickling and bubbling models of propagation. We also found out that the third argument to addEventListener is used make the event handler use the trickling model. The removeEventListener method's third argument, just like addEventListener, is called useCapture. If we pass a truthy value for this argument, the method will detach the trickling event handler, and if we pass a falsy value, it will detach the bubbling event handler.

```
var trickling = function(event){
    console.log('Trickling');
};

var bubbling = function(event){
    console.log('Bubbling');
    event.target.removeEventListener('click', trickling, true);
};

var item = $('item');
item.addEventListener('click', trickling, true);
item.addEventListener('click', bubbling, false);
```

The first time we run this and click on the element with the id item, we'll get the following console output:

```
Trickling
Bubbling
```

Our bubbling handler will then detach the trickling event handler; then, clicking on the same element will produce only the following in the console log:

```
Bubbling
```

Dispatching Events

The IE model's explicit dispatch API is quite simple: create a new event object using the document.createEventObject function, and then dispatch the event on the element using the fireEvent method. The standard model's dispatch APIs, though, are much more complex.

First, you need to create an event object, using the document.createEvent function. This function takes a single argument, eventType, which is a string that denotes the prototypal type of the event. It can be one of these four values:

- 'HTMLEvents' – for general events that will inherit from the Event type.

- 'UIEvents' – for user-interface events that will inherit from the UIEvent subtype.

- • 'MouseEvents' – for mouse events that will inherit from the MouseEvent subtype.

- • 'KeyboardEvents' – for keyboard events that will inherit from the KeyboardEvent subtype.

You must supply the document.createEvent function with one of these four strings as an argument. Take note of the spelling: the eventType argument has to be in proper case and should always be plural. Failing to pass a proper eventType value to document.createEvent will result in an exception.

The document.createEvent function returns an event object. However, it does not end there. The event object returned by this function is uninitialized, which means its properties haven't been properly set to their values. In the IE model, we simply set these properties by directly assigning them a value. In the standard model, however, all event properties are read-only, so we'll need to use methods to set the values of these properties.

Each event type has its own initialization method. For events of the Event type, it's called initEvent, and it takes three arguments: eventType, which is a string that denotes the actual name of the event like 'blur' or 'focus'; canBubble, which is a Boolean that will be the value of the bubbles property of the object; and cancelable, which is a Boolean that will be the value of the cancelable property.

```
var event = document.createEvent('HTMLEvents');
event.initEvent('blur', false, true);
```

The snippet above will create a new Event object with a type property value of 'blur', a bubbles property value of false, and a cancelable property value of true.

Do you see a pattern? The arguments of the initialization method map directly to the properties of the event object. While this is an interesting way to do it, the approach becomes quite problematic when working with complex events, like those that inherit from MouseEvent or KeyboardEvent. Just to show you how complex it can get, here are the function signatures for those two events:

```
initMouseEvent: function(
    type,
    canBubble,
    cancelable,
    view,
    detail,
    screenX,
    screenY,
    clientX,
    clientY,
    ctrlKey,
    altKey,
    shiftKey,
    metaKey,
    button,
    relatedTarged
)

initKeyboardEvent: function(
    type,
    bubbles,
    cancelable,
    view,
    key,
    location,
    modifiers,
    repeat
)
```

Yes, you're seeing that correctly: the initMouseEvent method does indeed have 15 parameters in total, while the initKeyboardEvent has 8 parameters. This means that if you're initializing a MouseEvent, you have to provide fifteen arguments—in that order. That's quite a lot of arguments for a single event!

So let's say that we're gonna keep it simple and use a simple Event instance for our dispatch. In the IE model, we use the fireEvent method to dispatch an event object, passing in the event type as a string and the event object itself. The standard model's dispatch method, appropriately called dispatchEvent, works the same way. However, it only requires the event object argument—the type of the event is determined by the type property of the event object:

```
var event = document.createEvent('HTMLEvents');
event.initEvent('mouseover', false, true);
document.dispatchEvent(event);
```

This snippet will dispatch an event called mouseover in the document object. Note that the basic event dispatcher in the standard model doesn't take into account actual event types when dispatching events. This means that the mouseover document handlers of the document object will be invoked by the dispatcher in this example, even if mouseover should have been initialized using initMouseEvent and not with initEvent.

The complexity of the standard model's dispatch API is one of the reasons why most JavaScript libraries provide their own event system—and the MooTools event system is what we'll learn about next.

The MooTools Event System

The existence of two event models is a constant source of problems for web developers. While writing applications that use either one is easy enough, writing applications that work with both event models is much more difficult. Factor in the implementation-dependent inconsistencies of both APIs, and you get a ton of headaches.

MooTools solves this problem by providing its own event system. This event system is an abstraction of the native event system, and is built to work with both the IE model and the standard model. Instead of writing code that targets one of the two native models, we can write code that uses the MooTools events API that works no matter what model the current browser uses.

The MooTools event system is a hybrid that combines elements from the two native models. From the IE model it takes the bubbling-only propagation model, the use of a single event type and the succinctness of the dispatch API. From the standard model it takes the idea of passing event objects as handlers, the binding of event handlers to the current target, and the use of event object methods to perform actions. It also provides powerful features of its own, like custom events and event pseudo-functions.

We will discuss each of these items in turn, but first we have to go over the common operations involving events: attaching events, preventing default actions, stopping event propagation, detaching events, and dispatching events.

Attaching Event Handlers

All element objects inherit the event handler attaching method, addEvent, from Element.prototype. This method takes two arguments: type, which is a string denoting the type of event to handle, and fn, which is the handler function to attach:

```
var handler = function(){
    console.log('Clicked');
};

var item = $('item');
item.addEvent('click', handler);
```

This snippet attaches the function "handler" as the click event handler for the element with the id "item". Like the standard model, the type argument should be the real name of the event, and should not have an "on" prefix. Clicking on the element with the id "item" will then invoke the event handler function and log 'Clicked' in the console.

Like the standard model, event handlers in the MooTools event system are invoked with an event object argument:

```
var handler = function(event){
    console.log(typeOf(event)); // 'event'
};

var item = $('item');
item.addEvent('click', handler);
```

Here we added a formal parameter to the handler function so that we'll get an identifier to the event object argument. When we click on the item element, we get console output equal to the result of the typeOf(event) call, which in this case is 'event'. This means that the event objects passed to the event handler are instantiated from the Event type, which we'll discuss in a little bit.

Also like the standard model, the event handlers in MooTools are bound to the current element. This means that the this keyword inside the handler functions reference the element where the event was attached:

```
var item = $('item');

var handler = function(event){
    console.log(this === item); // true
};

item.addEvent('click', handler);
```

In this example, we check whether the this keyword inside the handler function is the same as the item element. Since we attach the event handler to the item element, the this keyword is therefore bound to this element and so our output is true.

The MooTools event system, like the IE model, only supports event bubbling, which means that you won't be able to attach trickling event handlers to elements. This decision is due to the fact that there's no way to implement a capturing phase to Internet Explorer, which makes it quite impossible to support trickling event handlers.

Because the addEvent method is an Element method, it means we can use it on Elements instances as well:

```
var links = $$('a');
links.addEvent('click', function(event){
    console.log('I was clicked');
});
```

Here we attached a click event handler to all the links in the page. This is a very nice shortcut for attaching event handlers to multiple items at once.

Another Element method, addEvents is used to attach several event handlers at once. It takes a single argument, events, which is an object containing the event handlers to attach. The keys of the events object correspond to the name of the events to attach, while the values are the event handler functions:

```
var item = $('item');
item.addEvents({

    'click': function(event){
        console.log('Clicked');
```

```
    },

    'dblclick': function(event){
        console.log('Double-Clicked');
    },

    'focus': function(event){
        console.log('Focused');
    }

});
```

Here we attached three different event handlers to the item element using addEvents. We passed an object to the method containing the keys of the events we wanted to handle—'click', 'dblclick', and 'focus'—together with their corresponding handler functions. This attaches all three event handlers in a single method call, making addEvents a very nice shortcut for attaching multiple event handlers at once.

In the Chapter 8, we learned about the universal modificator functions: get, set, and erase. We learned that these functions depend on the Element.Properties hash for dynamic properties, such as styles or html. One of the dynamic properties available is Element.Properties.events, which can be used for attaching multiple events using set. We can therefore rewrite our example as the following:

```
var item = $('item');
item.set('events', {

    'click': function(event){
        console.log('Clicked');
    },

    'dblclick': function(event){
        console.log('Double-Clicked');
    },

    'focus': function(event){
        console.log('Focused');
    }

});
```

Here we replace the call to addEvents to set('events'). This example and the previous one work the same way, because the Element.Properties.events object uses addEvents internally for this dynamic setter.

While this may not be that interesting when it comes to attaching events to existing elements, the fact that the set method understands events gives us a nice shortcut for attaching events during element creation. Remember that the Element constructor takes a second argument, properties, which is an object that the constructor passes to the set method. This makes it possible to combine the element-creation and event-attaching calls:

```
var div = new Element('div', {
    events: {
        'click': function(event){
            console.log('Clicked');
        }
    }
});
```

290

Here we created a new div element and attached a click event handler to it. Instead of separating the calls to addEvents, we simply included an events object in the properties argument to the Element constructor. This gives us a very handy way to attach event handlers to new elements.

Like its counterpart from the native event models, the MooTools addEvent method allows event handlers to be attached only once.

```
var handler = function(){
    console.log('Clicked.');
};

var item = $('item');
item.addEvent('click', handler);
item.addEvent('click', handler);
item.addEvent('click', handler);
```

In this snippet, we tried attaching the handler function as a click event handler to the item element three times. Like in the native event models, though, the handler function will only be attached once in order to prevent us from accidentally attaching the function more than once.

One tricky part is the dispatch order of event handlers. We learned that in the IE model, event handlers are invoked randomly, while in the standard model, they are invoked according to the order they were added. The MooTools event system, being built on top of these two native models, inherits the dispatch order of whatever model the current browser uses.

```
var handlerA = function(){
    console.log('Handler A.');
};

var handlerB = function(){
    console.log('Handler B.');
};

var item = $('item');
item.addEvent('click', handlerA);
item.addEvent('click', handlerB);
```

If we run this snippet on a browser that uses the standard model, we're guaranteed that handlerA will always be called first before handlerB. But if we run this on IE, we'll also get the same behavior as the IE model where event handlers are invoked randomly. This is because, as we'll see later on, MooTools uses both models internally in its implementation of an event system.

Preventing Default Action

Remember this example?

```
<a href="home.html">Home</a>
<a href="about.html">About</a>
<a href="projects.html">Projects</a>
```

We have a set of links that point to different pages and we wanted to stop the browser from doing the default click action, which is to load the page referenced by the href attribute of the links. In the IE model, we used window.event.returnValue = false to do this, while we used the preventDefault method of the event object in the standard model.

MooTools takes its inspiration from the standard model, and provides its own preventDefault method for its event object:

```
var links = $$('a');
links.addEvent('click', function(event){
    event.preventDefault();
});
```

Here we attach a new event handler to all the links using addEvent. Inside our handler function, we use the preventDefault method of the event object argument to stop the browser from performing the default action associated with the event.

Stopping Event Propagation

Let's take a look at a rewriting of an earlier example that let us observe event propagation at work:

```
<html>
    <head>
    <script src="mootools.js"></script>
    <script>
        window.addEvent('domready', function(){
            var items = $$('img, body, html');
            items.addEvent('click', function(event){
                console.log('Clicked: ' + this.get('tag'));
            });
        });
    </script>
    </head>
    <body>
        <img src="hello.png">
    </body>
</html>
```

In this example, we attach a click event handler to the <img>, <body>, and <html> elements. When we run this example on the browser and click on the <img> element, we get the following output:

```
Clicked: img
Clicked: body
Clicked: html
```

We already know that this is event propagation at work: the events that happen on the target node are propagated upwards to its parent nodes. This model of propagation, where the event dispatch happens from the bottom up, is called the bubbling model and it is the only propagation model supported by all event systems—including MooTools'.

In instances when we don't want propagation to happen, we can stop it using native techniques. In the IE model, we use the window.event.cancelBubble property, and in the standard model, we use the stopPropagation method. Like preventDefault, the MooTools event system also takes its cue from the standard system:

```
<html>
    <head>
    <script src="mootools.js"></script>
    <script>
        window.addEvent('domready', function(){
            var items = $$('img, body, html');
            items.addEvent('click', function(event){
                event.stopPropagation();
                console.log('Clicked: ' + this.get('tag'));
```

```
            });
        });
    </script>
</head>
<body>
    <img src="hello.png">
</body>
</html>
```

Event objects in MooTools also have a `stopPropagation` method that halts the event propagation process. Here we invoke the `stopPropagation` method of the event object inside our handler function, making the propagation halt when any of the elements is clicked. Running this in a browser and clicking on the image element, we get the following output:

```
Clicked: img
```

The event bubbling was stopped after that first click, and the event handlers of the parent nodes of the image element were not fired.

Stopping Events All Together

There are some cases when we'll want to prevent the default action of an event as well as stop the event propagation process. Take the following example for instance:

```
<html>
    <body>
        <a href="index.html">Home</a>
    </body>
</html>
```

Here we have a simple HTML snippet. We want to prevent the default behavior when the link is clicked, and we want the event propagation to also be halted. We can do the following to achieve this:

```
var link = $$('a');
link.addEvent('click', function(event){
    event.preventDefault();
    event.stopPropagation();
});
```

We attach a click event handler to our link and inside the event handler, we call the `preventDefault` and `stopPropagation` methods of the event object argument to stop the browser from performing the default click action for the link, as well as to prevent our click event from being propagated.

MooTools, however, provides another method called `stop`, which can be used as a shortcut to replace these two calls:

```
var link = $$('a');
link.addEvent('click', function(event){
    event.stop();
});
```

Instead of calling `preventDefault` and `stopPropagation` separately, we call the `stop` method of the event object. Internally, this method combines the `preventDefault` and `stopPropagation` methods into one function, making it easier to call both functions at once. The results of this snippet and the previous are the same: the link's default click action is stopped, and the event propagation process is halted.

Detaching Event Handlers

The MooTools event system provides the removeEvent method that can be used to detach event handlers from elements, which is similar to IE's detachEvent and the standard removeEventListener. It takes two arguments: type, which is a string denoting the event name, and fn, which is the handler to detach.

```
var counter = 0;
var handler = function(event){
    if (counter < 3){
        console.log('Hello!');
    } else {
        this.removeEvent('click', handler);
    }
    counter++;
};

var item = $('item');
item.addEvent('click', handler);
```

Here we rewrote our self-detaching handler example to use the MooTools event API. Like its native counterparts, the removeEvent method expects that the fn argument is the exact same handler function that was attached using addEvent in order to properly detach the event handler.

Like addEvent, removeEvent has a multiple-handler version called removeEvents. It also takes a single argument, events, which is an object containing the events to detach:

```
var item = $('item');

var clickHandler = function(){},
    dblclickHandler = function(){},
    focusHandler = function(){};

item.addEvents({
    'click': clickHandler,
    'dblclick': dblclickHandler,
    'focus': focusHandler
});

item.removeEvents({
    'dblclick': dblclickHandler,
    'focus': focusHandler
});
```

In this snippet, we create three event handlers: clickHandler, dblclickHandler, and focusHandler. We then use the addEvents method to attach all three handlers to the item element. Next we call on removeEvents to detach the dblclick and focus handlers. Our item method now has only one event handler, the one for click.

Take note that unlike addEvents and set, the removeEvents handler can't be used with the universal modificator function erase. This is because the Element.Properties.events object doesn't define an erase function, so the erase method won't have a dynamic property function to use.

Dispatching Events

The MooTools event dispatch API is patterned after the IE model, which is much simpler than the standard model. Internally, though, it's much more complex than either model, but we'll talk about that later.

To dispatch events in MooTools, we use the fireEvent method. This method takes two arguments: type, which is the type of event to dispatch as a string, and event, which is an object that will be passed as the event object to the handlers:

```
var handler = function(){
    console.log('Clicked');
};

var link = $('main');
link.addEvent('click', handler);

// dispatch a click event
setTimeout(function(){
    link.fireEvent('click');
}, 5000);
```

In this snippet, we dispatch the click event of the link element after 5 seconds. This will call the handler function, and give us a log output of 'Clicked'.

You'll notice that we didn't supply fireEvent with a second argument. This is because the event argument to fireEvent is optional. For native events, MooTools automatically creates an Event object for fireEvent, but you can also supply this argument yourself—or omit it if necessary, like what we did in our example.

You can pass any object argument to fireEvent, even if it's not a true event object:

```
var handler = function(event){
    console.log(event.foo); // 'bar'
};

var link = $('main');
link.addEvent('click', handler);

// dispatch a click event
setTimeout(function(){
    link.fireEvent('click', {foo: 'bar'});
}, 5000);
```

Here we passed a basic object with the property foo to fireEvent. When fireEvent dispatches our handler function, it passes the object we used as an argument. The console will then output the value of the foo property, which is 'bar'.

Another great feature of fireEvent is that you can have more than one argument for the event handler by providing an array argument to event:

```
var handler = function(a, b){
    console.log(a); // 'foo'
    console.log(b); // 'bar'
};

var link = $('main');
link.addEvent('click', handler);
```

```
// dispatch a click event
setTimeout(function(){
    link.fireEvent('click', ['foo', 'bar']);
}, 5000);
```

In this example, we dispatch the click event of link using the fireEvent method, but we pass an array of two strings as the event argument. These two strings are then passed to the event handlers of the element. In this case, the first string corresponds to the a parameter of handler, while the second string corresponds to b.

As you can see, the MooTools event dispatch API is a far cry from the complex dispatch APIs we've seen so far. This simplicity of the dispatch API—and the whole events system—is in part due to nifty tricks that MooTools uses for its event system. And these tricks are what we're going to look at now.

Event System Internals

Now that we've seen the external API that we'll use to work with the MooTools event system, it's time to dig deeper and look at how MooTools implements its event system. There are several moving parts that we need to put together to get a full view of the MooTools event system, and we'll discuss each one in turn.

The Event Type

Unlike the standard model (and like the IE model), there's just one event type in MooTools, represented by the Event type object. And unlike all other types we've seen so far, the Event type is special because it does not directly override the native event type of the browser. Instead, the Event type acts as a "proxy" for the native event type.

This might be confusing, so let's have an example:

```
var item = $('item');

var firstEvent;

item.addEventListener('click', function(event){
    firstEvent = event;
}, false);

item.addEventListener('click', function(event){
    console.log(firstEvent === event); // true
}, false);
```

Here we attach two click event handlers to the item element. The first event handler stores the value of its event object into a variable called firstEvent, while the second event handler compares whether the event object passed to the first handler—as stored inside firstEvent—is the same as the event object passed to it. When we run this on a browser and click on the item element, we get a console output of true, which means that they're the same objects.

However, take a look at this example

```
var item = $('item');

var nativeEvent;

item.addEventListener('click', function(event){
```

```
    nativeEvent = event;
}, false);

item.addEvent('click', function(event){
    console.log(nativeEvent == event); // false
});
```

In this snippet, we also attach two click handlers to the item element, but we do so using both the standard event API and the MooTools event API. Like the previous example, the second event handler also compares the two event objects. However, as we'll see if we run this in the browser, the event object passed to the first event handler is a different object from the one passed to the second event handler.

These examples are interesting because they show us that the MooTools event system uses a different event object from the native one. Unlike with Elements, MooTools does not directly extend the native event objects, but rather creates a new type that "wraps" the original event object. This new type is, of course, the Event type.

The Event constructor requires a single argument, event, which should be a native event object. The event constructor then takes this native event object and stores it as a property of the Event instance, making it accessible via the event property name. This means you can access the native event object that a MooTools event object wraps via the event property:

```
var item = $('item');

var nativeEvent;

item.addEventListener('click', function(event){
    nativeEvent = event;
}, false);

item.addEvent('click', function(event){
    console.log(nativeEvent == event.event); // true
});
```

In this example, we modified our second event handler so that it compares the nativeEvent object to the event property instead of directly comparing the two event objects. The console output in this case is true, telling us that the event property of the MooTools event object is the original native event object passed by the browser's event dispatcher.

In order to make the Event type cross-browser, it needs to support the IE model as well. Because the IE model does not supply individual event objects, the Event constructor makes use of window.event for this browser. We can confirm this with the following snippet:

```
var item = $('item');

item.addEvent('click', function(event){
    console.log(window.event == event.event); // true
});
```

This snippet, works in Internet Explorer only, confirms that the event property of the event object passed to our click handler is the same object as the global event object.

This native event wrapping is essential because it enables MooTools to have a flexible Event type that works regardless of which event model the browser uses. Internally, the MooTools uses feature detection—which we discussed in Chapter 7—to implement the methods of the Event type.

Let's take the preventDefault method of MooTools event objects, for example. In the IE model, we have to use window.event.returnValue = false to stop the browser from performing the default action for an event. On the other hand, we use the preventDefault method to achieve the same in the standard model. The MooTools preventDefault method is implemented like so:

```
Event.implement('preventDefault', function(){
    if (this.event.preventDefault) this.event.preventDefault();
    else this.event.returnValue = false;
    return this;
});
```

Using the wrapped event object, MooTools detects whether the current browser supports the standard model's preventDefault method, and then calls the method if so. If the current browser doesn't, MooTools falls back to the IE model's returnValue technique.

Similarly, the stopPropagation method is implemented using feature detection:

```
Event.implement('stopPropagation', function(){
    if (this.event.stopPropagation) this.event.stopPropagation();
    else this.event.cancelBubble = true;
    return this;
});
```

Like native event objects, the MooTools event object has properties that give us more information about the event.

- type is the string name of the event, such as 'click' or 'mouseover'.

- target is a reference to the element where the event originated.

- shift, alt, meta, and ctrl are Booleans that denote the state of the modifier keys during the event. These properties are similar to the shiftKey, altKey, metaKey, and ctrlKey properties of native event objects.

- code is a property is similar to the keyCode value in the IE model, which means that it has a different value depending on the keyboard event. For the keydown and keyup events, this property will be a number that represents the keycode value of key pressed, such as 77 for the M key or 118 for the F7 key. Meanwhile, this property, when used in conjunction with the keypress event, will be the Unicode value of the specific character, such as 77 for the uppercase M and 109 for the lowercase m.

- key event is a lowercase string that contains the name of the key pressed during a keyboard event. For example, if the user pressed the Enter key, the value of this property will be 'enter'. Other possible values are 'up', 'down', 'left', 'right', 'space', 'backspace', 'delete', and 'esc'.

- wheel is a special numeric property used for the mousewheel event that indicates the amount of scrolling of the user's mousewheel that triggered the event.

- page and client are coordinate objects that indicate the position of the mouse pointer during a mouse event. The page object has two properties, x and y, which indicate the horizontal and vertical coordinates of the pointer in relation to the document. The client object also has two properties, x and y, which indicate the coordinates of the pointer in relation to the window.

These properties are added directly by the Event constructor to the event object instance by going through the native event object. Like the IE model, the MooTools event object does not differentiate between different event types, but uses a single type to handle all events. Most of these properties are compatible with the native event objects from both models, but some don't have native equivalents. If you need to access the native properties, though, remember that you can always access the native event object using the event property.

Two Layers

There are actually two layers to the MooTools event system. One layer deals with making the event system work with the native event layer, and the other deals with the MooTools-specific event features. These two layers are intertwined, and you won't notice this unless you dig through the source.

At the native level are two Element methods called addListener and removeListener, which are cross-browser wrappers for the event handler attachment and detachment functions. The addListener method takes two arguments, type and fn, which correspond to the same arguments used for attachEvent and addEventListener. When we invoke the addListener method of an element, it attaches the fn handler function using addEventListener if the browser supports the standard model, or attachEvent if the browser supports the IE model.

The removeListener method also takes the same two arguments, and it corresponds to the detachEvent and removeEventListener methods from the native models. Like the addListener method, the removeListener method is also aware of the event model used by the browser and switches between using detachEvent and removeEventListener automatically.

These are the two methods that allow MooTools to attach and detach handlers in a cross-browser function. When we call the addEvent and removeEvent methods, MooTools automatically calls on addListener and removeListener from inside these methods to add the native event handlers for the browser.

The Event Table

However, things aren't as straightforward as that. The addEvent and removeEvent methods actually perform several operations before attaching and detaching the native event handlers. Like the class system, MooTools adds powerful new features to the native event system using JavaScript, and these new features depend on addEvent and removeEvent to work.

The first feature that MooTools adds is an internal event table. The event table is an object where the event handlers for an element are stored. Each element has its own internal event table, which is kept inside an element's storage object:

```
var item = $('item');

console.log(typeOf(item.retrieve('events'))); // 'null'

var handler = function(){};
item.addEvent('click', handler);

console.log(typeOf(item.retrieve('events'))); // 'object'
```

An element's event table can be accessed through the storage method retrieve that we saw in the Chapter 8, and it is kept under the key events. In this example, we first try accessing the element's event table by calling on retrieve('events'), but because our element has no event handlers yet, we get null. After this line, we attach an empty click event handler to the same element, and then try retrieving its event table again. This time we don't get null; instead we get an object. And this object is the element's newly created event table.

The event table is actually a collection of *weakmaps* that are used to keep track of your event handlers. A weakmap is a special object that has two properties, keys and values. Unlike a regular object where the mapping is direct, a weak map uses index-based mapping. For instance, look at the following object map:

```
{
    'keyA': function A(){},
    'keyB': function B(){}
}
```

This object has two keys, keyA and keyB, which have two function values. The mapping here is direct: keyA is a direct reference to function A, while keyB is a direct reference to function B. In contrast, a weakmap uses indirect mapping:

```
{
    'keys': ['keyA', 'keyB'],
    'values': [function A(){}, function B(){}]
}
```

Here the object has two properties, keys and values, which are both arrays. The keys array stores the keys of the objects, while the values array stores the values of the keys. The mapping here is indirect: the first item in the keys table corresponds to the first item in the values table, and so on. So the value of the key keyA, which has the index 0 in the keys array, is function A(){}, which has the index 0 in the values array. Because the mapping between items is indirectly done using indices of the array, the mapping is considered "weak". Thus, the name "weakmap."

Why does the event table use weakmaps? The answer lies in the fact that weakmaps have a very interesting feature: because the keys of a weakmap are stored using an array, you can use any value as a key. That means you can use objects, functions, or even arrays themselves. You'll understand why this is important in a little while.

An element's event table is composed of several weakmaps, one for each event. In the example above, the event table of the item element would look like this:

```
{
    'click': {
        'keys': [handler],
        'values': [function(){ return handler.call(element); }]
    }
}
```

Here we see that the event table has one property, click, which contains the weakmap for the element's click event handlers. When we attached the handler function as the event handler of the item element, MooTools first pushed the handler function to the click weakmap's keys array.

But what about the value? We see in this example that the value isn't the handler function, but another function that calls handler. This is because the MooTools event system (like the class system), does function wrapping. What this means is that the handler functions we pass to addEvent are wrapped in another function.

Event Handler Wrapping

In the chapter on classes, we saw how the MooTools implement method wraps the methods of a class in a special wrapper function in order to provide features such as this.parent() and protected functions. In the MooTools event system, the addEvent method also wraps the handler function to provide additional features.

The MooTools event system makes a distinction between user events and native events. A user event is an event that's not natively supported by the browser, and is therefore never dispatched by the native event dispatcher. For instance a foo event or a bar event are user events: these events may be created by the user for his own use, and are dispatched in the code using the MooTools fireEvent method. However, because the browser doesn't understand these events, they will never be dispatched by the native event systems, so we don't need to add native event handlers for these.

Native events, on the other hand, are the events that the browser supports. These include events like click and mouseover, as well as a host of other events defined by the environment and the different DOM standards. Because they are dispatched by the browser directly, we need to add native event handlers for these events using the addEventListener or attachEvent methods.

In the MooTools event system, handler functions are processed depending on whether they're user events or native events. For user events, the handler function will be wrapped with a very simple wrapper function that looks like this:

```
function(){
    return fn.call(self);
}
```

This is the basic wrapper used in MooTools for user events. The fn identifier in this case is the actual event handler function passed to addEvent, while self is a reference to the element. The wrapper uses fn.call(self) in this case to make sure that the handler function is called with its this keyword pointing to the element. This solves the problem in the IE model, where the event handlers have their this keyword pointing to window.

Because user events aren't understood by the browser, no native event handler is added to the element. This means that after wrapping the handler function, the addEvent method will simply store this wrapped function inside the element's event table, under the values array of the particular event weakmap.

On the other hand, native events are much more complicated. MooTools keeps track of which events are native events using a special object called Element.NativeEvents:

```
Element.NativeEvents = {
    // mouse click events
    click: 2, dblclick: 2, mouseup: 2, mousedown: 2, contextmenu: 2,

    // mouse wheel events
    mousewheel: 2, DOMMouseScroll: 2,

    // mouse movement events
    mouseover: 2, mouseout: 2, mousemove: 2, selectstart: 2, selectend: 2,

    // keyboard events
    keydown: 2, keypress: 2, keyup: 2,

    // mobile events
    orientationchange: 2,

    // touch events
    touchstart: 2, touchmove: 2, touchend: 2, touchcancel: 2,

    // gesture events
    gesturestart: 2, gesturechange: 2, gestureend: 2,

    // form events
    focus: 2, blur: 2, change: 2, reset: 2, select: 2, submit: 2,

    // window events
    load: 2, unload: 1, beforeunload: 2, resize: 1,
    move: 1, DOMContentLoaded: 1, readystatechange: 1,

    // misc events
    error: 1, abort: 1, scroll: 1
};
```

This is the actual `Element.NativeEvents` object. Each key of this object corresponds to the name of a known and supported native event. Here you'll see all the common events like `click`, `dblclick`, and `keypress`.

When we call the `addEvent` method, MooTools will check the value of the type string argument against the properties of the `Element.NativeEvents` object to check whether we're attaching a user event or a native event. If the value of the type argument corresponds to a property of the `Element.NativeEvents` object, `addEvent` will wrap the event handler argument and then attach it using the `addListener` method we discussed a few sections back before pushing the wrapped function to the `values` array of the event's weakmap.

And there lies the distinction between user events and native events. For user events, MooTools doesn't attach a native event handler to the element using `addListener`, but simply stores the wrapped event handler inside the `values` array. On the other hand, MooTools does attach a native event handler for native events before storing the wrapped function in the events table.

Notice, however, that the events defined in the `Element.NativeEvents` object have different values. Most of the events have the value 2, but some events, like unload and resize have the value 1. Those values group the native events into two categories: events with the value of 1 are non-bubbling and non-cancelable, while the events with the value of 2 are bubbling and cancelable.

This distinction is important. For non-bubbling and non-cancelable events, their event objects become somewhat useless: they can't be canceled, so we can't use `preventDefault` and they can't bubble so we don't have to use `stopPropagation`. In contrast, bubbling and cancelable are more interesting because they enable us to control the event itself.

This grouping becomes even more important in MooTools. For events that are non-bubbling and non-cancelable, MooTools does not create event objects:

```
window.addEvent('resize', function(event){
    console.log(event); // undefined
});
```

Here we attached a resize event handler to the window object. When we run this in a browser and resize the window, we see that MooTools does not pass an event object to the handler function, which is why we get undefined. This is because the resize event falls under the non-cancelable and non-bubbling category.

This behavior is controlled by the function wrapping. If the native event we're adding falls under the non-bubbling, non-cancelable category, MooTools wraps the event handler function like a simple user event:

```
function(){
    return fn.call(self);
}
```

As with simple events, this wrapper function takes the `fn` function—which is the original event handler passed to `addEvent`—and invokes it via the `call` method, binding it to the current element. This wrapped function will then be added as a native event handler to the element using the `addListener` method.

Notice that the wrapper function doesn't have an event formal parameter. This means that the event object passed by the native event system will be discarded by this wrapped event handler—which is why we don't get event objects in our handler function.

On the other hand, bubbling, cancelable events are wrapped in a different function:

```
function(event){
    event = new Event(event, self.getWindow());
    if (condition.call(self, event) === false) event.stop();
}
```

Here you can see that the event formal parameter is now in place, making this wrapped function able to receive the event object from the native event system. Inside the function, the native event received from the native event system is first turned into a MooTools event object by passing it to the Event constructor. The condition identifier in this case is a reference to a function, which we'll discuss later. For now, think of the condition as the same function as the original event handler passed to addEvent. This wrapped function is then attached as a native event handler to the element using addListener.

It's easy to get confused in the process, so let's recap it using two examples. Let's start with a basic user event:

```
var item = $('item');
item.addEvent('foo', function(){
    console.log('Foo');
});
```

Here we call addEvent to attach a foo event handler to the item element, passing in the value 'foo' for the type argument and a function for the fn argument. The process then proceeds as follows:

1. First, addEvent checks whether the item element has an event table by calling item.retrieve('events'). Since this is the first time an event was attached to the item, no event table for the element exists yet, so addEvent will create a new one.

2. The addEvent method then looks for the foo weakmap in the newly created event table. Since there's no foo weakmap yet, it creates a new one by assigning item.retrieve('events')['foo'] = {keys:[], values: []}, before pushing the event handler fn to the foo weakmap's keys array.

3. The Element.NativeEvents object is then checked to see if there's a native event called foo. Since there's no native event with that name, no native event handler will be added.

4. The event handler function is then wrapped using the simple wrapper function.

5. The addEvent method then pushes the wrapped event handler to the values array of the foo weakmap.

Now let's trace the process for a native event:

```
var item = $('item');
item.addEvent('click', function(){
    console.log('click');
});
```

For this example, we're attaching a click event handler to the item element.

1. The *addEvent* method checks for the item element's event table, creating a new one if it doesn't exist.

2. The click weakmap of the item element's event table is checked, and a new one created if one doesn't exist.

3. The Element.NativeEvents object is checked to see if there's a native event called click, and the value of this native event will be checked, too.

4. Since Element.NativeEvents.click exists with the value 2, the event handler will be wrapped in a special wrapper function that takes the passed event object and turns it into a MooTools event object.

5. The wrapped event handler is then attached as a native event listener for the element's click event using `addListener`.

6. The `addEvent` method then pushes the wrapped event handler to the values array of the click weakmap.

One thing we have to understand is that the handler function we pass to `addEvent` is never really attached directly as a native element event handler. Rather, it's the wrapped version of the handler function that is attached for native events. This enables MooTools to do two things: first, it makes the event handlers bound to the element by ensuring that they are invoked using the `call` method, and second, it gives MooTools the chance to turn the native event object into a MooTools event object before it is passed to the actual event handler.

Event Handler Detachment and Dispatch

Because event handlers are wrapped, we get a very interesting problem when it comes to detaching them. Remember that to work properly, the native handler detachment functions, `removeEventListener` and `detachEvent`, depend on being provided with the exact same attached handler function. However, the native event handlers that the MooTools event system adds are wrapped versions—which means we don't have access to them. How do we remove them then?

This brings us to the importance of weakmaps in the event table. Because the weakmap allows us to use non-string keys, we're able to use the original handler function as the key. We can then associate the handler function by making it the value of the particular key in the weakmap. As long as we can provide the original handler function to it, the MooTools event system will be able to locate the wrapped event handler in our event's weakmap.

When we call `removeEvent`, the method first searches the event's weakmap to find the handler function and its associated wrapped version. Then it deletes the handler function from the keys array of the weakmap, before checking if the event is a native event handler. If it is, it calls on `removeListener`, passing in the wrapped handler function, in order to detach the native event handler from the element. Finally, the wrapped version is removed from the weakmap.

And that leaves us with just one item: the dispatch API. One interesting feature of the dispatch component of the MooTools event system is that it does not rely on explicit dispatch. For the MooTools event attachment and detachment APIs, we saw that they used native APIs in order to provide these features, explicitly calling native methods such as `addEventListener` and `removeEventListener`. The MooTools event dispatcher, however, doesn't call on native methods directly, so there are no calls to the IE `fireEvent` or standard `dispatchEvent` methods.

Instead, MooTools relies on implicit dispatch for the native event system. Remember that in addition to storing the event handlers in its own internal event table, MooTools also attaches native event handlers to elements that call the original event handlers. These act as the "dispatchers" for the MooTools event system.

Explicit dispatch using the MooTools `fireEvent` method, on the other hand, is a whole different matter. Like the native explicit dispatchers, `fireEvent` expects us to provide our own event objects for the dispatch. The great thing, though, is that the `fireEvent` method is flexible enough that we can pass any kind of value to it to serve as the arguments for our event handlers.

When we call the `fireEvent` method of an element, it first searches the event table of the element for handlers attached to that particular event. It then loops through each one in turn, invoking them with the arguments you've passed for the event handler. This is very similar to how the native dispatch systems work.

Custom Events

Let's look at that native event handler again:

```
function(event){
    event = new Event(event, self.getWindow());
    if (condition.call(self, event) === false) event.stop();
}
```

As I mentioned some paragraphs above, the `condition` identifier here is a function, and I said that it's the event handler we passed to `addEvent`. Of course, that was a simplification. While there are some cases where `condition` is indeed the handler function, it can also be something else—something that highlights one of the best features of the MooTools event system.

Recall that there are two kinds of events supported by MooTools: user events, which are created by the user but not understood by the native event system, and native events, which are events defined by specifications and the browser's own event system. We said that the main difference between these two is that MooTools attaches native event handlers to the elements for native events, while user events don't get any native handlers attached.

MooTools actually supports a third kind of event, a hybrid between user events and native events called custom events. A custom event is a user-defined event that's based on a native event, and therefore uses native event handlers. We can think of native events as our own modified version of native events, which we can define and use for our own programs.

To see how custom events work, let's try creating our own event. First, though, let's see how we might use it:

```
var item = $('item');
item.addEvent('click', function(event){
    if (event.shift) console.log('shift click!');
});
```

Here we have a simple event handler attached to the item element. Inside our event handler, we check the event object's `shift` property to see if the shift key was pressed while the user was clicking on the element. When we run this in the browser and try clicking on the element, we get no console output. However, if we click on the element while holding down the shift key, we'll get the console output 'shift click!'.

So let's say we're going to use this kind of handler a lot. Wouldn't it be easier if we could simply attach an event handler directly to a shiftclick event so that we don't have to check `event.shift` every time? This is where custom events come in.

All custom events are stored in a special object called `Element.Events`. To define a new custom event, we simply have to augment this object with a new custom event object. A custom event object is a simple object that has two main properties: `base`, which is a string that defines the native event where the custom event will be based from, and `condition`, which is a function that's going to be used to test whether the event has happened.

Going back to our shiftclick event, let's see how to define it. First we need a base event, and in this case, it'll be the click event. Second, we need a test, which is simple enough in our case: check if the shift key was pressed during the event. And with that, we have our custom event:

```
Element.Events.shiftclick = {

    base: 'click',

    condition: function(event){
        return event.shift;
```

```
    }
};
```

Now that it's defined, we can rewrite our original example to something much simpler:

```
var item = $('item');
item.addEvent('shiftclick', function(event){
    console.log('shift click!');
});
```

In this new snippet, we attach an event handler for the new shiftclick event. Now when we click on the element, MooTools will automatically run our condition function to check whether the shift key was pressed during the event by looking at the value of the event.shift property. If is the shift key was pressed, our event handler will be invoked, and we'll get a nice console output of 'shift click!'.

Since we now know about custom events, we'll need to revisit our addEvent and removeEvent processes to take custom events into account. When we attach a new event handler using addEvent, the first thing MooTools does after pushing the event handler function to the event table is to check the Element.Events object to see whether the type argument we passed is a custom event. If it is a custom event, MooTools will wrap the event handler in a wrapper function that looks like this:

```
function(event){
    if (custom.condition.call(this, event)) return fn.call(this, event);
    return true;
}
```

This function will become the value of the condition identifier we saw earlier in this section, which is invoked inside the native event handler. The custom.condition identifier in this new wrapper function actually points to the condition function defined in the custom event object. If the custom.condition function returns true, our real handler function will be invoked.

The next thing that MooTools does is to check the base property of the custom event object. The base property of the custom event object is used to determine the native event that will be the basis of the custom event. MooTools will then add a native event handler to this native event, which will be used to fire the condition function.

The result is a very powerful addition to the event system that allows us to define a multitude of new events based on native events already understood by the browser. This gives us freedom to design new and much more complex events that we can use to write rich and powerful applications for the browser.

The Wrap-Up

And here ends this loopy chapter. We started out with the basics of event-based programming: main loops, event loops, event systems, and events themselves, and then we examined the browser's own event system. We took a look at the two main models of event systems, then moved on to saner grounds as we explored the MooTools event system and how it enables us to create truly cross-browser event-based programs.

The next chapter brings us back to elements and how they are selected. We won't talk about functions and methods to do this, though—no, that was done in Chapter 8. What we will explore is the Deus behind the Machina: the thing that enables us to actually find that elemental needle in the DOM Tree haystack.

So line up at the concession stand and get yourself a soda and some popcorn because the show's about to begin: the supporting cast is the CSS Selectors, and the star is the Selector Engine.

CHAPTER 11

■■■

Request

There is perhaps no bigger revolution that propelled JavaScript to where it is today than Ajax. This paradigm shift that started in the early 2000s brought JavaScript back to the center of Web development and restored the luster it had lost during its early years. And this whole revolution happened because of the rediscovery of a very interesting object called the XMLHttpRequest.

In this chapter, we'll learn about the HTTP request and response process, and how XMLHttpRequest fits into the equation. We'll also talk about the MooTools Request class, a simple abstraction of the native XMLHttpRequest API, and how it makes working with requests easier and more MooToolsian.

Requests and Responses

At the most basic level, *browsers* are tools for displaying resources on the Web, resources that are stored in special places called *servers*. At the heart of the Web is the communication between browsers and servers, and it is this communication that underlies everything we do online.

The communication between browsers and servers is a very complex topic, one that touches subjects we don't really need in our discussion. However, a certain part of browser-server communication—the **request-response flow**—is integral to understanding web applications, and we need a basic understanding of this process in order to fully grasp the things we'll see later.

When a browser loads a resource, it first sends a request to the server. A **request** is a set of directives containing information about what exactly we're requesting, as well as other criteria for the resource we're trying to fetch. Let's say we're loading http://foo.com/index.html in our browser. The browser first connects to the server for foo.com and then sends a request that looks like this:

```
GET /index.html HTTP/1.1
User-Agent: BrowserX/1.1
Host: foo.com
Accept: text/html
```

This request has several parts. The first line starts with the *method*, which is a verb that describes the action we want to perform on the particular resource. In this example, we use the GET method, which tells the server we would like to fetch the particular resource. Other supported verbs include POST and PUT for sending user data to a particular resource, DELETE for removing a particular resource, and HEAD for retrieving the headers for a resource.

Right after the method comes the *resource URI*, which describes the path of the resource we want to access. In our example, we told the server for foo.com that we want to access the resource called /index.html. Finally, the first line ends with an *HTTP version identifier*, which tells the server which version of the HTTP protocol we'd like to use.

The first line, which is called the **request line**, is the most important part of the request because it contains the essential information about the request. The next lines, called **headers**, contain other information about the request. A header is a key-value pair that takes the form <Header Name>:

Value>. Each header appears on a separate line, and each describes a specific criterion or property of the request.

Our example has three headers. The first is User-Agent, which identifies the current browser to the server. In our example, the browser is called BrowserX and its version identifier is 1.1. Normally, the value of the User-Agent header is exactly the same string as the value of the navigator.userAgent property we saw in Chapter 7. Next is an Accept header, which tells the server what kinds of files we'd like to receive. In our example, we tell the server to give us files that have the mimetype text/html, a common mimetype for HTML files. Finally, we have the Host header, a required header in HTTP/1.1.

After sending this request to the server, the browser waits for a response. A **response** is a set of directives and properties the server sends back as an answer to a particular request. Our hypothetical foo.com server, for example, could send us back this response in answer to our request:

```
HTTP/1.1 200 OK
Content-Type: text/html
Content-Length: 87

<html>
<head>
    <title>Hello World!</title>
</head>
<body>
    Hello World!
</body>
</html>
```

The first line of the response begins with the *HTTP version identifier*, which tells the browser which version of the HTTP protocol the server used to answer the request. This is followed by the *status code*, a numeric value that determines the nature of the response. A 200 status code, for example, means that the request was correctly answered by the server and there were no errors in putting together a response. A 404 status code, on the other hand, means that the server couldn't find the particular resource asked for by the request. The status code is followed by the *status text*, which is a textual representation of the status code, in our case **OK**.

Because the first line of the response contains information about the status of the response, it's also called the **status line**.

Just as with requests, the headers come after the first line. The response headers, of course, describe the nature of the response, and they also give the browser some instructions regarding how to interpret the particular response. In our example, we have two headers: Content-Type, which describes the mimetype of the response data, and Content-Length, which is the length of the response data.

Right after the final header comes a mandatory blank line, followed by the most important part of the response: the *body*. In most cases, the body contains the actual file data for the particular resource, like in our example where we received the HTML source of the page as a body. This part of the response is the actual content, and is therefore the part we're most interested in.

With the response in hand, the browser can start parsing the HTML source and display the page. When a new resource is needed, the whole process is repeated. This request-response cycle is the lifeblood of browser-server interaction, and it affects the way we develop web applications in a massive way.

The basic request-response cycle fits the model of the web as a collection of hyperlinked documents. A browser first sends a request for a document to a server, and the server then sends a response back to the browser with the requested document. When the user clicks on a hyperlink, the process is repeated. The cycle of requesting a resource and then parsing the response for the resource is suitable for this model of the web because we're working with documents with a very limited interaction framework: open a resource, click links to open more resources, repeat.

Many web applications actually implement this same document-style interaction, and it works for the most part. First a page is shown to the user, then the user performs an action, such as filling in a form and submitting it, which triggers the browser to send a request to the server containing the data provided by the user. The server processes the data and sends a response containing the updated page, which is then displayed to the user by the browser. This process is repeated when the user performs another action.

While this works for simple applications, building more complex web applications that somehow mimic the desktop application model is hard to fit in this style. Desktop applications, which most users are familiar with, are often very dynamic: an action is immediately reflected in the interface, no loading or reloading involved. Simple web applications, on the other hand, feel a lot less like applications and more like web sites because they are too constrained by the hyperlink-style request-response cycle: if a part of the interface needs to be updated, the entire page has to be reloaded.

The problem isn't about developers not being smart enough to create desktop-style applications. Rather, it's about the lack of an API for issuing HTTP requests using JavaScript. Requests happen at the browser level: a default event or piece of JavaScript code triggers the browser to load a page, and the browser does the appropriate HTTP requests to load or reload a page. In the past, there was no infrastructure in place that let developers request data from servers directly using JavaScript.

The landscape changed, however, in the early years of the 21st century, with the rediscovery of a then obscure API. This API, originally developed for loading XML documents into JavaScript, became an instant hit because it enabled developers to make direct HTTP requests using JavaScript. Suddenly, JavaScript gained the necessary ingredient to create powerful web applications.

Using this API, web applications could load or post new content from the server without having to refresh the whole page. This helped developers create rich, complex applications that can rival desktop applications. Users no longer have to wait for a page to reload in order to see their changes, because applications can now make those changes in the background and then update the interface to reflect the changes.

JavaScript-based HTTP requests made web applications less like web sites and more like desktop apps, and the browser became the platform that enabled these rich, dynamic applications to run. JavaScript, as the language of the browser, became the old new cool thing, and the language regained popularity and regard within the developer community. And all of this is because of an obscure object called the XMLHttpRequest.

The XMLHttpRequest Object

That obscure object called the XMLHttpRequest, or **XHR**, is at the heart of the new model of internal requests. First introduced by Microsoft in 1999, XHR is a special object that can be used to make HTTP requests—as well as receive appropriate HTTP responses—from within JavaScript. This object gives us a very simple API that can be used to build a request and send it to a server, as well as the appropriate means to handle the responses the server sends back. As its name implies, an XHR was originally used for retrieving XML documents, but it is flexible enough to be used for any kind of data.

You create an XHR object using the XMLHttpRequest constructor:

```
var xhr = new XMLHttpRequest();
```

This snippet creates a new instance of XMLHttpRequest, which we can now use to send requests to servers. Unlike most other constructors, the XMLHttpRequest constructor takes no arguments, but rather depends on methods to set the appropriate values for the request.

▓ **Note** Older versions of Microsoft Internet Explorer do not have an XMLHttpRequest constructor. Instead, XHRs are created by instantiating ActiveX objects that implement the XMLHttpRequest API. Because this topic has already been covered in numerous books and articles, we won't talk about cross-browser XHR instantiation here.

The first of these methods is open, which is used to initialize a request. It takes two required arguments: method, which is an uppercase string indicating the HTTP method of the request, and url, which is a string that points to the location of the resource we're trying to access. A third argument, async, is used to determine the mode of the request. We'll look at how this third argument affects requests later, but for now we'll pass false as the value of this argument.

```
var xhr = new XMLHttpRequest();
xhr.open('GET', 'http://foo.com/index.html', false);
```

In this snippet, we created a new XHR object called xhr, then called its open method to initialize it. We passed three arguments to open: 'GET', which corresponds to the HTTP method GET, 'http://foo.com/index.html', which is the resource we're trying to load, and a false value, the use of which we'll find out later.

There are several important things you need to remember about these arguments. First, the method argument should always be in uppercase, so it's 'GET' and 'POST', not 'get' or 'Post'. Second and more important, the value for the URI should be in the same domain as the current domain running the script. In our example, we assume that the script is running in the foo.com domain, not www.foo.com or dev.foo.com.

▓ **Note** That last point is important. One of the limitations of XHRs is imposed by the *same-origin policy*. This is a security concept that limits XHRs to requesting resources only from the same domain in which they are running. This security "feature" was put into place to prevent malicious scripts from sending or loading data from other malicious sites.

You'll notice that these arguments correspond to the request line of the HTTP request message:

```
GET /index.html HTTP/1.1
```

The HTTP version identifier, which is the last part of the request line, isn't included in the formal parameters of the open method, because the browser itself sets which version of the HTTP protocol to use.

Another method of XHRs is setRequestHeader, which is used to add appropriate headers to the request. It takes two arguments: header, which is a string name of the header we're adding, and value, which is the value of the header.

```
var xhr = new XMLHttpRequest();
xhr.open('GET', 'http://foo.com/index.html', false);
xhr.setRequestHeader('Accept', 'text/html');
```

Here we added a single request header called 'Accept', which tells our server the kind of file we want to receive. Our request message now looks like this:

```
GET /index.html HTTP/1.1
Accept: text/html
```

Note that some common or required headers, such as Host or User-Agent, are added automatically by the browser, so we no longer need to add them explicitly.

At this point, our request is ready to be sent to the server. We do this using the send method:

```
var xhr = new XMLHttpRequest();
xhr.open('GET', 'http://foo.com/index.html', false);
xhr.setRequestHeader('Accept', 'text/html');
xhr.send();
```

Here we send the original example above by calling the send method of our XHR object. This tells the browser to send an HTTP GET request to foo.com to retrieve the /index.html resource.

Sometimes you'll need to send data with your request, especially for requests that use the POST and PUT methods. In that case, you'll need to pass the optional body argument to the send method. This argument should be a string that contains the data you want to send.

```
var data = 'name=Mark&age=23';

var xhr = new XMLHttpRequest();
xhr.open('POST', 'http://foo.com/data/', false);
xhr.setRequestHeader('Content-Type', 'application/x-www-form-urlencoded');
xhr.setRequestHeader('Content-Length', data.length);
xhr.send(data);
```

In this snippet, we need to send the value of the data variable to http://foo.com/data. First we create a new XHR object, then we initialize it using the open method, specifying the POST method and the URL endpoint. We then set two necessary headers, Content-Type and Content-Length, which are used by the server in parsing the data. Finally, we send the request using the send method, passing in the data variable that becomes the body of our request. Our request message will look like this:

```
POST /data HTTP/1.1
Host: foo.com
Content-Type: application/x-www-form-urlencoded
Content-Length: 16

name=Mark&age=23
```

Now that we've sent the request, it's time to parse the response. When the data is received back from the server after sending the request, the browser will update the XHR object and put the data from the response into properties. Let's say that after sending our GET example above, the server responds with the following:

```
HTTP/1.1 200 OK
Content-Type: text/html
Content-Length: 87

<html>
<head>
    <title>Hello World!</title>
</head>
<body>
    Hello World!
</body>
</html>
```

We can access the parts of this response using the properties of the XHR object itself. The first property is status, a numeric value that corresponds to the status code of the response:

```
var xhr = new XMLHttpRequest();
xhr.open('GET', 'http://foo.com/index.html', false);
xhr.setRequestHeader('Accept', 'text/html');
xhr.send();

console.log(xhr.status); // 200
```

Here we sent the original GET example, which returns the response we saw above. We then retrieve the status code of the response by accessing xhr.status, whose value in this example is 200, just like our response.

A related property, statusText, gives us the status code plus the status text of the response as a string:

```
var xhr = new XMLHttpRequest();
xhr.open('GET', 'http://foo.com/index.html', false);
xhr.setRequestHeader('Accept', 'text/html');
xhr.send();

console.log(xhr.statusText); // 'OK'
```

Response headers can be accessed using the getResponseHeader method. This method takes a single argument, headerName, and returns the value for that particular header:

```
var xhr = new XMLHttpRequest();
xhr.open('GET', 'http://foo.com/index.html', false);
xhr.setRequestHeader('Accept', 'text/html');
xhr.send();

console.log(xhr.getResponseHeader('Content-Type')); // 'text/html'
console.log(xhr.getResponseHeader('Content-Length')); // '87'

console.log(xhr.getResponseHeader('Fake-Header')); // null
```

The getResponseHeader method always returns a string containing the value of the header if the header is present, and null if the header doesn't exist in the response. In this example, we used the getResponseHeader method to retrieve the values of the Content-Type and Content-Length headers of the response. Because these two headers exist in the response, getResponseHeader returns their values as strings. However, when we tried retrieving the value of Fake-Header using the same method, we get null because the response doesn't have this header.

You can retrieve all response headers using the getAllResponseHeaders method. This method returns a string containing all the headers of the request, one header per line.

```
var xhr = new XMLHttpRequest();
xhr.open('GET', 'http://foo.com/index.html', false);
xhr.setRequestHeader('Accept', 'text/html');
xhr.send();

console.log(xhr.getAllResponseHeaders());
```

This snippet will log the following string:

```
'Content-Type: text/html
Content-Length: 87'
```

Finally, you can access the body of the response itself using responseText, which is a string containing the raw response body:

```
var xhr = new XMLHttpRequest();
xhr.open('GET', 'http://foo.com/index.html', false);
xhr.setRequestHeader('Accept', 'text/html');
xhr.send();

console.log(xhr.responseText);
```

This will give us the following console output:

```
'<html>
<head>
    <title>Hello World!</title>
</head>
<body>
    Hello World!
</body>
</html>'
```

The responseText property contains the actual body of the response and is not parsed by the browser. This allows us to retrieve any kind of resource from the server for use in our applications.

One thing to note is that the value of responseText can be null or an empty string in some cases. If the server returned a response with no body, or if there was a server-based error, the responseText property will be empty. However, if there was an error in the request itself or an error from the server side that resulted in a wrong response, the value of the property will be null.

An easy way to guard against errors is to check the status code of the response. Usually, a response with a status code greater than or equal to 200 but less than 300 is considered a "successful" response from the HTTP protocol point of view. Therefore, we can add a simple if statement to our code to check for success:

```
var xhr = new XMLHttpRequest();
xhr.open('GET', 'http://foo.com/index.html', false);
xhr.setRequestHeader('Accept', 'text/html');
xhr.send();

if (xhr.status >= 200 && xhr.status < 300){
    console.log(xhr.responseText);
} else {
    console.log('Unsuccessful Request.');
}
```

Our if statement in this example checks the status code of the XHR object to see whether its value is greater than or equal to 200 but less than 300. If it is, it logs the responseText property of the XHR. Otherwise, it will log 'Unsuccessful Request.'. Because the response status for this example is 200, we'll get a proper console output like the previous one.

Because the XMLHttpRequest API was originally created with XML documents in mind, there's another property called responseXML, which is a document object. If the content-type of the response body is an XML document, the browser will automatically try to parse the responseText value into a DOM Tree object, and set it as the value of responseXML. However, if the response is not an XML document—as in our case—the responseXML property is set to null.

There are times you'll need to cancel a request, and you can do that using the abort method:

```
var xhr = new XMLHttpRequest();
xhr.open('GET', 'http://foo.com/index.html', false);
```

```
xhr.setRequestHeader('Accept', 'text/html');
xhr.send();
xhr.abort();
```

There are many reasons you might want to abort a request, such as if the user decides to cancel the action. Or you may want to set some sort of timeout for the request. The XMLHttpRequest object doesn't natively support timeouts, which means it will wait for a response from the server as long as possible. You can use abort together with the setTimeout function to automatically cancel a request after a specific time:

```
var xhr = new XMLHttpRequest();
xhr.open('GET', 'http://foo.com/index.html');
xhr.setRequestHeader('Accept', 'text/html');

// timeout
setTimeout(function(){
    xhr.abort();
}, 5000);

xhr.send();
```

Here we combined the abort method with setTimeout to cancel the request after 5 seconds. If the request hasn't received a response after 5 seconds, the timeout function will automatically cancel the request, making it possible to create some sort of timeout function that can be used to cancel long-running requests.

Going Async

The requests we made above using XHR objects are **synchronous**, which is a fancy term for blocking: after sending the request, the browser halts all processes in the current window until it receives a response. Only after getting a response back from the server will the browser continue execution.

While that's fine in some cases, synchronous requests are problematic in general because loading resources takes time. Since the browser blocks all processes during synchronous requests, your application will remain unresponsive during this time and the user won't be able to interact with it. If you're loading a large file, for instance, it might take a few seconds for the browser to finish loading the response from the server—a few seconds that might be enough reason for your bored user to stop using your application. Factor in the slow speed of some Internet connections plus the latency between the user's physical location and the server, and you get a user-experience nightmare.

Thankfully, we have an alternative: **asynchronous requests**. An asynchronous (or **async**) request happens in the background and is therefore non-blocking. Using an async request, we can send a request to the server and continue without waiting for a response. Because it doesn't block the browser from performing other processes, our application remains interactive while the request is being processed, and users won't notice anything happening until we get the response back and update the interface.

To use the async mode of XHRs, we must initialize our objects with the third argument for the open method. This third parameter, called async, takes a Boolean value: if the value is true, the request will be asynchronous. In the previous examples, we passed false to this argument, which made our requests synchronous. To make our request asynchronous, we simply have to change that value to true:

```
var xhr = new XMLHttpRequest();
xhr.open('GET', 'http://foo.com/index.html', true);
xhr.setRequestHeader('Accept', 'text/html');
xhr.send();
```

In this snippet, we changed the synchronous example from the last section into an asynchronous version by passing a true value as the async argument to open. When we send our request using the send method, it will now be done in the background, and the lines after the send invocation will immediately be interpreted. This behavior is different from the synchronous example, where the script waits for a response from the server before executing the next lines.

The use of async requests, though, requires a different approach. Until the previous example, all of our code snippets were written with the synchronous calls in mind. This enabled us to access the values of the XHR object directly after our send invocation:

```
var xhr = new XMLHttpRequest();
xhr.open('GET', 'http://foo.com/index.html', false);
xhr.setRequestHeader('Accept', 'text/html');
xhr.send();

console.log(xhr.responseText.length); // 87
```

Since synchronous requests block further execution until the response arrives, we're able to get the response values like this. By the time our first console.log line is evaluated, the response has already been received, so we can read the data immediately.

But what about async requests?

```
var xhr = new XMLHttpRequest();
xhr.open('GET', 'http://foo.com/index.html', true);
xhr.setRequestHeader('Accept', 'text/html');
xhr.send();

console.log(xhr.responseText); // undefined
```

Here we modified the example to use an async request instead of a synchronous one. Even if both examples point to the same URL, this example will always log undefined for the responseText property. This is because, unlike in our previous example, the JavaScript interpreter will not wait until the response is received before interpreting the line after the send call. Instead, the interpreter triggers the browser to perform a non-blocking background request and then goes on to interpret the rest of the program.

Because the request is asynchronous, we won't be able to access the properties right after we invoke send, because we don't know for sure whether the response has arrived from the server by the time the interpreter evaluates our access code—and often, the response arrives much later.

To work with asynchronous requests, then, we need a new plan of attack. Instead of immediately accessing the properties of the XHR after sending it, we need to defer this access until we actually get a response. In other words, we need to wait for the response to actually arrive before processing it. And the technique we'll use to do that should already be familiar to us, since we just discussed it in the previous chapter: events.

An XHR object supports one main event: the readystatechange event. This event is dispatched by the XHR every time its ready state changes, which we'll discuss in a bit. In order for us to effectively use async requests, we must therefore attach an appropriate event handler for this event.

Attaching an event handler to an XHR, however, is a bit tricky. In browsers that support the standard model, we can use the addEventListener method for this purpose. Internet Explorer, on the other hand, does not implement event methods such as attachEvent on XHR objects. We must therefore use an older style of event attachment that's supported by all browsers—**event handler properties**:

```
var xhr = new XMLHttpRequest();

// attach handler
xhr.onreadystatechange = function(){
    console.log('Ready State Change.');
};
```

Instead of using a method to attach an event handler, we attached the event handler directly to the object through a property name that's composed of the "on" prefix plus the name of the event. In this case, we attached a readystatechange event handler by assigning a function to the onreadystatechange property of the XHR object. This method of attaching the event handler is part of the legacy event model, which comes from the DOM Level 0 days of the browser but is still supported by all major browsers.

Of course, attaching the event handler is just part of the equation. Take a look at the following example:

```
var xhr = new XMLHttpRequest();
xhr.open('GET', 'http://foo.com/index.html', true);

// attach handler
xhr.onreadystatechange = function(){
    console.log('Ready State Change.');
};

xhr.setRequestHeader('Accept', 'text/html');
xhr.send();
```

If we try running this in the browser, we'll get the following console output:

```
'Ready State Change'
'Ready State Change'
'Ready State Change'
'Ready State Change'
```

We got four log outputs, which means that our event handler was dispatched four times. Instead of just dispatching the event when it receives a response from the server, the XHR dispatches the readystatechange event for every phase of the request-response cycle.

If we look back at the request-response cycle, we can see that there are four phases. The first phase is connecting to the server where the HTTP request message will be sent. The second phase is sending the actual request message to the server. The third phase is downloading the response data. The fourth phase is ending the download phase and parsing the data from the response. So the four phases are connect, send, download, and complete.

These four phases are connected to the "ready state" of the XHR. An XHR object has a special property, readyState, that contains a numeric value that tells us the current phase the XHR object is in:

- 0 - the XHR has just been created, but its open method hasn't been called yet so it remains uninitialized. This XHR phase does not correspond to a request-response flow phase.

- 1 - the XHR has been initialized, but the request hasn't yet been sent to the server using send.

- 2 - the XHR's request has been sent, and the preliminary data—headers and status codes—are available.

- 3 - the XHR's response is being downloaded and the responseText property already has partial data.

- 4 - the XHR's response has been downloaded completely and we can now process the data.

As the XHR moves from one phase to the next, it dispatches the readystatechange event to inform us of the change of state. We can then use the readyState property to check which phase it is in.

Let's modify the previous example:

```
var xhr = new XMLHttpRequest();
xhr.open('GET', 'http://foo.com/index.html', true);

// attach handler
xhr.onreadystatechange = function(){
    switch(xhr.readyState){
        case 1: console.log('1: Connect'); break;
        case 2: console.log('2: Send'); break;
        case 3: console.log('3: Download'); break;
        case 4: console.log('4: Complete'); break;
    }
};

xhr.setRequestHeader('Accept', 'text/html');
xhr.send();
```

In our readystatechange event handler, we used a switch statement to check for the value of the readyState property. Here's the corresponding console output from our snippet when run on the browser:

```
'1: Connect'
'2: Send'
'3: Download'
'4: Complete'
```

The first line in our output, '1: Connect', is logged after we call the open method. The open method changes the state of the XHR from 0 to 1, which dispatches the readystatechange event. The second line is logged after we call send, which changes the state from 1 to 2, triggering another dispatch of the readystatechange event. As the browser starts receiving data from the server, it changes the state of the XHR to 3, dispatching a third readystatechange event that logs our third line. Finally, the last readystatechange event is dispatched when the browser finishes downloading the whole response from the server, thereby logging our fourth and last line.

The last phase is perhaps the most important of these four phases, because it's only when we have all of the response data that we can start parsing it for our purposes. This means that until the readyState of our XHR object is 4, we can't access the complete data from our response. With this in mind, we can now create a proper event handler for our async request:

```
var xhr = new XMLHttpRequest();
xhr.open('GET', 'http://foo.com/index.html', true);

// attach handler
xhr.onreadystatechange = function(){
    if (xhr.readyState == 4){
        console.log(xhr.responseText);
    }
};

xhr.setRequestHeader('Accept', 'text/html');
xhr.send();
```

Here we changed our readystatechange handler by adding an if statement that checks whether the readyState property is equal to 4. If the value of this property is anything other than 4, the data isn't ready yet and we won't be able to read the full response body. But if the value is equal to 4, our response has been completely downloaded, and we can begin using it or parsing it for our needs.

One thing we also have to factor in is the simple guard we included to check for failed requests. Remember that we checked the value of the response's status code in the previous section to determine whether the response was successful or not. We should also add that into our new event handler:

```
var xhr = new XMLHttpRequest();
xhr.open('GET', 'http://foo.com/index.html', true);

// attach handler
xhr.onreadystatechange = function(){
    if (xhr.readyState == 4){
        if (xhr.status >= 200 && xhr.status < 300){
            console.log(xhr.responseText);
        } else {
            console.log('Unsuccessful Request.');
        }
    }
};

xhr.setRequestHeader('Accept', 'text/html');
xhr.send();
```

Finally, we can also add a timeout that will automatically cancel our request if it takes too long:

```
var xhr = new XMLHttpRequest();
xhr.open('GET', 'http://foo.com/index.html', true);

// attach handler
xhr.onreadystatechange = function(){
    if (xhr.readyState == 4){
        if (xhr.status >= 200 && xhr.status < 300){
            console.log(xhr.responseText);
        } else {
            console.log('Unsuccessful Request.');
        }
    }
};

xhr.setRequestHeader('Accept', 'text/html');
xhr.send();

// timeout
setTimeout(function(){
    xhr.abort();
}, 5000);
```

And with that, we now have our complete asynchronous XHR code.

The MooTools Request Class

Now that we've looked at the native XMLHttpRequest implementation, you might have noticed a few things:

- The initialization method open has to be called separately from the constructor function, which doesn't fit with the normal JavaScript (or MooTools) style.

- Native XHRs dispatch only a single event type in most browsers, which means that we have to cram all our code into a single event handler for both successful and failed requests.

- Timeouts aren't natively implemented, so we need to add separate code to handle this for us.

- We don't have the flexibility to handle different response types, and we have to parse the responses ourselves.

Because XHRs are used a lot these days, you'll probably encounter these issues in most applications you build. Therefore, we need a somewhat better API for working with XHRs to streamline the process for us.

Thankfully, MooTools provides us with the API we need: the Request class. This special class is an abstraction of the native XHR class, and can be used as a replacement for native XHR code. Like the Event type, the Request class is a wrapper: it does not override the native XMLHttpRequest type, but instead wraps it in order to add functionality. Unlike most of the constructors we've discussed so far, Request is implemented as a class rather than as a type object in order to enable subclassing—which, as we'll see later in this chapter, makes Request a really powerful feature of MooTools.

In the sections to come, we'll translate the following native XHR code to a version that uses the Request class:

```
window.addEvent('domready', function(){
    var notify = $('notify'),
        data = 'name=Mark&age=23';

    var xhr = new XMLHttpRequest();
    xhr.open('POST', 'http://foo.com/comment/', true);

    xhr.onreadystatechange = function(){
        if (xhr.readyState == 4){
            if (xhr.status >= 200 && xhr.status < 300){
                notify.set('html', xhr.responseText);
            } else {
                notify.set('html', '<strong>Request failed, please try again.</strong>');
            }
        }
    };

    xhr.setRequestHeader('Accept', 'text/html');
    xhr.setRequestHeader('Content-Type', 'application/x-www-form-urlencoded');
    xhr.setRequestHeader('Content-Length', data.length);

    xhr.send(data);
    notify.set('html', '<strong>Request sent, please wait.</strong>');
```

```
    // timeout
    setTimeout(function(){
        xhr.abort();
        notify.set('html', '<strong>Request timeout, please try again.</strong>');
    }, 5000);
});
```

In this snippet, we send a POST request to http://foo.com/comment/ in order to send the data to the server. We then wait for a response from the server to tell us whether the operation was successful, and this response is composed of an HTML string that we'll insert into the notify element.

Creating New Requests

The first thing we need to do is to create a new request object using the Request constructor. This constructor takes a single argument, options, which is an object containing options for our request object.

```
var data = 'name=Mark&age=23';

var request = new Request({
    url: 'http://foo.com/comment/',
    method: 'post',
    async: true
});
```

Unlike the native XMLHttpRequest API, the Request API doesn't have a separate open method to initialize the request. Instead, we pass the values that we'd normally pass to open as values in our options argument. In this snippet, for example, we passed three options: url, which is the URL of the location we're requesting; method, which is the HTTP method to use for the request; and async, which tells the Request class that we want to use the asynchronous mode for this request.

You'll notice that the method option isn't in uppercase, and that's okay. The Request class allows any case for the method option: we could have used 'POST', 'Post' and even 'PoST'. It's common, however, to use the lowercase style with Request class instances.

Another thing we need to know is that most of the options for Request have default values. For instance, the method option is 'POST' by default, and the async option is true by default. If the default values of these options are already set to what we need, we can simply omit them from our options object:

```
var data = 'name=Mark&age=23';

var request = new Request({
    url: 'http://foo.com/comment/'
});
```

This snippet is the same as the previous one, even if we didn't include values for the method and async options.

When we create a new instance of Request, the constructor automatically creates a native XHR object that will be used for the request. As I mentioned, the Request class is a wrapper object, like the Event type: it doesn't create a new object type of its own but only creates an abstraction for the native object. We can access this wrapped XHR object by accessing the xhr property of our request object:

```
var data = 'name=Mark&age=23';

var request = new Request({
    url: 'http://foo.com/comment/'
});

console.log(typeOf(request.xhr)); // 'object'
```

Adding Request Headers

Now that we have our request object, we need to add the headers, and we do this using the setHeader method. This method takes two arguments, name and value, which correspond to the header name and value:

```
var data = 'name=Mark&age=23';

var request = new Request({
    url: 'http://foo.com/comment/'
});

request.setHeader('Accept', 'text/html');
request.setHeader('Content-Type', 'application/x-www-form-urlencoded');
request.setHeader('Content-Length', data.length);
```

Here we set three headers for our request: Accept, Content-Type, and Content-Length. You'll notice that the setHeader method is very similar to the setRequestHeader method from the native API, and they actually are somewhat similar in style.

One nice feature, though, is that we can actually pass these headers to the Request options. This saves us three function invocations:

```
var data = 'name=Mark&age=23';

var request = new Request({
    url: 'http://foo.com/comment/',
    headers: {
        'Accept': 'text/html',
        'Content-Type': 'application/x-www-form-urlencoded',
        'Content-Length': data.length
    }
});
```

Instead of calling setHeader separately, we just pass a headers option to the Request constructor. This option should have an object value, with the keys of the object corresponding to the name of the header, and the value corresponding to the header value. This cleans up our code considerably, and makes the Request declaration more expressive.

All request objects have a default Accept header with the value 'text/javascript, text/html, application/xml, text/xml, */*'. This means we can remove the Accept header declaration in our code:

```
var data = 'name=Mark&age=23';

var request = new Request({
    url: 'http://foo.com/comment/',
    headers: {
```

```
        'Content-Type': 'application/x-www-form-urlencoded',
        'Content-Length': data.length
    }
});
```

Another feature of MooTools is the special urlEncoded option, which automatically encodes our data into the application/x-www-form-urlencoded type. It also automatically adds a Content-Type and Content-Length header to our request if the method used is POST. We can therefore remove those two headers and use the urlEncoded option instead:

```
var data = 'name=Mark&age=23';

var request = new Request({
    url: 'http://foo.com/comment/',
    urlEncoded: true
});
```

By default, the urlEncoded option of a request object is set to true, which means we don't even need to explicitly add it. So, we can go back to our original request code once more:

```
var data = 'name=Mark&age=23';

var request = new Request({
    url: 'http://foo.com/comment/'
});
```

Sending Data

At this point, we've replaced about half of our original native code with this simple code block. Now we need to consider the data to be sent. In the native model, we passed the data to the send method of the XHR object. In MooTools, we can do the same using its send method:

```
var data = 'name=Mark&age=23';

var request = new Request({
    url: 'http://foo.com/comment/'
});

request.send(data);
```

Like the native send method, the Request send method can be invoked with an argument to send data to the server. Here we send the value of the data variable to the server by passing it the send method.

However, we don't need to use the send method to pass data to the request; we can also declare the data to be sent using the Request options:

```
var data = 'name=Mark&age=23';

var request = new Request({
    url: 'http://foo.com/comment/',
    data: data
});
```

Here we added a new option called data to the options object. This option is used to declare the data that will be sent to the server, and in our case, we declared the value of this option to be the string value of our data variable.

We aren't limited to using strings as data values in the Request class though. MooTools allows us to send other values, such as objects:

```
var request = new Request({
    url: 'http://foo.com/comment/',
    data: {
        'name': 'Mark',
        'age': 23
    }
});
```

In this example, we declared the value of the data option to be an object with two properties. When we send this request, MooTools automatically turns the object into a string that's readable by the server. The Request class is able to process different kinds of objects like this: plain objects, arrays, and even form elements. This gives us flexibility in our code and enables us to transparently send complex JavaScript objects to the server.

Attaching Event Handlers

The next thing we have to deal with is events. With native XHRs, we needed to attach a readystatechange event handler and check the readyState property, and then put our processing code inside the handler. For our example, we had a readystatechange event handler that looked like this:

```
xhr.onreadystatechange = function(){
    if (xhr.readyState == 4){
        if (xhr.status >= 200 && xhr.status < 300){
            notify.set('html', xhr.responseText);
        } else {
            notify.set('html', '<strong>Request failed, please try again.</strong>');
        }
    }
};
```

The MooTools Request class, on the other hand, lessens the complexity of the readystatechange event by providing not one but five main events:

- The request event is dispatched right after the request is sent.

- The complete event is dispatched when the request has finished.

- The success event is dispatched for a successful request.

- The failure event is dispatched for an unsuccessful request.

- The cancel event is dispatched when a running request is stopped.

You can manage event handlers for these events to your request object using the MooTools event methods such as addEvent or removeEvent.

The request Event

The first event, request, is dispatched right after the request is sent. It is useful for displaying notification messages or loading images in your interface to tell the user that something is happening. In our native example, we logged a message right after the request was sent. This is a good candidate for use with our request event:

```
var notify = $('notify');

var request = new Request({
    url: 'http://foo.com/comment/',
    data: {
        'name': 'Mark',
        'age': 23
    }
});

request.addEvents({

    'request': function(){
        notify.set('html', '<strong>Request sent, please wait.</strong>');
    }

});
```

When our request object is sent in this example, the request event will be dispatched, which in turn invokes the event handler we attached. The HTML source of our notify element will then be updated, informing our users that an action is taking place.

The complete Event

The next event, complete, is dispatched when the request has been completed. This event, however, does not tell us whether the request was successful or not—it simply tells us that the request has been done. Therefore, this event shouldn't be used for data processing event handlers. Instead, it should be used for "cleanup" purposes, such as removing elements you've added during the request event.

```
var spinner = new Element('img', {src: 'spinner.gif'});

var request = new Request({
    method: 'get',
    url: 'http://foo.com/index.html'
});

request.addEvents({

    'request': function(){
        spinner.inject(document.body, 'top');
    },

    'complete': function(){
        spinner.destroy();
    }

});
```

In this separate example, we attached event handlers for the request and complete events. For the request event, we displayed a spinner image in our interface to tell the user that we're loading something. We then removed this spinner during the complete event to signify that we finished loading the data. Since we're not doing anything like this in our original native example, we didn't attach a complete handler in the earlier example.

The isSuccess Function

The next two events, success and failure, are the two most important events when it comes to requests, since these events are dispatched right after the complete event to inform us whether our request was successful or not. To determine whether an event was successful, the Request class uses a function named isSuccess. When the request is completed, the request object will invoke this function to check whether the request was successful. If the function returns true, then the request is successful and the request object will dispatch the success event. If the function returns false, the request is considered unsuccessful and the request object will dispatch the failure event.

The default isSuccess function looks like this:

```
isSuccess: function(){
    var status = this.status;
    return (status >= 200 && status < 300);
}
```

As you can see, the criteria used in the isSuccess method are the same as those we used in the native example: if the status of the response is greater than or equal to 200 and is less than 300, the request was successful.

There are times, though, when the default isSuccess criteria doesn't suffice for your applications. Thankfully, the Request class allows you to define your own isSuccess function by passing it using the options object:

```
var request = new Request({
    method: 'get',
    url: 'http://foo.com/index.html',
    isSuccess: function(){
        return this.status == 200;
    }
});
```

Here we define a different isSuccess method by passing it as an option in our Request declaration. The criterion used by our isSuccess function in this case is stricter than the default one: only responses with the status code of 200 will be considered successful.

The success Event

After consulting the isSuccess function, the request will fire one of two events. The first event, success, is dispatched when the request is successful:

```
var notify = $('notify');

var request = new Request({
    url: 'http://foo.com/comment/',
    data: {
        'name': 'Mark',
        'age': 23
```

```
        }
});
```

```
request.addEvents({

    'request': function(){
        notify.set('html', '<strong>Request sent, please wait.</strong>');
    },

    'success': function(text, xml){
        notify.set('html', text);
    }

});
```

The event handler for a request's success event receives two arguments when invoked: text and xml. The second argument, xml, is simply the value of the responseXML property of the wrapped native XHR object. The text argument, on the other hand, is a stripped version of the responseText property value: all scripts tags are removed from the original responseText value. For example, say we received the following response data:

```
<div>Hello World</div>
<script>
    alert('Hello World');
</script>
```

The request object will parse this response data and strip out the script tag. The text argument that our success event handler receives will therefore look like this:

```
'<div>Hello World</div>
'
```

The script tag was removed, leaving us with only the HTML source for the div.

MooTools strips out scripts for security reasons to prevent malicious scripts from being injected directly into the page. However, there are instances when you'd want to use those scripts and evaluate them in your application. The Request class, therefore, provides a special option called evalScripts. If you pass this option with the value of true, the Request object will automatically evaluate your scripts after stripping them.

▓ **Note** The evalScripts option, however, only works for <script> tags with bodies, such as <script>alert('Hello World');</script>. Tags that are implemented with the src attribute, such as <script src="hello.js"></script>, will not be automatically loaded or evaluated, but will still be stripped.

Another option related to evalScripts is evalResponse. If you set this option to true in your request declaration, MooTools will automatically evaluate the whole body of the response as a script. MooTools will also automatically evaluate the value of the response body if the Content-Type of your response contains the words ecmascript or javascript.

Of course, there are cases where the automatic script stripping will not be what you want to do. In such cases, you can access the raw responseText and responseXML values using the response object property of your request object, which stores the unprocessed response data from the server:

```
var notify = $('notify');

var request = new Request({
    url: 'http://foo.com/comment/',
    data: {
        'name': 'Mark',
        'age': 23
    }
});

request.addEvents({

    'request': function(){
        notify.set('html', '<strong>Request sent, please wait.</strong>');
    },

    'success': function(){
        notify.set('html', this.response.text);
    }

});
```

In this snippet, we removed the formal parameters for our success event handler, and instead accessed the raw response body using the response object property of the request.

The failure Event

In contrast to the success event, the failure event's handler functions receive only one argument: the wrapped native XHR object. MooTools passes the native XHR object so we can handle the failure ourselves. Take note, though, that even if we're not passed the response text and response xml values, we can still access them using the response property object in our failure event handler.

```
var notify = $('notify');

var request = new Request({
    url: 'http://foo.com/comment/',
    data: {
        'name': 'Mark',
        'age': 23
    }
});

request.addEvents({

    'request': function(){
        notify.set('html', '<strong>Request sent, please wait.</strong>');
    },

    'success': function(){
        notify.set('html', this.response.text);
    },

    'failure': function(){
```

```
            notify.set('html', '<strong>Request failed, please try again.</strong>');
    }

});
```

We didn't need any fancy error handling in our original native example, so we just attached a basic failure event handler.

Timeouts

The next thing we need to do is to add a timeout. In our native example, we used the abort method of the XHR object together with a setTimeout call to cancel the request after a specific amount of time. The Request class has a method called cancel that is equivalent to abort, and we can use that here:

```
var notify = $('notify');

var request = new Request({
    url: 'http://foo.com/comment/',
    data: {
        'name': 'Mark',
        'age': 23
    }
});

request.addEvents({

    'request': function(){
        notify.set('html', '<strong>Request sent, please wait.</strong>');
    },

    'success': function(){
        notify.set('html', this.response.text);
    },

    'failure': function(){
        notify.set('html', '<strong>Request failed, please try again.</strong>');
    }

});

setTimeout(function(){
    request.cancel();
    notify.set('html', '<strong>Request timeout, please try again.</strong>');
}, 5000);
```

You'll notice that after we canceled our request, we updated our notify element to show that our request has timed out. Instead of putting this directly in our setTimeout function, we can also implement this as an event handler.

```
var notify = $('notify');

var request = new Request({
```

```
    url: 'http://foo.com/comment/',
    data: {
        'name': 'Mark',
        'age': 23
    }
});

request.addEvents({

    'request': function(){
        notify.set('html', '<strong>Request sent, please wait.</strong>');
    },

    'success': function(){
        notify.set('html', this.response.text);
    },

    'failure': function(){
        notify.set('html', '<strong>Request failed, please try again.</strong>');
    },

    'cancel': function(){
        notify.set('html', '<strong>Request timeout, please try again.</strong>');
    }

});

setTimeout(function(){
    request.cancel();
}, 5000);
```

Request objects dispatch the cancel event every time a running request is cancelled. In this example, our cancel event handler will be dispatched when our request times out after 5 seconds.

While our snippet looks good right now, we can actually make it cleaner. The MooTools Request class actually adds support for timeouts using the timeout option. So instead of writing our request code as we did above, we can modify it to look like this:

```
var notify = $('notify');

var request = new Request({
    url: 'http://foo.com/comment/',
    data: {
        'name': 'Mark',
        'age': 23
    },
    timeout: 5000
});

request.addEvents({

    'request': function(){
        notify.set('html', '<strong>Request sent, please wait.</strong>');
```

```
    },

    'success': function(){
        notify.set('html', this.response.text);
    },

    'failure': function(){
        notify.set('html', '<strong>Request failed, please try again.</strong>');
    },

    'timeout': function(){
        notify.set('html', '<strong>Request timeout, please try again.</strong>');
    }

});
```

Instead of using the cancel method with setTimeout, we simply added a timeout option to our Request declaration. The request class will automatically handle the timeout for us, and dispatch a timeout event when the request times out. You'll notice that we also changed our cancel event handler to a timeout event handler since we're no longer handling the cancel event.

Event Handler Declarations

At this point our code is almost complete, and we can now add the send invocation to finish it. Before we do that, however, we need to check out one more feature of the request declaration. Instead of attaching event handlers using addEvent or addEvents, we can actually include them in the request declaration by using the "on" prefix form:

```
var notify = $('notify');

var request = new Request({

    url: 'http://foo.com/comment/',

    data: {
        'name': 'Mark',
        'age': 23
    },

    timeout: 5000,

    onRequest: function(){
        notify.set('html', '<strong>Request sent, please wait.</strong>');
    },

    onSuccess: function(){
        notify.set('html', this.response.text);
    },

    onFailure: function(){
        notify.set('html', '<strong>Request failed, please try again.</strong>');
    },
```

```
onTimeout: function(){
    notify.set('html', '<strong>Request timeout, please try again.</strong>');
}

});
```

We moved the event handlers from a separate addEvent call to the actual Request declaration by capitalizing their names then attaching an "on" prefix to them. This declaration form is similar to the one above, but it's cleaner and tighter and therefore used more often in development.

Sending the Request

This brings us finally to the part where we send the request. To complete our code, we simply have to send the request by invoking the send method:

```
var notify = $('notify');

var request = new Request({

    url: 'http://foo.com/comment/',

    data: {
        'name': 'Mark',
        'age': 23
    },

    timeout: 5000,

    onRequest: function(){
        notify.set('html', '<strong>Request sent, please wait.</strong>');
    },

    onSuccess: function(){
        notify.set('html', this.response.text);
    },

    onFailure: function(){
        notify.set('html', '<strong>Request failed, please try again.</strong>');
    },

    onTimeout: function(){
        notify.set('html', '<strong>Request timeout, please try again.</strong>');
    }

});

request.send();
```

You already saw the send method a few sections back when we discussed how to factor in the data being sent to the request. The MooTools send method looks very similar to the native send method for XHR objects: we can pass the string data to be sent by making it an argument to the send method.

However, the send method will only use the argument as the data for the request if the argument is a string or an element. If you pass an object to the send method, for example, it won't be sent to the server. Thus, something like request.send({name: 'Mark'}) won't work.

This is because the send method's argument isn't actually called data—it's called options. This options object is similar to the options object you pass to the Request constructor, but it understands only three options: url, method, and data.

When you pass a string or element argument to send, the method actually transforms it into the data property of an options object. Thus, send('name=Mark') is the same as doing send({data: 'Mark'}). If we want to send an actual object using the send method, we have to use a real options object, like send({data: {name: 'Mark'}}).

Passing an options object to send makes it possible to create reusable request objects.

```
var request = new Request({
    link: 'chain',
    onSuccess: function(){
        console.log(this.response.text);
    }
});
```

```
request.send({url: '/index.html', method: 'get'});
request.send({url: '/comments', method: 'post', data: {name: 'Mark'}});
```

Here we created a single request object, then used options objects with the send method so that we can send different requests using a single request object. Note that passing in different values for the options to send does not change the actual option values of the request object. This means that even if we used a different url value in our send options, the actual url of the request object won't be changed—it will still be a blank string, which is the default value.

Request Sending Modes

You'll notice from our last example that we added a new option to the request declaration called link. This option is used to set the behavior of the request object if a send call is issued while a request is still running.

By default, the value of this option is 'ignore'. In this mode, the request object will ignore additional calls to send while it is running.

```
var request = new Request({
    link: 'ignore',
    onRequest: function(){
        console.log(this.response.text);
    }
});
```

```
request.send({url: '/index.html', method: 'get'});
request.send({url: '/comments', method: 'post', data: {name: 'Mark'}});
```

In this snippet, only the first request—the GET request to /index.html—will be honored. Because we called send immediately after sending the first request, the second request will be ignored. This is because the second time we invoked send, our original request was still running. By default, all request objects use the ignore mode.

The second possible value for link is 'cancel'. In this mode, subsequent calls to the send method will cancel the current running request.

```
var request = new Request({
    link: 'cancel',
    onRequest: function(){
        console.log(this.response.text);
```

```
    }
});
```

```
request.send({url: '/index.html', method: 'get'});
request.send({url: '/comments', method: 'post', data: {name: 'Mark'}});
```

In this example, the second send call will cancel the previous one. Therefore, the POST request to /comments will be the one honored by the request object and the first GET request will be canceled.

The last possible value for link is 'chain'. In this mode, requests will be "chained": if the send method of the request object is called while it is running, the request will wait for the currently running request to finish before sending the new one.

```
var request = new Request({
    link: 'chain',
    onRequest: function(){
        console.log(this.response.text);
    }
});
```

```
request.send({url: '/index.html', method: 'get'});
request.send({url: '/comments', method: 'post', data: {name: 'Mark'}});
```

Both requests will be sent in this example. First, the GET request will be sent, and the second POST request will be added to the request chain. When the GET request is finished, the request object will automatically send the POST request.

Our Final Code

This brings us finally to the part where we send the request. To complete our code, we simply have to send the request itself by invoking the send method:

```
window.addEvent('domready', function(){

    var notify = $('notify');

    new Request({

        url: 'http://foo.com/comment/',

        data: {
            'name': 'Mark',
            'age': 23
        },

        timeout: 5000,

        onRequest: function(){
            notify.set('html', '<strong>Request sent, please wait.</strong>');
        },

        onSuccess: function(){
            notify.set('html', this.response.text);
        },
```

```
        onFailure: function(){
            notify.set('html', '<strong>Request failed, please try again.</strong>');
        },

        onTimeout: function(){
            notify.set('html', '<strong>Request timeout, please try again.</strong>');
        }

    }).send();

});
```

You'll notice that the original request variable assignment was removed from this snippet. Since we don't need to store the request, we can simply do away with the assignment and send the new instance directly. We also wrapped the whole snippet in a domready event handler, as in our original example.

Let's take another look at the original native request code:

```
window.addEvent('domready', function(){

    var notify = $('notify'),
        data = "name=Mark&age=23";

    var xhr = new XMLHttpRequest();
    xhr.open('POST', 'http://foo.com/comment/', true);

    xhr.onreadystatechange = function(){
        if (xhr.readyState == 4){
            if (xhr.status >= 200 && xhr.status < 300){
                notify.set('html', xhr.responseText);
            } else {
                notify.set('html', '<strong>Request failed, please try again.</strong>');
            }
        }
    };

    xhr.setRequestHeader('Accept', 'text/html');
    xhr.setRequestHeader('Content-Type', 'application/x-www-form-urlencoded');
    xhr.setRequestHeader('Content-Length', data.length);

    xhr.send(data);
    notify.set('html', '<strong>Request sent, please wait.</strong>');

    // timeout
    setTimeout(function(){
        xhr.abort();
        notify.set('html', '<strong>Request timeout, please try again.</strong>');
    }, 5000);

});
```

I think we will all agree about which code is better. Our Request-based code is cleaner, easier to read, and more modular, and it fits the MooTools style perfectly.

Subclassing Request

A great thing about Request is that it's implemented as a class rather than a type object. This gives us the opportunity to create subclasses that extend the functionality of Request.

Request Internals

To understand how Request subclassing works, we must first get a feel for the internals of the MooTools Request class. Request is a very simple class. It uses all of the three mixin classes we discussed in Chapter 5: Options, Events, and Chain. We use the Options mixin for the initialize method, which is how we're able to pass an options object when we create a new object. We use the Events mixin to enable the request object to use event handlers and dispatch events. And we use the Chain mixin to power the "chain" mode of request sending.

When a new Request instance is created, the initialize method does two things. First, it creates the internal XHR object that will be used to send the requests and stores it in the xhr property of the instance. Second, it takes the options object argument and merges it with the default options using the setOptions method from the Options class. Remember that this method enables us to define event handlers using the onEventName format, which is how we're able to combine the event handler declaration with the other options in our request object instantiation.

At this point, the Request instance contains a non-initialized native XHR object. Request doesn't actually call the open method of the XHR until later in the process. Rather, all processes at this point are "buffered" internally. For example, when we add new request headers using the setHeader method, the Request instance doesn't actually add them immediately to the XHR object using setRequestHeader. Instead, it stores the headers first in the internal headers property. This makes the class flexible enough so that changes can be easily made without having to reset the XHR instance.

The send Method

The bulk of the Request processes happens in the send method. When called, it first sets the current request as "running," so that subsequent calls to it will be controlled. The method then prepares the internal options: it combines the options object passed to it (if there is one) to the option values defined during the creation of the request object.

The send method then prepares the data for sending. If our data is a simple string, it does no further parsing. If our data is an element, it will first call the toQueryString method of Element to turn form elements into a query string value. And if our data is an object, it'll use the Object.toQueryString generic to turn the object into a proper query string. Thus, no matter what kind of data we pass to Request, it always turns it into a string.

The next step the method takes is to initialize the native XHR object by calling its open method. It uses the prepared values from the options to perform this task: an uppercase version of options.method for the method argument, options.url for the url, and options.async for the async argument. It then attaches the readystatechange handler for the XHR object: a method called onStateChange, which we'll discuss in a second. Next, it adds the appropriate headers to the XHR object by looping through the internal header property and adding them using setRequestHeader. Finally, it dispatches the request event before sending the native XHR object.

The onStateChange Method

The send method, however, is only half of the puzzle. The other half is the readystatechange event handler method, onStateChange. After the send method sends the request, control of the request goes over to the onStateChange method, which waits for the wrapper XHR object to reach the ready state of 4. When this happens, onStateChange prepares the response object property of the request, setting the raw responseText value for response.text and raw responseXML value for response.xml.

The onStateChange method then calls the isSuccess function to check whether the request was successful. If the request was successful, the method calls the success method, which parses and prepares the response.text value to strip out script tags. This success method then passes this new formatted value to the onSuccess method, which dispatches the complete and success events.

Unsuccessful requests, in contrast, will make the onStateChange method invoke the failure method, whose main job is to invoke the onFailure method that dispatches the complete and failure events.

These four methods—success, onSuccess, failure, and onFailure—are the usual points for subclassing. Most Request subclasses will override these four methods in order to create a specialized version of the class.

Success Overriding

The most basic kinds of Request subclasses add additional options and use a different parsing method for the responseText value. Because it is the job of the success method to parse the response data before passing it to success event handlers, most subclasses override only this method for their purposes.

For example, let's take one of the Request subclasses included in MooTools Core: Request.JSON. This is a specialized request class used for JSON requests that automatically turns the response data into a JavaScript object. Normally, if we want to include a JSON request using the Request class, we do this:

```
var request = new Request({
    url: 'myfile.json',
    method: 'get',
    headers: {
        'Accept': 'application/json'
    },
    onSuccess: function(text){
        var obj = JSON.decode(text);
        if (obj){
            console.log(obj.name);
        } else {
            console.log('Improper JSON response!');
        }
    }
}).send();
```

Here we requested a JSON file from the server. We made sure that the server will only send us JSON back by attaching an Accept header that has the value of the JSON mimetype. In our success event handler, we then parse the text response from the server using JSON.decode to turn it into a JSON object. If the parsing is successful, we'll get an object result, the name property of which we output to the console. If the parsing fails, we log an error message.

Request.JSON automates this process, and handles the parsing process using JSON.decode internally.

```
var request = new Request.JSON({
    url: 'myfile.json',
    method: 'get',
    onSuccess: function(obj){
        console.log(obj.name);
    },
    onFailure: function(){
        console.log('Improper JSON response!');
```

```
    }
})).send();
```

Instead of passing a string to the success event handler, Request.JSON passes an object that is the parsed value of the JSON response. This saves us from having to call JSON.decode ourselves. Request.JSON also automatically dispatches the failure event in the case of the response failing the JSON.decode parsing.

The source itself of Request.JSON is very simple:

```
Request.JSON = new Class({

    Extends: Request,

    options: {
        secure: true
    },

    initialize: function(options){
        this.parent(options);
        Object.append(this.headers, {
            'Accept': 'application/json',
            'X-Request': 'JSON'
        });
    },

    success: function(text){
        var secure = this.options.secure;
        var json = this.response.json = Function.attempt(function(){
            return JSON.decode(text, secure);
        });

        if (json == null) this.onFailure();
        else this.onSuccess(json, text);
    }

});
```

The Request.JSON class is a direct subclass of Request. It overrides the original initialize method in order to add the appropriate headers to the request instance, but it also retains the original initialize process from Request using this.parent(). You'll see that the success method is the only real method that's overridden. The Request.JSON version of the success method first tries to turn the response data into a proper JSON object using JSON.decode. If the process fails, it calls the onFailure method, which dispatches the failure event. If the process succeeds, it calls the onSuccess method, passing in the newly parsed object. The onSuccess method will then dispatch the event handlers for the success event, passing the parsed object.

As this example shows, subclassing the Request object is a very simple affair. The flexibility of the original Request class itself makes the process really simple, and gives Request the ability to be subclassed into new and more useful classes.

The Wrap-Up

In this chapter we learned all about the HTTP request-response cycle and how it affects the design of our applications. We also found out about asynchronous requests, and how the native XMLHttpRequest object enables us to issue requests from inside our code to create more powerful and dynamic applications. Finally, we talked about the MooTools Request class, and how it provides a nice abstraction of the native XHR API.

In the next chapter, we'll learn about another fancy technique for improving our interfaces: animation. We'll talk about how animation is done in JavaScript, as well as how the Fx classes give us a very powerful framework for complex animations.

So if you're ready, follow my lead and jump into the magic of animation.

■ ■ ■

CHAPTER 12

Animation

In the previous chapter, we talked about the Request class, which is the old new thing in the recent JavaScript revolution. Now we'll talk about an "old old thing:" animation.

In this chapter, we'll learn about the basic theory of animation and how objects are actually animated from one state to another. We'll then explore the elements that come together to create these animations in JavaScript, before finally diving into the MooTools Fx classes, the pinnacle of JavaScript animation today.

Getting Animated

When we hear the word animation, what generally comes to mind is motion—the movement of an object with regard to its original horizontal or vertical position. Animation tasks such as moving a square from left to right or bouncing a ball up and down are good examples. When animating the square, we might move it from its original position to another position to the right of the original, thus relocating the object horizontally. The bouncing ball animation, on the other hand, requires us to shift the ball vertically, first moving it up from its original position, then moving it back from the new position to the original.

These two examples give us an idea of some of the basic elements of animation. First we have the object to be animated, called the *subject*. In our examples, the subjects are the square and the ball. Then we have the particular property of the object that we need to change, which in our examples is the vertical or horizontal position of the square and ball subjects. And, finally, we have the value of that property itself.

Motion occurs when the original value of the property—which we designate as the initial value—changes. So when our square, which was originally 10 pixels to the left of the screen, moves 20 pixels to the right, we have apparent motion.

This changing of the initial value happens over time, which is another element of animation. When we start, our square will be 10 pixels to the left of the screen; then, after a second, it moves to a new position 20 pixels to the right of its original position. The time it takes for the initial value to change to the new value is the *duration* of the animation.

Each change of the initial value is called a *frame*. In our square example, for instance, we might have two frames: our first frame would show the square 10 pixels from the left of the screen, while the second frame would show the square 30 pixels from the left. Our first frame therefore represents the initial value of the property, while the second frame represents the change of the initial value equal to 20 pixels to the right of the initial value.

If our animation's duration is 1 second, we'll see our first frame, followed by the second frame after a second. We'll see the motion, of course, but it's a very jumpy sort of motion. It will seem that our square suddenly jumped 20 pixels to the right without any smooth movement in between. This happens because our eyes detect the abruptness of the movement: the change is so big that our eyes notice it immediately.

In order to make the animation smoother, we must be able to trick our eyes so they don't notice the abruptness of the movement. We can do this by making the change in the properties value smaller. In our example, this means that instead of simply changing the value of the square's position from 10 pixels left to 30 pixels, we must slowly increase the original 10 pixel value over time until it reaches 30 pixels from the left of the screen.

The way to do this is to add more frames. We could add, for example, another frame that will go in between the first and last frames. The first frame will show the square at 10 pixels to the left, the second will show it at 20 pixels and the last at 30 pixels. We then divide the duration—which is one second—accordingly, which means that frame 1 will be shown first, frame 2 will be shown half a second later, and frame 3 is shown after a full second. When done like this, the animation still won't look smooth, but it won't look so jumpy either. Because the amount of change was spread through the duration of the animation, our eyes won't complain as much.

But in order to make the animation really smooth, the number of frames should be sufficient that the change in each frame is small enough to go undetected by our eyes. The number of frames to use in an animation is called the frame rate and is measured in frames per second, or fps. The frame rate of an animation is simply the number of frames to be displayed each second of the animation's duration. If you have a two-second animation at a 24fps frame rate, for example, it means that 48 frames will be displayed during the span of two seconds. In our first frame example, we had a 1fps frame rate, while our second example had a 2fps frame rate.

Note The first frame, which shows the initial state of the subject prior to any changes, isn't included in the framerate.

The frame rate of an animation is also used to determine the amount of change per frame. We do this by dividing the amount of change we want by the number of frames we'll have. In our square example, we want to change the value of the square's horizontal position from 10 pixels from the left to 30 pixels from the left, which means that the amount of change is 20 pixels. If our animation runs for 1 second at the frame rate of 1fps, then the amount of change per frame will be 20 pixels. On the other hand, if our animation runs for 1 second at the frame rate of 24fps, then the amount of change per frame will be around 0.8 pixels, which means that the horizontal position of our square will change 0.8 pixels for each frame until it reaches the final frame.

At this point we can formulate a good definition: animation is the process of gradually changing the value of a property over a specific period of time. Take note that while we've discussed animation here using the concept of motion (the change in the value of the horizontal or vertical position property), animation isn't limited to motion, especially when we're animating in JavaScript. For example, if we change an element's height or width through animation, the object remains in the same position—yet this is still considered animation. This is also true for animating things such as opacity or color, which have nothing to do with motion.

So now that we have a basic understanding of the concepts involved in animation, we can turn our attention to the implementation details. But before we actually animate anything in JavaScript, we must first understand how the animation concepts of property and time apply.

Being Stylish

The most common properties that are animated in JavaScript are the visual properties of elements, such as positions, dimensions, and colors. And these visual properties are controlled by CSS styles.

CSS Styles

At a global level, CSS styles are added to the page using style sheets, which contain style declarations:

```
div.post {
    color: #CCCCCC;
    display: inline-block;
    height: 20px;
}
```

This is an example style declaration, which should be familiar to you by now, since we saw something like this in Chapter 9, on Slick. At the start of the declaration is the selector, which defines which elements to apply the style to, followed by the style rules that are surrounded by the curly braces.

Each of these style rules defines the value of a particular visual property of the elements to which the rules apply. This declaration, for example, tells us that all div elements with the class post will have a font color of light gray (color: #CCCCCC), a visual display that makes it both an inline and a block element (display: inline-block), and a vertical dimension of 20 pixels (height: 20px).

A style rule—and therefore a visual property of an element—is usually one of four types:

- Numeric rules are rules whose possible values are numbers, such as font-size, line-height, or opacity.

- Color rules are rules whose possible values are colors defined using either hexadecimal notation, such as #CCCCCC or #09FA0C, or a color function, such as rgb(255,0,51) or hsl(120,100%,75%).

- String rules are rules whose possible values are strings (i.e., a sequence of characters), such as font-family or display.

- Mixed rules are rules whose possible values can be a number, a color, a string, or combinations of these. Examples are shortcut rules like background and font, or rules like height or margin, which can accept both numbers and strings. Strictly speaking, all rules are mixed rules, since you can assign string values to them, such as auto and inherit.

All these rule types can be animated in one way or another, and we'll see how each of them is handled later on. An important thing to know right now, though, is that some rules—particularly color and numeric rules—are easier to animate than others.

We use style sheets to define these rules on a global level: style declarations in a style sheet are applied to all elements on a page that satisfy the selectors. But specific elements can also have their own set of styles that are defined using inline styles, which are style rules that are defined only for a specific element.

An inline style can be defined in HTML using the style attribute:

```
<div class="post" style="color: #000; display: inline;"></div>
```

Here we have a div element with a style attribute that defines its inline style. For this element, the color rule is given the #000 value, while the display rule is given the inline string value.

If this element appeared in the same document with a style sheet that includes the style declaration we have above, what would be the color and display visual property values of the div be? Would they be #CCCCCC and inline-block respectively, or #000 and inline? The answer, of course, is the latter. Inline styles take precedence over global styles, which means that if an element has an inline style rule declared, it will override any global styles for the same rule—except global rules declared with !important.

This precedence of inline styles over global styles is important because animation happens using inline rather than global styles. As we'll see later, it is the value of these inline styles that change rather than the global styles. This is because animation needs to be localized: if we change the value of an inline rule, it affects only the element where the inline rule is declared.

Explicit, Implicit, and Computed

The global styles and inline styles that we define for our documents are called *explicit* styles, because we explicitly define them using style rules in style sheets or inline styles. We can find out the explicit styles in our documents in two ways.

For global style rules, we can inspect the document.styleSheets object, which is a node collection containing all the style sheet objects in a page. Inspecting this object can sometimes be complicated, though, because it uses multiple interfaces and objects.

Inline styles, on the other hand, are available directly by accessing the style object property of an element. For our div example, for instance, we can get the value of its color style by accessing div.style.color, which should give us the hex string '#000'. For CSS rule names that are hyphenated, such as background-color, the style object will use a camelcase variation of the name, like backgroundColor. If an element doesn't have an inline style defined, the value of the property will be an empty string, which means that accessing div.style.background in our example will yield "".

Explicit styles are only one piece of the puzzle, though. All style rules have, in fact, a default value. For example, the default value of the height rule is auto, which means that the item's height depends on its content. When creating style sheets or inline styles, we usually don't write down the values for all rules, but only for the rules whose default values are different from the ones we want. Styles whose values are not defined directly in the style sheet are said to be *implicit* styles. Included in the implicit styles category are styles that are inherited by an element from an ancestor or parent, such as color.

When it comes to styles, explicit styles trump implicit styles. Inline explicit styles are honored more than global explicit styles, and both inline and global explicit styles come before implicit styles. When you combine both the explicit and implicit styles that apply to an element, you get the complete set of styles for an element, and thus you get the element's *computed* styles.

Computed styles represent the final style that's applied to an element. For our div snippet, for example, the computed style for the color of the div will be #000, which is equal to the definition in the inline style, while the computed style for the height of the div will be 20px, which is equal to the definition in the global style sheet. And since there was no definition for it, the computed background-color style of the div will be transparent—the default implicit value for the style.

When dealing with computed styles, it's important to note that values such as auto don't exist because computed styles have concrete values. An auto value usually represents a value that automatically changes depending on the state of an element, like height based on the content of the element. When computed styles come into play, these auto values are turned into actual pixel values—so an element with a height set to auto in a declaration will have a height value equal to X pixels in computed styles.

This concreteness of computed styles is important because we need to deal with real values in animation. If we want to animate the height of a div by adding 20 pixels to it, for example, we need to be able to get the initial pixel value of the element's height so that we can increment it per frame. We can't do this using ambiguous values like auto—we need the actual, concrete numeric value.

Revisiting Style Methods

In Chapter 8, when we talked about the Element type, we learned about the basic style methods such as getStyle and setStyle. We said that these methods are used to return and set the specific styles of the elements, and in part that's true. But since we now know more about CSS styles in general, we need to expand our discussion a bit.

The getStyle and setStyle methods can be considered "unified" methods: both can be used as interfaces to other related functions. The setStyle method, for instance, is mainly a wrapper for assigning properties to an element's `style` object. This means that doing something like `el.setStyle('height', 'auto')` is the same as doing `el.style.height = 'auto'`. Well, almost the same: aside from this simple `style` object assignment, `setStyle` can also handle things like setting opacity, which is really done using `set('opacity')`. Thus, we go back to the original premise: `setStyle` is a single interface to several different operations.

Like `setStyle`, `getStyle` is largely concerned with the `style` object. When we try to access an element's `style` value using `getStyle`, the method first checks the `style` object of the element to see if the specific rule is present. If it is, the value of this rule is simply parsed into a usable form and returned. However, if this rule isn't present in the `style` object, `getStyle` will call another method: `getComputedStyle`.

The `getComputedStyle` method has the same API as `getStyle`, but it checks the computed style of an element directly rather than checking the `style` object first. When we retrieve an element's style rule value using `getComputedStyle`, we actually access the final style value that's applied to the element. This means that all rules—both explicit and implicit—are available using `getComputedStyle`, which makes it very valuable.

One typical question about `getStyle` and `getComputedStyle` goes like this: "If `getComputedStyle` can give us the final value for any element style rule whatsoever, then why doesn't `getStyle` simply use `getComputedStyle` for everything?" This is a valid question. The truth is that for most cases, `getStyle` does use `getComputedStyle` for everything, since most elements won't have inline styles, which means they'll have blank style object properties. But on the other hand, MooTools does check the `style` object as much as it can for two reasons: because it's faster and because the value of the rule in the `style` object is actually the same as the value of the element's computed style, since inline styles have the highest precedence order.

Time for Some Action

Now that we've seen how properties come into play, let's take a look at the other piece of the animation puzzle: timers.

Timers

The existence of a main loop lets browsers provide special functions called *timers*. A timer is a function that enables us to execute a function at a particular time. There are two timer functions in JavaScript: `setTimeout` and `setInterval`.

The `setTimeout` function takes two arguments: `func`, which is the function to run, and `delay`, which is a number representing the amount of time to wait before executing the function.

```
setTimeout(function(){
    console.log('Hello World!');
}, 1000);
```

Here's an example of `setTimeout` that executes a function after a second. You'll notice that the delay number is in milliseconds, where one thousand milliseconds is equal to a second. When this snippet is run in the browser, the JavaScript interpreter will wait one second before invoking the function.

The other timer function, `setInterval`, also takes two arguments: `func`, which is the function to run, and `interval`, which is a number representing the amount of time to wait before executing the function. This function works similarly to `setTimeout`, but instead of simply delaying the execution of the function, it invokes the function at regular intervals.

```
setInterval(function(){
    console.log('Hello World!');
}, 1000);
```

In this snippet we use the same arguments as we did for the `setTimeout` function. And as with `setTimeout`, the JavaScript interpreter will again wait one second before invoking the function. Unlike `setTimeout`, though, which invokes the function only once, `setInterval` will continue invoking the function regularly for an indefinite period of time. So after the first invocation, the interpreter will wait another second before invoking the function again, and then repeat this wait-invoke process indefinitely.

▓ **Note** The `setTimeout` and `setInterval` functions aren't actually limited to functions, but can also be passed strings representing code to be evaluated using the `eval` function. This form is discouraged, however, because of the limited scope of the `eval` function and also because it can lead to some security issues regarding unescaped user input.

One important thing to know about these functions is that they're scheduling functions, not blocking ones. What this means is that when the interpreter sees an invocation of `setTimeout` or `setInterval`, it does not stop further execution in order to wait for these functions to finish. Instead, it takes the function arguments and the delay or interval value and stores them in a stack in order to access them later before continuing the execution. For example:

```
console.log('A');
setTimeout(function(){
    console.log('B');
}, 1000);
console.log('C');
```

In this example we have a `setTimeout` call surrounded by two `console.log` invocations. When we run this on the browser, we get the following console output:

```
A
C
B
```

You'll notice that the order of the log is different from the order of `console.log` invocations in the snippet. This is because the interpreter doesn't wait for the function argument to be executed, but instead stores that function first. So what happened here is that the first log output, A, was logged first, then the interpreter saw the call to `setTimeout`. It then stored the function argument to `setTimeout` in a stack before proceeding to the next line to output C. When the delay period specified for `setTimeout` passed, the interpreter finally called the function argument, so the B value is logged.

Both `setTimeout` and `setInterval` return a number value, called a timer identifier. This number is used if we need to disable the timer, which is especially useful for `setInterval`. Disabling a timer is called "clearing," and can be done using two functions: `clearTimeout` and `clearInterval`.

The `clearTimeout` function takes a single argument, `id`, and disables a `setTimeout` timer associated with that id:

```
var id = setTimeout(function(){
    console.log('Hello World!');
}, 1000);

clearTimeout(id);
```

In this snippet, we first stored the identifier of the timer in a variable called id. We then immediately called on clearTimeout, passing the identifier we stored. This means that the function will never be called, because we disable the execution of the timer function immediately.

As you might guess, clearInterval is used to disable a setInterval timer. Like clearTimeout, it also takes a single id argument:

```
var count = 0;

var id = setInterval(function(){
    console.log('Hello');
    count++;
    if (count === 3) clearInterval(id);
}, 1000);
```

Here we have an example of a self-disabling interval function. We first set up a counter that increments for each invocation of the function argument. We then set the function argument to run every one second using the setInterval function. When the function argument has been invoked three times, we call clearInterval to disable the timer, stopping our function from further executing.

Since the setTimeout and setInterval functions are mostly concerned with executing function arguments, MooTools implements two Function methods that employ these two timer functions, delay and periodical, which we've already seen in Chapter 2. Like setTimeout and setInterval, these two function methods return a timer identifier that can be used with the clearTimeout and clearInterval functions.

Timer Execution

JavaScript's single-threaded nature has a very interesting effect on timers. Remember that the global scope and function scopes have separate execution contexts, which the interpreter "enters" and "exits" during the course of a program. Because JavaScript is single-threaded, only a single execution context can be active at any point in the program's lifetime.

This one-context-at-a-time design affects timers immensely because timers are run in a separate execution context. For instance, take a look at the following example:

```
var fn1 = function(){
    setTimeout(function fn2(){
        console.log('fn2');
    }, 0);
    console.log('fn1');
};

fn1();
```

In this snippet we created a new function called fn1. Inside this function, we created a new delayed function called fn2 using setTimeout. What's different about this delayed function is that we set the delay amount to 0—which is like saying we don't want any delay in execution. So, we would likely assume that since there is no delay, fn2 will be executed immediately and our output will be 'fn2' and then 'fn1'. But when we run this, we see the following output:

```
fn1
fn2
```

Even though our fn2 function had a delay of 0, it wasn't executed immediately. Instead, the interpreter finished executing fn1 first before invoking fn2.

345

This is an important point to consider when working with timers. Because JavaScript is single-threaded, only a single execution context can be active at a time. In our example, fn2 can't be executed immediately even if the delay is 0 because at the point the timer went off, the interpreter was still busy interpreting fn1.

But timers aren't only competing with regular functions for execution, they are also competing with other timers. If a function delayed using a timer is executing, other timers that are set off during that time won't be able to execute as well, which means they'll be queued for later execution.

It is imperative that you remember this because it shows us a "flaw" in the timer system: most of the time, we can't trust timers to execute at exactly the time we specified. If there are no functions currently being executed, our timers will probably execute with a delay that's equal to what we specified. But if our application is busy with other things, we can't expect the timer to be really on time.

A Basic JavaScript Animation

At this point we have all the elements we need to get started working with JavaScript animation. We know the basics of animation theory, we know about styles, and we know about timers. So let's go ahead and try implementing a simple animation with JavaScript.

For our purposes, we'll reuse the square example: a square that is 10 pixels from the left of the screen needs to be moved 20 pixels to the right until it reaches a position of 30 pixels from the left of the screen. For this attempt, we'll make everything really simple so that we can focus on the animation itself.

First, here's our element:

```
<div id="square" style="
    background: #000;
    height: 20px;
    width: 20px;
    position: absolute;
    left: 10px">
</div>
```

The element we're animating is a basic div element. To keep things simple, we've defined the dimensions and position of the element using an inline style. This makes it easier for us to get these dimensions in our code using the style property.

Now that we have our element, it's time to start writing our animation code. The first thing we need is to declare a few variables:

```
// the element
var square = $('square');

// time/frames variables
var duration = 1000;
var rate = 50;
var frames = duration / 1000 * rate;

// property variables
var amount = 20;
var increment = amount / frames;
```

The first variable, square, is a reference to the element we're animating. The next three variables are our time and frames variables: duration tells us the length of the animation in milliseconds, rate tells us the frame rate or number of frames per second, and frames tells us the total number of frames for the whole animation sequence. Finally, we have the property values: amount, which tells us the total amount of change for the element's property, and increment, which is the amount to change per frame.

Now we need to create the step function. This function will be the one called to update the value of the div's property. There are many ways to do this, but we can simply code it like this:

```
var step = function(){
    // get the current value
    var left = parseFloat(square.style.left);

    // increment the value
    left += increment;

    // set the new value
    square.style.left = left + 'px';
};
```

The first thing the step function does is to get the current value of the property being animated, which it stores in the left variable. It then increments this original value with the amount we calculated by dividing the total change amount by the number of frames for the animation. Finally, the function sets this new value as the value of the left property of the element—thereby visibly moving the object on the screen.

We're almost done with this animation example. The last thing we need to do is to add the timer. Since we'll need to call the step function at regular intervals, we'll use the setInterval function:

```
var stepInterval = setInterval(step, Math.round(duration / frames));
```

Here we used setInterval to get the interpreter to run our step function at a regular rate. The speed of our interval function is defined as Math.round(duration / frames), which gives us a nice whole number to work with, since timer functions aren't that good with floating points.

Now we have everything in place. Let's take a look at our complete code:

```
// the element
var square = $('square');

// time/frames variables
var duration = 1000;
var rate = 50;
var frames = duration / 1000 * rate;

// property variables
var amount = 20;
var increment = amount / frames;

var step = function(){
    // get the current value
    var left = parseFloat(square.style.left);

    // increment the value
    left += increment;

    // set the new value
    square.style.left = left + 'px';
};

var stepInterval = setInterval(step, Math.round(duration / frames));
```

The first time the step function is called by the interpreter's timer, the square will be moved a little bit to the right, and will continue moving for each subsequent invocation. The result is a nice animation sequence.

There's a problem with our implementation though: we didn't add anything that will make it stop! If we run this on the browser, the square will continue moving right indefinitely. Remember that we only want to move the square a few pixels to the right—20 pixels to be exact—but our previous example moves the square way past that amount.

```
// the element
var square = $('square');

// time/frames variables
var duration = 1000;
var rate = 50;
var frames = duration / 1000 * rate;

// property variables
var initial = parseFloat(square.style.left);
var amount = 20;
var increment = amount / frames;

var step = function(){
    // get the current value
    var left = parseFloat(square.style.left);

    if (left < (initial + amount)){
        // increment the value
        left += increment;

        // set the new value
        square.style.left = left + 'px';
    } else {
        // stop the timer
        clearInterval(stepInterval);
    }
};

var stepInterval = setInterval(step, Math.round(duration / frames));
```

Here we added a new variable called initial, which stores the initial value of the property we're animating. We also modified our step function to check the value of the element's left property each time it's called. If the value is less than the sum of the initial value and the total change amount, then our animation isn't done yet, so we can continue incrementing the value. If it's not smaller, however, it means that the target amount of change has been satisfied, so we can stop the animation by clearing the timer.

Our example is pretty easy to understand, and the whole implementation is straightforward enough. As it shows, basic animation isn't that complicated: you only need to declare some basic variables with simple mathematical formulas, and employ a single function that will be repeated using a timer. Even with this simple code, the result is still quite exciting.

MooTools Fx Classes

While our animation example is great for showing the elements of animation in action, it has flaws that make it unsuitable for real-world use.

The first problem is the hard-coded property change. We're animating a single property in our example, but what if we need to add more properties to animate? Or what if we need to change this property? All the property-related elements in our example are hard-coded as variables, and the change process itself defines our property explicitly.

Another issue is reusability. What if we want to animate other things on our page? Do we copy the same function and just change it? That would be wasteful, not to mention impractical. In order to make animations really practical, we need a reusable way of adding animations to our page.

If we want to fully take advantage of animation in our applications, we need a better solution. Animation was one of the most common uses of JavaScript in the early days of the language—the other being validation—and even today, animation plays a big role in browser-based JavaScript applications, not only for the purpose of "eye-candy" but also to provide visual clues about UI changes to users.

The usefulness of animation was apparent to many early framework developers, and almost all frameworks include some animation facilities in their APIs—and MooTools is no exception. Most of these animation APIs address the two issues I noted, as well as other implementation details that might not be apparent to most of us.

The MooTools animation system—which is embodied by the Fx class and subclasses—is one of the oldest APIs in MooTools. As we learned in Chapter 1, MooTools started out as Moo.Fx, an animation framework for another JavaScript library. What we know now as MooTools evolved from these original Moo.Fx animation classes, which should give you an idea of just how important these APIs are.

Animation Objects

Unlike our native animation example, which uses variables and functions, the MooTools Fx system uses animation objects to perform the same set of tasks. An animation object is an instance of an Fx subclass like Fx.Tween or Fx.Morph that encapsulates the basic elements of the process, like timers and calculation functions, and controls the whole progression of the animation sequence.

```
var square = $('square');

var tween = new Fx.Tween(square, {
    duration: 1000,
    fps: 50
});
```

```
tween.start('left', 30);
```

Here we reimplemented our previous native animation example using an animation object that is an Fx.Tween instance. Unlike our native example, we didn't need to write a whole bunch of variables and functions, but instead simply instantiated a new animation object. Our tween object in this case contains all the necessary elements for performing the animation, and we triggered this by simply calling the start method.

Notice that the style property we're animating, left, and the value we want this item to take, 30, are passed as arguments to the start method rather than passed as options to the constructor. This is because all animation objects are generic by default: they don't describe the actual properties being animated, only the duration and speed of the animation itself. This makes animation objects reusable in a way that a single animation object can be used to animate different properties by changing the arguments to the start method.

```
tween.start('height', 30);
tween.start('width', 30);
```

However, this doesn't mean that it'll work as we'd expect. After our first call to start, the animation object will be in a working state, which means that it'll be busy performing the necessary actions to animate the height of the element.

If we call start again while the animation is in this state, the animation object will behave according to the value of its link option. If the link option has the value 'ignore', it will simply ignore the second call.

```
var square = $('square');

var tween = new Fx.Tween(square, {
    duration: 1000,
    fps: 50,
    link: 'ignore'
});


tween.start('height', 30);
tween.start('width', 30);
```

In this snippet we passed a link option with the value 'ignore' to our constructor. This tells the animation object to ignore any subsequent calls to start while the animation object is still busy with the previous call. Note that all Fx classes use 'ignore' as the default value for the link options, which means we don't need to include it explicitly:

```
var square = $('square');

var tween = new Fx.Tween(square, {
    duration: 1000,
    fps: 50
});


tween.start('height', 30);
tween.start('width', 30);
```

This example is the same as the previous one even if we didn't include the link option, because all animation objects have 'ignore' as their default link value if the option isn't specified.

Another possible value for the link option is 'cancel'. This tells the animation object that if the start method is called while it is in a working state, the new call should cancel the previous one and replace it:

```
var square = $('square');

var tween = new Fx.Tween(square, {
    duration: 1000,
    fps: 50,
    link: 'cancel'
});


tween.start('height', 30);
tween.start('width', 30);
```

In this snippet the second call to start will cancel the previous call, and then replace it. This means that the animation sequence that's changing the height property of the element will be stopped and the animation object will proceed with animating the width property.

Finally, animation objects can have the link option of 'chain', which stores subsequent calls to start for later processing.

```
var square = $('square');

var tween = new Fx.Tween(square, {
    duration: 1000,
    fps: 50,
    link: 'chain'
});


tween.start('height', 30);
tween.start('width', 30);
```

Here our animation object will store the second call to start in a queue. After the first animation sequence has finished, the animation object will then call the next one in the chain, making it possible to chain several animation sequences in order. We'll see how to combine animation sequences when we look at Fx.Morph later in the chapter.

Tween and Morph

Tween and Morph are the two main Fx classes are used for animation in MooTools. These classes have very similar APIs, with the exception of having different signatures for their start methods. Because they're inherently similar, we'll take a look first at their differences before discussing the common methods of their APIs.

Fx.Tween

We've already seen Fx.Tween. This class is used to animated single CSS properties. The Fx.Tween constructor takes two arguments, element, which is the element to animate, and options, which is an optional object that can be used to set various internal properties.

```
var square = $('square');

var tween = new Fx.Tween(square, {
    duration: 1000,
    fps: 50
});
```

Here we created a new Fx.Tween instance called tween. We passed the value of our square variable, which is an element, to the constructor to tell it that we're animating that element. We also passed an options object argument containing two options: duration, which sets the length of time for our animation, and fps, which sets the number of frames per second to display.

Internally, the Fx.Tween constructor passes the value of the element argument to document.id, which means we can either pass a real Element instance or simply the id of the element we're animating. The following snippet is the same as the one above:

```
var tween = new Fx.Tween('square', {
    duration: 1000,
```

```
    fps: 50
});
```

At this point, we have our generic tween animation object. In order to activate the animation sequence, we need to call the start method. This method takes two arguments: property, which is a string denoting the CSS style property to animate, and value, which is the target value of the CSS property.

```
tween.start('height', 30);
```

In this snippet we're triggering the tween object to start animating the height style property of the element. The animation object will then take the initial value of the element's height property and animate it until it reaches the value of 30.

■ **Note** The MooTools Fx system uses pixels as its main unit for numeric values, which means any number passed to the start method is interpreted as pixels.

However, the start method also has another form, which uses three arguments instead of two: property, from, and to.

```
tween.start('height', 20, 30);
```

Here the second argument, from, is used to explicitly set the initial value of the property before it is animated. In the previous form we simply used the current value of the property, but here we explicitly tell the animation object that we want to start the animation with our element's height property set to 20 before it's animated to 30.

Fx.Morph

While Fx.Tween is concerned with animating single properties at a time, Fx.Morph is used to animate several CSS properties together in the same animation sequence. This makes it useful for complex animation sequences that change an object's properties in several ways.

As with Fx.Tween, the Fx.Morph constructor takes two arguments: element, which is the element to animate, and options, which is an object containing various animation related options. Also like the Fx.Tween constructor, Fx.Morph passes the value of the element argument to document.id, so we can pass both Element instances and string ids.

```
var morph = new Fx.Morph('square', {
    duration: 1000,
    fps: 50
});
```

The main difference between the APIs of the Fx.Tween and Fx.Morph classes is the signature of their start methods. For Fx.Morph, start takes only a single argument, properties, which is an object. The keys of the properties object correspond to the CSS style properties to animate, while their values correspond to the target values for these properties:

```
morph.start({
    'height': 30,
    'width': 30
```

```
});
```

Here we called the start method of our Fx.Morph instance, passing in a properties object with two properties: height and width. This triggers the animation object to animate both the height and width properties of the element at the same time.

Like Fx.Tween, Fx.Morph also allows us to set the initial value of the property. We can do this by putting the values in our properties object arrays.

```
morph.start({
    'height': [20, 30],
    'width': 30
});
```

In this example we changed the value of the height property to an array containing two numbers. The first number will be used as the initial value of the property before animating it, while the second value will be the target value for the property.

Fx Methods and Events

As you'll notice above, both Fx.Tween and Fx.Morph have almost the same APIs, except for signature differences in the start method. These two classes actually inherit from the same base class as we'll see later, which gives them the same set of methods. Some of the shared methods, like start, are overridden by these two classes, but most of them are shared.

▓ **Note** From here on we're just going to use Fx.Tween instances in our examples in order to avoid repeating the code for both classes.

One of these shared methods, cancel, is the opposite of the start method and triggers the animation to stop:

```
var square = $('square');

var tween = new Fx.Tween(square, {
    duration: 1000,
    fps: 50,
});

tween.start('left', 30);

tween.cancel();
```

Here we called the cancel method immediately after calling start, which forces the animation sequence to halt entirely.

Of course, there are times when you don't want to completely cancel an animation sequence, but simply stop it for a bit and continue later. You can do this using the pause and resume methods:

```
var square = $('square');

var tween = new Fx.Tween(square, {
    duration: 1000,
```

```
    fps: 50,
});

tween.start('left', 30);

tween.pause();

setTimeout(function(){
    tween.resume();
}, 500);
```

In this snippet we called the pause method of our object immediately after calling start, halting the animation sequence. We then set a timer function to continue the animation using the resume method. The result is that our animation will stop for a bit, before continuing after half a second.

Animation objects, like other MooTools classes, function as event dispatchers, which means we can add event handlers that will get invoked at particular stages of the animation sequence. This is because Fx implements the Events mixin internally, which gives our animation objects the necessary event APIs.

There are three main events dispatched by the Fx classes:

- start is dispatched right after the start method is called.

- cancel is dispatched when the cancel method is called.

- complete is dispatched when the animation sequence has finished.

You can add event handlers for these events using the addEvent methods we've already seen in previous chapters. Another way would be to pass the event handlers using the options argument:

```
new Fx.Tween('square', {
    onStart: startFn,
    onCancel: cancelFn,
    onComplete: completeFn
});
```

All event handlers for these events are invoked with a single argument, element, which is the element that's being animated.

Fx Internals

Without knowing about the basic principles of animation that we've discussed, the MooTools animation system might come off as overly complicated. Unlike the other internal systems we've seen so far, the main Fx animation system is composed of several interconnected classes, most of which aren't directly used. In order to understand the system, we need to take a look at these classes separately, then connect them at the end of our discussion.

The Fx Base Class

The Fx class is at the root of the MooTools animation system. This class defines the most basic components required to produce animations, and all animation-related classes inherit from Fx.

The Fx class uses all of the three built-in mutators: Options to allow passing option objects during instantiation, Events to enable animation objects to dispatch events and have event listeners, and Chain to enable the chaining of calls to the start method.

Initialization and Class Options

Initializing the Fx class method takes two arguments: subject and options. The method takes the first argument, subject, and sets it as the value of the subject property of the instance, while the second argument is passed to the setOptions method.

As we saw in the previous section, all Fx classes have three main options: duration, fps, and link. These three options are given default values by the explicit options property declared in the Fx class declaration, and these default values are 500, 50, and 'ignore' respectively.

Of special note is the duration option, which can actually take either a numeric value that represents the length in milliseconds, or one of the special "duration values." These duration values are stored in a special object called Fx.Durations:

```
Fx.Durations = {'short': 250, 'normal': 500, 'long': 1000};
```

So instead of putting duration: 250, we can use the equivalent duration value, like duration: 'short'. And since the Fx.Durations object is public, we can augment it directly to define our own duration values.

The step Method

If you look back at our native animation example, you'll see the function called step, which is used to control the animation operation. We call this function the animator function, and it's in charge of computing the amount of change to be applied for a particular frame as well as stopping the animation when the desired value has been reached.

The Fx class implements the animator method that's used by all animation objects: step. This method is called at each frame of the animation, and like its native counterpart, it performs the necessary calculations for each frame as well as checking whether to stop the animation when it's done.

Unlike our native step function, which uses the actual values of the animated property, the step method takes a different approach that uses the elapsed time. At the start of the animation sequence, the current timestamp is stored in the time property of the object. When the duration of the animation (which is expressed in milliseconds) is added to this timestamp value, we get another timestamp value, which is the target time when the animation will be completed.

When the step method is called, it checks the current time to see if it's less than the target time. If it is, the animation should still be in progress, and should therefore continue. However, if the current time is greater than the target time, the animation should be done and the step method will finish the animation sequence.

This time-based technique is also used for calculating the amount of change that needs to happen at a particular frame. In our native example, we simply divided the total amount of change by the number of frames and incremented the property value for each frame. In contrast, the step method computes the value based on the time elapsed using special equations called *easing equations*.

Timers

While the animator function is concerned with changing the value of the property per frame, the timer function is concerned with keeping the animation sequence moving by invoking the animator function at regular intervals.

In our native animation example, we created a single function called step, which we then ran periodically using the setInterval function. The step function therefore acted both as the timer and as the animator. In other words, the function that's in charge of changing the properties is the same function that gets called repeatedly by the setInterval function. If we were to animate multiple objects this way, we'd end up with a different timer function for each object we're animating. Because each object would have its own periodical function, we could say we have multiple timers.

MooTools, on the other hand, doesn't merge the animator and timer. Instead, MooTools creates private timer functions that call the step method of the animation objects. All timers are private and can only be accessed by the Fx class. The startTimer method of the Fx class is the method used to associate the current instance to a particular timer, while the stopTimer method is used to remove this association. These two methods are used by the other Fx methods, and are never actually invoked outside the class.

MooTools will group animation objects using the values of their fps option. All animations that run at 50fps, for example, will share the same timer function, and the same is true for all other animation objects that share the same fps value. Because a single timer function can be used for multiple animation objects, we can say that MooTools uses unified timers.

The use of unified timers gives the MooTools Fx system some great benefits. First, using unified timers minimizes the problem of multiple timers blocking each other due to JavaScript's single-threaded nature. Because multiple animation objects can share a single timer, the number of timer functions vying for execution time is lessened, which means less execution conflict.

The second—and perhaps more important—benefit of unified timers is animation synchronization. With multiple timers, only a single timer function (and therefore a single animator function) can run at a time, which means that multiple objects being animated won't have synchronized animations. In contrast, unified timers enable several animator functions to run for each pass of the interval, synchronizing the change for all objects.

The start Method

The Fx class implements the main start method that's used by all Fx subclasses. Some subclasses will override this method in order to add class-specific functionality, but these overriding methods will still call the original start method implemented by Fx.

The first thing the start method does is to check whether the animation is currently running. If it isn't, start proceeds to set various flag properties for the animation. These include items like the initial value and the target value for the property being animated, as well as the easing equation to use for the animation. The start method then calls the startTimer method of the instance, which associates the current instance to a private timer function. The startTimer method also saves the current timestamp that will be used by the step function for its calculations. Finally, the start method calls the onStart method, whose job is to dispatch the start event using fireEvent.

However, if the start method is called while the animation object is still busy with a previous sequence, it will either ignore or store this new call, or cancel the previous one and replace it with this new call—a behavior that's dependent on the value of the link option.

CSS Animation

As we've seen, the Fx base class is mostly concerned with setting up a framework for the basic elements of animation. Fx itself is very important in the MooTools animation system, but it remains incomplete because it does not implement the higher-level parts.

In order to make Fx usable, it has to be subclassed, and new methods that handle the actual property computation and change need to be implemented. Fx is actually very flexible in that you can subclass it to handle any kind of animation. Luckily, MooTools does the grunt work for us by including an Fx subclass that handles CSS style animation—the most common animation done on the DOM— called Fx.CSS.

The Fx.CSS class implements all the necessary methods that are used for CSS style animations. These include basic methods like render and serve, which are concerned with the actual computation and setting of the properties using setStyle, and more complex methods like search, which is used to parse the document's style sheets to find default values for CSS class declarations.

The most interesting part of Fx.CSS, though, is the set of parsers used for computing the changes for CSS style values. There are three default parsers for Fx.CSS: String, Number and Color. These parsers, which are stored in `Fx.CSS.Parsers`, are used to parse values that will be employed in the animation sequence, and turn them into JavaScript objects that can be used in computational operations.

Like `Fx`, though, `Fx.CSS` is still unusable on its own. The API for `Fx.CSS` is a bit unpolished, so subclasses are needed to add a more refined abstraction for the class.

MooTools provides two of these abstractions: `Fx.Tween` and `Fx.Morph`. These two classes are subclassed from the `Fx.CSS` class, and implement the abstractions for tweening and morphing elements. We've already seen them at work, and I think we all can agree that they give us a very elegant API for working with CSS animations.

The Wrap-Up

Animation is usually seen and not read, but we did learn a thing or two about it in this chapter. We've seen what animation actually is, and what elements that come together in the animation process. We also learned a little about CSS styles and JavaScript timers, and the roles they play in animation. Finally, we discussed how to do JavaScript animation using native JavaScript and the MooTools Fx classes.

With this chapter, our tour of JavaScript and MooTools on the browser has ended. In the next chapter we'll break free from the window, from the DOM and from elements and visuals.

So put on those riding boots and mount your space horse, as we explore JavaScript beyond the browser.

PART III

Breaking from the Browser

CHAPTER 13

■ ■ ■

JavaScript without Limits

In the first two parts of this book, we explored topics that are more or less "old stuff" in terms of JavaScript development. The JavaScript language has been around for quite some time, and the things we've learned so far have been explored and re-explored many times before. For some of us, the previous chapters were refreshers; for others, they're advanced information waiting to be applied.

But now we leave the comfort of the familiar and delve into a very young topic: CommonJS. Barely two years old, CommonJS has pushed JavaScript into an area it has never been successful in before: it has turned JavaScript into a powerful, general-purpose scripting language.

Breaking out of the Browser

JavaScript has always been a language of the browser—and will remain so for quite some time. This, of course, is beneficial to the language: because the Internet has become a ubiquitous part of most people's lives, the browser—the application that helps us navigate this vast network of information—has also established itself as one of the most important applications today. And JavaScript, as the only DOM scripting language currently supported by all major browsers, benefits greatly from the continuous effort browser developers put toward making their applications faster and better.

But, at the same time, this binding of JavaScript to the browser is too limiting. JavaScript is a very powerful language that has lots of potential outside of browsers. It's a quirky language, yes, but its quirks don't make it less powerful by any significant mark.

One of the potential uses of JavaScript outside the browser is as a general-purpose scripting language. In the browser, JavaScript functions mainly as a DOM scripting language: a language for manipulating documents. Outside the browser, though, JavaScript would be a great language for handling a multitude of programming tasks: servers, text-processing, and file manipulation—just to name a few.

For JavaScript to reach this potential, though, it must lose some of its parts: no more browser-based APIs and no more DOM Trees and nodes. It needs to be lean, a language that has no other association to anything except itself. To go back to the idea of the first part of this book, JavaScript as JavaScript.

This, of course, has been done several times already. A lot of platforms have appeared over the years that tried taking JavaScript outside the browser and bringing it to the realm of the server, but mostly these didn't capture the attention of developers. This all changed in January of 2009, when for the first time, a glimmer of hope for a general-purpose JavaScript showed itself through a movement.

CommonJS

The **CommonJS** movement started in early 2009 with an effort by Kevin Dangoor. In an article called "What Server Side JavaScript Needs" (www.blueskyonmars.com/2009/01/29/what-server-side-javascript-needs/), Dangoor outlined the pitiful state of server-side JavaScript implementations at the time. He raised several points that needed to be addressed:

- The lack of a standard set of libraries that can be used in any server-side JavaScript implementation.

- The lack of a standard way of importing and exporting modules for use in multiple implementations.

- The lack of a usable packaging system for server-side JavaScript.

To address these points, Dangoor created a new group called *ServerJS*, which included developers of existing server-side JavaScript implementations as well as other JavaScript developers interested in the area. The group gained quite a following, and discussions about the topics presented in the article grew into firm plans that have affected the state of JavaScript outside the browser for good.

In August of 2009—just about six months after the initial introduction of ServerJS—the group decided to rename the effort CommonJS to reflect the new direction they were taking. Instead of simply defining a set of specifications that could be used in server-side implementations, the CommonJS group wanted to make these specifications usable in any kind of JavaScript environment—the browser included.

The name CommonJS actually refers to two things: It refers to the group itself, of course, the loose organization that came into being via the ServerJS initiative. And it also refers to the set of technologies that emerged from the proposals the CommonJS group created.

The CommonJS group came out with a handful of proposals for language and API extensions, dealing with everything from modules and packages to file I/O and unit testing. As of the time of this book's writing, the group has approved and released several important specifications:

- Modules (1.1)

- Packages (1.0)

- System Interfaces (1.0)

- Unit Testing (1.0)

These four specifications—together with the dozen others that are currently being discussed—form the core set of APIs that all CommonJS-compliant engines support.

In addition to the specifications themselves, the CommonJS group is responsible for another important effect—the development of several powerful implementations that are compliant with these specifications. There are now more than a dozen implementations available, each created using the original open-source interpreter from popular browsers such as Mozilla's SpiderMonkey and Rhino engines, and Google's v8 engine. This enables a multitude of platform possibilities for JavaScript development outside the browser.

Common Modules

Perhaps the most important specification to come out of CommonJS is Modules. This specification is one of the first efforts of the group to be widely accepted, and it has gained support in all CommonJS engines—as well as in other platforms both inside and outside the browser.

The Modules specification—the current version is 1.1—describes a working system for creating and reusing JavaScript modules. At its center is the concept of a **module**, a group of related JavaScript functionalities that can be imported into CommonJS programs for reuse.

For the most part, an implementation of the Modules specification is the only requirement a platform needs in order to be called CommonJS-compliant. Any platform—from standalone JavaScript engines to fully-fledged application frameworks—can therefore be considered a CommonJS engine if it enables the use of CommonJS Modules. As such, the Modules specification plays an important role in the CommonJS ecosystem for determining which implementations can be compatible with the CommonJS philosophy.

Export and Require

To understand how the Modules specification—and thus the module system of all CommonJS-compliant engines—works, we'll have to implement a basic module. Let's take a module composed of some math-related functions.

```
var sum = function(a, b){
    return a + b;
};

var increment = function(num){
    return sum(num, 1);
};
```

Here we have two simple functions, sum and increment, which we'd like to turn into a CommonJS module. In the CommonJS specification, a module is simply a file with the name of the module as the file name, followed by the file extension .js. What we want is a math module, so we'll name our file math.js:

```
// math.js

var sum = function(a, b){
    return a + b;
};

var increment = function(num){
    return sum(num, 1);
};
```

Now we have a file called math.js, which includes our two math functions. However, we still don't have a module. To create a module, we have to define the things a module provides. A module is said to provide something if by importing the module, we can access that functionality.

In our math example, we want importers of our module to be able to access the two functions. To do this, we have to use a special object called exports:

```
// math.js

var sum = function(a, b){
    return a + b;
};
```

```
var increment = function(num){
    return sum(num, 1);
};

exports.sum = sum;
exports.increment = increment;
```

The exports object is a special global object created by a CommonJS implementation. Any properties or methods you add to this object will be available to packages that import the module. Here we added two lines at the end of our file that define the export of the sum and increment modules, thereby making these two functions importable.

Now we already have a fairly simple yet usable math module. The next step is to import it into a program that's going to use these functions. To do this, we have to use the require function:

```
// program.js

var math = require('math');

console.log(math.sum(2, 3)); // 5
console.log(math.increment(303)); // 304
```

In this example we have a very simple program stored in a file called program.js. Since our program needs both the sum and increment functions defined in our math module, we decided to import this module. We did this by invoking the require function and passing in the name of the module without the extension. This function executes the contents of the math module, and then returns the value of the exports object. Thus, the return value of the require('math') call in our example is the exports object of the math module, which is why we are able to access the sum and increment functions.

Modules are executed in their own context, and any local variables defined in a module are private to that module.

```
// math.js

var sum = function(a, b){
    return a + b;
};

var increment = function(num){
    return sum(num, 1);
};

exports.increment = increment;
```

Here we only exported the increment function, which means that importers of this module won't be able to access the sum function. However, since modules are run in their own context, the increment function is still able to access the local function sum, which means we can use closures for our modules.

Loosely speaking, all CommonJS programs are treated as "modules" by the engine. This means that in our example, both math.js and program.js are modules, and thus any module-related API available to math.js is also available to program.js. This is an important point to remember, because it tells us we're allowed to import modules into other modules:

```
// sum.js

var sum = function(a, b){
    return a + b;
};
```

```
exports.sum = sum;

// increment.js

var sum = require('sum').sum;

var increment = function(num){
    return sum(num, 1);
};

exports.increment = increment;

// program.js

var increment = require('increment').increment;

console.log(increment(302)); // 303
```

Here we split up the math module into two modules: sum and increment. The sum module, in sum.js, is simply a declaration of the function together with an exports declaration. In increment.js, which is a separate module, we first import the sum module, then define the increment method that uses the sum function we imported. Finally, we import the increment module into the program itself. Thus, we are able to put together three separate modules into one program transparently.

Module imports using the require function are done linearly: when a module imports another module, the engine first interprets the contents of the imported module before returning the value of the exports object and continuing to interpret the rest of the importing module.

In our example, the engine will first interpret the program.js file and see that we're importing the increment module, so it will pause execution of program.js and open increment.js to start interpreting this file. In the increment.js file, it'll see that there's another call to require, so it'll again halt execution and perform the import by opening and interpreting sum.js.

After interpreting sum.js, the engine will take the value of the sum module's exports object and return to the importing module, which is increment.js. The increment.js file will then continue execution, thereby defining the increment function and exporting it. Then the engine will again take the value of the exports object and return to the main program.js file where execution will continue.

This linear execution of modules is done in order to prevent race conditions on dependencies. In our example, the increment module depends on the sum function from the sum module. Because of this dependency, the engine needs to make sure that the sum function will be available before the increment module can use it. Thus, the modules are interpreted in a linear fashion.

Module Paths

Those of you who are runners more than readers would probably have hit a snag in trying out the examples above. In particular, you might be getting errors about modules not being found. You probably just typed in those examples, placed them in a directory, and tried running program.js—which will lead to an error about module locations.

This error occurs because of how require works. If you notice, we didn't specify the exact location of the file to the require function, only the name of the module. How then does require know where to look for these modules?

The answer lies in a special property of the require function called paths. The require.paths property is an array of file-system locations expressed as strings. When require is invoked, it searches for the module by looking at each of these locations starting from the one indexed at 0 and moving on until it finds the particular module.

Each CommonJS engine will have a different set of default locations for require.paths, so there's not so much compatibility there. But let's say, for example, that our require.paths array looks like this:

```
[
    '/home/mark/.commonjs',
    '/home/shared/commonjs',
    '/usr/local/commonjs'
]
```

Now suppose we called require('math'). The first thing the require function will do is to inspect its paths property to determine which locations are to be searched. It takes the first location, /home/mark/.commonjs, and looks for a file called math.js in that directory. If it finds the file there, it stops the search, opens the file and interprets it. If the file doesn't exist, it will continue searching through the locations in require.paths until it finally finds the module. If all the locations have been exhausted without finding the file, require will throw an error to halt the execution of the program.

All engines allow you to add your own locations to the require.paths array. This enables us to store our modules in common locations that can be used in any CommonJS engine.

```
require.paths.unshift('/home/mark/.commonjs_modules');
```

Here we added a new location to the start of the require.paths array using the unshift method. Since paths are inspected using their indexing order, the require function will first search for an imported module in the new path before moving on to the other paths. If you want to add a new path to the end of the array, you can simply use the push method instead of unshift.

In this light, require seems to be quite absolute in its searches: in order to import a module, it needs to be stored in a location included in the require.paths array. However, this isn't always the case. The require function actually allows you to import modules relative to the current file.

Suppose our three files—program.js, increment.js, and sum.js—are stored in the /home/mark/code/example directory, which is a path that's not included in require.paths. If we run the original example without modification, our program will terminate with an error, because our modules can't be resolved. What we have to do, then, is modify our examples:

```
// sum.js

var sum = function(a, b){
    return a + b;
};

exports.sum = sum;


// increment.js

var sum = require('./sum').sum;

var increment = function(num){
    return sum(num, 1);
};

exports.increment = increment;


// program.js
```

```
var increment = require('./increment').increment;
```

```
console.log(increment(302)); // 303
```

Here we changed the `require` invocations by prefixing the module names with `./`. This tells the `require` function that we want to search for the modules using a path that's relative to the location of the importing module. Therefore, `require('./increment')` will look for the `increment.js` file in relation to the location of the `program.js` file, which is at `/home/mark/code/example`.

Because the location is relative, we can also use the conventional directory notation. For example, say we have the following directory structure:

```
/example
    /libs
        increment.js
        sum.js
    program.js
```

Now in order for `program.js` to be able to import `increment.js`, it needs to do `require('./libs/increment')`. On the other hand, `increment.js` can use `require('./sum')` directly because they are both in the same location.

MooTools and CommonJS

We saw in the first part of this book that, unlike other frameworks, MooTools does not limit itself to DOM scripting. If anything, the DOM scripting functionality in MooTools is only an extension to the real core of the framework: a powerful extension to the native JavaScript language. This makes MooTools a very good library for use with CommonJS.

Preparing MooTools for CommonJS use is as simple as building a MooTools package without browser-based extensions such as the `Element` type or the `Request` class. All other parts of the framework can be used in CommonJS, and MooTools, in fact, offers a special server-side build that can be used for CommonJS.

There is, however, a slight snag. Remember that CommonJS uses modules for much of its functionality, and to use MooTools with CommonJS engines, MooTools needs to be turned into a proper CommonJS module. The problem is that the current version of MooTools does not directly support the CommonJS module specification, which means that it doesn't use `exports` declarations. Instead, MooTools "exports" all its public APIs using the implicit global object, which makes exported objects like `Class` or `Type` inaccessible through `require`.

Thankfully, this isn't such a big problem. The structure of the MooTools library actually makes it very easy for us to add a simple importer function to make MooTools a CommonJS module. There are several available importer functions, but this one (which I've written myself) is what we'll use here:

```
(function(){

var $top = this,
    $exports = (typeof exports === 'object') ? exports : {};

Array.each([
    "MooTools",
    "typeOf", "instanceOf",
    "Type", "Class",
    "Events", "Options", "Chain"
], function(item){ $exports[item] = $top[item]; });
```

```
$exports.into = function into(globalObj){
    if (globalObj && globalObj !== $top){
        for (var i in $exports) {
            if ($exports[i] !== into) globalObj[i] = $exports[i];
        }
    }
    return globalObj;
};

})();
```

To use this importer function, you have to add it to the end of the MooTools server-side build file. This adds a new function called into, which can be used to import MooTools. To use into, you simply have to call it directly and pass the global object of the CommonJS implementation you're using:

```
require('mootools').into(global);
```

This example, which works in almost all major CommonJS implementations, will import MooTools and add commonly used objects such as Class or Type to the program's global object. Importing MooTools this way means that all modules—regardless of whether they import MooTools or not—will be able to use all MooTools functionality, making it easier to craft MooToolsian JavaScript programs for CommonJS.

Meso: MooTools in the Middle

There is, however, a simpler way that doesn't involve modifying MooTools to add an importer function: **Meso**.

The Meso project, which I started with the help of members of the MooTools development team and other MooTools community developers, is a cross-engine runner and library that aims to provide a cross-compatible API for using MooTools with CommonJS. Instead of targeting individual CommonJS engines, developers can target Meso to make their programs compatible with all supported implementations.

At the time of this writing, Meso supports four major engines: NodeJS, v8cgi, Flusspferd, and RingoJS, This means that all programs written using the Meso API will be able to run in all of these engines, making it easier to craft programs that can run on the user's choice of implementation.

Meso provides a simple set of classes for handling things like file system access, basic I/O, and server requests. But perhaps the most interesting feature of Meso is the runner, which not only provides a cross-engine way of running programs but also automatically imports MooTools.

Say we have the following CommonJS program:

```
var Person = new Class({

    initialize: function(name, age){
        this.name = name;
        this.age = age;
    },

    log: function(){
        return this.name + ', ' + this.age;
    }

});
```

```
var cassiopeia = new Person('Cassiopeia', '21');

print(cassiopeia.log);
```

You'll notice that we're declaring a new class in this program, but we're not importing MooTools. Because we didn't import MooTools here, the Class constructor won't be available if this program is run in a CommonJS engine, and therefore it will terminate with an error. However, if we run this on Meso, we won't get any errors because MooTools is automatically imported—which means all of those nice features we saw in the first part of this book will be usable.

Because Meso makes it quite easy to work with multiple CommonJS engines, we're going to use it instead of a specific engine for this book. You'll therefore need to install Meso on your system to be able to work through the next chapter. Because there are different installation instructions for different systems and different engines, I advise you to visit the official Meso site, http://mesojs.com, and follow the instructions there.

The Wrap-Up

This chapter introduces JavaScript as a potential general-purpose scripting language—outside the browser. We learned how CommonJS and the CommonJS Modules system make this possible. We also got a glimpse of MooTools on the server side and Meso, a cross-engine toolkit for MooTools and CommonJS.

In the next chapter, we'll expand on some of the concepts we learned here and take a look at a real-world example of how MooTools can be used on the server side.

So put on that astronaut suit you stashed in your closet and get ready for launch, as we explore the space beyond the browser.

CHAPTER 14

■ ■ ■

MooTools on Deck

Before CommonJS, there was ServerJS, a movement to advance the state of JavaScript on the server. Server-side JavaScript isn't something new: there have been several attempts to bring JavaScript to the backend of applications, but none of them was really successful. ServerJS (eventually renamed CommonJS) changed that.

The idea of JavaScript on the server might seem weird to some people. After all, there are already dozens of established languages that can be used to write the backend of web applications. There's a big allure, however, to being able to write both parts of an application—server and client—in the same language, and that alone is enough to warrant exploration into server-side JavaScript.

In this chapter, we'll take a quick look at the server-side aspect of applications and how CommonJS expands JavaScript to work on the backend. We'll also take a look at Deck, a cross-engine server-side JavaScript application layer written in MooTools.

Revisiting Request and Response

In Chapter 11, we learned about HTTP requests and responses in the context of the browser. We learned that when a browser needs to load a resource, it sends a *request* to a server, which the server answers with a *response*. The browser then parses this response to display the data or update the interface.

This side of the process should be familiar to you by now. However, we still haven't considered the other piece of the puzzle: the server itself. We know how to send requests and process the received response, but we don't know anything about how the server actually creates those responses.

Web servers come in different forms, from simple ones written in languages like Lua or Io, to much more complex systems like the Apache HTTP Server and Nginx. All of them, however, follow a very simple formula when it comes to the request and response cycle.

It begins, of course, with the web server software itself. As I said, web servers take a multitude of forms, and there's really no general engineering format that can describe them all. There is, however, a similarity in their architecture: all web servers will have some form of *listening loop* that lets them listen for incoming connections. Like the long-running programs we discussed in Chapter 10, web servers will sit and wait for events to happen. In this case, the events are client connections and requests.

When a client, such as a browser, connects to a server and sends a request, the server performs an inverse operation from the one we saw in Chapter 11. Say we have the following GET request:

```
GET /index.html HTTP/1.1
User-Agent: BrowserX/1.1
Accept: text/html
Host: example.org
```

The server, like the browser, understands the HTTP protocol, and therefore knows how to parse this message. In this case, the server knows that the client is requesting to retrieve (GET) a resource named /index.html and wants to receive files of the text/html type.

Most web servers have the capability of serving two kinds of resources: static and computed. A **static resource** is simply a resource that's stored as a file in some location on the server. For example, images and style sheets are almost always served as static resources; they are stored directly on the server and sent as is. For static resources, the web server only needs to locate the particular file on the server, process its contents to get its mime-type and length, and then send the whole resource back as a response.

If our /index.html is a static resource, for example, the web server simply looks for a file named index.html in the site's root directory, reads this file to get its contents and length, and then sends a response back to the client with the contents of the file included. The process is quick and straightforward, and there's not much processing involved.

On the other hand, **computed resources**, as their name implies, are resources that are the result of some computational process that's generally done using scripts and programs. In this category are the resources generated by PHP scripts, Rails or Django applications, or other dynamically created resources.

If static resources are stored directly as files on the server, does that mean that computed resources aren't stored as files? The answer is it depends. What makes a resource computed isn't actually whether it's stored in a file, but how the server retrieves the data associated with a resource.

Let's take PHP scripts, for instance. A PHP script is simply a plaintext script containing code that can be interpreted by a PHP interpreter. Say we have a PHP script file called program.php in the root of the server. If we request GET /program.php and the server responds with the actual content of the PHP file, then we are served a static resource. But if the server runs the PHP script file first by passing it to the PHP interpreter and then takes the result of that execution and sends it back to us, the resource we received is computed—the result of running a PHP script.

The decision as to whether to serve a resource as static or computed is therefore up to the server. Of course, this decision is aided by the configuration that the server administrator sets: a user can specify that a particular file type always be sent as static, while another file type should always be interpreted first to yield a computed resource.

Aside from this static versus computed resource distinction, web servers also distinguish between **direct** and **routed resources**. Remember that when we request a resource, we send a resource URI to the server that identifies the location of the resource we want to access. The location of the resource, therefore, determines whether the resource is direct or routed, which adds another dimension to the web server process.

In our examples, both index.html and index.php are files that are stored in the root directory. Therefore, the resource URIs /index.html and /index.php both correspond to the actual location of the files on the server. Thus, these resources are said to be direct because their resource URIs directly correspond to their locations in the file system. The resource index.html is therefore a *direct static resource*, while index.php is a *direct computed resource*.

However, web servers also allow us to define "virtual" locations for our resources. For example, we can set up our web server so that the resource URI /home would access the resource /index.php. The resource URI is therefore not directly connected to the actual location of the resource, and it is up to the web server to match the resource URI to the real resource location. Thus, this resource is said to be *routed*, because the web server needs to determine the route from the resource URI to the actual location.

Of course, all these ideas are transparent to the clients requesting resources from a server. To them, the web server is simply a black box: send a request, get a response. However, these ideas are important in our current discussion because we're moving away from the client-side of the equation and moving into the realm of the server.

JavaScript on the Server

Most simple web sites are served using direct static resources. Write a bunch of HTML pages, add in some images and style sheets, upload to a server, and you're done. Sometimes the resources are mapped so that they become routed resources, which make their external URLs prettier and more accessible, yet they still depend on static files.

Web applications, meanwhile, are built to be computed resources. Some parts of the web apps, such as the client-facing site, are sometimes built using static resources, but the server end of a web application is always computed. The computed parts of a web application are always written as programs, usually using one of the popular web programming languages such as PHP, Ruby, or Python, or more "arcane" yet interesting ones like Smalltalk or Lua.

In the early days of JavaScript, writing the computed, server-side part of a web application in JavaScript was an almost impossible idea. The technology was there, but there wasn't enough interest yet to capture the attention of developers. This gradually changed through the years, and eventually led to CommonJS. In fact, this was exactly the goal of ServerJS, the precursor to CommonJS: to provide a viable way to create web applications with a JavaScript backend.

And that's no longer just a pipe dream. Nowadays, lots of server-side JavaScript applications are being launched, and more companies are starting to test the usefulness of the language for building their next web application.

This confuses quite a lot of people, of course: why would we want to write a web application in JavaScript when there are already a lot of other languages to choose from? The most common answer is reuse. By using JavaScript, you can use the same language to develop both the client-side and the server-side parts of the application. JavaScript is the *de jure* language of the browser, and it now has the blessed status of being natively supported by both the client-side and the server-side—something that no other language can claim.

JSGI

One thing that's needed, though, to make JavaScript work on the server side is a set of language APIs that deal with application servers. In order for it to be used on the server side, JavaScript must learn the language of requests and responses from a server's point of view.

The CommonJS specification that deals with web applications is called the **JavaScript Gateway Interface** specification, or simply **JSGI**. This specification defines a model for creating JavaScript server-side applications using a very simple flow via function decoration.

In the JSGI model, an application is a simple JavaScript function that receives an object argument called the *environment*. It should then return a response object that contains the details of the response. Here's a very simple JSGI application:

```
var app = function(env){
    return {
        status: 200,
        headers: {
            'content-type': 'text/plain',
            'content-length': 12
        },
        body: ['Hello World!']
    };
};
```

When this application is called by the JSGI server, it's invoked as a function and passed a single env argument. This is the environment object that contains details about the request and the current environment. It has the following main properties:

- `method` is the HTTP method of the request in an uppercase string form, such as `'GET'` or `'POST'`.

- `pathInfo` is the request URI in string form. Like in our examples, this value is always prefixed with /.

- `queryString` is the query string portion of the request URI, if available.

- `host` and `port` give information about the host and port used to connect to the server.

- `scheme` is the string representation of the URL scheme used to access the server, such as `'http'` or `'https'`.

- `headers` is an object containing the request headers. Each header is defined as a key-value pair, with the key being the lowercase equivalent of the name of the header. For example, the HTTP header Content-Type will be available from this object through `headers['content-type']`.

- `input` is a special *stream* object that can be used to read the body of the request.

- `jsgi` is an object that contains special JSGI model values that are used to determine the nature of the engine's JSGI implementation.

- `env` is an object to which you can add new application- or host-defined properties, since the top-level environment object should not be augmented with new properties.

In JSGI applications, the environment object is used to determine the nature of the request, and its properties are inspected so we can properly serve a response. Since we're not doing any complex procedure in our application example, we simply ignore the environment object.

To properly respond to a request, the JSGI application needs to return a response object. This is a basic JavaScript object with the following properties:

- `status` is a number property that defines the HTTP status of the response.

- `headers` is an object containing the response headers. Like the `response` property of the environment object, each header is defined as a key-value pair with keys being lowercase header names.

- `body` is a collection object that contains the response body. For simple applications, a basic array is used as the body property, while more complex applications can use special *byte-array* objects provided by the CommonJS engine. When the response is sent to the client, the body property is either concatenated into a single string or sent in chunks using streams depending on the CommonJS engine.

In our example, the application sends back a simple response that will look like this to the client:

```
HTTP/1.1 200 OK
Content-Type: text/plain
Content-Length: 12
```

```
Hello World!
```

Because JSGI applications are simply functions, they can be extended and changed using simple function decoration, which we discussed in Chapter 2. For example, let's say we want to add the string `'Hi Universe'` to the end of the response body. We can do this using a simple decorator:

```
// decorator
var decorate = function(app){
    return function(env){
        var response = app(env);
        response.body.push('/nHi Universe!');
        response.headers['content-length'] = response.body.join('').length;
        return response;
    };
};

// jsgi application
var app = function(env){
    return {
        status: 200,
        headers: {
            'content-type': 'text/plain',
            'content-length': 12
        },
        body: ['Hello World!']
    };
};

// decorate app
app = decorate(app);
```

Here we defined a decorator function that takes a JSGI app and returns a new decorated app. What this decorated app does is call the original application and store its response object. It then pushes a new value to the body of the response object before returning it. This will yield the following response:

```
HTTP/1.1 200 OK
Content-Type: text/plain
Content-Length: 26

Hello World!
Hi Universe!
```

Without the decoration, the original application is invoked directly by the JSGI server and passed the environment object as an argument. When decorated, however, the application is no longer called directly. Instead, the new decorated function is the one called by the server, and it is this new decorated function that invokes the original application. The decorated function is therefore said to be in the middle between the server and the application, which gives functions like this their JSGI designation of **middleware**.

In JSGI, middleware is simply JSGI applications that call other JSGI applications. These applications are stacked much as in our example, which makes it possible to create complex transformations that let us create powerful applications. There is no limit to the amount of middleware that can be added to an application, and middleware functions can be used to produce simple transformations, as we did above, or more complex ones like changing the environment object itself.

JSGI and CommonJS Engines

The JSGI model is very simple to understand and, when used properly, lets us create really powerful applications. It is the de facto model for application development in CommonJS.

However, the JSGI model isn't supported by all CommonJS engines, often because of the different nature of the engine implementation itself. This creates a problem when it comes to developing applications that can run on several engines, and is therefore an interesting issue to look at.

Meso, the MooTools runner and toolkit for CommonJS that we'll be using here, currently supports four popular CommonJS implementations: Flusspferd, RingoJS, NodeJS, and v8cgi. In the following sections, we'll look at each one of these and take a peek at how they implement a web application model.

Flusspferd

Flusspferd (`http://flusspferd.org`) is a CommonJS implementation first released in April 2009. It is written in C++ and uses the Mozilla SpiderMonkey JavaScript engine, which is written in C.

Flusspferd itself doesn't have a web application module, but one is available in the form of Zest, an HTTP server implementation for Flusspferd written by Ash Berlin. Zest natively supports JSGI, and is therefore compatible with the CommonJS spec.

Here's an example of a Zest-based JSGI application:

```
// the application
var app = function(env){
    return {
        status: 200,
        headers: {
            'content-type': 'text/plain',
            'content-length': 12
        },
        body: ['Hello World!']
    };
};

// zest module
var Zest = require('zest').Zest;

// create a server
var server = new Zest({
    handler: app,
    port: 8081
});

server.start();
```

We used our original application example and then included the Zest module using the `require` function. The Zest module exports a main constructor function called `Zest`, which is used to create an HTTP server. In the last part of our snippet, we created a new Zest HTTP server and we passed two options: `handler` is a reference to our JSGI application and `port` is the local port where the server will listen for connections. Finally, we called the `start` method of the server object to start the HTTP server.

RingoJS

RingoJS (http://ringojs.org) is the successor to the Helma project, which came into being in 1998. As such, it's one of the older server-side JavaScript projects around, and is representative of just how far server-side JavaScript has come.

RingoJS is written in Java and is based on the Mozilla Rhino engine, which is also written in Java. This CommonJS implementation is meant to be a full stack implementation, and it has one of the more extensive core libraries available. Like Flusspferd, RingoJS's web application module is fully JSGI-compliant.

Ringo uses Jetty—a popular Java HTTP server implementation—for its web application stack. The Jetty parts of RingoJS, though, are abstracted into the HTTP server module of the framework. Rewriting our previous example, we get this:

```
// the application
var app = function(env){
    return {
        status: 200,
        headers: {
            'content-type': 'text/plain',
            'content-length': 12
        },
        body: ['Hello World!']
    };
};

// http server module
var Server = require('ringo/httpserver').Server;

// create a server
var server = new Server({
    app: app,
    port: 8081
});

server.start();
```

The first part of this snippet is similar to our previous one. The main changes are with the module import statement, which now imports the Ringo HTTPServer module. This module exports a Server constructor that can be used to create a new HTTP server object. We used this to create a new server instance, passing in two options similar to those in Zest, with the exception that the key for the JSGI application is app instead of handler. We then start the server using the start method, just like with Zest.

NodeJS

NodeJS (http://nodejs.org)—or simply Node—was introduced to the world by Ryan Dahl in early 2009 and has since gained the distinction of being the most popular CommonJS engine today. It is written largely in C and C++, and uses the Google v8 JavaScript engine, also written in C++.

Node's main difference from other CommonJS engines is its event-based nature. Like a regular browser environment, Node employs an event loop that enables it to have asynchronous features that depend on event loops and JavaScript timers.

Because of this different paradigm, Node doesn't support JSGI by default, but instead uses a different model that can support asynchronous event-based code. Like in JSGI, a basic Node application is a function. However, it does not receive a single environment argument but instead receives two special objects called the *request* and the *response* objects.

The request object is similar to the JSGI environment object, and it has properties and methods that can be used to determine the nature of the client request. The response object is a unique object that corresponds to the response object from JSGI—but isn't exactly like it. The main difference is that you can't recreate a response object like you do in JSGI; instead, you have to reuse the same object passed by the node server. You also don't need to return this response object in your application, since Node automatically tracks and reads this object to retrieve the response.

Here's an example Node application:

```
var app = function(request, response){
    response.writeHead(200, {
        'content-type': 'text/plain',
        'content-length': 12
    });
    response.write('Hello World!');
    response.end();
};
```

Unlike the JSGI version of this same application, this Node example uses methods to output the response details. The `writeHead` method is used to prepare the status code and the headers of the response, while the `write` method is used to send chunks of data to the client. Finally, the end method is used to signal that the response is finished, and that the requesting client should be informed that no more data will be sent.

Like Flusspferd and RingoJS, Node uses its own HTTP server implementation for its web application stack. Node's HTTP module is used to create servers, and here's an example of a basic one:

```
var app = function(request, response){
    response.writeHead(200, {
        'content-type': 'text/plain',
        'content-length': 12
    });
    response.write('Hello World!');
    response.end();
};

var http = require('http');

var server = http.createServer(app);
server.listen(8081);
```

Here we used the `createServer` function to create a new HTTP Server object, passing in the application function. We then used the `listen` method of the server to start it, passing in the number of the port where the server will listen.

v8cgi

Of all the CommonJS engines we've seen so far, v8cgi (http://code.google.com/p/v8cgi/) is probably the most unique. First released by Ondrej Zara in the middle of 2009, v8cgi was originally meant to be a way to run JavaScript applications via a module for the Apache HTTP Server. Like Node, it is written in C++ and also uses the Google v8 JavaScript engine.

Because of its close ties with the Apache HTTP Server, v8cgi's paradigm is much more like PHP than the other CommonJS implementations. Scripts that run on the v8cgi stack are simply uploaded to the server and are handled directly by Apache, just like PHP. Thus, v8cgi does not require setting up an HTTP server in the application itself, since the HTTP part is automatically handled by Apache.

Applications written in v8cgi do not need to be functions, and are often written in a very linear fashion. Inside these scripts, the application handles requests and responses through the global `request` and `response` objects. These two objects are similar to the Node objects of the same name, but are automatically created and are globally available throughout the application.

Here's an example of our Hello World! application for v8cgi:

```
response.status(200);
response.header({
    'content-type': 'text/plain',
    'content-length': 12
});
response.write('Hello World!');
```

You'll notice that this script is the simplest application example we've seen so far. This snippet goes in a simple file that is then uploaded to a v8cgi-enabled server. The resource will then have to be accessed as a computed resource, and will yield the same response as all our other examples.

A Common Deck

One thing you've probably noticed by now is that there's no single cross-compatible solution for CommonJS application development. As we've seen, not all CommonJS implementations agree on how to do things, and each one provides its own APIs for handling the work of application development.

This is not a big problem if we're going to target only a single platform. Unlike with browser-based development, we have the freedom to choose the implementation we want to support, without having to worry about our application not being able to run on other platforms. We're no longer bound to external constraints like the browser preference of our target users or the different bugs in the implementations of these browsers.

There is, however, the question of risk. The CommonJS effort is very young and the various engines available today are mostly still under development. Targeting a particular engine is inherently risky, since you're locking yourself into a very particular set of APIs. This is very disconcerting once you take into account the "bus factor" of some CommonJS projects: some of these projects need only one developer to get hit by a bus to send the whole project into disarray (a bus factor of one).

Also worth considering are projects that are meant to be cross-platform. If you're building open-source discussion software or a blog engine, for example, you'll probably want to be able to deploy the end product to as many engines as possible. You therefore have to take into account the different APIs involved, and write your application so it can use all those APIs.

In fact, there are a whole lot of reasons why a common application development model would be useful, aside from those we already discussed. While the choices are no longer bound by our end users, they are still bound by external factors.

Enter Deck

In early 2009, Jabis Sevon and I decided to create a new View-Controller application framework for the v8cgi engine called *Raccoon*. After our initial development period, we successfully deployed a set of Raccoon applications on our server, which prompted the first documented use of the MooTools framework for server-side development.

During this time, however, the newer CommonJS engines like Node and Flusspferd started gaining more traction, and we decided that it would be great to be able to deploy Raccoon applications on different engines aside from v8cgi. To do this, though, we had to rewrite the internals of the Raccoon framework to be able to take into account the various application models used in these implementations.

This was bound to complicate the Raccoon stack, so we decided to do something different: instead of rewriting Raccoon to be able to understand all these APIs, why not simply write a lower level framework that Raccoon—or any other framework—can use. Thus, DeckJS was born.

DeckJS—or simply **Deck**—is a cross-platform server abstraction layer for CommonJS. It was created to provide a simple way to allow application and framework developers to build cross-implementation server-side JavaScript applications without having to worry about implementation-specific details. Deck is written using the MooTools framework, and exposes the MooTools framework to the application as well.

Getting Decked

You can download Deck from the official website at http://deckjs.com/, and use the instructions on the site to install Deck on your system. There are a few ways to use Deck, but we recommend using it together with Meso, which you saw in the previous chapter. For simplicity, we'll assume you're running the following example using Meso.

```
var app = function(request, response){
    response.setStatus(200);
    response.setHeaders({
        'content-type': 'text/plain',
        'content-length': 12
    });
    response.write('Hello World!');
    response.finish();
};

var Deck = require('deck').Deck;

var deck = new Deck({
    app: app
});

deck.serve({port: 8000});
```

When we run this program and load http://localhost:8000, we're greeted with the 'Hello World!' message as with the other implementations.

You'll notice that the code has elements from all the APIs we've seen so far. Like the previous APIs, the application is simply a regular JavaScript function. We create a new instance using the Deck constructor, passing in an options object with the app property to define our application. We then start the application using the serve method, passing in an options object that defines the port to listen to. Like in Node, application functions in Deck receive two arguments: request and response. These objects represent the actual HTTP request and response messages, and they're used to determine the nature of the request and set the response appropriately.

It might not seem like a big deal right now, since we can pretty much do the same thing in other engines—and for the most part, we've proven that already. However, this Deck example is unique because it runs on all the engines we've seen so far: the same code can be used whether we're using Flusspferd, RingoJS, NodeJS, or v8cgi—and those are only the engines that have adaptors so far! This means that with proper adaptors, we can run this same example anywhere.

It's also interesting because underneath this single API, Deck uses the same per-engine APIs we've seen above. This means that Deck is using Zest when it's running on Flusspferd, or http.createServer when running on Node. However, we don't notice this because everything is done transparently.

Routing

Of course, Deck isn't limited to just abstracting low-level APIs. Aside from providing an API that works on multiple engines, Deck also has additional features that make writing applications and frameworks easier.

One of these features is **routing**. In creating applications, it's rare that we use a single request URL. Each point of the application is usually accessed using a different URL, so applications must be able to handle each URL differently.

Imagine we're creating an application that changes its behavior depending on the requested path. If our users access the /hello path, the application will respond with Hello World!, while if they request the /hi path, it'll respond with Hi Universe!. To achieve this, we can rewrite our previous app function to look like this:

```
var app = function(request, response){
    response.setStatus(200);
    response.setHeaders({
        'content-type': 'text/plain',
        'content-length': 12
    });

    if (request.pathInfo == '/hello'){
        response.write('Hello World!');
    } else if (request.pathInfo == '/hi'){
        response.write('Hi Universe!');
    }

    response.finish();
};

var Deck = require('deck').Deck;

var deck = new Deck({
    app: app
});

deck.serve({port: 8000});
```

Here we add an if-else statement to our app function to check the pathInfo property of the current request. We then serve the appropriate response body according to the requested path: 'Hello World!' for /hello and 'Hi Universe!' for /hi, which you can check for yourself by running this example and going to http://localhost:8000/hello or http://localhost:8000/hi.

While this style works for simple examples like the one above, it becomes hard to use once we start working with more complex applications. As our applications become bigger, the internal logic for each part of our application increases: our /hi path might require some database access, while /hello might have to write some files. If we're going to use a single application function for all our paths, our code will very quickly become unmanageable.

To make our code easier to work with, we need to split up our monolithic application function. Deck makes this easy by allowing you to have multiple application functions using **routes**. A route is a special rule that's checked against the request object. If the request satisfies the rule, the application associated with that route is served. If it doesn't, Deck will continue comparing the request object against other routes until it finds one that matches.

We use the addRoute method of a Deck instance to add new routes. It takes two main arguments: matcher, which is used to match the pathInfo property of the request, and app, which is the application function to serve.

```
var appHello = function(request, response){
    response.setStatus(200);
    response.setHeaders({
        'content-type': 'text/plain',
        'content-length': 12
    });
    response.write('Hello World!');
    response.finish();
};

var appHi = function(request, response){
    response.setStatus(200);
    response.setHeaders({
        'content-type': 'text/plain',
        'content-length': 12
    });
    response.write('Hi Universe!');
    response.finish();
};

var Deck = require('deck').Deck;

var deck = new Deck();

deck.addRoute('/hello', appHello);
deck.addRoute('/hi', appHi);

deck.serve({port: 8000});
```

Here we split up the original app function into two separate functions: appHello and appHi. We also removed the app option object from the Deck instantiation code, which tells the Deck class that we want to use multiple routes. Finally, we added two routes using the addRoute method, one for the appHello function and another for appHi.

Running this example, we'll get the same behavior as with the previous one: 'Hello World!' for http://localhost:8000/hello and 'Hi Universe!' for http://localhost:8000/hi. What happens is that when we request these URLs, Deck automatically compares the path of the requested URL to the defined routes. If the path is /hello, it serves the appHello function, and if it's /hi, it serves appHi.

Middleware using Modules

I mentioned earlier that in the JSGI model, application functions can be chained together to form more complex applications, and these decorator functions are called middleware because they sit in between the application and the server implementation. Deck also allows for middleware, which in Deck terms are called **modules**.

Like in the JSGI model, Deck modules lie between the application and the server implementation. However, modules and application functions aren't chained using function decoration. Instead, Deck implements a stack-based model for using modules.

In this model, the modules and the application are placed in an array, with the application function always sitting in the middle. Deck will call each of the functions one after the other, passing in the request and response objects to each one. The chaining therefore occurs inside the Deck instance, and not through explicit decoration on the part of the user.

Also unlike the JSGI model, Deck modules are actually objects and not functions. The functions that are invoked from each module come from **handlers**, which are methods of the module objects.

```
var module = {

    preHandler: function(request, response){
        request.next();
    },

    postHandler: function(request, response){
        request.next();
    }

};
```

Here we have a simple Deck module object, with the two handler methods. The preHandler method of the module object is added to the front of the application, while the postHandler method is added at the back. This means that Deck modules can be invoked before, after, or before and after the application function, depending on the handlers they define.

Adding a module to a Deck instance is simply a matter of calling the addModule method:

```
var app = function(request, response){
    response.setStatus(200);
    response.setHeaders({
        'content-type': 'text/plain',
        'content-length': 12
    });
    response.write('Hello World!');
    response.next();
};

var module = {

    preHandler: function(request, response){
        request.next();
    },

    postHandler: function(request, response){
        request.next();
    }

};

var Deck = require('deck').Deck;

var deck = new Deck({
    app: app
});

deck.addModule(module);

deck.serve({port: 8000});
```

Deck Internals

Deck is, in essence, an abstraction layer that sits on top of the implementation-specific HTTP server APIs we've seen. Deck provides a layer of abstraction that enables us to use the same API for any application model the engine uses. Because the underlying implementation-specific APIs are abstracted by Deck, we are able to create projects that will run on any supported CommonJS implementation without changes, removing any platform-specific lockdowns.

At the center of Deck is a single class called Base, which is exported as Deck. This class is a unifier class that implements all other minor classes using mixins. There are about half a dozen classes that make up Deck itself, each of them controlling a different aspect of the system, and we'll look at the most important ones in turn.

Request and Response

The bulk of Deck's internals focus on the creation and manipulation of Request and Response objects. For every request received by the underlying HTTP server, Deck creates an object representation of the request and a corresponding response object. These objects are passed to the application, which then processes and manipulates them before passing them back to the Deck instance to be sent to the originator of the request.

The Request object contains several properties that describe the request, including the HTTP method, the requested resource, the user-agent, and other headers. It also has several utility methods that can be used to modify its properties, add additional headers, or change the requested resource. The Response object represents the response to be sent back and has methods to set the HTTP status of the response, add headers, and modify the response body.

The Request and Response objects are always created as pairs: both are created when a request is received and both are passed to the application for access and modification. Unlike the existing CommonJS JSGI standard that expects the application to create and return its own Response object, it is the work of the Deck instance to create the Response object that the application modifies.

The Filtered Model

Deck implements a *filtered* model for server requests and responses. In a simple model, a request is made to the server-side application by the browser and the application then sends a corresponding response. In Deck's filtered model, several "filters" sit before and after the application and they modify the request or response in order to change behavior.

The filtered model can be viewed like a deck of cards (from which Deck gets its name): the application sits in the middle of the deck and several modules are placed on top and on the bottom of the application. The Request and Response objects are then passed to each of these items in turn, starting from the topmost module and ending at the bottom module.

With this model, complex applications can be simplified by separating common tasks into several modules. An example might be a Rewrite Module, which could modify the Request object's pathInfo property before it reaches the application, thereby changing the request. The application would then be able to serve the appropriate response without having to do further checks on the Request object. Another example might be a Logger Module that logs every Request and its corresponding Response. Instead of having to do this within the application, you could simply add the module to the Deck instance.

Deck uses a *double-ended queue* (or a *deque*, pronounced "deck") to keep track of the application and the modules. In the middle of the deque is the application and the modules are added either before or after so that the application always remains in the middle. The addition of modules also follows the deque's two ends: the preHandler method of a module is always added in the front of the deque and the postHandler is always added at the end of the deque.

Dispatching

After creating the Request and Response objects, the Deck instance "dispatches" the modules and the application by invoking the first function in the deque, passing the Request and Response objects as arguments. The Deck instance waits until it is signaled to move on to the next item in the deque, and then repeats the process until all items have been dispatched before sending the response back.

The signal to the Deck instance to move to the next item is done by the modules and the application themselves. The Request object has a special method called next that's called by the modules and the application within their function bodies to tell the Deck instance to move to the next item. All Modules and Applications are required to call this method; otherwise, the Deck instance won't be able to move to the next item in the deque and the response will timeout.

Additionally, the Response object has a special method called finish that tells the Deck instance that the response has been finalized. Calling this method will stop the dispatching of the next items on the deque and return the response immediately.

Because the dispatching of items is done using an explicit signal, Deck is able to support asynchronous applications natively.

The Router

Deck includes a built-in router that dynamically changes the internal module and application deque before dispatching. Multiple routes can be set for a Deck instance, describing the rules and the corresponding application function to dispatch for a specific request.

The base of the routing rule is a string or a regular expression describing the request's requested path and the HTTP request method. After the Deck instance creates the Request and Response objects, it checks the Request object's pathInfo property and HTTP request method to see whether it matches any of the routing rules set for the Deck instance. If it does, it builds a new deque with the application function described in the route rule before dispatching the deque.

Additionally, a *constraint* object can be passed when setting a new route that will be used to check other rules before dispatch. The constraint object is a simple JavaScript object with keys corresponding to the Request objects properties and values that can be strings, regular expressions, or functions that will be used to check the info against.

The Wrap-Up

In this chapter we learned about JavaScript on the server side, and how different CommonJS engines implement their application server APIs. We also learned about Deck, a server-side framework for application development that's written on top of MooTools.

Deck itself is a very complex framework, and it's unfortunate that it will take at least another book to discuss it in full. It is a young project, but it does offer a glimpse of how complicated JavaScript applications and frameworks can be written on top of MooTools.

If you're hungry for more information about Deck, I suggest you visit the official site at http://deckjs.com. You'll find a more extensive coverage of both the API and the framework itself on the website, and I personally invite you to try it out and contribute to the next iterations of the framework.

The Wrap-Up to Conquer All Wrap-Ups

Whew! It's been quite a ride, hasn't it? We've covered a lot, rested at a few pitstops and learned a trick or two from roadblocks. We've explored the nooks and crannies of JavaScript and the internals of MooTools, and we've seen things that will gladly go to our development arsenal.

My hope is that you've learned a thing or two from this book. We can't cover everything in a single volume, but at least now you have enough material to start your own experimentation. Remember that learning a language doesn't end with reading a single book. It takes experimentation, more reading and lots of application in order to really become a great coder.

So fire up your text editor, get your fingers moving and start exploring!

APPENDIX

■■■

Resources

To help you out with your further exploration of JavaScript and MooTools, I've compiled a very short list of resources that you can check out. The selection isn't exhaustive in any sense, but simply reflects base points for further study and experimentation.

JavaScript

The recent resurgence of JavaScript has certainly raised the number of JavaScript related resources, both in print and online form. The following are the ones that stand out as being essential references that are consulted by most developers.

- **ECMAScript Language Specifications**. The official language specifications are, of course, the first resources that any serious JavaScript developer should consult. Because they are formal documents, the language specifications can be hard to get through at times. However, it is important that you take time reading through the specifications, since all implementations are judged by their conformance to these documents. Since the third edition is still the most widely supported version of the language, I recommend that you read through third Edition specification first (http://www.ecma-international.org/publications/standards/Ecma-262-arch.htm). Afterwards, you should read the fifth Edition specification (http://www.ecma-international.org/publications/standards/Ecma-262.htm) to familiarize yourself with the new features of ECMAScript 5.

- **JavaScript the Definitive Guide** by David Flanagan (Fifth Edition; 2006, O'Reilly). Often called the *Rhino Book* because of its cover, this book is one of the best JavaScript books in terms of scope and content. There have certainly been a lot of changes since this book was first published, but it still remains an essential reference for any serious JavaScript developer.

- **Mozilla Developer Network** (https://developer.mozilla.org/). The Mozilla Developer Network or MDN (formerly MDC), is the official reference site for the Mozilla Foundation. The JavaScript section of this site contains a ton of free data regarding the language, its implementation within Mozilla, and other development-related information. Also worthy of perusal are the DOM and CSS sections of the site.

MooTools

Because of the large size of its community, MooTools has a fair share of developer resources. Here are some of the recommended resources that you should explore:

- **The Official MooTools Documentation** (`http://mootools.net/docs/`). This one needs no further introduction. Any serious MooTools developer should have the official documentation site bookmarked.

- **The MooTools Source Repository** (`http://github.com/mootools/`). A lot of the material in this book wasn't discovered by reading the docs but by reading and examining the MooTools source code. I therefore recommend that you spend some time working with the MooTools source code itself, which is available from the official repositories.

- **The MooTools Forge** (`http://mootools.net/forge`). The Forge is the official MooTools community plugin and extension resource site. You'll see applications of the information from this book in some of the plugins and extensions published on the Forge, and I advise you to peruse the Forge and examine the published extensions as an exercise in understanding how they use the MooTools API.

- **The MooTorial** (`http://mootorial.com`) and **MooTools 1.3** (`http://ryanflorence.com/issue-004/`). These two online resources are geared towards MooTools beginners. The first is a little outdated (uses MooTools 1.2), but is still useful in understanding general MooTools development; while the second is a new series that was created for the MooTools 1.3 release.

- **MooTools Essentials** by Aaron Newton (2008, Apress), and **MooTools 1.2 Beginner's Guide** by Jacob Gube and Garrick Cheung (2009, Packt). Like the previous resources, these two are targeted towards MooTools beginners, but in book form. Both are really good introductions to the framework, but they are a little outdated since they still discuss MooTools 1.2.

Index

■ ■ ■

Breinigsville, PA USA
23 December 2010
252067BV00006B/63-206/P